The Prevention of
Racial Discrimination in Britain

The Prevention of Racial Discrimination in Britain

Edited by

SIMON ABBOTT

Published for the
United Nations Institute for Training and Research
and the
Institute of Race Relations
by
OXFORD UNIVERSITY PRESS
LONDON   NEW YORK   TORONTO
1971

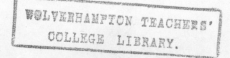

Oxford University Press, Ely House, London W.1

GLASGOW   NEW YORK   TORONTO   MELBOURNE   WELLINGTON
CAPE TOWN   SALISBURY   IBADAN   NAIROBI   DAR ES SALAAM   LUSAKA   ADDIS ABABA
BOMBAY   CALCUTTA   MADRAS   KARACHI   LAHORE   DACCA
KUALA LUMPUR   SINGAPORE   HONG KONG   TOKYO

ISBN 0 19 218199 8
UNITAR SERIES NO. 4

Printed in Great Britain by
Ebenezer Baylis and Son Limited
The Trinity Press, Worcester, and London

Contents

PART IV CONCLUSIONS

Acknowledgements

Thanks are gratefully given to the members of the advisory panel, to the staff at UNITAR for their co-operation and patience, and to all the contributors. But perhaps especially to those who worked on the surveys: Jyothi Kamath, Margot Levy, Ronnie Manderson-Jones, Martin Davies, Roger Jowell, and S.C.P.R. Also to Nicholas Deakin who mapped out the first research design, to Brian Cohen who assisted in the general discussion and development only at the earlier stages, to A. Sivanandan for some advice on reading but without blame for the results, to Rose-Ann Mitchell for her as ever thorough editing, and to Chye Neo Choo for much of the administrative labour and conversion with little dissent of too dull long-hand pages into typescript. Finally, thanks to Phyllis McDougal for compiling the index.

SIMON ABBOTT

Note

The bibliographical references are started anew in each chapter, i.e. the first reference to a work in each chapter is a full one. A small point of editorial discrimination is that Black has generally been capitalized and white has not: earlier, IRR styling had been to capitalize Negro, and this practice when extended has produced some contradictions, for example, in Chapter 12, that would have been better avoided. In some cases, however, the use of Black is correct, because it then reflects a group consciousness of identity.

Foreword

Racial discrimination is not confined to one country or even to one continent. It takes many forms, depending on history, the ethnic composition of the population, social structure, and the stage of economic development. It is a universal problem because when men of one race come into contact with men of another, there is tension. It is faced by the American living in the great Northern cities just as much as by those whose home is the old Confederacy. It is faced by the Londoner and Mancunian. In different forms, it appears in Paris and Amsterdam, in Nairobi and Kuala Lumpur. The Indians and Eskimos in the Canadian Northland are becoming restive at what they consider to be paternalistic treatment. It can involve relations between Black and white, Black and brown, yellow and brown, and even white and white or Black and Black where ethnic and linguistic differences exist. No longer can race relations be regarded as an esoteric subject of interest only to the sociologist or the anthropologist. It concerns us all.

To take effective action against such a phenomenon, it is first necessary to understand it; and to understand it on a global scale involves a series of comparative studies, using a standard set of references or guide-lines. The experiences of one country will be valuable in showing another what can be accomplished and what mistakes should be avoided. The particular circumstances will naturally vary, but it should be possible to find in the techniques used for combatting racial discrimination some common ground that can be applied universally.

The United Nations Institute for Training and Research (UNITAR) has attempted to lay the foundation for such comparative studies. Its interest stems from the concern of the United Nations to see racial discrimination eliminated. UNITAR is part of the United Nations, established by resolution of the General Assembly to carry out training and research to improve the effectiveness of the Organization. It is an autonomous body with an independent Board of Trustees and its own budget, based on voluntary contributions from both governments and non-governmental sources. The statute establishing UNITAR says that it 'shall conduct research and study related to the functions and objectives of the United Nations'. In establishing priorities for its research programme, the Board of Trustees decided that 'emphasis would be placed on studies concerned with the effectiveness of United Nations action, techniques and machinery . . . ' and that 'UNITAR should not only attempt to fill the research gaps which are not yet adequately covered by the existing United Nations services and facilities, but it should be prepared to initiate studies in fields of its own choosing which fall within its terms of reference'. Specifically, the Board also agreed that among the principal research areas should be 'United Nations methods and techniques for the promotion and protection of human rights'. With this mandate, it was decided that one of the first projects would be a comparative study of the effectiveness of measures against racial discrimination. If it was to achieve its purpose, it would have to be trans-national and each individual study would have to be based on empirical data gathered under the same set of guide-lines. Only in this way would a true comparison be possible.

The decision to begin research in this field came at a time when the General Assembly had decided to convene an International Conference on Human Rights. In the work of the Preparatory Committee for this conference, it became clear that many delegations were anxious to see a review of progress in the field of human rights which would enable the international community to evaluate the methods and techniques employed to promote the objectives of the Charter. This might involve looking behind and beyond the periodic reports made by governments and the Specialized Agencies to the Economic and Social Council. These reports could tell of the legislation passed to protect human rights, but they would not explain the social, personal, and emotional factors which would be involved in making it effective. The Preparatory Committee agreed that UNITAR was the appropriate body to undertake 'effectiveness studies' and specifically requested it to begin work on them.

The International Conference on Human Rights was held in Teheran in April 1968. Three documents prepared by UNITAR were submitted to it, and one is the basis on which this study of the Prevention of Racial Discrimination in Britain was undertaken. It was titled 'Guidelines for a Study of the Effectiveness of Policies and Measures against Racial Discrimination' (A/CONF. 32/11).

The purpose of these studies is to analyse and compare policies and measures to combat racial discrimination and the results obtained by them in various national societies. Three criteria were established for the societies to be studied: each must have a multi-racial population, a significant degree of tension between the ethnic groups, and some accumulated experience in concerted action against discrimination.

UNITAR's aim is to discover the respective importance and weight of the policies and methods deliberately used and of the dynamics of structural change in national societies in determining the intensity and direction of trends in the pattern of race relations since the end of World War II. To quote from the 'Guidelines':

The present situation will be approached as the historically accumulated result of the effectiveness, or lack of effectiveness, of the policies applied and the methods used during the last quarter of a century to build desirable patterns of racial relations in the society under study. An attempt should be made to extract, from the analysis and comparison, possible guidelines for better performance in the future. To a great extent, it will be a study of the social structure of multi-racial societies, of the social values, and of the different types of social action that are causing multi-directional change in prevailing models of inter-ethnic relations.

Any national study should make an objective characterization of the situation existing at the end of World War II, an analysis of the factors that have acted to change that situation, and the identification and evaluation of the role played by deliberate policy measures to combat discrimination. Obviously, certain basic information would be required in each case. There would have to be statistical data on the size, growth, and social status of the different ethnic elements. There would have to be an account of the trends affecting relations between these elements. There would have to be an analysis of policies and measures to combat racial discrimination. Finally, there would have to be an assessment of the effects and an evaluation of the results of these policies and measures, compared with other factors such as the dynamics of the racial situation itself. This research methodology is a pioneering step for the United Nations in the field of comparative studies. It should be possible to apply the same, or similar, techniques to a variety of multi-national studies on other aspects of human rights.

This is the first study using these guide-lines to be published, and it is appropriate to ask: Why Britain? Historically, Britain is a country that has been largely free of domestic racial prejudice. Within a single generation, race relations had become a problem serious enough for the Government to introduce legislation designed to combat discrimination. History has shown that all too often, such action was not taken in time. On this occasion, it was taken deliberately to forestall what could become a major confrontation.

The reasons why this problem had arisen are easy to understand. They rest largely in the concept of a British subject, which embraced the Commonwealth, and in economic interdependence. As British subjects, the citizens of all parts of the Commonwealth were free to emigrate to Britain if they wished. This freedom of movement led to an influx from the Indian subcontinent and the Caribbean in the post-war years and, in turn, to the growth of a colour problem. A country largely free from racial tensions suddenly found itself in a position where the Government decided to limit immigration precisely because of the large number of non-whites coming to live there and to take measures to prevent discrimination against those who had already arrived. Britain was facing issues that had arisen in other parts of the world but had previously been absent within her shores. In short, it was no longer an island.

This leads one to ask questions. Are the reasons for the growth of racial tensions connected with what one might call the bread and butter issues of life and living—with competition for jobs and housing? Or is there something more fundamental? Have we been seeing in Britain an indication that if you scratch a white man, any white man, you will find in him a prejudice against his Black brothers? Is it just a question of numbers? If Britain had been free of prejudice, was this because an individual could be accepted where a thousand people of a different colour were rejected? And further, one must ask whether there is a time frame to racial discrimination. Is it the sudden arrival of substantial numbers which alter social patterns that breeds discrimination? Will this decline as these strangers become part of British life? Or will they never be absorbed into the community?

To ask these questions is to indicate the gaps in our know-ledge. It was important to look for answers. More important still would be an examination of the effectiveness of legislation to prevent the growth of some of the uglier manifestations of dis-crimination and prejudice. Britain seemed a good place for such a study. Almost without warning, race relations had become a subject which could not be ignored, and the Government had acted. Here, it seemed, might be a perfect laboratory experiment. The issue of race had grown, and yet not to such proportions that the entire fabric of British society was in danger. The Government had taken steps to control a crisis before it got completely out of hand. How effective had these measures proved in practice? Would others be necessary?

If the UNITAR study was to be complete, the co-operation of the Government would be important, and we are fortunate that this was forthcoming. It was more than simply a tacit decision not to oppose. We have had the co-operation of the various Ministries, the Home Office, the Race Relations Board, and the Community Relations Commission. We are extremely grateful for this. Without it, our work would have been severely hampered. With it, we have produced a study which we believe will be helpful to the authorities in furthering their efforts to prevent racial discrimination in Britain.

The UNITAR 'Guidelines' call for extensive research carried out by qualified experts who know what information will be significant, how it can be gathered, and how it should be in-terpreted. Only by systematic surveys can one find answers to such questions as these: Do people of one race find it more difficult to get jobs? Are they charged higher rents? Are mortgages more expensive and harder for them to obtain? Do they have trouble finding a place to live when their opposite numbers of a different race do not? Is the education given their children of an inferior quality? Do they have more trouble with the law and the bureau-cracy? If so, is this because of racial bias or because they have different standards of life and living? All these are examined in this volume. It shows that there is discrimination in employment, and that in part this can be attributed to the traditionally con-servative attitude of the trade unions (Chapters 6 and 7). While a substantial proportion of the immigrant population owns their own homes, these are frequently old, in poor condition, and

located in run-down areas likely to be slated for urban development. Often there is overcrowding, which leads to violations of
health regulations and to difficulties with the authorities. The
newer council houses are harder to come by, and there is a strong
suggestion that the local officials are not always free of bias. Finally,
when the immigrants try to move 'up and out' to the suburbs,
racial discrimination becomes much more evident (Chapter 4).

Traditionally, Britain has not concerned itself with race. One
example of this is the virtual impossibility of obtaining accurate
data on the size of the coloured population. The census does not
provide it. There is a question about where a man is born, but
not about his race. Thus, the statistics of people born in India, for
example, will include children of the British Raj as well as immigrants from that country (Chapter 3). Since the end of World
War II, Britain has received the largest and most variegated
influx of immigrants in her history; yet it is extremely difficult
to determine its extent or to discover precisely what has happened
to the newcomers.

The colour problem arose after the arrival of considerable
numbers of West Indians, Indians, and Pakistanis. Successive
Governments in London were reluctant to control the flow. They
were equally reluctant to introduce legislation to prevent discrimination. However, the pressures for action built up and the
result was the Race Relations Acts of 1965 and 1968. Louis
Kushnick has written a penetrating account of the origins of these
two laws as well as a critique of the loop-holes they have failed to
close (Chapter 9). As elsewhere, it was easier to start with forma-
lizing declarations of principle than with punitive legislation. In
examining the various statutory bodies set up under this legislation, it should be no surprise to discover that they have had their
teething troubles (Chapters 10 and 11). They were, after all,
something completely new in British life and it is only possible
to proceed by trial and error. The role of the police in dealing
with racial tensions is vital, and here too it should not be a surprise
to discover that immigrants have had complaints. Brian Cohen
has contributed a valuable analysis of the role of the police in an
earlier draft paper. He shows that there has been some discrimination and that serious efforts are being made to eliminate
it. However, in contrast to some other societies, police brutality
does not appear to have been a major issue in Britain. Some of the

indirect results of attempts to prevent discrimination are reflected in other parts of the study. Julia McNeal's account of education shows that the policy of dispersal has had some unexpected repercussions. It was designed to prevent schools from becoming all white or all Black, and in this it may have succeeded. However, sending the children by bus out of their own neighbourhood has disrupted normal community relations. It has been harder for parents and teachers to get to know each other, and the children are unable to extend friendships from the home to the classroom and vice versa. At the other end of the spectrum, it is interesting to discover that no attempt is being made in the schools to prepare white children for living in a multi-racial society (Chapter 5).

Of course, government policy is not, and should not be, the only way of combatting discrimination. A great deal can be done by voluntary groups. These have existed in Britain longer than the official bodies, and they have made a useful contribution (as told in Chapter 12). However, one is left with the impression of a number of individuals anxious to help but not quite sure how best to set about it, and with virtually no co-ordination between them.

While Britain seemed a good place for the study of the effectiveness of measures to combat racial discrimination, UNITAR had no intention of singling it out for special attention. This is one of a series of national studies to be made under the Institute's guide-lines, and it is the first to be completed. Studies on Peru and the United States are now in progress, and others are under consideration.

We believe UNITAR's 'Guidelines' will be helpful in encouraging this work. Our concern has been on a trans-national rather than a national level, and with the elimination of racial discrimination as a United Nations goal of universal application. In a purely national study, there would be a tendency to be inward-looking and to cast the findings in what might be called insular terms. By using a trans-national framework, each study takes on a wider perspective. Naturally, each will be concerned with a domestic situation, but this in turn is related through the guide-lines to what is happening in other countries.

This study has been a co-operative effort to an unusual degree, and UNITAR owes a debt of gratitude to many people. We are fortunate that the Institute of Race Relations has undertaken this study for us, and the members of its staff who have been involved in it have done a fine job. It is impossible to name them all, but special mention must be made of Simon Abbott, who has not only contributed three important chapters but has acted in the role of co-ordinator of the work. Without him, our task would have been much harder. At UNITAR, the Director of Research, Oscar Schachter, has supervised our contribution, providing guidance and advice and encouragement. His Deputy, Alexander Szalai, has kept a close eye on the work as it progressed and made many valuable suggestions to ensure that we stayed on the right track. The initial groundwork was laid by Professor L. A. Costa Pinto of Brazil, then a Senior Research Fellow at the Institute, and it was followed up by Joseph Therattil of the research staff. We owe a great deal of gratitude to David Ennals, then Minister of State for Health and Social Security, for helping us obtain the co-operation of the British government. The Institute of Race Relations established an Advisory Panel to assist in the study. Its members were Mrs. Brenda Bailey, Geoffrey Bindman, N. D. Deakin, Professor Fernando Henriques, Professor Hilde Himmelweit, Anthony Lester, Dr. Alan Little, Professor Kenneth Little, Professor Richard Longaker, Dipak Nandy, Dr. R. E. Pahl, and E. J. B. Rose, with Mrs. Lucy Syson and Nadine Peppard acting as observers. Members from the panel read the various chapters as they were completed and made important suggestions for improving them. To them we must give special thanks. In accordance with UNITAR practice, the complete manuscript was submitted to an international panel of experts. Finally, of course, there are the authors, the men and women who undertook the research and who have given life to their findings: Simon Abbott, Sheila Patterson, Brian Cohen, Elizabeth Burney, Julia McNeal, Bob Hepple, Roger Jowell, Patricia Prescott-Clarke, R. Manderson-Jones, Jyothi Kamath, Marna Glyn, Louis Kushnick, Hannan Rose, Margot Levy, and Nicholas Deakin. Without them, this book would have been immeasurably the poorer. This has been a joint endeavour in the true sense of that phrase. However, the opinions and conclusions expressed are those of the authors and not necessarily of UNITAR. We hope that our co-operation will lead to a greater knowledge and understanding of the problems of racial discrimination. Only then will we be able to eradicate this evil from the world.

Executive Director   CHIEF S. O. ADEBO

CHAPTER 1

Introduction

SIMON ABBOTT

This introductory chapter attempts to consider four factors: the general aims of the UNITAR national studies; the significance of the terms 'racial discrimination' and 'effective measures'; some relevant factors of the British situation; and, finally, an introduction to the study in fact carried out in Britain.

1. *The General Aims of the UNITAR National Studies*

UNITAR have produced several papers dealing with the national studies. The guide-lines for the selection of countries were that there should be: '(a) a multi-racial population; (b) a significant degree of tension between the ethnic groups; and (c) some accumulated experience in concerted action against discrimination'.[1] Five countries were to be chosen 'at different stages of social, political and economic development'.[2]

The objectives of the study at the national level were to assess: (i) 'Structural characteristics of the multi-racial society', in terms of 'demographic data' and 'position of groups in the stratification system'; (ii) 'Main traits and trends', being 'historical background, and analysis of the origins and orientations of the patterns of values, assumptions and goals connected with the prevailing racial policies'; (iii) 'Policies and measures', being 'analysis of the policies and measures applied to combat racial discrimination'; and (iv) 'Successes and failures', being the 'assessment and evaluation of the results of the policies applied, compared with other factors connected with the dynamics of the racial situation itself'.[3]

The ultimate intention of the national studies is that there should be a comparison of anti-discriminatory measures and resulting recommendations on improving the effectiveness of such measures.

[1] UNITAR, 'Comparative Study of Effectiveness of Measures Against Racial Discrimination, Draft Guidelines for Research', 10–11 July 1967, p. 1.
[2] Ibid., p. 2.   [3] Ibid., p. 4.

These in brief detail were the guide-lines given for the present British study, which was the first of the national studies to be undertaken.

2. *The Significance of the Terms 'Racial Discrimination' and 'Effective Measures'*

(a) DISCRIMINATION

It seemed important to attempt some definition of what were the substantive terms or ideas from which this study started. Even between those engaged in study and research in the testing of discrimination, there can be some disagreement as to the meaning of this term. For example, the question can be put: 'When measuring the extent of discrimination, do you consider the range of housing that members of minorities do apply for, or the housing they could apply for?'[1] It has been replied that if 'the majority of housing in some localities is closed to some immigrant communities, and so they avoid these districts ... ' then, 'If this were really true, there would be no discrimination in housing.'[2] But it might be added that, in such circumstances, even if there were then no discriminatory acts, there would appear to be evidence of a more general discriminatory situation.

Is it not possible to achieve a more exact and extensive definition of 'racial discrimination'? It is fairly clear that many legal or administrative descriptions are simply concerned with the *act* of discrimination, as when the Home Secretary of the United Kingdom argued that 'a person will be held to discriminate if, on grounds of colour, race, ethnic or national origins, he treats a person less favourably than he treats other people'.[3] The definition of discrimination in the Race Relations Act 1968 is similar: 'a person discriminates against another if on the ground of colour, race or ethnic or national origins he treats that other ... less favourably than he treats or would treat other persons'.[4] The description employed in the Report of Political and Economic Planning was: 'By "discrimination" is meant a practice or policy which affects members of minority groups differently because of

---

[1] W. W. Daniel in *Race* (Vol. XI, No. 3, January 1970), p. 355.
[2] Robin Ward, ibid., pp. 364–5.
[3] *The Times* (10 May 1969).
[4] *Race Relations Act 1968* (London, H.M.S.O., 1968), p. A2.

colour or country of origin, in ways that are either of significance to them personally or of significance socially.'[1] This extends the concept by introducing (i) the idea of a practice or policy, that is a series of discriminatory acts; and (ii) the notion of groups. But it is not altogether clear how to draw the line between what is significant personally and socially; nor what meaning to attach here to the term 'significant'. A different description is that which takes discrimination 'to mean the use, by a superordinate group, of its superior power to impose customary or legal restrictions and deprivations upon a subordinate group in order to maintain a situation of privilege and inequality'.[2] A minor objection to this definition is that the use of the terms superordinate and subordinate may, on rare occasions, be misleading: a West Indian householder in London may discriminate against prospective white tenants although the West Indians as a group may in the London conurbation be discriminated against in the housing field. However, it will generally be agreed that the situation of racial discrimination usually involves a sequence of discriminatory acts. The terms in-group and out-group might nevertheless be preferred, if indeed it is necessary to distinguish between the groups in this way.

Further factors that can usefully be explored are attitudes, especially those of prejudice, and in general the psychological aspects of discrimination. Simpson and Yinger regard 'discrimination [as] the overt expression of prejudice; it is the categorical treatment of a member of a group because he is a member of that group, and supposedly, therefore, of a "particular type"'.[3] This view must, however, be modified by noting that discrimination is not always the result of prejudice: for example, social roles may dictate discriminatory behaviour upon individuals who are not themselves prejudiced. One writer has suggested that, 'Discrimination, far from being pathological or deviant, has generally been normative.'[4]

[1] Political and Economic Planning and Research Services Ltd., *Racial Discrimination* (London, P.E.P., 1967), p. 2.

[2] A. H. Richmond, in G. Duncan Mitchell (ed.), *A Dictionary of Sociology* (London, Routledge & Kegan Paul, 1968), p. 58.

[3] G. E. Simpson and J. Milton Yinger, *Racial and Cultural Minorities*, 3rd edn. (New York, Harper & Row, 1965), p. 13.

[4] Richard M. Burkey, 'Discrimination and Racial Relations: A Theoretical Perspective' (UNITAR, CIRR, Denver, Aspen Institute 1970 conference).

...don W. Allport defines more fully two aspects of dis-
...nation: the nature of the action undertaken by a group and
the position of the individual in relation to a group.

We often separate ourselves from people whom we find uncongenial.
It is not discrimination when we do so, so long as it is *we* who move
away from them. 'Discrimination comes about only when we deny
to individuals or groups of people equality of treatment which they
may wish.' It occurs when we take steps to exclude members of an
out-group from our neighborhood, school, occupation, or country.[1]

It may reasonably be objected that the wish for equality of
treatment is not a necessary condition of discrimination, although
it is often an indication of it. West Indian immigrants in an urban
area of the United Kingdom may have been offered inferior
accommodation at a superior price, and may have accepted it
without knowledge of the general prevailing market prices and
availability of accommodation in the area. In other words, had
the seeker of accommodation not been adversely distinguished
by race as West Indian, the supplier might have offered the
accommodation at a lower price, or have offered better accommodation. They might not have wished for better because, in this
instance, they did not know that better was—in the absence of the
race factor—available. Yet such a circumstance might well be
called discriminatory. Allport goes on to say:

Our definition of discrimination must be further amplified. A criminal,
a psychotic, a filthy person may desire 'equality of treatment' and
we may without compunction deny it to him. Differential treatment
based on individual qualities probably should not be classed as
discrimination. Here we are interested only in differential treatment
that is based on ethnic categorization.[2]

A further important component is the relationship of the
discriminatory situation to the general society. Robin M. Williams
has suggested that: 'Discrimination may be said to exist to the
degree that individuals of a given group who are otherwise
formally qualified are not treated in conformity with these
nominally universal institutionalized codes.'[3] He repeats this

[1] Gordon W. Allport, *The Nature of Prejudice* (Cambridge, Addison-Wesley, 1954),
p. 51; quote from U.N. publication, 1949, xiv, 3, 2.
[2] Allport, op. cit.
[3] Robin M. Williams, *The Reduction of Inter-group Tensions* (New York, S.S.R.C.,
1947), p. 39.

idea in his definition of group discrimination: it is 'the differential treatment of individuals, in so far as this is based upon their membership in a given social group which conflicts with important institutional rules within a society'. [1] The insistence on a system of values may, however, be misleading and seems not so much necessary to a description of discrimination as the expression of a hope, along with Gunnar Myrdal and others, that the American global democratic ideals would overcome the segmentary situation of the Negroes. It may be argued, for example, that a Pakistani in the United Kingdom might pay an inflated price for a house: the seller and buyer might accept this as an integral part of their ethics, but the transaction might still remain an unequal one because of the race factor, and may therefore be termed discriminatory. It is probably better to start from a more simple definition, such as that by Oliver Cromwell Cox, who writes that: 'Both cultural and race prejudices are dynamic group attitudes varying in intensity according to the specific historical situation of the peoples involved.'[2] In short, the general situation cannot be omitted from the evaluation of the discriminatory situation. And this can be expressed in terms extending to the suggestion that generally cases of racial discrimination are rooted in the inequitable structuring of a society.

Finally, it is important to remember that discriminatory situations are not necessarily static: if one looks, for example, at Michael Banton's analysis of role theory and discrimination,[3] one can see both how roles have exemplified discriminatory situations, and how the calling into question of traditional roles has heralded a new and changing phase of discrimination.

It is possible to bring these views into focus against the analysis of discrimination in terms of effective anti-discriminatory measures. Quite clearly, a measure may be directed primarily at one part of the discriminatory situation; for example, a legislative measure may be designed to reduce or eliminate the incidence of a particular discriminatory act. In order fully to describe discrimination, it is therefore necessary to employ some such concept as that of a 'discriminatory process'. This process may be further

[1] Ibid., p. 43.

[2] Oliver Cromwell Cox, *Caste, Class and Race* (New York, Monthly Review Press, 1959), p. 318.

[3] Michael Banton, *Race Relations* (London, Tavistock Publications, 1967), p. 60, *passim*.

defined as containing a number of interrelated, overlapping, but to some extent recognizably different, component parts: in-group; act of discrimination; out-group; and relationship of those to society as a whole. The operation of this discriminatory process would involve: aspects of attitude and behaviour of the in-group; these aspects expressed in an act that denies members of out-groups equality of treatment; the attitudes and behaviour of members of out-groups; and, finally, the relationship of these factors to the more general social situation. Under these terms, an anti-discriminatory measure may be seen to be directed particularly at one or more parts of the discriminatory process described. It is suggested that this concept of a discriminatory process may be employed for both a particular situation, say, over recruitment to a particular employment in a particular place, and for the general situation, relating to the relative positions and discrimination between a minority group or groups and the general society.

However, it has been argued that: 'The concept of discrimination belongs to a class of concepts which are defined theoretically in terms of factors that are themselves only indirectly measurable.' And that: 'When we attempt to measure discrimination we usually obtain measures of inequality.' Further, that: 'One of the problems in measuring discrimination is that of identifying the unit to be measured. Is it the number of discriminatory *acts*, the number of discriminatory *actors*, or the number of persons affected by discrimination?'[1] Perhaps confusions of this kind can be lessened by the use of a concept of a discriminatory process, and that the succeeding measurement of some part of this process may be related not only to indices of a static inequality but also to a mobile social situation.

There remains one fundamental problem to the study of racial discrimination: what is the racial factor and what distinguishes it from—simply—discrimination? It is not difficult to agree that by 'race' we here mean 'social race', or attitudes and behaviour conditioned by beliefs of one group about another. (There is at present no real evidence that 'genetic' race affects group behaviour, and this approach should, therefore, be discarded at this time.) It is next quite easy to postulate a dis-

---

[1] H. M. Blalock, *Toward a Theory of Minority-Group Relations* (New York, John Wiley & Sons, 1967), p. 17.

criminatory act in which, say, one person of one racial group is preferred for a job or promotion, and another, similar in every way except for 'race', is excluded on the conscious and deliberate grounds of race by a member of a second racial group. This may easily be termed racial discrimination and, for the sake of clarity, will be called first-order racial discrimination. It would, though, be naive to suppose that all such incidents could be so easily defined; very often there are a variety of factors (such as appearance, motivation, education, experience, socio-economic class, language ability, cultural background, residence in area or country, etc.) that complicate a clear decision. Nevertheless, by controlling as many variables as possible (as, for example, in the study of racial discrimination and white-collar testing in Chapter 7), it is possible to show that the factor of race is of dominant and primary importance. This situation may therefore be termed first-order discrimination.

There is a rather different sort of situation where members of one racial group may, for example, be consistently denied access to jobs controlled by another racial group on the grounds, *inter alia*, of low educational achievement; and it can be shown that the group denied jobs indeed have low educational attainments that apparently debar that group from satisfactorily performing jobs on the same basis as the other group. It can be argued that this is not racial discrimination, since it is not race but low education that is the dominant and primary factor. However, this argument can to some extent be countered. There exist racial groups that have received unequal treatment because of their race and are not now in a position in a society to receive equal treatment irrespective of their race.

One example of this might be of certain Negroes in certain cities in the northern United States. Put simply, proposition A is that the great majority of such Negroes have been consistently denied equality in such facilities as housing, education, and employment primarily because they are Negroes. This cannot be said to be true of all Negroes; but it can be said to be true of the majority in certain towns.[1] In contrast, other groups have

---

[1] For example, Horace R. Cayton and St. Clair Drake in *Black Metropolis* (London, Jonathan Cape, 1946), p. 176, found that, as long ago as 1930 in Chicago, '90 per cent [of Negroes] were in districts of 50 per cent or more Negro concentration. Almost two-thirds [63 per cent] lived where the concentration was from 90 to 99 per cent Negro!'

either not been deprived or have not been deprived to the same extent. Proposition B is that the group of deprived Negroes are now denied housing because of low educational attainment, and so forth. Of course, race may still be a contributory factor, but it is not now the primary one. It is, however, still the dominant factor, although operating as it were at one remove. Race is primary in proposition A, and proposition B is said here to follow from proposition A. This cyclical process may be termed second-order racial discrimination. The study of such situations is very necessary in assessing broad change within a society. It is open to argument as to how far and with exactly what force this proposition of second-order discrimination can be applied; but it can, for example, be seen to have some effect within historical relationships as between Britain and the West Indies. One writer has commented: 'I regard my relationship with the Englishman in his own country as an extension of the colonial relationships which existed in my native country.'[1] From the colonial relationship has come a further relationship, affecting the new arrivals to the metropolitan receiving country.

The discriminatory process outlined above may be applied to situations of first-order and second-order discrimination.

(b) EFFECTIVE MEASURES

The second main problem discussed in this section, is the definition of effective measures. An initial distinction can be drawn between specific and general measures: specific measures are those directed deliberately at some part of the discriminatory process; general measures are those directed at situations not primarily of racial discrimination, but which in operation affect a racial group or groups. As has been suggested, it is necessary to distinguish between different parts of the discriminatory process: for example, a legislative measure may reduce incidence of an act, but may increase awareness of discrimination amongst the group discriminating or the group discriminated against.[2] This means that a measure effective in one direction, may appear to be the reverse in another.

The method of measuring effectiveness will vary: the act of discrimination and related behaviour can be measured by incidence; by certain variations, e.g., of time and of differences

---

[1] A. M. Gomez, unpublished MS.   [2] For example, see Chapter 8.

between groups; by fairly precise measures of group attainments in terms of such factors as occupational classification, job engagement and promotion, education, housing, and so forth. The attitudes of groups can be found from surveys, and some work on quantifying subjective attitudes and the incidence of racial discrimination has been done.[1] But it is in respect of what people think that it is difficult to estimate effectiveness; and it cannot, of course, be maintained that attitudes and behaviour are here related in a constant and consistent way. Indeed, it is one of the aims of much legislation to achieve an immediate change in behaviour, with the knowledge that conflicting attitudes may persist. The difficulty considerably disappears when situations are considered historically—that is to say, when they are studied over a period of time. Here the differential between behaviour and attitudes is obviously much diminished. Even for the shorter time study, it is very necessary to consider attitudes. Many of the definitions and discussions of discrimination—which are usually carried on by the dominant group—omit sufficient attention to the feelings of the subordinate group. For example, the race relations legislation in the United Kingdom has been established without very much attention to the views of the groups it is designed to protect; although it would not be very easy to gauge these accurately.

The effectiveness of measures may therefore be found by such methods as time-scale, comparisons between groups, and the attainments of groups. The *kind* of measures that are effective will, of course, be considered at length in the main part of the text of this study, and in the 'Conclusions'. At this stage, it may simply be useful to note that attempts have been made to categorize such measures: for example, Simpson and Yinger list a variety of methods or 'strategies with major emphasis on changing the personality': First, exhortation, although 'It is easy . . . to exaggerate the influence of exhortation . . . . This uneasiness, in fact, may lead to stronger intolerance.'[2] Secondly, propaganda, although 'anti-prejudice propaganda has not been very effective'.[3] Thirdly, contact, although this seems effective sometimes in

---

[1] For example, Franklin J. Henry, 'The Measurement of Perceived Discrimination: A Canadian Case Study', *Race* (Vol. X, No. 4, April 1969), pp. 449–61.
[2] Simpson and Yinger, op. cit., pp. 498–9.
[3] Ibid.

reducing and sometimes in increasing prejudice and discrimination. Fourthly, education: 'One is justified in a modest optimism that when a program has been set in motion, particularly with children, it can be fairly effective in preventing or reducing prejudices.'[1] Fifthly, 'personal therapy' and 'group therapy'. It may not be inappropriate here to recall Adorno's views that analysis of prejudiced people is more likely to provide information for the non-prejudiced and information about the broad nature of prejudice, than to suggest very specific and effective measures that may be aimed directly against prejudice:

. . . counter-measures should take into account the whole structure of the prejudiced outlook. The major emphasis should be placed, it seems, not upon discrimination against particular minority groups, but upon such phenomena as stereotypy, emotional coldness, identification with power, and general destructiveness. . . . [It] is not difficult to see why measures to oppose social discrimination have not been more effective. Rational arguments cannot be expected to have deep or lasting effects upon a phenomenon that is irrational in its essential nature. . . . Although appeals to his reason or to his sympathy are likely to be lost on him, appeals to his conventionality or to his submissiveness to authority might be effective . . . he [the prejudiced man, here 'the potentially fascist personality'] would be impressed by legal restraints against discrimination.[2]

Whether one agrees with Adorno or not, it may be worthwhile to note some of the difficulties involved in attempts to change 'personality'. Simpson and Yinger go on to review methods or 'strategies with major emphasis on changing situations'. These include the 'place of law and administration', and 'organizations opposing discrimination', this last ranging from public agencies to civil rights and protest movements. Many of the measures that have been taken in the United Kingdom can, to some extent, be fitted within these categories.

A measure, in the light of the discussion above, would seem to have certain characteristics: it may be either general or aimed specifically at lessening some aspect of racial discrimination; it may possibly be aimed at affecting personality and prejudice, or at changing situations. It can further be suggested that a measure is an intended act, or more usually a series of acts, carried out

[1] Ibid., p. 511.
[2] T. W. Adorno et al., *The Authoritarian Personality* (New York, Harper & Brothers, 1950), p. 973.

probably by a group. An effective measure might then be said to be such a measure of the nature described that is found—by such methods as historical study or comparisons between groups or attainments of groups—to have achieved some amelioration of racial discrimination, or, presumably, to have at least prevented a worsening of a situation of racial discrimination.

3. *The Situation in the United Kingdom*) *Why there will be a wide range of race in U.K.*

There will be no attempt here to reproduce in number or extent the many factors that relate the United Kingdom situation to this particular study, for these are later discussed in the various chapters. But an attempt will be made to review, very briefly, a few dominant factors.

( ) Firstly, the race relations situation in the United Kingdom is still—for the purpose of this study—to a considerable extent a migration one. (But it must also be remembered that the migration factors are of diminishing importance, and many observers feel that they are now of less importance than the 'race relations' factors discussed below.)[1] Of the approximately one million

[1] The relative importance of the migration factor and the race relations factor is difficult to define exactly. This is, firstly, because definitive evidence is hard to come by in the early stages of immigration: it can be agreed that the break-out rates for both white and non-white groups, from their initial migrant situations to positions of greater symbiosis with the host communities, are small. Hence, it is difficult to isolate and calculate the effect of the colour factor since one is, for example, attempting to compare one small degree of change for one group with another small degree of change for a different group. It is also difficult to define because the factors interact: Sheila Patterson describes some white supervisors and workers who 'were not colour-conscious to anything like the same degree as the newcomers', and found it irksome to have to watch their words and behaviour so closely with individuals whom they would otherwise have regarded as quite acceptable; but Dipak Nandy finds this 'the familiar "chip-on-the-shoulder" hypothesis to account for allegations of discrimination which did such sterling work through the 1950s in sustaining "colour blindness"'. See Sheila Patterson, *Immigrants in Industry* (London, Oxford University Press, for Institute of Race Relations, 1968), p. 258; and Dipak Nandy, in *New Society* (19 December 1968), p. 924. Were the whites colour prejudiced? Were the non-white newcomers wrongly attributing inevitable and initial migration difficulties to colour prejudice? And so on. At later stages, the migration factor will be of much reduced importance, and the race factor will stand out more clearly. But in the initial stages they will both be present and potent. It is probably a safe conclusion that, even in these early stages, the race factor *is* potent; from the evidence of a variety of more 'developed' race relations situations elsewhere and from increasing evidence on the British situation, the behaviour and attitudes of the white hosts are strongly affected by race. Yet, this apart, the factors of language and culture, among others, are still at this time of considerable importance. Both factors must therefore be considered.

non-white people in the United Kingdom in 1966, towards four-fifths were immigrants and the remainder had been born in this country. Furthermore, the immigrants are comparatively recent arrivals: the considerable majority have entered the country in the last fifteen years. There are three main groups: West Indians, Indians, and Pakistanis. Of these, in late 1968 the West Indians (immigrants and their children born in the United Kingdom) numbered about 445,000 with their families largely complete and relatively few dependants likely still to enter; the Indians numbered about 230,000 with their families near half-way completed; and the Pakistanis, about 125,000 with a considerable number of dependants still to come. Generally, all visibly non-white persons are loosely lumped together and called 'coloured'. This points to the potential rigidity of British race relations and apparently also serves to conceal from the British that the 'coloured' immigrants form only a minority of all the immigrants in Britain. These main groups from Commonwealth countries have clearly come from different social and economic systems and, often, from a different part of the system from that in which they now find themselves (that is, most immigrants originate from rural areas and very nearly all are now in urban areas). In the case of the Indians and Pakistanis, the differences are fairly obvious in such terms as dress, language, or education; in the case of the West Indians, these differences are rather less obvious but are still considerable (although the image of the 'British Caribbean' as the Southern States of the United Kingdom remains a useful one). It therefore follows that in terms of discrimination in employment, housing, education, etc., allowance must be made for the migration factors: so far, the applicant for a job is likely on average to have had his education in a different country, to speak English not at all, poorly, or with a noticeably different accent from the usual styles, etc. This also means that, for example, one cannot easily examine discrimination along the line of engagement, promotion, etc., because there has not yet been sufficient time for a clear pattern to emerge. These migration factors are relevant not only to host-immigrant relationships, but also to relationships between immigrant groups: as yet, there is very little co-operation at any level between the Indians, Pakistanis, and West Indians, and this has important repercussions particularly in terms of activist organizations and political activity. Comparisons to

conceal
conceive

illustrate the migration factor can in many ways best be made between the United Kingdom and certain other European countries, particularly the Netherlands and France. Both these countries have, as metropolitan powers, received a considerable number of immigrants from former colonies, as well as a more general labour migration. It may prove an important difference that a lower percentage of the immigrants in these countries have been regarded as Black or coloured; but, the general position of immigrants in France has by no means been trouble-free.[1] However, at the time of this study few European comparisons had been made;[2] and comparisons have more frequently been made with the situation in the United States.

The fact that there is now a permanent and sizeable coloured minority of over one million makes it clear that there is a race relations situation. It is, at this stage, fundamentally different from that of the United States. The size of the non-white population is much smaller in over-all and relative terms; there are the transcontinental migration factors previously mentioned; and the economically active immigrants have a high level of employment, do not mainly live in ghetto areas, nor do their children go to *de facto* segregated schools. Compared to American race relations,[3] then, the United Kingdom is at what seems to be a critically formative stage: broadly, there is the road to an integrated society, on the one hand, and, on the other, the road to segregation and ghettos. If there is not yet massive unemployment, nor segregated housing and education, neither are the non-white minority groups integrated into the general society. Of course, this argument is partly based on the premise that the general society is itself 'integrated' or can become so. Other viewpoints can be advanced, such as that the general society is far from integrated, with the class divisions so deep that the coloured immigrants will be subsumed into the underclass, and that what is called for is a radical restructuring of society. A third viewpoint might be that the coloured or Black immigrants (and

[1] See, for example, Godula and Stephen Castles, 'Immigrant Workers and Class Structure in France', *Race* (Vol. XII, No. 3, 1971).
[2] But see Christopher Bagley, *Race Relations in the Netherlands and the United Kingdom* (London, Oxford University Press, for Institute of Race Relations, forthcoming).
[3] This term is used because British race relations are often discussed in relation to the United States. Neither country, of course, encompasses many of the situations occurring in other areas that may also be termed 'race relations'.

'Black' is here particularly appropriate as denoting common political consciousness) will act as the Third World vanguard in Europe, and that a restructuring of the general inequity of international relations is necessary. But the point being made here is more preliminary and basic: in race relations terms, the situation in Britain seems to be flexible to the extent that the coloured minorities do not yet form a rigid, distinct, and separate group from the rest of society. The pattern of race relations can therefore be regarded as still relatively unformed and mobile. In 1968, it was still broadly true that the immigrant non-white groups and the British Government favoured integration or, at least, accommodation.

The third factor to note is that the anti-discriminatory measures operating in the United Kingdom are very new, even within the time-span of the main coloured immigration. The Commonwealth Immigrants Act 1962 first limited coloured immigration, and the introduction of the earliest Governmental anti-discriminatory measures was in 1965. The Government have claimed that restriction over entry has been accompanied by measures to promote equality and integration for those already admitted; and, in August 1965, the White Paper on *Immigration from the Commonwealth* further restricted immigration and re-constituted the National Committee for Commonwealth Immigrants as the main body concerned with host-immigrant relations. In November 1968, this organization was re-formed as the Community Relations Commission. Also in 1965 came the first Race Relations Act, containing anti-discriminatory legislation effective only in public places and also legislation against incitement. Under this Act, the Race Relations Board was set up to administer the provisions of these race relations laws. In 1968, the scope of the legislation was much extended. The United Kingdom has, therefore, had two main specific measures, and bodies, effective since 1965: the 'National Committee', now the Community Relations Commission, and the Race Relations Board. Apart from this, the Government have attempted a few additional measures, such as monetary aid to certain areas with immigrants, and the issuing of special instructions to Government employment exchanges. Generally, however, there have been very few measures introduced either by local government, or in the area of private business and initiative. It is not, perhaps, surprising that the history of anti-discriminatory measures has been a short one: the migration is itself recent, and the belief was widely held for some time that special measures were not necessary.

The fourth main factor here briefly delineated is that of the society into which these heterogeneous coloured groups have come. Compared again to the United States, it is a relatively homogeneous society and earlier immigrants have largely been absorbed within the British social structure. The net population movement has generally been outwards: for example, there has been a net inflow for only six years since 1945. Whereas in the United States it has been possible to maintain a binary approach of ethnic separatism and over-all national consciousness, here there has been perhaps a dominant 'Britishness' with less important internal regional variations. No comparably large non-white groups have entered in the past and it would seem that, to absorb these new groups, an extension of British national consciousness must be developed. (It is not, of course, intended to suggest that British society is literally homogeneous; for example, the importance of class divisions is very great; but, compared to American society, it can be represented in certain aspects of political consciousness as *relatively* homogeneous.) These new groups are clearly conditioned by the ordinary operation of the society into which they arrived: those in traditional, relatively deprived reception areas, have had access to housing and other facilities in those areas. Quite apart from matters of race, they are therefore subject to the ordinary factors affecting recently arrived migrant groups in this country; and, additionally, if they live in a relatively deprived area (as many of the urban centres are), they will be subject also to general discriminatory factors (for example, access to public services as outlined in a variety of poverty research). Apart from considering the general discriminatory factors, what of race discrimination in Britain? That racial discrimination does exist has been established by a number of research studies and by both Government and private bodies working in this field. For example, a further volume based on the P.E.P. project[1] reported that: 'In the sectors we studied—different aspects of employment, housing and the provision of services—there is racial discrimination varying in extent from the massive to the substantial.' It goes on

---

[1] W. W. Daniel, *Racial Discrimination in England* (Harmondsworth, Penguin, 1968), p. 209.

to say that: 'The experience of white immigrants, such as Hungarians and Cypriots, compared to black or brown immigrants, such as West Indians and Asians, leaves no doubt that the major component in the discrimination is colour.' The study of white-collar applicants reported in this volume shows that: 'Using colour as an independent variable, we found substantial differences between the success rates of white and coloured immigrants. . . .' Britain's long history of colonialism overseas does not sufficiently explain the present racialism in this country. Indeed, some of Enoch Powell's apparent success may come from the fact that individuals and institutions generally are only beginning to be aware of the size of the problem and its significance for British society. It is possible, for example, to regard the comments of some of the judges and others concerned with legal cases involving apparent racialism as based on the belief that the matter was isolated and largely irrelevant to British affairs. The importance of colonialism is nevertheless great, both as providing a socio-economic link that—as in some other European countries—brought an immigrant influx, and as a factor moulding the minds of many of the British host population towards prejudice. Yet colonialism was overseas and the presence of a significant number of non-whites in English schools and streets, courts and pubs, presented a new situation: the basic challenge of racialism to a national democracy is perhaps still not yet fully recognized in Britain. However, although Britain has had little history of racialism at home—fascism has been a relative failure in the United Kingdom—it can now be recognized that racialism is present, as one of many factors, in British society today: there undoubtedly are tensions between the racial groups. These should not, of course, be exaggerated; the disturbances of 1958 have not so far been repeated and there has been very little violence. Also racialist tendencies have been countered by the Government and other measures described in this study.

4. *The United Kingdom Study*

The applicability to the United Kingdom of the three pre-conditions laid down by UNITAR was first considered: there was a multi-racial population; there was a significant degree of tension between ethnic (and racial) groups; but there could hardly be said to be much accumulated experience in concerted action against discrimination, and the study was to take place at the time of the introduction of more comprehensive measures. Despite this, it was thought reasonable to undertake a study during 1968: evaluation of measures during their early stages would provide useful comparable material for the future; and the United Kingdom, despite the relatively recent introduction of legislative measures as compared to, say, the United States or Canada, had in fact already achieved more specific measures in this field than had most countries with racial minorities.

The study design had to take into account not only the declared objectives of UNITAR, but the very short period of time available for the study, existing research material and published work, and various of the factors outlined earlier in this Introduction. The approach that was adopted involved, firstly, specially commissioned papers based on existing knowledge in the fields of migration history and theory, law, employment, housing, and the development of the voluntary committees. A second category was work undertaken by the Institute's permanent or temporary staff, based on the use of documentation, interviews, etc., and covering the operation of the Race Relations Board and the N.C.C.I. and some of the local committees; the activities of the police and Government; education; the attitudes of West Indian and Asian immigrant leaders; the demographic and statistical background. A third category was work commissioned through Social and Community Planning Research. Because relatively little was known about developments in the critical sector of employment, it was decided to supplement the existing work by testing the degree of discrimination in white-collar employment, using postal applications. It must be noted that many of the chapters were written in 1968, that the interviewing and testing were done in 1968 and 1969, and that a few chapters were written more recently or have been up-dated.

The UNITAR objectives called for 'structural characteristics of the multi-racial society' in terms of 'demographic data' and 'position of groups in the stratification system'. In Chapter 3, Brian Cohen provides this and, in terms of our analysis, considers the general situation relating to the discriminatory process and gives the data on which to assess the possible growth of the situation earlier described as second-order discrimination. In

Chapter 2, Sheila Patterson not only surveys the passage of the main immigrant groups, but also provides a review of theories and concepts of migration upon which the comparative discussion of the groups and of the receiving society can be based.

Also called for was information on the 'main traits and trends', being 'historical background ... connected with the prevailing racial policies'. The chapters on employment by Bob Hepple, housing by Elizabeth Burney, and education by Julia McNeal, provide summaries of the process of discrimination in the three critical areas of immigrant-host contact. The report by Roger Jowell and Patricia Prescott-Clarke, of Social and Community Planning Research (S.C.P.R.), offers fresh evidence in an important but largely unstudied part of the employment field. Additionally, the evidence in Chapter 8, from the interviews undertaken by R. Manderson-Jones and Jyothi Kamath, makes available information on the attitudes of leaders of minority groups: it will be remembered that the importance of testing the perceptions of minority group members within the social process of discrimination was stressed.

'Policies and measures' can best be considered together with some assessment of their success or failure. The most obvious policies and measures have been in the legislative field: Louis Kushnick's paper employs historical material to evaluate intentions as well as to record the legislation achieved. Brian Cohen reviews the working of the Race Relations Board, and Marna Glyn, the analysis of complaints, involving the use of incidence (although the data must, of course, be interpreted as incidence of reported discrimination and not of racial discrimination *per se*). The second main body, the National Committee for Commonwealth Immigrants, now the Community Relations Commission, and the local committees are assessed in papers by Hannan Rose, Margot Levy, and myself. Additional Governmental and private measures and activities, including the role of employers, are discussed by N. D. Deakin and Brian Cohen. Finally, the evidence is reviewed in the 'Conclusions', which also attempt briefly to review the larger structural relationships that underlie social change and anti-discriminatory measures.

Part I

The Immigrants and the Receiving Society

CHAPTER 2

Immigrants and Minority Groups in British Society

SHEILA PATTERSON

1. *Climates of Opinion*

Any discussion of discrimination or attempts to evaluate the effectiveness of various anti-discrimination measures in different countries must clearly take into account the over-all social situations, patterns, and dynamics that are specific to each country.[1] Thus, whilst the issues of discrimination and anti-discrimination measures are dealt with in other chapters, this chapter will be primarily concerned with the observed processes of immigrant-receiving society and minority-majority relations in Britain, and will endeavour to provide a theoretical framework which appears to be applicable to the British and a number of related situations —notably complex developed societies which have received considerable inflows of immigrants, often from less developed areas.

This attempt at a two- or three-generational overview may have some value at a time when the prevailing climate of opinion on coloured immigration has undergone an almost polar change in recent years: from *laissez-faire* indifference to nervous preoccupation on the part of most national political leaders and a wide range of public opinion; and from 'multi-racial' optimism to 'race war' pessimism among liberal and left-wing élites.

At the time of the earlier extreme of *laissez-faire* optimism, dissent was seemingly voiced only by small groups of illiberal or pathological anti-immigrationists. There were, however, others whose misgivings and warnings were either drowned out by or confused with the clamour of the anti-immigrationists, and were thus little heard from or listened to, particularly in the metropolis. These included a growing number of individuals with close

[1] See UNITAR paper on the 'Comparative Study of the Effectiveness of Policies and Measures Against Racial Discrimination' (Teheran Conference, 1968) pp. 3–4.

knowledge of the situation, including some local government officers, welfare workers, trade union officials, and others in the areas most affected by large-scale immigration from the 'coloured' Commonwealth countries. The dogged, uneuphoric pragmatism of such people may have acquired a more sombre expression in recent years, but it has not swung as far as the prevailing climate of opinion. Their approach has withstood the test of time and has been extended to an increasing number of people from the same and other fields (for example, teachers and the immigrant groups themselves). Given the added incentive of encouragement and large-scale financial assistance at national level, the existence of a sizeable body of people with such an approach and such expertise is an essential precondition for the effective operation, at face-to-face level, of legal and other anti-discrimination measures, among which must be included programmes aimed at positive integration rather than the prevention of discrimination.

The nature of the shift in the climate of opinion, and the major reasons for it, are discussed in detail in Nicholas Deakin's excellent article on 'The Politics of the Commonwealth Immigrants Bill'.[1] Here, however, it may be relevant to add a brief personal comment, as I was one of the relatively few people actively involved in the study and discussion of race relations in Britain for the whole period since 1955, when interest was beginning to focus on the 'new' mass migration movement of West Indian economic immigrants, not to the docks and ports, but to Britain's labour-hungry industrial areas.

Since 1955, the change of social climate has been immense, nor is there any reason not to anticipate future shifts. For instance, in the mid-1950s immigration controls were rarely discussed in public, and anti-discrimination legislation hardly at all.[2]

Late summer 1958 brought the shock of the Notting Hill disturbances, which left a widespread sense of disquiet. At this time, some voluntary associations were beginning to tackle certain aspects of integration, and there was a small but growing anti-immigration lobby in Parliament. Nevertheless, the issue of immigration was politically peripheral and the prevailing climate of opinion remained basically *laissez-faire*, voluntaristic, and non-

---

[1] In *The Political Quarterly* (Vol. 39, No. 1, January–March 1968).

[2] This is not to overlook the repeated attempts, since 1953, by Fenner Brockway and R. Sorensen (then M.P.s, now peers) to introduce anti-discrimination legislation.

discriminatory (not only in the sense of rejecting immigration controls or planning, but in such matters as refusing to keep separate statistics). This formal allegiance to non-discrimination was maintained not only by most British politicians, at national and even local levels, ranging from Tory Commonwealth traditionalists to left-wing internationalists, but was also insisted upon by the West Indians, who were the Commonwealth peoples most involved. With the exception of the Barbadian Government project, any talk of planned migration, selection, phasing, reception, or dispersal was generally rejected as contrary to the somewhat euphoric conception of an egalitarian, multi-racial Commonwealth and of a common Commonwealth citizenship which, during this transition period between an imperial past and an uncertain future, was shared by many opinion-formers on the Right as well as on the Left.

A major reason for the continued existence of this climate of opinion through the 1950s was that the dimensions of the problem posed by free immigration, particularly as viewed from the metropolis, were not large enough to warrant official action at a time when it might have been less drastic in content and less odious in manner. At the end of 1958, there were, according to a Home Office estimate, about 210,000 coloured Commonwealth residents of the United Kingdom, of whom 115,000 were West Indians (the total population of the British Caribbean at that time being about three and a half millions) and only 55,000 from India and Pakistan (total combined population about 550 millions). In 1959, another 16,400 West Indians entered and in 1960, the total entry jumped to nearly 50,000. Meanwhile, there was increasing concern over the possibility of rising entry figures from India and Pakistan, whose Governments had until 1959 effectively maintained voluntary controls. By 1961, however, the net inward movement was rising steeply (66,300 West Indians, 23,750 Indians, 23,100 Pakistanis). Whether or not this rise was stimulated by fears of controls or was one of the factors that led to their introduction, *laissez-faire* attitudes began to give way to the increasingly restrictive and negative climate of opinion that has since characterized British reactions to Commonwealth immigration.

Immigration controls were announced in September 1961 and came into force in mid-1962, after a further beat-the-ban net

2*

increase in the first six months of 75,930 (including over 44,000 Indians and Pakistanis). Thereafter, arrivals dropped, but soon picked up to reach over 41,000 in 1963 and 1964 and more thereafter (mostly dependants of the beat-the-ban immigrants). By the year 1968, therefore, the over-all number of coloured Commonwealth immigrants, including their British-born children, had more than quadrupled in a decade,[1] and its ethnic and socio-cultural make-up had been radically diversified by the large post-1960 inflow of Asians. (This change in the composition of the immigrant population has inevitably contributed to the change in orientation among those concerned with promoting absorption, with the emphasis shifting from accommodation with hopes of ultimate assimilation—probably via the class hierarchy— to an as yet rather vaguely conceived pluralistic integration.)

Over the same period, there has also been increasing disillusionment within the Commonwealth, and within Britain, over the Commonwealth in its present form; an intensified preoccupation with the problems, as opposed to the possibilities, of multiracial societies everywhere, focused increasingly on the deteriorating American situation; a growing self-consciousness among immigrants and hosts alike about colour and race; and a burgeoning tendency to view situations everywhere in terms of simple Black-white confrontations. These trends have been for some years stimulated or supported by sensationalism in the mass media and increasingly virulent activity at both extremes and among a minority of immigrants themselves. Latterly, the expression of extreme anti-immigrant views has increased as a result of the respectability conferred on them by a prominent Conservative M.P. and ex-Cabinet Minister, Mr. Enoch Powell, in his blood-and-funeral-pyre speech of 20 April 1968 and subsequent speeches. The concentration of immigrants in decaying areas of large industrial cities has exacerbated existing shortages and problems, in such fields as housing, education, and welfare, thereby gravely impeding the work of positive integration. At national level, support for positive policies of integration has been meagre, tardy, and half-hearted. Anti-discrimination measures, which are

---

[1] The fact that I cite increased numbers as a factor in the changed situation does not mean that I accept without qualification the proposition that the size of the group determines the size of the 'problem', or the naive and superseded notion of 'economic' absorptive capacity in relation to immigration.

preventive rather than positive, have been introduced—but only after years of opposition—as a counterbalance to increasingly rigid controls and a substitute for expensive positive action. For the time being, the general climate of opinion remains overcharged, negative, restrictive, legalistic, and 'discriminatory' in a number of senses, including the widespread underlying assumption that the problems of 'coloured' peoples everywhere are not only identical but different from those of other groups.

Looked at in the immigration perspective, the social climate which has developed in recent years may be seen as a phase that almost inevitably follows a wave of uncontrolled, unselected, undirected immigration, when the receiving society, or considerable local sections of it, feels threatened not only because of excessive pressure on inadequate social facilities and services but also with regard to the 'community core' or 'cultural core', which has been defined as the 'essence of a nation'.[1] A general sense of widespread threat to this core may be discerned behind the uglier manifestations of anti-immigrant and anti-colour feeling that characterized the massive outburst of approval of Mr. Enoch Powell's anti-immigration speech in April 1968. As London's Sunday *Observer* commented in a major editorial on 28 April:

The citizens of Bradford and Birmingham are neither enlightened philosophers nor political extremists. But what few liberals have dared to face quite frankly is that these people are no more inclined to welcome a crowd of black people (as distinct from an occasional individual) into their clubs and pubs than liberal intellectuals would be to admit a lot of people holding a blatantly different set of values into whatever they regard as their social group. It may be argued that skin colour and matters of opinion are utterly different. But both generate powerful feelings of identity. In Northern Ireland a man's religion is treated like a racial difference. Anti-Semitism itself is based more on cultural prejudices and beliefs than on physical differences. Skin colour is only the most irreducible, inescapable, senseless but probably strongest of our means of recognising a group identity. And only if we are conscious of our own sense of group identity can we gauge the strength of feeling that infringement of that sense arouses. . . .

In times of change and confusion, it is usual that people feel their security and sense of identity is threatened; often, as in Germany

[1] See W. D. Borrie, *The Cultural Integration of Immigrants* (Paris, UNESCO, 1959), pp. 114–15.

in the 1930s, they look for a scapegoat to explain their difficulties. The accidental arrival of many coloured people at this time in our history has confused the problems of colour with the unrelated frustration and grievances widely felt among both the workers and much of the middle class.

Situations in which a sense of threat to the community and cultural core has led to an outburst of hostility to newcomers and aliens have occurred in Britain before, notably in relation to large-scale Irish and Jewish immigration, and they are part of the history of all countries of immigration. The outburst of hostility has normally been followed by a period in which immigration declined or was cut back, with a consequent slowing-down of inter-group tensions and, at least in earlier days, of economic development. Then would come a phase in which, to quote W. D. Borrie again, 'the society had to choose between a relatively low rate of economic growth with little social tension and a rapidly growing community core on the one hand, and a rapid growth with considerable tension and a weakening of the community core on the other'. The problem of the interrelation of economic and socio-cultural factors was 'to keep the tensions below the point of disruption'.

2. *Some Concepts in Immigration Theory*

The theoretical approach employed in this chapter is an extension of that outlined in *Dark Strangers*[1] and elaborated in the discussion on the industrial sphere in *Immigrants in Industry*.[2] The emphasis is basically sociological and historical, rather than psychological; it is more concerned with groups than with individual relations, and with behaviour rather than attitudes.[3]

[1] Sheila Patterson, *Dark Strangers* (London, Tavistock Publications, 1963; and Harmondsworth, Penguin Books, 1965).

[2] Sheila Patterson, *Immigrants in Industry* (London, Oxford University Press, for Institute of Race Relations, 1969).

[3] At this juncture, too, no systematic attempt will be made to review or apply other theoretical approaches or general hypotheses about minority-majority relations in all types of society. For some recent reviews of these, see Brewton Berry, *Race and Ethnic Relations* (Boston, Houghton Mifflin & Co., 1958); Charles A. Price (ed.), *Australian Immigration: A Bibliography and Digest* (Canberra, A.N.U., 1966); Michael Banton, *Race Relations* (London, Tavistock Publications, 1967); Pierre van den Berghe, *Race and Racism* (New York, Wiley, 1967); Tamotsu Shibutani and M. Kwan Kian, *Ethnic Stratification: A Comparative Approach* (New York, Macmillan, 1965); Herbert Blumer, 'Recent Research on Racial Relations in the U.S.A.', UNESCO *International Social Science Bulletin* (Vol. X, No. 3, 1958).

Apart from a debt to such pioneer American social historians of immigration as Hansen and Handlin, the theoretical approach adopted here owes most to the work of such scholars as R. E. Park, Everett Hughes, S. N. Eisenstadt, Michael Banton, and W. D. Borrie. It has arisen rather out of an 'integration' (or 'consensus') than a 'conflict' view of society.[1] On the other hand, various concepts of the 'plural society' (see, for example, J. S. Furnivall, M. G. Smith, Freedman and Willmott, H. S. Morris) have stimulated thought as to the true nature of the over-all British society, the differing types of minority and immigrant groups that it contains, and the relationships between them and the majority society (and also between different minority groups) in a variety of situations.

(a) THE PROCESSES AND PHASES OF ABSORPTION

I have adopted Eisenstadt's term 'absorption' to cover the whole situational range of the two-way processes of 'adaptation and acceptance' that occur between immigrant or minority groups and the absorbing or majority society. Both the general term and those indicating different phases denote both a process leading to an end-product and the end-product itself (static or ideal).

(i) Assimilation

The term 'assimilation' has been defined in a number of senses, ranging from Park's minimal definition[2] to complete incorporation, acculturation, adaptation, and acceptance between a minority and the majority society.[3] Where the latter definition is accepted, there has in recent years been a tendency to criticize

---

[1] See Banton, pp. 62–76, for a discussion of sociological theory in relation to the study of race relations and majority-minority situations. However, he finds the consensus theory not well suited to the 'study of circumstances in which two societies interact or in which social patterns are maintained by force rather than agreement' and puts forward a tentative new set of sequences based on, *inter alia*, the differing stimuli of group alignment and George C. Homans's model of social behaviour as a 'transaction'.

[2] In *Encyclopaedia of the Social Sciences*, Vol. 2, pp. 281–2. Elsewhere, however, he defined it as a far more thorough-going process.

[3] See discussions in the *Cultural Assimilation of Immigrants* (Cambridge, International Union for the Scientific Study of Population, Cambridge University Press, 1950), pp. 3, 115.

or avoid its use,[1] whether because it has sometimes been associated with one-way political pressures and misleading biological associations, or is found polemical and offensive by certain minority groups, or again because it is not seen, at least on a short-term view, to reflect over-all social reality. None the less, there have been numerous instances of full assimilation, group as well as individual, in Britain, as well as the United States, Canada, Australia, France, Israel, and elsewhere. We are here concerned less with value judgements and goals than with social facts, and it is, therefore, proposed to retain the term here to refer to complete adaptation by immigrants or a minority and complete acceptance by the absorbing society in all areas of social relationship, private as well as public.[2]

The process of assimilation is not necessarily one-way, but is often two-way, in that the majority society may move some way towards the newcomers; nevertheless, the main effort of adaptation does fall on the latter, particularly in a relatively homogeneous and stable society such as Britain. Except for a minority of highly adaptable and energetic individuals, complete assimilation rarely occurs in the first immigrant generation. This applies even in cases where an immigrant group is not only 'assimilating' in intention but culturally akin and socially acceptable to the receiving society (e.g. the British in the 'old Commonwealth' or the United States and vice versa; Latin immigrants in South

---

[1] Cf. Price (ed.), op. cit., pp. A1–2, for some historical instances of this. The much quoted definition of integration as an official goal, as opposed to assimilation, given by the then Home Secretary, Mr. Roy Jenkins, in the latter part of 1966, is a recent instance of this tendency. (See Commons debate on the Expiring Laws Continuance Bill on 8 November 1966.)

[2] Once full assimilation is achieved it may, of course, lead to biological amalgamation, as with such groups as the Dutch, Germans, and Scandinavians in Canada and the United States, the Huguenots and Flemings in Britain, and also the more than ten thousand Negro slaves in the population of London during the nineteenth century. With small dispersed groups, there is, of course, the possibility that amalgamation may precede or aid social assimilation, but this depends to a great extent on the social context of inter-group relations. The assumption that the social problems involved in the absorption of large minority groups can be averted or solved by physical amalgamation is, however, generally an example of wishful thinking. In 1947, Ralph Linton wrote: 'Most anthropologists agree that there will be no Negro problem in another two hundred years: by then there will not be enough recognisable Negroes left in this country to constitute a problem.' See 'The Vanishing American Negro', in *American Mercury* (February 1947). This prediction may well be accurate, but in 1969, one must ask: What of the intervening period when Negroes are still recognizable and increasingly recognize themselves as different?

America; 'Western' Jewish immigrants in Israel; etc.). In other cases it may even take three or four generations, particularly in countries of immigration where the 'cultural core' and 'core community' are relatively new and weak,[1] or where there is apparently no common cultural core but a complex balance of ethnic communities and ethno-religious cultures (for example, in American sub-societies such as New York). On the other hand, complete assimilation may never occur at all for some if not most ethnic groups, particularly in such situations as New York, although the ethnic group will have changed and adapted itself and its institutions to its new role.[2] Instead, a situation of pluralistic integration or cultural pluralism prevails.

(ii) *Integration*

'Integration' will henceforward be used in the specific sense of 'pluralistic integration' or 'cultural pluralism', a process whereby, and a phase in which, a group adapts itself and is accepted as a permanent member in certain universal spheres of association within the absorbing society (e.g. employment, political life, and civil rights and duties); at the same time it remains 'integrating' in type, retaining a group existence and institutions (although some individuals may break away and become assimilated), and a community sub-culture based on such elements as religion, language, and perhaps geographical concentration or proximity to the country of origin, sometimes even on the retention of

[1] Cf. Borrie, op. cit., pp. 114–15. Israel is a partial exception here, since massive immigration is the only means by which a community core can be brought into existence. Nevertheless, despite a massive programme of assimilation or, later, of integration, there has been in recent years (at least until the Six Days' War in the summer of 1967) some evidence of the sort of problems and tensions that face all countries with a large, unselected intake of groups with widely differing socioeconomic and cultural backgrounds.

[2] In *Beyond the Melting Pot: The Negroes, Puerto Ricans, Jews, Italians and Irish of New York City* (Cambridge, Mass., M.I.T. Press and Harvard University Press, 1963), N. Glazer and D. P. Moynihan describe how the ethnic group in American society has ceased to be a survival from the age of mass immigration and has become a new social form, an interest group. Immigrant groups have fused into larger minority groups linked by language, culture, and religion; and even after language and culture have been lost, they have merged into groups linked by religion and/or race. (See also S. N. Eisenstadt, *The Absorption of Immigrants* [London, Routledge & Kegan Paul, 1954], pp. 251–2, for the transformation of 'ethnic' into 'religious' minorities.) On the other hand, some groups, notably the Germans, have virtually disappeared as ethnic groups, to be assimilated by the original Anglo-Saxon 'core'. This once again underlines the fact that groups differ not only in type but also in their interactions with the same over-all society.

secondary loyalties to that country. These 'alternatives' or 'specialities' should, in a universalistic, egalitarian society, be of a kind acceptable to the absorbing society, if the integrity of the latter's social and cultural core is not to be strained and endangered. Integration may be a seemingly final phase, or it may lead on to full assimilation.

There are a number of types of pluralistic situation arising out of the nature of the majority society and the type of the minority group. We are here basically concerned with modern mass migrations (political or economic) and the processes of absorption into complex, universalistic societies, with a more or less open-class stratification and a single basic social core. We should not, however, overlook the related situations in the 'federal' type of society, such as Switzerland, Belgium, Canada (and even to a lesser extent Britain in so far as the Scottish, Welsh, and Irish sub-cultures are concerned). Here the founding groups are long settled and usually have firmer territorial and cultural anchors than do most ethnic groups in societies of immigration and also later immigrant groups in their own countries. This territorial link seems to be one of the most important reasons for the stability and survival of many ethnic and cultural minorities; in the case of immigrant groups it has a different function: as a temporary oasis, and not as a permanent repository of group pride and values.

In so far as a pluralistic structure exists or develops, its nature would appear to be governed to a large extent by the criteria of the absorbing, majority or over-all society, although the character and orientations of the minority group are obviously important as well. There are a number of types of plural or pluralistic societies, as has been said, but we are not here primarily concerned with the classic type of colonial and multi-racial or multi-cultural 'plural society' identified by Furnivall from his experience in Burma and the Netherlands Indies: in such a society, relations between diverse groups are confined to the market-place; and for lack of a commonly held set of wants and values, the society can only be held together by the use of political force exercised by one dominant section.[1] Instead, the model

---

[1] For a discussion and critique of this and other models of the 'plural society', see H. S. Morris, 'Some Aspects of the Concept Plural Society', *Man* (Vol. 2, No. 2, June 1967), pp. 169–84.

would seem to be a 'federal' one, as in Switzerland, Canada, or Belgium. H. S. Morris has described the relations among the English, the Welsh, and the Scottish Highlanders as 'federal' rather than stratified.[1] While stressing the relative homogeneity of English society, the pressures to conform exerted on the Scots, Welsh, and Irish, as well as people from overseas, and the inclusiveness and consistency of the class system, Michael Banton suggests that, since World War II and the subsequent changes in the British social structure, British society is no longer as homogeneous as it was towards the end of the nineteenth century.[2]

That British society has been moving from homogeneity to heterogeneity over the last century is, of course, open to argument in cultural as well as social and political terms. From the viewpoint of the immigrant, however, as we shall show later, it would seem that a considerable amount of heterogeneity has been encountered as between classes and regional sub-cultures and latterly between generations. It should be stressed once more that the ethos and mores of an absorbing society (or particular sections of it) are a major factor easing or hampering the absorption of various immigrant and minority groups.[3] Thus, whereas a universalistic society such as Britain can, it appears, tolerate and accept certain degrees of pluralistic integration provided that certain universal roles are accepted by the newcomers, it may be asked whether and in what circumstances such a society can extend this toleration and acceptance to self-segregating groups that refuse to adapt themselves even to universal roles.

(iii) *Self-segregation*

We are not here concerned with segregated and rejected groups such as those found in many former conquest and colonial situations,[4] but with groups that voluntarily segregate themselves from

[1] Morris, op. cit., p. 175.

[2] Banton, op. cit., pp. 369–71, 387.

[3] Eisenstadt (p. 18) points out that complete transplantation of an immigrant community with all its customs, associations, and so on, is not feasible; some social transformation according to the demands of the new country must occur, since even the criteria of pluralistic absorption imply performance of the universal roles of the absorbing country.

[4] Much of the segregation and rejection that have so far occurred in Britain seems to have occurred on a class, and particularly a colour-class, basis; and as there is a fairly open class-stratification, it has not been permanent or total. One should, however, consider the possibility that a rigid and fairly visible under-class may evolve in

the majority society, resisting all forms of adaptation, even in universal spheres—in fact, groups that behave like those in the colonial type of plural society described by Furnivall. Such self-segregating groups are also found in a number of universalistic societies with a single social and/or structural core (e.g. the Mennonites in the United States and the Doukhobors in English-speaking Western Canada). A minimal amount of adaptation has nevertheless been found necessary by such groups if they are to avoid clashing with the majority society and its institutions (the Doukhobor Sons of Freedom refused even this and in consequence have clashed repeatedly and violently with the Canadian authorities).

In the early years of a migration, self-segregation in everything but the economic sphere may be regarded as part of the process of accommodation (for which see below). Later it is arguable whether it is not merely an extreme version of the process of integration, into which it may pass as the processes of absorption grind on. Certain groups in Britain have, however, succeeded in maintaining a voluntary self-segregation for a generation or more (e.g. the Chinese, and some Arab and Jewish communities) and it is perhaps worth regarding this as a separate category of process and looking at the conditions and factors which have made its endurance possible (for instance, the existence of specialized or 'niche' occupations in which the group can find work without competing with the over-all labour force, such as work in Chinese restaurants).

(iv) *Accommodation*

Granted that full absorption, whether by assimilation or integration, takes one or more generations, it seemed reasonable to adopt another term—'accommodation'—for the earlier phase of migrant-host relations. This may last out the first generation or at least the first five or ten years of migration. I have elsewhere[2] defined 'accommodation' as the attainment of a minimum *modus*

---

certain urban areas that are heavily settled by coloured immigrants, if special measures are not taken. One must also not overlook the fact that self-segregating groups can evolve out of rejection and alienation (e.g. the Black Muslims, Rastafarians, some orthodox Jewish communities, and others).

[1] See Berry, op. cit., pp. 274-5, 277.

[2] See *Dark Strangers*, op. cit., pp. 13-16; and *Immigrants in Industry*, op. cit., pp. 6-9. As used here, 'accommodation' is a modified version of Park's concept.

vivendi between newcomers and the receiving society. The immigrants establish themselves tolerably in the spheres of work and housing, and begin to conform, at least outwardly, to the new society's 'universal' patterns. This limited adaptation is met by a limited acceptance from the receiving society—both adaptation and acceptance being greater (though not complete) in some areas of association than in others (e.g. in such institutionalized and universalistic spheres as employment, legal and political rights, social services, etc.). Considerable social difference nevertheless remains, particularly in less defined and more intimate areas of association, such as neighbourhood life, informal social intercourse, and intermarriage.[1]

Accommodation is thus the lowest degree of adaptation and acceptance that is consistent with peaceful co-existence between immigrants and the absorbing society in the earlier period of contact (this does not, of course, preclude tensions and conflict). Migration involves wide social changes, including a shrinkage of social roles and some 're-socialization'. The phase of accommodation sees the beginnings of 're-socialization' in the new society. While the newcomers begin to adapt themselves in the necessary universal roles, they are enabled to retain, rebuild, or reorient their own patterns, norms, and values in other spheres. It is possible that this process may differ as between groups that are potentially assimilating, integrating, or self-segregating.

It should be emphasized that the phases of absorption defined and described above are not as self-contained and straightforward as they sound. In the first place, they move at different rates in different spheres or situations (e.g. immigrants can be assimilated at work and in the neighbourhood, but live an integrated ethnic life; or again, they can be integrated in an ethnic gang at work but be in an early phase of accommodation in the neighbourhood and all other spheres). This does not, of course, mean that progress towards absorption in one sphere does not influence adaptation

---

[1] The indices of accommodation and other phases of absorption vary considerably from one absorbing society to another (see Eisenstadt, op. cit., pp. 16–20). In *Dark Strangers* (pp. 16–18), I have suggested some indices of accommodation in various areas of social interaction in Britain; and made a later attempt to construct a more detailed set of indices of all phases of industrial absorption (see Table 3 in *Immigrants in Industry*, p. 206; see also explanatory section, pp. 205–27). It would also be possible to construct such a set of indices for interaction in, for instance, the neighbourhood and private social spheres (see Eisenstadt, op. cit., p. 109).

and acceptance in others. Another point is that the progression, over-all and in various spheres, is not necessarily an even or steady one (and in the same society it may differ for differing groups in different regions and in different socio-economic and cultural milieux). The history of immigrations shows how absorption can proceed in irregular strides and pauses—major efforts of adaptation or acceptance followed by years of an apparent *status quo*, or even regression as a result of such developments as economic, cultural, political, and other forms of conflict, the latter being inherent in every phase of the absorption process; nativistic movements or hostile reactions from the community core of the receiving society; or the re-infusion of 'old country' values in the minority groups through renewed or continuing migration particularly when the newcomers are conscious culture-bearers (as with the Polish and Ukrainian post-1939 exiles who reinforced the 'old' emigrations in the United States and Canada).[1]

Adaptation and acceptance do not usually proceed side by side. Some groups may achieve an almost complete adaptation but, for a time at least, remain only partially acceptable (e.g. anglicized European exiles in Britain, Jews in parts of the United States). On the other hand, other groups may adapt themselves only partially but meet with a large measure of acceptance (e.g. Australians, Canadians, or Americans in Britain).

Finally, even integrating or self-segregating groups are not monolithic. Thus, there are likely to be individual members who break away from an integrating-type group towards the goal of assimilation. There may also be segregating sub-communities within a given integrating-type group (e.g. Pentecostalists in a West Indian settlement, or Orthodox sects within Anglo-Jewry).

(b) FACTORS INFLUENCING THE PROCESSES OF ABSORPTION

The processes of absorption are the outcome of the interplay between immigrant or minority groups and the absorbing society, and cannot be studied in isolation.[2] Immigrant-host relationships are influenced by a considerable range of variables on either side. These may, for convenience, be subsumed under four main

[1] This refers to more than M. L. Hansen's 'third generation reaction' statement and the extension of it by Oscar Handlin and others. See Price (ed.), op. cit., pp. A23–47.

[2] This is not to underestimate the value of monographs concerned with particular groups studied from the inside.

headings: demographic; socio-economic and cultural; structural
(this, to some extent, overlaps with socio-economic and cultural)
and specific.

(i) *Demographic*

This covers such variables as: the relative size of the groups
involved; the number of immigrant or minority groups; the rate
of entry and the duration of the migration; the mode and density
of settlement (rural or urban; concentrated, isolated, or dispersed); the age and sex composition of the groups; lengths of
settlement; proximity to homeland (which facilitates continued
migration and slows full absorption).

(ii) *Socio-economic and Cultural*

This covers the socio-economic and cultural characteristics of both
immigrants and the absorbing society, and the degree to which
they coincide or are compatible.[1] Variables include: educational
levels and goals; occupational background and training; rural
or urban provenance; religion; language; 'core' patterns, values,
and norms (e.g. those concerned with family, kinship, class, and
regional ties; work and leisure; political and ideological beliefs,
etc.); motivations for migration of the newcomers (economic or
ideological); migrant intentions (seasonal, migratory, settler);
migrant expectations of, and attitudes to, the absorbing society
and that society's expectations of, and attitudes to, particular
groups and all newcomers (where there is a policy for immigration
and integration this may or may not reflect popular attitudes and
expectations: if it does not, this further complicates relations).

(iii) *Structural*

This covers such variables as the complexity, range, rigidity or
flexibility, and degree of exclusiveness of membership of the
organizational and stratificatory framework of the host society
and the organizations brought with them or set up by the newcomers. It may also extend to the different policies of immigration
control, selection, and integration that are operated by the absorbing society (and also any legal and other provisions relating to

[1] While the processes of absorption seem to a lesser or greater extent to get to work
whenever groups of people come into contact, there is no doubt that cultural kinship,
in the main elements and values of the cultures of the groups involved, speeds and
eases accommodation and absorption.

newcomers), and to any emigration policies and subsequent organizational arrangements (for representation, welfare, civil rights, etc.) made by the sending societies (such provisions can clearly affect the character of the migration and also the subsequent relations of the migrants with the host society).

(iv) *Specific*

Many of the variables above involve an historical perspective, but there are also particular historical events and trends that can exert a powerful influence on a particular situation and relationship, at the time of occurrence and later. For instance, the American Civil War and the myths of Reconstruction helped to determine the development of white-Negro relations for a century; likewise, Britain's abandonment of Empire and a world role and the emergence of a world-wide race issue cannot but influence the situation of over one million coloured immigrants and their children from that former Empire now in Britain.[1]

Another kind of specific variable is found in the presence and intervention of individuals or groups, usually from the absorbing society, in sponsoring or black-balling roles, and the emergence among the newcomers of various kinds of leadership and pioneer enterprise. Such interventions are more frequent than is generally realized, and they are partly responsible for the wide range of variations and the differing degree and forms of immigrant absorption found in seemingly similar situations within a given society.[2]

The importance of such variables, singly or more usually in differing combinations, in retarding or promoting the processes of absorption, will vary considerably between one society and another, one group and another, one situation or social context and another. Moreover, a particular factor may operate differently —in conjunction with differing clusters of other factors—in Society A than it does in Society B.[3]

[1] Events since February 1969 (the Kenya Asian crisis and the subsequent panic controls, and the rise of Powellism) afford a vivid example of this. An earlier instance is the stimulus provided by World War II for the acceptance of the Irish in Britain.

[2] Cf. Sydney Collins, *Coloured Minorities in Britain* (London, Lutterworth, 1957), pp. 30f., 247–8, 253; Patterson, *Immigrants in Industry*, op. cit., pp. 269–73.

[3] Cf. Price (ed.), op. cit., p. A55; Eisenstadt, op. cit., p. 16; Patterson, *Dark Strangers*, op. cit., p. 29 (of Penguin edition). One such variable is race or colour as a role sign, which clearly differs as among for instance, the United States (North and South), Brazil, South Africa, Mozambique, Britain, and France.

(c) THE IMMIGRATION PERSPECTIVE AND THE RACIAL PERSPECTIVE

Until one has produced a sufficiently detailed study of inter-group relations in a particular society, there is much to be said for caution in applying the criteria established for another society. In studying the absorption of coloured immigrants in Britain, for instance, there is a strong temptation to apply uncritically criteria from the Negro-white situation in the United States, instead of looking at the much more useful corpus of studies of immigration over several generations in American society (including the Negro migration from South to North and Puerto Rican migration) and others, such as Australia, Canada, France, and, most important, Britain itself. There is at present a tendency to single out the factor of race and colour and to posit unique racial or colour confrontation, identical in all societies, in which other and differing local factors are of relatively little importance. Quite apart from the fact that this approach may have a self-fulfilling quality, it is a gross over-simplification which is bound to obscure the real complexities and the full chiaroscuro of the fluid British scene.

The 'racial perspective' was, understandably enough, stressed by students of the small, established coloured settlements in ports and docks, but a number of those who after 1955 set out to study the new, larger settlements of West Indians, Indians, and Pakistanis, found the 'immigration perspective' more useful. Lately, with the accumulating evidence of anti-assimilationist tendencies among both the receiving society and the immigrants, and the growing international concentration on race problems, there has been a swing back to the 'race perspective'. In his recent study, for instance, Banton writes:

In general, there are grounds for thinking that, since the middle of the 1950s, the immigration perspective has become less appropriate to studies of the British scene and the racial one more so. Experience in the industrial cities of the United States has become more relevant to British problems. The changes that prompt such a conclusion have been brought about by the political significance that questions of immigration and race relations have acquired, and by the further development of tendencies within the British economic and social structure.[1]

[1] Banton, op. cit., p. 384.

In the same chapter, however, he mentions other developments which militate against this: for instance, there is no single
'coloured population' but several entirely distinct socio-cultural
groups between which the receiving population is increasingly
well able to differentiate; and the members of the second generation, even if British-born, are rarely fully acculturated, but are at
best socially and culturally marginal between their various
parental groups and the absorbing society. The implication must
surely be not that an 'immigration perspective' is of diminishing
utility but that it is often focused too short: it should have, at the
least, a three-generational sweep.

It is fashionable today to say that the second generation of
coloured immigrant[1] children will differ from their coevals only
in colour; they will, therefore, expect equal opportunities and
treatment from the society at large, and will become alienated and
rebellious if they do not receive them. Such expectations do
undoubtedly arise, and it is necessary and laudable that the
absorbing society and its agencies should endeavour to meet them
and to provide all possible opportunities. But a true 'immigration
perspective' will show that 'second generation blues', including
marginality, uncertain identity, excessive expectations, alienation,
stress, deviance, and at times delinquency, are found in a wide
range of majority-minority situations whether or not the colour
factor is present (e.g. Ukrainians in Canada; Puerto Ricans in
New York; rural Negroes and whites from the South in Northern
American cities; Yemenis and other Oriental Jews in Israel, the
Irish in Britain). Moreover, receiving societies do from time to time,
and for a variety of reasons, go through periods of apprehension,
resentment, and even rejection of any large group of newcomers.

Instead of falling back on the 'racial perspective' through
which to view and try to explain the events and trends of the next

---

[1] The use of this term in relation to people born in this country is often queried
and meets with considerable resentment from immigrant or minority groups themselves. It is, in fact, derived from studies of earlier immigrations elsewhere (e.g. the
United States, Canada, Australia) and reflects the obvious sociological fact that birth
in a particular area and/or possession of formal documents of citizenship do not of
themselves involve 'belonging' or even wishing to 'belong' to the majority community as a full member. While one may, as a matter of policy, use the more precise
'children of immigrants', one cannot overlook the fact that some second- and sometimes even third-generation children are torn between the old-country cultures and
values and those of the new society, even without taking into account any non-
acceptance of them or their group by the majority society for this or other reasons.

decade or so, it might be more useful (if one is trying as an academic or a policy-maker to understand the long-term processes
and mechanisms of absorption) to consider the whole complex
of circumstances in which these host society reactions arise;
and, in the case of the second immigrant generation, it would be
instructive to compare the situations in which there is little
marginality and alienation and those in which there is a great
deal, and the reasons for this. In the former category we may place
the Jewish, Polish, and Baltic second generations in Britain; in
the latter, the Irish, Anglo-coloured (even in the case of this
group, colour is only one of the factors influencing their situation),
and, as reported, some Cypriots. Those who deplore the very
notion of assimilation, however long-term, and indiscriminately
advocate cultural pluralism, overlook the fact that not all cultures
are sufficiently compatible with that of a particular absorbing
society or sufficiently adaptable to meet its basic minimum
demands without a clash which falls most heavily on the second
and perhaps even later generations.

(c) *Modes of Absorption and Integrative Action*

Looking at the history of earlier immigrations, it seems possible
that, in the British context, absorption, whether in the form of
integration or assimilation, proceeds more smoothly for those
minorities[1] which have come from a complex, urbanized society
with an inclusive, comprehensive, and flexible system of stratification—particularly when they are drawn not from the lowest
stratum but from various levels in the hierarchy. Greater difficulties appear to arise in the case of newcomers from rigidly
stratified estate-like societies (in which the élite and the masses
are alienated from one another, and the middle class is likely to
be small and ineffectual), and also those immigrants from simple,
rural societies in which a complex stratificatory system has not yet
evolved.

Clearly, many other factors have contributed to the smoother
absorption of certain immigrant and minority groups: for instance,
strong intra-group kinship and organizational links and loyalties,

[1] This does not refer only to newcomers from societies whose social and cultural
kinship with Britain is so close that their children are assimilated without difficulty
or trace in the second generation (e.g. immigrants from Australia, New Zealand,
Canada, and the United States).

and the presence of centrally-placed sponsors. Nevertheless, it seems worth-while to examine the past, present, and future role of Britain's strong, all-embracing, complex, and flexible class system in the absorption of immigrant and minority groups.[1]

It may well be that, as it has done for past immigrations, this mechanism can provide a more satisfactory long-term solution than the alternative of culturally and racially pluralistic minorities, incipient self-segregating and segregated 'ghettos' or 'coloured quarters', with a dark colour/low class/inferior culture identification persisting and perhaps even a genuine 'coloured' or 'black' under-class developing.

Pace the pessimistic liberals, Black Power advocates, and others, such a monolithic 'coloured' or 'black' minority or under-class is not likely to consolidate itself within the next ten years or so, although anti-integrationist pressures, ceaseless harping upon colour and race, and inability to recognize group differences and deal with each group according to its needs and aspirations,[2] on the part of the majority society, will certainly promote such a consolidation. This development could, however, be anticipated in the third generation and the later stages of the second generation —when old country cultural patterns and values are likely to have become tenuous and vestigial—if the grandchildren of Jamaicans, Trinidadians, Sikhs, Pakistanis, Somalis, and the remnants of a white proletariat are left to make common cause in the twilight areas of the West Midlands and Greater London.

If absorption is ultimately to take place via the stratificatory system (whether or not this means assimilation or pluralistic integration in cultural terms), certain pre-conditions and measures would now seem to be indicated, particularly in the universal areas of contact in which both integrative and anti-discriminatory measures are likely to be most effective. On the host side, policy-makers must promote a positive and informed tolerance among the general public, while endeavouring to remedy the general social

---

[1] Cf. Banton, op. cit., p. 370, and also p. 387.

[2] The use of 'coloured' liaison officers in some localities is a case in point. This may work well when the individual is British-born and trained, but in other cases West Indians may be found to object to an appointment of an Asian, while Hindus may prefer the services of an English officer rather than a West Indian or Pakistani. Yet in the case of 'white' European immigrants, it has generally been understood by the authorities that each immigrant or minority group tends to relate itself to the receiving society rather than to make common cause with all the others.

problems which have been exacerbated by the flow of immigrants. In such an improved climate of opinion, it will be easier to carry out policies of residential and educational dispersal, occupational training and differentiation, and cultural bridging (in such matters as the teaching of English, urban living, the use of local institutions), which will ultimately lead to social dispersal of the newcomers throughout the stratificatory system.

On the newcomers' side, there must be a will to acquire basic qualifications (including the English language), to participate and conform in universal areas of interaction, and to adapt or change in non-essentials.[1]

On both sides, policy-makers and opinion-formers must consider how the more essential social values and cultural elements that are at variance or incompatible with those of the receiving society can be adapted without losing their essence, to the point that the receiving society, educated to greater tolerance, can accept them as part of its over-all culture.[2]

3. *A Brief Review of the History of Immigration to Britain*

(a) THE 'OPEN DOOR' TRADITION

Up to 1905 there was free entry for all who wished to come to Britain, whether they were refugees from religious or political persecution, or migrants in search of work or skills. This long-standing permissive climate of official and public opinion may help to explain the later reluctance to impose barriers against British subjects from the Commonwealth and, indirectly, the

---

[1] A recent instance of this was the case of 'open' Moslem burials in Watford reported by the *Guardian* on 19 August 1968. Some doubts were expressed by the Deputy Town Clerk about the desirability of this practice on the grounds of public health. A prominent local Moslem spokesman said that 'open burial' was a preferred method because the emphasis in Islam is always on a simple burial which rules out distinctions between rich and poor: 'If there is a genuine fear of infection, I am sure we would be prepared to use a simple wooden box. Moslems are even more anxious than non-Moslems about hygienic matters.' The report added that a spokesman for the Ministry of Health said that they did not regard Moslem burials as in any way dangerous.

[2] For instance, Catholicism and Judaism have in the past entered or re-entered Britain as alien religions, but gradually they have been modified and adapted to this point. Buddhism and Confucianism seem to present fewer problems of acculturation, but this may not be the case with Islam and Sikhism. Other elements found among immigrant communities which can be at variance with British mores include: marital and family patterns, including the status of women (paternal responsibility, parent-child relations, polygamy, etc.); attitudes to authority (including tax officers, the courts, and the police); leisure patterns; political activities; etc.

haste and inadequacy with which controls were imposed when they seemed inevitable. The widespread reluctance to limit free entry to the Mother Country shown in the years immediately before the Commonwealth Immigrants Act of 1962, was more than paralleled by the passionate defence of the right of asylum throughout the nineteenth century; even today this right to asylum remains, though in a restricted form.

These, then, are the main strands in the history of immigration to Britain: unrestricted asylum for refugees and, until 1905, an open door for economic migrants, whether they were refugees from poverty and unemployment or those seeking after skills and learning.[1] With this open-door policy went an official *laissez-faire* attitude in economic and social matters. Once inside, most newcomers were left to fend for themselves. Nor were they welcomed with open arms by the man-in-the-street. For the British people have also traditionally been characterized by insularity and a certain xenophobia; as early as 1598, in his *View of London*, Stow wrote that the English nature was 'somewhat inhospitable to strangers' and 'jealous of their industry'. Nevertheless, the strains of absorption have been eased by the fact that, with two major exceptions, the exile communities and the economic immigrant groups of the past have either been relatively small in numbers or have consisted of élites—groups whose members were socially and culturally compatible with the host society, or who had special skills and knowledge to contribute to it.

Such were the Flemish weavers of the fourteenth century, invited by Edward III to come and bring their 'mystery' with them; the Protestant religious refugees from the Low Countries, Germany, and further afield during the Tudor period; the Huguenot craftsmen and mastermen who fled from France after the St. Bartholomew's Day massacre in 1572, and again after Charles II's invitation in 1681 and the Revolution of the Edict of Nantes in 1685; and Jews, at first mainly Sephardim from Spain, Portugal, and Holland after 1657, and then Western European Ashkenazim. Later, there were the European political refugees of the eighteenth and nineteenth centuries, who included anti-monarchist Frenchmen like Voltaire, anti-revolutionist *émigrés* like the Bourbon princes and Chateaubriand (most of

---

[1] Many of the latter have been quasi-immigrants, i.e. students and trainees, who subsequently returned home.

whom, however, returned to France after the downfall of Napoleon), and Bonapartists after Waterloo. The other political refugees were of all shades of opinion, by far the largest number being left of centre, from moderate liberal to deep red. They included Italians like Mazzini; Spanish constitutionalists; post-1831 Polish exiles; post-1848 radical exiles from all over Europe, like Herzen, Kossuth, and Victor Hugo; the French again in 1870 and 1871; and German and Russian socialists.

Other smaller groups whose members were to be gradually assimilated, and in some cases biologically amalgamated, in British society were the many lascar seamen who settled in Britain's ports and dock areas, the White Russian *émigrés* of the aristocracy and intelligentsia who came as a consequence of the Russian Revolution, and a group of some significance for today's situation, the 15,000 or so coloured ex-slaves who vanished into the London population by the mid-nineteenth century. Though the official host attitude has been one of *laissez-faire*, social pressures have gone to work slowly but inexorably on these and other groups; after two or three generations, all have been transformed into Englishmen, their passage marked only by a residue of faintly exotic surnames, a few churches and hospitals, some occasionally visible additions to the national genetic bank, and some solid contributions to the nation's economic and cultural life.

On the surface, therefore, Britain's ultimate solution to her internal minority problems seems to have been that of full assimilation. On the other hand, if we look at the situation of the two largest pre-1939 immigrant groups, the Irish and the Jews, it is clear that full assimilation has not yet taken place for a substantial proportion of their members; instead, we have a situation of pluralistic integration.

(b) THE IRISH MINORITY AND BRITISH JEWRY

Irish migrants, or refugees from poverty and hunger, have been coming to this island for many centuries. As early as 1413, a statute was passed ordering all Irishmen, Irish clerks, and beggars to be 'voided out of the realm'; and when the famine influx of 1845–8 began, there were already some 400,000 Irish-born residents here, or rather more than 2 per cent of the population (4.8 per cent in Scotland). In 1821, Southey described the fears of British workers that the starving Irish hordes would 'fill up every vacuum created in England and Scotland, and reduce the labouring classes to a uniform degree of degradation and misery'.

The Irish immigrants of this period were regarded not only as an economic problem, but as a police problem and a health problem. Arriving without money or urban and industrial experience, they appeared to constitute a threat to both the Englishman's livelihood and his standard of living. They were used to a low diet and a simple, rural way of life, which did not translate well into the dilapidated, insanitary 'rookeries' into which they crowded. Particular and well-documented sources of friction with neighbours were: extensive subletting (by dividing a single room between families or even letting a half-share in a bed to a workmate, or another family); the keeping of domestic animals in lodgings (dogs, pigs, donkeys, chickens), with the resultant smell and additional pollution of the streets by dung; and the funeral wake, which involved not only the risk of noise and brawls, but the danger to health which arose when a body lay for many days before burial on the only bed in the family's single room. In addition, the Irish at first constituted a highly distinctive minority, with their brogue or Gaelic tongue and their alien 'papist' faith.

After 1887, the proportion of the Irish-born to the rest of the population decreased substantially up to 1921. A second wave of immigration occurred in the 1920s, following the imposition of immigration controls by the United States, and a third wave began during and after the 1939–45 War, to meet the acute labour shortage in Britain. This inflow still continues, characterized by a high in-and-out movement: the 1961 Census gave a total of 644,398 Southern Irish-born migrants or settlers in Britain, and the 1966 Census showed a total of 698,600, figures that would not include their British-born children.[1] But whereas the great majority of earlier Irish newcomers had been restricted

[1] The Irish had the right of unrestricted entry into Britain until the outbreak of war and the policy of neutrality adopted by the Irish Republic in 1939. In June 1940, controls were imposed upon the immigration of persons born in the twenty-six counties of Southern Ireland; but because of the acute labour shortage, more and more permits were issued to Irish workers. It is interesting to note that during the war years it proved possible to work out and implement a centralized plan of controls, recruitment, and movement of Irish labour into Britain, including transit hostels. See J. A. Jackson, *The Irish in Britain* (London, Routledge & Kegan Paul, 1963), pp. 98–105.

to unskilled jobs that could not readily be filled by native labour (building, navvying, general labouring, and domestic service), a whole new range of occupations—from industry to nursing and clerical work—had now opened up for Irish men and women as a result of their war-time performance. There were also an increasing number of professionals (in 1951, Irish-born doctors formed 12 per cent of the medical profession in England and Wales).

Today the Irish minority in Britain presents the following picture: there is a large short-term migrant population in the initial phase of accommodation; an unknown number of more or less assimilated settlers at all socio-economic levels; and a large group of first- and second-generation Irish occupying a half-way house between England and Ireland, whose proximity helps to reinforce kinship, local, and patriotic ties. So, for some at least, does the strong Irish influence in many Roman Catholic parishes in Britain (in 1951, 21 per cent of all Roman Catholic priests in England and Wales were Irish-born).

By the end of the nineteenth century, the first wave of Irish migrants had been more or less absorbed in the general mass of the British urban poor. In the three decades preceding World War I, the Eastern European Jews who had fled from Tsarist and, later, Romanian *pogroms*, became the major problem and target for local hostility. Between 1870 and 1914, some 120,000 of these Yiddish-speaking Ashkenazim arrived in Britain, settling in London's East End and spreading into Northern cities such as Manchester, Leeds, Liverpool, and Glasgow. They brought no craft mysteries, and to both the British people and the established middle-class Anglo-Jewish community (Sephardim augmented by German and Dutch Ashkenazim), they seemed just as penniless, dirty, primitive, and outlandish as the Irish. They settled in the slums and embarked on street trading and tailoring, two of the few occupations permitted in the Eastern European ghettos. They were accused of undercutting local wages, refusing to trade with native shopkeepers, and sweating labour; of living in overcrowded and insanitary conditions; and of forming exclusive, non-assimilating communities, based on an alien religion, language, and culture.[1] This influx occasioned sociological enquiries, select committees, a Royal Commission on Alien Immigration in 1903,

---

[1] See Royal Commission on Alien Immigration, *Minutes of Evidence* (1903), Question 17, pp. 455–9.

and the imposition of mild restrictions under the Aliens Act of 1905.[1] Arrivals nevertheless continued at the rate of 5,000 a year until the outbreak of war in 1914 terminated the flow.

By this time, there were nearly 300,000 Jews in Britain, but the newcomers were already settling, fanning out residentially and occupationally, and becoming increasingly anglicized. This process was speeded and helped by the generosity and organized communal and integrative activity of the old, established Anglo-Jewry.[2] The new and enlarged community was well on the way to integration, both internal and external, by the time it received further accessions: nearly 20,000 refugees from Russia between 1914 and 1930; and by 1939, another 40,000 refugees from Nazi persecution in Germany, Austria, and the Sudetenland. This latter group was recently characterized by Elspeth Huxley as 'without doubt, in terms of intellect and skill, the most valuable batch of immigrants since the Huguenots'.[3]

In Britain today, there may be about 450,000 Jews (i.e. people who think of themselves as Jews and maintain some link, however slight, with organized Jewry or Jewish tradition), or just under 1 per cent of the population. Sixty-two per cent of them are reported to live in Greater London. Apart from this 450,000, thousands of individual Jews have broken away from the Jewish religion, culture, and community, often by marrying out, and have passed into local British society.[4] At the opposite pole, there is a hard core of self-segregating orthodox zealots[5] who fight the disarming assimilatory pressures of a host society more tolerant than Russia or Nazi Germany. In the middle, however, there is still a large community of British Jews, often of the second or third

[1] This forbade the entry of immigrants and the diseased, but not those seeking asylum from persecution, even if they were without means. On the motivations behind this legislation, see Lloyd Gartner, *The Jewish Immigrant in England: 1870–1914* (London, Allen & Unwin, 1960), p. 278.

[2] For Jewish communal organizations, see J. Gould and S. Esh (eds.), *Jewish Life in Modern Britain* (London, Routledge & Kegan Paul, 1964).

[3] *Back Street New Worlds* (London, Chatto & Windus, 1964), p. 19. For an account of the organized assistance provided for displaced scholars and scientists in Britain, see Walter Adams, 'The Refugee Scholars', *Political Quarterly* (Vol. 39, No. 1, January–March 1968).

[4] On the interaction between the British receiving society and the Jewish community, and particularly the diffusion of the 'gentleman ideal' among upwardly mobile Jews moving into the upper reaches of British society, see Gould and Esh, op. cit., pp. 196–200.

[5] See Gould and Esh, op. cit., p. 45.

migrant generation, with English as their only language, who are conscious of their Jewishness and maintain contact with some aspect of Jewish faith, tradition, or organization. Of this large intermediate group, a Jewish sociologist recently said it was questionable whether they should be described as *British* Jews or British *Jews*.

The Jews in Britain thus provide examples of individual assimilation, anti-assimilationist self-segregation, and also pluralistic integration. It must, of course, be asked whether the latter two solutions can be maintained, in the face of such factors as widespread upward socio-economic and occupational mobility, residential dispersal, drift from the synagogue and ritual, and a lowered birth-rate—all particularly characteristic of British Jews—and, last but not least, the comparative tolerance of a host society in which fears of anti-Semitism have virtually shrunk to what Percy Cohen has called the 'golf-club syndrome'.[1]

Looking at the evolution of these two large minority groups, one can discern certain similar features, all likely to slow absorption and impede assimilation. In each case the migration was large-scale, the rate of entry rapid, and the settlement concentrated.[2] Both groups came in at the bottom of the occupational ladder and both were conspicuously alien, at least in the nineteenth century, because of such characteristics as language, adherence to a minority religion, appearance, clothing, living standards, and customs. Both groups showed a fairly balanced sex-ratio, so that male immigrants were not compelled to marry out of the community. And both groups encountered not only economic hostility and resentment, but a set of bitter and pejorative stereotypes in the receiving society.

With the passing of time, the economic and cultural gaps have narrowed, the alien language has virtually disappeared, and the stereotypes have been modified. But for both Jews and the Irish, religion still seems to be one of the most powerful communal ties. And religious disaffiliation promotes favourable conditions for assimilation. Nevertheless, an assimilating Irishman can remain a Roman Catholic, although he may prefer to attend

---

[1] For an attempt to answer these questions in relation to Leeds Jewry, see E. Krausz, *Leeds Jewry: Its History and Social Structure* (Cambridge, Heffer & Sons, 1964), pp. 135-7.

[2] Reference is primarily to the late nineteenth-century Ashkenazim migration from Eastern Europe.

3

a fashionable church with an English, rather than a first-generation Irish, priest.

The history of the Irish and Jewish minorities in Britain also suggests that socio-economic class and occupational status are of considerable importance in the processes of absorption in this country. Firstly, assimilation appears to occur more easily in the upper and professional classes. And, secondly, absorption seems to proceed more smoothly once the group has begun to disperse residentially and to move up the socio-economic and occupational ladder. In this process, length of settlement is another important factor, and it is clear that full absorption, at least under more or less *laissez-faire* conditions, is likely to take two or more generations.

Here it may be noted that both groups of newcomers, and particularly the Jews, have not been entirely left to fend for themselves, but have received long-term advice, assistance, and education from their own established community organizations, notably the religious ones. No such established communal organizations existed for the West Indian, Hindu, and Moslem immigrants in the early years of their settlement.

(c) THE POST-1939 IMMIGRANTS

The story of the evolution of the Jewish and Irish communities in Britain, of their problems and relations with the absorbing society over several generations, indicates possible lines of development for more recent immigrant groups.

Since World War II, Britain has experienced the largest and most variegated influx of immigrants in her history, mainly because of full employment and an almost chronic labour shortage. In addition to the new wave of Irish migrants, Britain has taken in up to half a million immigrants from the European continent. These fall into two main categories: first, the Eastern European political exiles and refugees, of whom the Poles form the largest single group, numbering today about 130,000, including British-born children. There are also communities of Ukrainians, Balts, Czechs, Romanians, Yugoslavs, and Hungarians. The latter group received a reinforcement of some 16,000 in late 1956, after the abortive Budapest Rising. These groups of political exiles were in general characterized by a wide range of educational and occupational qualifications, by strong organizational links, and by resistance to assimilatory pressures.

The majority were Catholic (or Orthodox) by religion, and few spoke English well. Another feature was the preponderance of men and the comparatively high age of many members.

The second category consisted of selected economic migrants from Western and Southern Europe. These came mainly from Germany and Italy, followed by Austria and, more recently, Spain. They entered Britain, under strict controls and on Ministry of Labour permits, to fill jobs in the undermanned industries or to undertake specialized skilled work.

For the most part, these European migrants were widely dispersed through the British economy and formed no conspicuous settlements. An exception were those Italians who came in large batches to work in the brick-fields and market gardens of Bedford and the Lea Valley, bought houses, imported their families, and set up a facsimile of Italian back-street life which was not entirely congenial to their neighbours at the outset.

The third and largest group of post-war arrivals consisted of unselected economic immigrants, mostly coloured, from the colonies and the New Commonwealth countries. Unlike the non-British immigrants, and like their forerunners, the Irish, these newcomers were, until controls were introduced in July 1962, entitled to enter Britain unconditionally and to settle and work wherever they could find lodgings or a job. At first, they came mainly from the West Indies, with smaller contingents from West Africa, Aden, Somaliland, Cyprus, and Malta. Later, just before controls were introduced, immigration from India and Pakistan began to snowball and continued to do so even after the Act. At 1968, it is estimated that there were about one million 'new Commonwealth' immigrants in Britain, including their British-born children. Of these, about one-half were of West Indian origins, about 60 per cent of them being from Jamaica. The total number of Indians and Pakistanis is less easy to establish, but there may be up to 225,000 Indians, mostly Sikhs from the Punjab, with some Hindus, mainly from Gujarat,[1] and about 120,000 Pakistanis, Moslems drawn mostly from East Bengal (East Pakistan, c. 55,000),

---

[1] In 1968, there was a sizeable accretion of Asians from Kenya, many of them Europeanized, English-speaking, and from professional and commercial backgrounds. These newcomers could provide a middle-class bridge between the other Indians and the host community. Alternatively, they could set up another pluralistic community or go for assimilation like the Anglo-Indians.

the Punjab, Azad Kashmir, and the North West Frontier (West Pakistan, *c.* 75,000).

Apart from a small minority of professional, white-collar, and skilled workers, the bulk of these new Commonwealth immigrants were ill-equipped to enter a complex urban industrial society. So they have followed the Irish into the lowest levels of the British economy.

There has been a misleading and meaningless tendency to lump all these newcomers together under the description 'coloured immigrants'. In fact, the various immigrant groups differ at least as much as the Irish do from the Jews, or the Poles from the Italians or Germans. They differ not only in demographic and occupational composition but in social organization, socio-economic and cultural background, and, also, motives for migration and expectations of the host society.

Most West Indians come from an English-speaking, Christian, British-oriented sub-culture, albeit impoverished, rural, and colonial by contrast with British metropolitan culture. Although they settle together in family and local groupings, they are mobile and individualistic, and resist the imposition of strong internal social controls. They also tend to have high expectations of full and immediate acceptance by the Mother Country. Such acceptance is at present slowed by real differences of values, cultural background, attitudes, and behaviour. It is also slowed by the British society's general antipathy to and avoidance of all outsiders, and by a set of historical preconceptions associating dark skin and Negroid features with alien and primitive cultures and with low socio-economic status. In recent years, there has also been a predictably hostile reaction among some West Indians to British attitudes.

The West Indians are nevertheless a potentially assimilating immigrant group, although it is still too early for most of them to have passed through the earlier phases of absorption at work and perhaps in the neighbourhood. Some years ago, on the basis of field-work in Brixton, I hazarded a guess, thought by many to be over-optimistic, that the West Indians in Britain would move slowly in the direction of assimilation over the next decades, dispersing residentially, moving up on the socio-economic ladder, and intermarrying in larger numbers than at present. This was, however, before the 'coloured' immigrant population was diversified by large inflows of immigrants whose 'colour' visibility was combined with wide cultural differences.

By contrast with the West Indians, the other large Commonwealth immigrant groups (notably the Indians, Pakistanis, and Cypriots) are the least assimilating, in type and intention, of all recent immigrant groups. They have their own entirely distinctive cultures, their own religions and languages, and a high degree of internal organization and control. They are essentially economic migrants, still at the stage when they intend to stay only a few years in Britain to accumulate savings or skills. The majority avoid all contacts with the receiving society other than at work, and are self-segregating to a degree that we have hitherto seen only among the Chinese. Their intentions of avoidance and return are, however, being rendered increasingly difficult of fulfilment by British immigration policy and the arrival of families and young children, who are exposed to the assimilatory pressures of the host society in the schools.

Looking at the larger post-war immigrant groups, it is probably still too early to speak of anything but accommodation except in the case of the Poles and other war refugees. Most of them have managed to establish an acceptable half-way house of cultural pluralism for a large section of the first generation, while demonstrating a high degree of upward mobility and moving to virtual assimilation in the second generation.

This rapid move to assimilation, despite the resistance of older exiles, may be attributed to such factors as the wide dispersal and unusual occupational background of these newcomers, and also to the Government's positive resettlement measures. The Italians, a more traditional economic immigrant group than the Poles, could follow slowly in the path of the Irish. So, perhaps, may the Cypriots. The future of the Pakistanis and Indians is far from certain. Will they move out of their ethnic ghettos and work-gangs? Will they distribute themselves up and down the British socio-economic hierarchy without losing their leaders? Can they become acceptable religious minorities like the Jews or Catholics? Or must they or their children abandon their religion and culture in order to be accepted?

Or again, will the single factor of colour be restressed to keep them outsiders in the second or later generations? This is something that would affect the acceptance of the 'assimilating' West

Indians as well. Against this danger, however, must be set the fact that several smaller 'coloured' immigrant groups that have arrived since the war—notably the Anglo-Indians and thousands of Cape Coloured—are already being dispersed and even assimilated in British society, almost imperceptibly and with little or no strain.

A final element in the processes of absorption today and in the future is the host society, which is itself in a state of rapid evolution and change towards a more egalitarian and a less insular model which may make cultural pluralism more acceptable and moderate assimilatory pressures.

The history of past immigration to Britain shows, firstly, that, as elsewhere, rapid, large-scale immigration, uncontrolled and concentrated on certain areas, produced local resentment and hostility as well as demands for a closed-door policy; these have tended to subside as each wave diminished and the processes of absorption proceeded. Secondly, it underlines the importance of social and cultural factors, as opposed to the consideration of 'economic absorptive capacity' alone; or to put it in another way, of qualitative social thinking rather than the quantitative 'rabble hypothesis' of many old-time employers and others. And thirdly, it suggests that, whereas the over-all pressures exerted by British society have been assimilatory and aimed at achieving a homogeneous, unified, and, increasingly, egalitarian society, the British people, or certain local segments, have also tolerated a degree of pluralistic integration or cultural pluralism for certain larger groups, so long as they accepted certain basic values and behaviour patterns and evolved half-way houses acceptable to the host society.

This pressure for over-all uniformity combined with tolerance of certain differences was exemplified in Britain's only large-scale, official integration plan to date: the long-term plan to resettle some 150,000 Polish ex-servicemen and their families after the 1939–45 War.[1] This remarkably successful scheme of 'institutional resettlement' concentrated on the universal areas of association in which official action can be most effective. Friction over scarce housing was avoided by the use of camps and hostels, and special departments, hostels, hospitals, and schools, together

---

[1] For a detailed account of this, see J. Zubrzycki, *Polish Immigrants in Britain* (The Hague, Martinus Nijhoff, 1956).

with trained personnel drawn from the Polish exile authorities, were used to promote the 'economic assimilation' of the Poles. This term was understood to mean success in employment, ability to speak English, and a naturalization certificate. Beyond this, the Poles were left free to retain their own culture and language, worship in their own churches, and form their own organizations.[1]

Not all the provisions or restrictions of this plan are suitable for application to the 'coloured' Commonwealth immigrants of today, but its basic approach and intentions are of considerable relevance. It combined a traditional tolerance of difference with an insistence on the view that has been widely restated with reference to the Commonwealth immigrants: that all those who are part of British society must be treated, without discrimination, as first-class citizens.

Thus, whatever kind of British society evolves in the future, the Government have a clear pattern to follow: to aim at establishing equality of opportunity for all citizens in the universal spheres of jobs, education, civic rights, and public housing, and to inculcate a sufficient knowledge of the English language and culture to permit of contact, understanding, and cross-fertilization between the minorities and the host society.

---

[1] A smaller but successful scheme was instituted in 1956–7 for Hungarian refugees after the 1956 Rising in Budapest. During the post-War period, there was also a large-scale but less comprehensive programme for the selection and settlement of 90,000 European Volunteer Workers from the German camps. See J. A. Tannahill, *European Volunteer Workers in Britain* (Manchester, Manchester University Press, 1958), *passim*.

CHAPTER 3

The Demographic and Statistical Background

BRIAN COHEN

1. *The Migration Statistics*

(a) THE MIGRATION UP TO MID-1962

As explained by Sheila Patterson, the existence of coloured minority groups in the United Kingdom is almost entirely the result of the migratory movements—occurring after World War II —of population from the British Commonwealth. The most important sources of migration in numerical terms were the British Caribbean (especially Jamaica), India, and Pakistan. Lesser migration also occurred from a wide range of countries and territories such as Nigeria, Ghana, Kenya, Ceylon, and Hong Kong, but for most purposes these will not be discussed individually in this section. The dynamics of the migration and the political factors affecting the migration will only be referred to, in passing, where they have very direct relevance to the changing nature of the migration.[1]

The migration from the West Indies, which was the earliest of the large-scale movements, has its roots in World War II. During the War, many thousands of West Indians served in the British armed forces, most of them spending some time in the United Kingdom, and also workers were specially recruited from the West Indies for employment in the British war-time economy. After the War, most returned to the West Indies, but on their return some found economic opportunities far more limited than in Britain. It was from this group that had had experience of work in Britain that much of the original impetus for the migration was

[1] For a further discussion on the dynamics of the migration and the effect of political factors, see Ceri Peach, *West Indian Migration to Britain: A Social Geography* (London, Oxford University Press, for Institute of Race Relations, 1968); and E. J. B. Rose and associates, *Colour and Citizenship: A Report on British Race Relations* (London, Oxford University Press, for Institute of Race Relations, 1969).

to come. Although some had remained in Britain after 1945 and others soon filtered back very quickly, the starting date, if it is possible to identify such a thing for a migratory movement of this nature, was June 1948 when the S.S. *Empire Windrush* brought 500 West Indians to Britain. In the following years, occasional groups came over in other specially chartered ships, but the numbers involved were probably small. Until 1952, no counts had been made of the number of arrivals, but in 1951, the census showed only 15,000 people born in the Caribbean and living in England and Wales (see Table 3:1 and Section 3, 'An Evaluation of Census Data').

TABLE 3:1

POPULATION OF SELECTED BIRTH-PLACE GROUPS
1951 CENSUS OF ENGLAND AND WALES

Birth-place	Number enumerated	Amended total
India	110,767	31,000*
Pakistan	11,117	5,000*
Caribbean	15,300	15,300
West Africa†	5,000	5,000

* It is estimated that approximately 80,000 persons born in India and 6,000 born in Pakistan were 'white Indians', i.e. persons born in these two countries of European (usually English) parentage.

† West Africa includes Gambia, the Gold Coast (now Ghana), Nigeria, and Sierra Leone. The remaining African countries are excluded as it is considered that a very high proportion of the enumerated population were the children of expatriate English parents.

Source: 1951 Census. Amended estimates from Mrs. V. Jackson in Rose and associates, op. cit.

From 1952 onwards, the Migrant Services Division (M.S.D.) of the West Indies made counts on the number of arrivals, and from 1955, the Home Office took unofficial estimates of arrivals and departures. The Home Office figures, which were generally more reliable and comprehensive, are about 10 per cent higher than the M.S.D. data, but both estimates generally agree as to the rise and fall of levels of migration.[1] The main movements in the migration up until mid-1962 are shown in Table 3:2.

[1] See Peach, op. cit.

3*

TABLE 3:2

NET INWARD MIGRATION 1955–JUNE 1962

	Caribbean	India	Pakistan
1955	27,550	5,800	1,850
1956	29,800	5,600	2,050
1957	23,020	6,620	5,170
1958	15,020	6,200	4,690
1959	16,390	2,930	860
1960	49,670	5,920	2,500
Total 1955–60	161,450	33,070	17,120
1961	66,290	23,750	25,080
First six months of 1962	31,800	19,050	25,090
Total 1961 and first six months of 1962	98,090	42,800	50,170
Total 1955– June 1962	259,540	75,870	67,290
% arriving before 1961	62%	44%	25%

Source: Home Office statistics.

During 1952 and 1953, the migration from the West Indies remained at a low level (about 2,000 per annum) but then rose sharply in 1954, and again in 1955, to over 20,000. In 1956, the level of migration remained about the same and then fell in the following two years. By 1959, the fall had ceased and the next two years (1960 and 1961) both saw very large increases to higher levels than had been seen previously. By 1961, the net inflow from the West Indies was over 60,000 per annum, and this rate continued for the first six months of 1962 until the Commonwealth Immigrants Act 1962 came into effect.

The origins of the migrations from India and Pakistan were far more diverse than that from the West Indies and reflect in part the diversity within both India and Pakistan. For the past fifty years, Indians have visited Britain in increasing numbers and a minority have settled in Britain throughout this period. Amongst the early settlers were ex-seamen, Sikh pedlars, professionals, and ex-students. It is estimated[1] that by 1945, a thousand Indian seamen had settled in Birmingham and another estimate[2] in 1949 suggested that about a thousand Indian doctors were practising in Britain. After 1945, other sources of migration included landless ex-Army officers and others who lost land-holdings in the communal disturbances around the time of partition. From the 1951 Census, it is possible to estimate that approximately 31,000 Indians and 5,000 Pakistanis were residents in England and Wales (see Table 3:1).

Up to 1955, no record of the levels of migration from India and Pakistan was kept; the net inflow for Indians during this period was probably less than 5,000 per annum and for Pakistanis probably less than 1,500 per annum. Both movements stayed at a fairly low level from 1955 up to and including 1960, with a trough in 1959. In 1961, migration from both countries showed a very sharp increase, with the net inflow from India increasing fourfold, and from Pakistan tenfold, over the previous year. The rate of flow continued to rise in the first six months of 1962. From Table 3:2, which summarizes the net inflows from India and Pakistan as well as from the West Indies, it can be seen that the bulk of the Pakistani migration was among the most recent arrivals, followed by the Indian—the West Indian migration occurring first and having its highest levels prior to 1961.

Up until 1960, the determining factors for these migrations were the state of labour demand in Britain, the availability and cost of transport, and the controls imposed by countries of emigration. From 1960 onwards, the very sharp rises in the levels of migration seemed to be due primarily to the fear of impending legislation for the control of entry into the United Kingdom. [3]

All three migratory events were of a two-way nature. For Indians and Pakistanis in every year up to 1960, the number of departures equalled more than half the total of arrivals. West Indians showed a much lower rate of returnees from the United Kingdom; but in 1958 and 1959, this was equivalent to over 25

[1] R. Desai, *Indian Immigrants in Britain* (London, Oxford University Press, for Institute of Race Relations, 1963).

[2] C. Kondapi, *Indians Overseas 1938–1939* (New Delhi, Oxford University Press, for Indian Council of World Affairs, 1951).

[3] Peach, *West Indian Migration to Britain: A Social Geography*, op. cit.

per cent of arrivals.[1] The small size of the net inflow of Indians
and Pakistanis in comparison to total arrivals makes it more
difficult to assess the changing flow of migration, over the years
up to 1960, as compared with the West Indians.

From the M.S.D. data, it is possible to estimate the number of
males, females, and children in the West Indian migration (see
Table 3:3). It will be seen that from the start (in 1952), when
figures were collected, women—although in a minority—were
already a sizeable proportion of the migration and that this proportion increased after 1956. Separate statistics for children were only
kept from 1955 onwards, and it will be seen that their number
grew every year although their proportional share of the
migration did fluctuate.

TABLE 3:3

WEST INDIAN MIGRANTS ENTERING THE UNITED KINGDOM

	Men	Women	Children
1952	1,500	700	—
1953	1,700	600	—
1954	6,600	2,600	—
1955	13,900	7,300	300
1956	13,900	9,400	600
1957	11,400	9,400	900
1958	7,700	7,800	1,000
1959	10,100	8,200	2,100
1960	29,600	19,900	3,200
1961	28,900	27,600	5,100

Source: 1952–4 figures from House of Lords Parliamentary Answer, 15 February
1956; 1955–61 figures from Migrant Services Division.

Information about the sex ratio of Indian and Pakistani
immigrants is sparse, but the evidence points to very much lower
proportions of females in these migrations. A study in the late 1950s
of one Sikh community estimated that the proportion of women
in the community was as low as 4 per cent.[2] With the threat of
control, many more Sikhs brought their wives to England in the
1960–2 period.[3] Amongst the other elements of the Indian migration

[1] R. B. Davison, Black British (London, Oxford University Press, for Institute of
Race Relations, 1966), pp. 2–4; and G. C. K. Peach, 'West Indian Migration to
Britain: The Economic Factors', in Race (Vol. VII, No. 1, July 1965), p. 41.
[2] G. S. Aurora, The New Frontiersman (Bombay, Popular Prakashan, 1967).
[3] A. Patnaik, 'Sikhs in Southall' (unpublished Institute of Race Relations research
paper available in the Institute's Library).

(Gujaratis, Bengalis, Anglo-Indians, etc.), it is likely that there was a very much higher proportion of women in their number. As far as it is known, the proportion of women amongst Pakistani migrants was extremely low. Evidence from the 1961 Census and from later investigations suggests that the pre-1952 migration from Pakistan was over 90 per cent male.[1]

(b) THE MIGRATION FROM MID-1962

With the coming into effect of the Commonwealth Immigrants Act on 1 July 1962, the balance of the migration changed in three ways. Firstly, the main source of the migration moved from the Caribbean to India and Pakistan. Secondly, the main component of the migration switched from new entrants to the labour market to dependants, and this, in effect, meant a switch from males to females and of adults to children. The third change was that within the migrating labour forces there has been an increasing proportion of skilled and professional workers as opposed to unskilled workers. The 1965 White Paper reinforced these changes, especially the latter two.

The 1962 Act controlled the entry of Commonwealth immigrants into the United Kingdom through the issue of labour vouchers by the Ministry of Labour. Three types of labour voucher were introduced by the Act: Category 'A' was for those who had a specific job to come to; Category 'B', for those who possessed special skills or qualifications; and Category 'C', for unskilled workers without a definite job. The 1965 White Paper discontinued Category 'C' vouchers and gave preference to Category 'B' (persons with skills) over Category 'A' (those with jobs to come to). It also imposed an upper limit of 8,500 vouchers in any year, of which 1,000 were reserved for Malta.

The 1962 Act and the White Paper allowed the continued free entry of the dependants of voucher holders and of Commonwealth citizens already resident in the United Kingdom. Wives and children under the age of 16 were allowed free entry and older children and parents could be admitted under discretionary powers. The tightening-up of procedures and categories of

---

[1] In Bradford in 1961, there were 3,376 Pakistani males and only 81 females; see 1961 *Census Yorkshire West Riding Country Report*. See also Eric Butterworth, *Immigrants in West Yorkshire* (London, Institute of Race Relations Special Series, 1968).

dependant has continued since 1962 and children under 16 are
not now normally admitted to join their father unless their mother
is also present in this country.

TABLE 3:4

COMMONWEALTH CITIZENS ARRIVING IN THE
UNITED KINGDOM, JULY 1962–DECEMBER 1967,
HOLDING MINISTRY OF LABOUR VOUCHERS,
OR AS DEPENDANTS

	India		Pakistan		West Indies	
	Voucher holders	Dependants	Voucher holders	Dependants	Voucher holders	Dependants
1962*	646	1,565	391	505	1,600	3,730
1963	8,366	6,616	13,526	3,304	2,077	7,896
1964	3,828	8,770	3,296	7,046	2,635	11,461
1965	3,794	12,798	2,520	6,763	2,987	11,147
1966	2,433	13,357	721	9,319	628	9,878
1967	2,175	15,822	754	17,506	630	11,211
	21,242	58,928	21,208	44,443	10,557	55,323

* 1 July to 31 December.
Source: Commonwealth Immigrants Act 1962, Statistics (London, H.M.S.O., published
annually).

As can be seen from Table 3:4, which summarizes the main
migratory movements since July 1962, the growing importance of
dependants in the migration is readily apparent. Amongst the
dependants, the ratio of wives to children has varied between the
three areas of origin and over time. For all three groups, the
number of children arriving has been greater than that of wives,
and for the Pakistani and West Indian migrations, the proportion
of children has steadily risen between 1962 and 1967. The differing
rates and composition of the migrations since 1962 is undoubtedly
a reflection of the migrations prior to control in 1962. In the case
of the West Indies, the high rate of female migration before 1962
is the prime reason for the steady fall in the number of wives
arriving in the United Kingdom since 1963. Conversely, the
relative absence of women in the Indian and Pakistani migrations
before control has meant that the number of wives arriving in the
United Kingdom has steadily increased since 1962.

2. *Population and Distribution*

(a) POPULATION

The number of coloured people living in Britain has been the subject of much discussion and it is extremely difficult to give an accurate estimate. The census, which is the most reliable single source of social data, only enumerates people by place of birth— and not by race—and, therefore, all census estimates have to be adjusted. The figures given in Table 3:5 summarize the birth-place data from the 1961 and 1966 censuses and provide a good starting-point for any estimate. As can be seen, the number of persons resident in England and Wales born outside the British Isles has increased substantially between 1961 and 1966. This increase has not been confined to the coloured Commonwealth countries, but also includes the white Commonwealth and some foreign countries. The largest rises numerically and proportion-ately have, however, been among New Commonwealth countries, especially Pakistan, Africa, the Caribbean, and India.

Estimates of the total coloured population have been made by eliminating white persons born in India and Pakistan and by estimating the number of children born in this country to Com-monwealth immigrants. A further complication is the apparent under-enumeration of the two censuses, and there have also been attempts to correct this, using entry dates. A recent attempt at an over-all estimate of the coloured population is shown in Table 3:6. This estimate was based on the following:

(i) An estimated 68,600 white Indians and 5,400 white Pakistanis were excluded.

(ii) Using entry figures into the United Kingdom, it was calcula-ted that the census enumerated only 84 per cent of the coloured population born overseas; under-enumeration was particularly severe among Pakistanis, of whom only 62 per cent were enumerated.

(iii) Census data on the number of children under 15 years old living in households where the head was born in one of the Commonwealth countries under examination, provided a basis for estimating the number of coloured children born in the United Kingdom.

Following these operations, it was suggested that at the time of the 1966 Census, the coloured population of England and

TABLE 3:5

BIRTH-PLACES OF RESIDENT POPULATION OF ENGLAND AND WALES: 1961 AND 1966

	Males		Females	
	1961	*1966*	*1961*	*1966*
Total population	22,303,833	22,840,580	23,800,715	24,294,930
Total born in British Isles	21,452,941	21,808,510	22,993,701	23,298,920
Scotland	335,475	364,620	318,151	352,420
Northern Ireland	97,873	92,130	89,676	87,800
Eire	316,409	322,120	327,989	352,440
Total born outside British Isles resident in England and Wales	732,358	953,120	687,168	889,510
Total Commonwealth countries, colonies, and protectorates	363,107	520,050	296,655	422,260
Africa	25,860	50,530	16,939	37,980
Nigeria	8,557	15,350	4,496	9,780
America	121,042	164,350	100,390	156,890
Canada	24,972	25,790	24,081	26,830
Jamaica	55,746	78,330	44,305	73,510
Rest of Caribbean	40,058	59,850	31,687	56,160
Asia	159,780	256,610	113,709	173,260
Cyprus	23,468	32,180	18,430	27,010
India	85,645	129,850	71,790	102,360
Pakistan	25,919	59,150	4,818	13,980
Europe	16,504	20,680	16,827	19,970
Malta	12,629	16,500	12,050	15,080
Oceania	22,904	27,880	28,243	34,160
Australia	16,151	19,510	20,579	24,970
Foreign countries and at sea	369,251	397,810	390,513	440,480
Europe	235,502	251,970	284,110	307,880
Germany	40,379	48,230	80,572	85,820
Italy	36,017	46,090	45,310	50,570
Poland	82,468	73,690	37,035	36,760
Africa (excluding Commonwealth)	31,801	35,350	35,195	39,710
America	61,061	54,750	48,929	49,270
U.S.A.	53,961	47,150	40,233	39,920
Asia and Oceania	23,544	25,170	21,810	25,450
U.S.S.R.	33,337	30,040	20,095	17,560

Notes:
1. Separate enumerations are shown only for those Commonwealth countries, colonies, and protectorates with 25,000 or more enumerated residents in England and Wales, and for foreign countries with 50,000 or more, either at 1961 or 1966.
2. Rest of Caribbean includes Guyana.
3. The Republic of South Africa is included under Africa ('Foreign countries') at both dates.

4. Figures for 1966 have been multiplied by 10 as the census at that date was a 10 per cent sample.
5. Visitors and those not stating birth-place have been excluded from all data except that for total population of England and Wales.
Source: 1961 and 1966 censuses.

Wales was 924,200, of whom 213,300 were children born in the United Kingdom. The largest single group was that of Jamaican origin, making up 30 per cent of the total. West Indians as a whole made up 49 per cent of the total, which was more than the combined percentages of Indians and Pakistanis (39 per cent). It was emphasized that the total of 924,200 was close to a minimum estimate.

TABLE 3:6

TOTAL ESTIMATED COLOURED POPULATION RESIDENT IN ENGLAND AND WALES, 1966 CENSUS, BY COUNTRY OF ORIGIN

Area of origin	Born overseas	Born in the United Kingdom	Total
India*	180,400	43,200	223,600
Pakistan*	109,600	10,100	119,700
Ceylon	12,900	3,200	16,100
Jamaica	188,100	85,700	273,800
Other Caribbean	129,800	50,500	180,300
British West Africa	43,100	7,600	50,700
Far East	47,000	13,000	60,000
Total	710,900	213,300	924,200

* Excluding white Indians and Pakistanis.
Source: Estimates by Mrs. V. Jackson in Rose and associates, op. cit., Table 10.2.

It will be clear that the calculations described above and the figures in Table 3:6 are only best estimates and there may well be an error factor on all or any set of figures. Apart from possible errors in the three operations mentioned above, there are other possible sources of error in calculating the total coloured population:

(i) Figures in Table 3:6 for countries, other than India and Pakistan, include an unknown number of whites born in those countries.

(ii) The table does not include such countries as Kenya, the Republic of South Africa, and others. An unknown percentage of those born in these countries will be coloured.

(iii) Coloured persons born in the United Kingdom who were 15 years and over in 1966, and their children, are not included in the table.

Despite these caveats, it would seem reasonable to suggest that the total coloured population of England and Wales was just over 900,000 in 1966 and had risen to just over one million by mid-1968 (i.e. just over 2 per cent of the total population). It should be emphasized that this population is in no way nationally, racially, or ethnically homogeneous and that the descriptive word 'coloured' covers West Indians, Indians, Pakistanis, Africans, and Chinese. Another point to be stressed is that the census provides no information on ethnic origin. Thus, it is not known how many people of Indian origin have migrated from the West Indies or Africa.

(b) DISTRIBUTION

A social geographer writing on the distribution of West Indians has suggested that 'they have gone to the decreasing urban cores of expanding industrial regions'.[1] It would seem that this applies as much to Indian and Pakistani migrants as to West Indians. West Indians, Indians, and Pakistanis have uniformly settled in areas of high labour demand. Those parts of the United Kingdom where labour demand has been lowest and unemployment highest over the past two decades, especially Wales, Scotland, and the North East, have signally not attracted immigrants from the Commonwealth.

The geographical distribution of immigrants within the areas of greatest labour demand has been determined by the availability of housing and jobs and, above all, by the migratory movements of the total population. The population of the centres of most of the large towns and urban concentrations has been steadily declining for decades, as people have moved to the suburbs or the country in search of better living conditions, and the coloured migrants have functioned as a replacement population, moving especially into those areas where demand for labour has remained high. In his analysis of the distribution of coloured immigrants in 1961, Peach found that concentration was greatest in the largest towns (with populations of 200,000 and over) and least in

[1] G. C. K. Peach, 'Factors Affecting the Distribution of West Indians in Britain', *Transactions and Papers 1966* (No. 38, Institute of British Geographers, 1966).

the small towns (50–100,000).[1] He also found that in those towns where population had decreased between 1951 and 1961, immigrant concentrations were greater than in those where population had increased.

TABLE 3:7

PERCENTAGE OF DIFFERENT IMMIGRANT GROUPS
RESIDENT IN ENGLAND AND WALES LIVING IN
THE GREATER LONDON CONURBATION AND THE
SIX CONURBATIONS COMBINED: 1961 CENSUS

Birth-place	Greater London conurbation	Six conurbations combined‡
Jamaica	53	80
Rest of Caribbean	68	76
India*	37	52
Pakistan	23	70
Africa†	47	60
Cyprus	81	86
Total population of England and Wales	18	37

* White Indians and Pakistanis are not excluded.
† Africa includes all Commonwealth countries, colonies, and protectorates (excluding the Republic of South Africa).
‡ The six conurbations are: Tyneside, West Yorkshire, South-east Lancashire, Merseyside, West Midlands, Greater London.
Source: Birth-place and nationality tables in 1961 Census.

The greatest concentrations of the different immigrant groups have been in the large conurbations, and especially in the Greater London and West Midlands conurbations. Table 3:7 shows the distribution in 1961 of the different immigrant groups in the six conurbations combined and in London. It will be seen that all the immigrant groups are over-concentrated in the conurbations, as compared to the total population. The concentration of West Indians is very high in London, but the concentration of Cypriots is far higher in comparison. Valerie Jackson[2] estimated that in 1961, excluding white Indians and Pakistanis, 71 per cent of coloured immigrants lived in the six

[1] Peach, 'Factors Affecting the Distribution of West Indians in Britain', pp. 76–82.
[2] Rose and associates, op. cit., Chapter 10.

conurbations and that in the London and West Midlands conurbations there were 47 per cent and 14 per cent, respectively.
She estimated that in 1966 the situation had hardly changed, with
72 per cent resident in the six conurbations.

TABLE 3:8

PROPORTION OF POPULATION RESIDENT IN SELECTED
AREAS BORN IN THE WEST INDIES, INDIA, AND
PAKISTAN: 1966 CENSUS

Area	Population	Birth-place			West Indians, Indians, and Pakistanis, as % of total population
		West Indies	India	Pakistan	
England and Wales	47,135,510	267,850	232,210	73,130	1·2
Conurbations					
Greater London	7,671,220	151,810	80,230	15,990	3·2
West Midlands	2,374,070	35,800	26,930	14,110	3·3
West Yorkshire	1,708,260	8,360	10,350	12,660	1·8
London boroughs					
Brent	282,490	15,580	4,510	780	7·4
Ealing	292,750	4,550	8,700	570	4·9
Hackney	244,210	14,640	2,340	420	7·1
Hammersmith	203,240	8,720	1,970	390	5·4
Haringey	246,570	10,460	2,810	550	5·6
Islington	235,340	10,760	1,440	520	5·4
Kensington and Chelsea	203,140	4,370	4,000	1,070	4·6
Lambeth	320,780	16,620	3,470	460	6·7
Lewisham	278,450	9,580	1,750	220	4·3
Wandsworth	318,970	11,040	3,260	1,060	4·8
City of Westminster	254,210	7,000	3,060	810	4·3
Local authority areas outside London					
Bedford	67,390	1,680	1,060	390	4·6
Birmingham	1,064,220	23,580	10,590	10,280	4·2
Bradford	290,310	1,690	3,600	7,030	4·2
Derby	125,850	1,940	2,390	830	4·1
Dewsbury	50,860	30	770	820	3·2
High Wycombe	53,920	1,600	350	680	4·9
Huddersfield	130,210	2,390	1,570	1,330	4·1
Leicester	283,260	2,650	6,010	270	3·1
Slough	81,980	1,040	1,940	860	4·7
Walsall	179,650	1,210	3,370	940	3·1
Warley	163,390	1,980	3,320	520	3·6
Wolverhampton	262,170	5,800	6,450	450	4·8

Notes:
1. White Indians and Pakistanis are not excluded.
2. Figures are given only for (a) those London boroughs with 4 per cent or more of the total population born in the specified areas; and (b) those local authority areas outside London with a total population of 50,000 or more and 3 per cent or more born in the specified areas.
3. (a) All the London boroughs are included in the Greater London conurbation.
   (b) Birmingham, Walsall, Warley, and Wolverhampton are in the West Midlands conurbation.
   (c) Bradford, Dewsbury, and Huddersfield are in the West Yorkshire conurbation.
4. In certain London boroughs there are large numbers of other immigrant groups, especially Cypriots. There are 10,300 Cypriots in Islington and 7,960 in Hackney.
5. All figures have been multiplied by 10 as they are derived from a 10 per cent sample.
   Source: 1966 10% Sample Census.

According to the 1966 Census, 1·2 per cent of the population was born in the West Indies, India, or Pakistan. Both in the West Midlands and Greater London, over 3 per cent of the population was born in these three countries. In local authority areas, the highest proportions were found in London boroughs (7·4 per cent in Brent), and in no local authority areas outside London was the proportion more than 5 per cent (see Table 3:8). It will be seen from Table 3:8 that there were considerable variations in the distributions of the three main groups, i.e. the West Indians, Indians, and Pakistanis. Thus, in London there were comparatively few Pakistanis, whilst in West Yorkshire they were the largest group; but even here, large differences were notable among different parts of the conurbation area. In Huddersfield, West Indians were the largest group and Pakistanis the smallest; but in Bradford, a few miles distant, the complete reverse was the case. Similarly in London, West Indians far outnumbered Indians in boroughs like Islington, Hackney, and Lambeth, but in Ealing there were about twice as many Indians as West Indians.

More detailed studies of the distribution of Commonwealth immigrants have been carried out using 1961 Census data.[1] In these studies the smallest of all census units, i.e. enumeration districts (average size under 1,000 persons), were studied for the Administrative County of London and the County Borough of Birmingham. In 1961, over half of all Commonwealth immigrants

[1] Ruth Glass and John Westergaard, *London's Housing Needs* (London, Centre for Urban Studies, 1965), pp. 30–45, esp. pp. 41–3; and Peach, 'Factors Affecting the Distribution of West Indians in Britain', op. cit., p. 88.

in London lived in enumeration districts where they constituted less than 8 per cent of the total population. On the other hand, over 10 per cent lived in areas where they were 16 per cent or more of the total population. The highest proportion in any of the 4,500 enumeration districts of London was 37 per cent of the total population. In Birmingham, it was found that just over 30 per cent of West Indians lived in enumeration districts where they were less than 5 per cent of the total population, and another 30 per cent where they constituted over 15 per cent of the total population.

The analyses of 1961 Census material showed that the concentration of different ethnic minorities had not gone so far as to form a majority group in any area even as small as an enumeration district. Examination of areas in which no coloured immigrants lived showed that half the population of Birmingham in 1961 lived in areas where no West Indians were enumerated.

A preliminary examination of 1966 Census data for Greater London has shown that while the number of Commonwealth immigrants has increased, their concentration has not increased as much as is sometimes popularly believed. In none of the more than 700 wards in Greater London did persons born in the New Commonwealth (excluding Australia, Canada, and New Zealand) constitute a majority of the population. The highest concentration was in one ward where just over 30 per cent of the population was born in the Commonwealth, mainly in India. In seven other wards, persons born in the New Commonwealth constituted between 20 per cent and 30 per cent of the total population. As far as the largest single immigrant group in London is concerned, i.e. those born in the Caribbean, there were only two wards where they constituted more than 20 per cent of the population. In over 100 wards in Greater London, persons born in the New Commonwealth constituted less than 1 per cent of the total population.

3. An Evaluation of Census Data

The most comprehensive source of social data for a very wide range of interests has been that gathered by the General Register Office in its censuses of population. These censuses have been conducted every ten years since the beginning of the nineteenth century and have enumerated the total population. Following the

1961 Census, it was decided as an experiment to hold a census based on a 10 per cent sample of the population midway between the 1961 and 1971 censuses. Thus, for the purpose of gaining any information about the position of racial minorities in the United Kingdom, only the 1961 and 1966 censuses are of immediate use; the 1951 Census serves as a reference point for changes taking place in the total British society. In this section, discussion will be limited to the 1961 and 1966 censuses.[1]

(a) DATA COLLECTION AND PRESENTATION

British censuses do not ask any questions relating to racial or ethnic origin, but they do collect information about birth-place. Furthermore, in 1961, a question was asked about the nationality of persons born outside the United Kingdom: were they citizens of Commonwealth states or British citizens by birth, descent, or naturalization. This question on nationality gives an estimate of the number of Anglo-Indians (i.e. persons of British descent who were born in India), thus making it possible to separate them out from the total figure for Indians.

Data on birth-place are generally not wholly reliable indicators of different racial groups, and the inherent degree of error is not known. The most problematic groups to estimate are those originating from areas in which it is known that large numbers of British people were also born. The number of persons of British, or more generally European, descent born in the Caribbean and Africa is not known. It is usually assumed that very few whites born in the Caribbean or West Africa are enumerated under these birth-places, and usually no correction is attempted. For birth-places in East and Southern Africa, the ratio of whites is believed to be higher and in some cases a majority, but little or no information is available. Attempts at measuring the coloured population in Britain at times include, and at times exclude, these groups.

One great failing of data on birth-place is that they do not give any indication of the coloured population born in Britain. This is obviated in part by the presentation of certain data according to the birth-place of the head of the household, thus

[1] Discussion of the 1966 Census is limited as at the time of writing many of the tables have not yet been published.

giving an estimate of the number of children born to immigrants. This does not, however, cover members of the small but fairly long-standing coloured communities in the ports, or others born in this country who now head their own household or are adopted into households with British-born heads. These are at present a fairly small minority; but, as time progresses, they will become a larger and larger element in the British coloured population. One proposal for the future, which has been examined and provisionally adopted, is that in the 1971 Census the General Register Office should ask a question on the birth-place of parents. This would, however, only delay the question as to whether future censuses should ask questions on racial, ethnic, and national origins.

In 1961, a total count of the population was made, but for certain types of information a 10 per cent sample was used. This meant that every tenth census form asked additional questions, mainly on employment. Thus, information on employment and certain other topics, especially in the case of Commonwealth immigrants, was based on the 10 per cent sample and not the full count. The 1966 data are all based on a national 10 per cent.

The information available from census data depends on their presentation and, essentially, two aspects of this: firstly, what tabulations are made relating birth-place to other variables such as age, housing, employment; and secondly, for what geographical areas are they presented. For nearly every topic, tabulations exist for birth-place against other variables, but in certain cases, groups of birth-places are combined and they are often national figures. A further complication (in the 1961 data) is that for many of the national tabulations, persons stating a birth-place and not stating nationality were excluded from the data. The major single source of information from the 1961 Census was the report on *Commonwealth Immigrants in the Conurbations* which is based on the 10 per cent sample and gives information for all residents of the six conurbations who were born in Jamaica, the rest of the British Caribbean, India, Pakistan, Africa (excluding the Republic of South Africa), Cyprus, and Malta.

What follows is a summary of the availability of certain census data:

(i) *Numbers and sex.* 1961 and 1966 for all birth-places for England and Wales, by region, by conurbation, by region less conurbation.

For 1961 only for all birth-places in those local authority areas with more than 2,000 persons born outside the British Isles and 50 or more with the specified birth-place.

For 1966, as above, available only from special unpublished tabulations for selected areas.

(ii) *Age structure and marital status.* For major birth-place groups with stated Commonwealth citizenship, for England and Wales. For selected birth-place groups by conurbation.

(iii) *Employment.* For major birth-place groups with stated Commonwealth citizenship, by sex, for England and Wales.

For selected birth-place groups, by sex, by age (15–24, 25 and over), for six conurbations combined and for the Greater London conurbation.

(iv) *Housing.* For selected birth-place groups: persons per room for six conurbations combined; and tenure for each conurbation.

Apart from the above, there exist certain special tabulations relating mainly to the London and West Midlands conurbations, which have been ordered by private research organizations.

As can be seen, the differing coverage of different topics, or, even, the differing coverage of the same topic, means comparability of data is often extremely difficult to obtain. In most cases, it is possible to present a wide range of social data for only four geographical areas:

(i) *England and Wales:* for 1961, this is limited to those persons who stated nationality; and for some of the groups of most interest, over 10 per cent of the population did not state nationality.

(ii) *Six conurbations combined:* this gives the most extensive coverage for all with stated birth-place.

(iii) *Greater London conurbation:* similar to (ii), and almost as extensive.

(iv) *Five conurbations outside London:* this is obtained by subtraction of data (iii from ii).

It will be noted that the geographical areas quoted above are all extremely large, and thus, many local variations are not amenable to examination. None of the areas has a total population of less than seven millions, and they all contain vast diversity within them. Of the two smallest areas, London is undoubtedly atypical of the country as a whole, while the other five conurbations combined are mixtures of urban areas of great diversity.

(b) UNDER-ENUMERATION

It has been suggested that the 1961 and 1966 censuses under-enumerated certain immigrant groups. Peach has suggested that in 1961 the West Indian-born population of the United Kingdom was under-enumerated by at least 20 per cent. Valerie Jackson[1] has estimated that the 1966 Census only counted 84 per cent of the total coloured Commonwealth population of Britain born abroad. For one group, the Pakistanis, she estimated that the count fell to 62 per cent in 1966.

Both Peach and Jackson used data on entries to the United Kingdom as a check on census figures and both stress that their corrections are only approximations. Using different methods, other investigators[2] have found that the census under-enumerated coloured immigrants in 1961. The General Register Office stated that for 1966 there was a 1·8 per cent underestimation of the total national population and that under-enumeration was higher for the conurbations. The General Register Office has not, however, presented any estimates for the under-enumeration of any particular birth-place group.

A further source of error through under-enumeration was suggested by Jenner and Cohen[3] who showed that the 10 per cent sample in 1961 was under-enumerated in comparison with the 100 per cent sample from which it was drawn. It was shown that the size of the 10 per cent sample varied among different birth-place groups, by sex, and among different areas: for example, West Indian, Indian, and Pakistani males were under-enumerated by more than 30 per cent. The importance of these errors was that the source of nearly all socio-economic data in 1961 was the 10 per cent sample and not the 100 per cent sample.

The effect of both types of under-enumeration discussed above is problematic as it is not known how the non-enumerated differ from the enumerated, if at all. The following probable differences between the two populations can be put forward: firstly, the non-enumerated live at a higher housing density, i.e.

[1] Rose and associates, op. cit., Chapter 10 and Appendix III.
[2] R. B. Davison, 'The Distribution of Immigrant Groups in London', *Race* (Vol. V, No. 2, October 1963); and C. S. Hill, *West Indian Migrants and the London Churches* (London, Oxford University Press, for Institute of Race Relations, 1963).
[3] P. J. Jenner and B. G. Cohen, 'Commonwealth Immigrants and the 1961 Census (10% Sample): Some Problems in Analysis' (unpublished paper, 1967).

persons per room, than the enumerated; secondly, the non-enumerated are more concentrated in low-paid occupations and industries; thirdly, a higher percentage are economically active (especially among the women); and fourthly, the non-enumerated are more recent arrivals than the enumerated population.

4. *Immigrants, Employment, and Change Between 1961 and 1966*

(a) INTRODUCTION

In this section, we use data from the 1966 Census to evaluate the comparative situations of the different coloured immigrant groups and the total population in the field of employment. We also try to examine these comparative situations over time by incorporating into our analysis all available data from the 1961 Census. In Chapter 1 it was suggested that the effectiveness of measures can be gauged by such measures as time-scale, comparisons between groups, and the attainments of groups. While the period for this examination, April 1961 to April 1966, was one in which there were hardly any specific measures in the field of employment, it is none the less felt that such an examination does illustrate the general direction of an evolving situation. Consequently, many of the underlying changes in the greater society and the complex factors relating to immigrants and to the receiving society, can be assessed in terms of what effect they have had on the attainment of immigrants in the key field of employment. Furthermore, a detailed analysis of the position in 1966 is a useful back-cloth to future examinations of the effect of specific measures such as the Race Relations Act 1968.

Some general words of caution are necessary before proceeding to an analysis of the employment position. As we have already stressed in our evaluation of the census data, these data differentiate not by race or ethnic origin, but by birth-place alone. Therefore, we will only be discussing immigrants (defined as persons born in the specified countries) and not persons, whatever their racial or ethnic origin, born in the United Kingdom. The omission of the 'Black British' is not a serious deficiency in this analysis of employment data, as these data refer only to those over the age of 15 in April 1966, and we are confident that their numbers were very small. A more serious deficiency is the inclusion of a large number of persons born in India of British or European descent. In the analysis that follows, we examine the position in the Greater London and the West Midlands conurbations. The problem of how to separate out the effects of white Indians is most difficult in London. For this reason, the situation in the West Midlands, where the proportion of white Indians is lower, is probably more representative of the migrations from India (and Pakistan) of the main immigrant groups such as the Sikhs and Gujaratis.

(b) ECONOMIC POSITION

The starting-point for any assessment of the position of Commonwealth immigrants in the field of employment is their economic position. How many of them are in employment or seeking employment, i.e. economically active? How many are economically inactive or outside the labour market? Of those who are economically active, how many are employed and how many unemployed; and of those who are economically inactive, how many are retired and how many are students? In Table 3:9, the percentage distribution in each of these categories is shown for each birth-place group and the total population 15 years and over.

TABLE 3:9

% OF TOTAL POPULATION (15 AND OVER)
ECONOMICALLY ACTIVE AND INACTIVE, IN
EMPLOYMENT AND OUT OF EMPLOYMENT, FOR
SELECTED BIRTH-PLACE GROUPS, 1966

	(a) *Males — Greater London Conurbation*						
	India	*Pakistan*	*Jamaica*	*Rest of Caribbean*	*British West Africa*	*Cyprus*	*All birth-places*
Total population 15 and over	41,290	10,500	35,680	32,720	13,070	20,910	2,875,530
% economically inactive	11·5	10·1	5·5	7·6	35·1	10·6	14·2
Retired, as % of total population	3·1	0·6	0·4	0·4	0·6	1·6	8·1
Students, as % of total population	6·4	6·9	2·2	5·2	32·3	7·0	4·1
% economically active	88·5	89·9	94·5	92·4	64·9	89·4	85·8
Out of employment, as % of economically active	2·9	3·2	3·9	3·0	6·4	4·1	2·3
% in employment of total population 15 and over	85·9	87·0	90·8	89·7	60·7	85·8	83·8

(b) *Males — West Midlands Conurbation*					
	India	*Pakistan*	*Jamaica*	*Rest of Caribbean*	*All Caribbean*	*All birth-places*
Total population 15 and over	13,590	11,750	13,940	3,460	17,400	888,270
% economically inactive	7·1	2·4	2·9	2·3	2·8	12·5
Retired, as % of total population	0·8	—	0·1	—	0·1	7·5
Students, as % of total population	4·0	1·4	1·1	1·2	1·1	3·0
% economically active	92·9	97·6	97·1	97·7	97·2	87·5
Out of employment, as % of economically active	1·4	2·6	3·5	2·7	3·4	1·8
% in employment	91·6	95·1	93·6	95·1	93·9	86·0

(c) *Females — Greater London Conurbation*						
	India	*Pakistan*	*Jamaica*	*Rest of Caribbean*	*British West Africa*	*Cyprus*	*All birth-places*
Total population 15 and over	32,230	3,040	35,380	30,380	8,180	17,420	3,245,570
% economically inactive	49·7	56·6	33·6	33·0	37·0	53·1	50·4
Retired, as % of total population	1·4	—	0·2	0·2	—	0·3	2·4
Students, as % of total population	3·9	4·6	3·1	4·0	14·4	3·7	2·9
% economically active	50·3	43·4	66·4	67·0	63·0	46·9	49·6
Out of employment, as % of economically active	4·3	5·3	6·7	5·7	7·6	3·3	2·7
% in employment	48·2	41·1	62·0	63·1	58·2	45·4	48·3

(d) *Females — West Midlands Conurbation*					
	India	*Pakistan*	*Jamaica*	*Rest of Caribbean*	*All Caribbean*	*All birth-places*
Total population 15 and over	8,390	1,000	11,620	2,970	14,590	929,730
% economically inactive	84·0	83·0	33·6	34·3	33·7	51·91
Retired, as % of total population	0·6	—	0·3	—	0·2	1·98
Students, as % of total population	2·7	1·0	2·2	3·0	2·3	2·4
% economically active	16·0	17·0	66·4	65·7	66·3	48·1
Out of employment, as % of economically active	8·2	—	7·4	8·7	7·7	2·2
% in employment	14·7	17·0	61·5	59·9	61·2	47·1

Source: 1966 10% Sample Census, special tabulations prepared for the 'Survey of Race Relations'; and for all birth-places, Table 13, *Economic Activity Tables*, Part I (London, H.M.S.O.).

As can be seen in section (a) of Table 3:9, which examines the position of males in the Greater London conurbation, all the selected birth-place groups (except British West Africa) have higher proportions of economically active males than the total population. The proportion of those out of employment (as a percentage of those economically active) is higher for the selected birth-place groups than for the total population. Despite this, however (except for British West Africa), the proportion of the selected birth-place groups in employment is higher than the corresponding proportion for the total population. The higher rates of economic activity for the selected groups and the deviance of the British West Africans are explained by differences in the proportions of students and retired persons in each group. All the immigrant groups, without exception, have many fewer retired persons than the total population, and all (except Jamaica) have higher proportions of students than the total population. Except for the British West Africans, of whom nearly one-third are students, the deficit in the number of retired persons in the immigrant populations outweighs the surplus of students.

Section (b) of Table 3:9 examines the position of males in the West Midlands conurbation. Persons born in British West Africa and Cyprus are not included, as the numbers enumerated in this area were very small; and Jamaicans and persons born in the rest of the British Caribbean are, additionally, shown together as well as separately. A very similar pattern emerges for the West Midlands as for London, as once again it can be seen that the immigrant groups have higher rates of economic activity and higher numbers in employment than the total population. The proportion of retired is again much lower, but the picture for students is different in that they are generally fewer than for the total population. Rates of unemployment are again higher except for the Indians. Too much reliance should not be placed on the differences for students and the unemployed, however, as the numbers involved are very small and may be due to sampling error. Comparing the two conurbations, one observes that the rate of economic activity is higher for all groups and, for that matter, the total population in the West Midlands. For the immigrant groups, this is mainly due to the fact that the number of students in the West Midlands is lower and one can also infer that there are fewer retired persons in the immigrant groups in the West Midlands; but once again, numbers are small and it would be unwise to place too great a reliance on them.

The position of females in the Greater London conurbation is shown in section (c) of Table 3:9. Here the situation is much more mixed and the selected birth-place groups vary more widely, with the rest of the Caribbean (67 per cent), Jamaicans (66·4 per cent), and the West Africans (63 per cent) having considerably higher rates of economic activity than the total population (49·6 per cent), whilst the Indians and Cypriots are at about the same level of economic activity as the total population and the Pakistanis (whose numbers are small) have a slightly lower rate (43·4 per cent). Rates of those out of employment for the selected groups are substantially higher for all groups than for the total population and in comparison with the males this is quite marked. The proportion of those in employment follows a similar pattern of rates of economic activity, with the two West Indian groups having the highest proportion, the Pakistanis the lowest, and the total population being intermediate. When examining the reasons for economic inactivity, one sees that in the same way as for the males, the immigrant female groups have lower numbers of retired persons and higher numbers of students; but the main reason for economic inactivity for women, in contrast to that for males, is, of course, the responsibilities of marriage and children, and also, for certain groups, cultural inhibitions to women working.

TABLE 3:10

% OF TOTAL POPULATION (15 AND OVER)
ECONOMICALLY ACTIVE AND INACTIVE AND
IN EMPLOYMENT, 1961 GREATER LONDON CONURBATION

| | (a) Males | | | |
	India	Pakistan	Jamaica	Rest of Caribbean
Total population 15 and over	26,520	4,510	21,490	17,900
% economically inactive	14·4	12·0	5·9	9·3
% economically active	85·6	88·0	94·1	90·7
% in employment	82·5	84·7	87·8	86·0

| | (b) Females | | | |
	India	Pakistan	Jamaica	Rest of Caribbean
Total population 15 and over	25,320	1,480	18,920	13,670
% economically inactive	51·8	51·4	31·8	34·7
% economically active	48·2	48·6	68·2	65·3
% in employment	46·7	48·0	63·5	60·6

Source: 1961 Census; Commonwealth Immigrants in the Conurbations (London, H.M.S.O., 1964).

In looking at the position of females in the West Midlands conurbation, as show in section (d) of Table 3:9, one immediately notes the similarity between the two conurbations for the two West Indian groups and the marked dissimilarity between the two Indian groups (this dissimilarity is equally marked for the Pakistanis, but because of the extremely small size of the sample they will generally be ignored for the purposes of analysis). In London, approximately one-half of the Indian group are economically active, whilst in the West Midlands only about one-sixth (16 per cent) are economically active. Apart from this, the pattern follows London in that the two West Indian groups have a higher level of economic activity (66 per cent) than the total population (48 per cent); the proportion out of employment is considerably higher (more so than for London), but despite this, the proportion of those in employment is higher for the West Indians than for the total population.

Between 1961 and 1966 in the Greater London conurbation, little change seems to have occurred in the participation rates of persons born in India, Pakistan, Jamaica, and the rest of the Caribbean. Table 3:10 summarizes the position of those groups in 1961; it is unfortunately not possible to compare either the West African or Cypriot groups, as in the 1961 data West Africans were included with persons from the rest of British Africa (excluding the Republic of South Africa) and the Cypriots were included with the Maltese. No data are available for the West Midlands conurbation. Between 1961 and 1966, males in all four groups showed a slight increase in the proportion of economically active and a slightly larger increase in the percentage in employment. Females in two groups showed marginal decreases and two marginal increases in the proportion economically active and in employment between 1961 and 1966.

Drawing together all the above data, it is possible to state certain general conclusions. In the two conurbations examined for 1966, males in the selected birth-place groups are proportionately more economically active than the total population in these areas. Despite a slightly higher number out of employment, the proportions in employment are still higher for these groups than for the total population. The main reason for these higher rates of activity amongst the immigrant population is the virtual absence of retired persons. A further point is that if one considers that persons coming to this country solely for the purposes of study are a separate, distinct group then the economic participation rates of the resident immigrant groups would be further increased, especially in Greater London.

For the females, the two West Indian groups have considerably higher participation rates in both conurbations than the total population. The other groups have generally similar rates to that of the total population in London; but in the West Midlands, the Indians (and the Pakistanis) have much lower rates. Numbers out of employment for females in the selected groups are generally much higher in both areas than for the total population and they are also higher in comparison to the males from the same birth-place groups.

The position of the Indians must be examined separately. Reference has already been made to the gross differences shown for Indian females in the two conurbations (sections (c) and (d) of Table 3:9); this points out the grave difficulties in interpreting information in the census about persons born in India. As has already been stated, the population in this country enumerated as being born in India is very heterogeneous and includes large numbers of children of British employees of the raj, professionals, and the more typical economic migrants. It would seem that the more typical groups, such as the Sikhs and Gujaratis, whose cultural orientation is far more Indian than Western, are a much higher proportion of those enumerated in the West Midlands than in London. It would also seem fairer to concentrate on these groups as they represent those Indian immigrants who are the subject of discussion when one talks of integration, discrimination, and related topics. Apart from the evidence of the females, a further pointer to the differences in the nature of the Indian population in the two areas, is the higher number of retired males in London.

Finally, from the data examined, it can be stated that very little change occurred in the economic participation rates for the main Commonwealth immigrant groups between 1961 and 1966 in the London area.

This is possibly a matter for some comment as far as West Indian females are concerned. In both 1961 and 1966, this group had very high rates of economic activity and it would have been reasonable to expect that, with the increasing number of children

4

in West Indian families, there would have been a fall in these rates. In fact, between 1961 and 1966, there was only a marginal fall in the proportion of Jamaican females economically active, while for those born in the rest of the Caribbean, there has been a marginal rise in the rate of economic activity.

(c) INDUSTRIAL STATUS

Having examined the economic position of the immigrant population 15 years and over, one can now proceed with an analysis of their industrial status—summarized in Table 3:11. In essence, this analysis leads to the identification of those groups within any population in employment who will always be in a minority in an industrial society, for example, the self-employed, managers, etc. The overwhelming majority of each birth-place group and of the total population will, of course, fall in the residual category of 'other employees'. Thus in this analysis, due to the often small numerical size of certain categories for certain birth-place groups, reference will also be made to this residual category.

Furthermore, this residual category can be used as a crude measure of the proportion of the total employed population that can be roughly described as the 'rank and file'. This 'other employees' category includes all those who are not their own bosses, who are not in some form of authority, or who are in part insulated from authority—or are not people who might hope to rise to these positions, i.e. trainees. Thus, it can be suggested that the 'other employees' category gives an appropriate indication of the proportion of any group that has not climbed the ladder of our hierarchical society. A possible parallel extension of this analysis is to state that this category is also a very approximate indicator of the degree of success different groups have had in reaching positions of economic power. The power to make the most central decisions in the world of employment lies almost entirely with the self-employed, the managers, and the professionals.

Section (a) of Table 3:11 shows the status of males in the Greater London conurbation and it is fairly clear that there are differences both between the immigrant groups and the total population and among the individual immigrant groups. An extremely high proportion of Cypriots (nearly one-fifth) are self-employed, whilst all the other selected birth-place groups have less than the 7·1 per cent self-employed of the total population.

TABLE 3:11

EMPLOYMENT STATUS OF THOSE IN EMPLOYMENT
FOR SELECTED BIRTH-PLACE GROUPS, BY
PERCENTAGE, 1966

(a) Males — Greater London Conurbation

	India	Pakistan	Jamaica	Rest of Caribbean	British West Africa	Cyprus	All birth-places
Total in employment	35,470	9,140	32,400	29,340	7,940	17,940	2,410,420
% self-employed	3·7	6·0	1·5	1·2	0·9	19·6	7·1
% all employees	96·3	94·0	98·5	98·8	99·1	80·4	92·9
Managerial, foremen, and supervisors	9·3	4·4	1·1	2·7	2·9	5·9	15·3
Apprentices, articled clerks, and formal trainees	4·2	4·7	1·9	2·5	7·9	3·2	4·1
Professionals	8·2	4·2	0·4	1·2	5·7	1·7	4·2
Other employees	75·6	80·7	95·1	92·4	82·6	69·7	69·3

(b) Males — West Midlands Conurbation

	India	Pakistan	Jamaica	Rest of Caribbean	All Caribbean	All birth-places
Total in employment	12,450	11,170	13,050	3,290	16,340	763,610
% self-employed	2·9	1·8	0·8	1·5	0·9	4·5
% all employees	97·1	98·2	99·2	98·5	99·1	95·5
Managerial, foremen, and supervisors	2·2	0·7	0·3	0·9	0·4	12·3
Apprentices, articled clerks, and formal trainees	2·9	0·3	1·8	3·3	2·1	4·8
Professionals	2·6	0·3	0·2	0·3	0·2	3·0
Other employees	89·5	97·0	96·9	93·9	96·3	75·3

(c) Females — Greater London Conurbation

	India	Pakistan	Jamaica	Rest of Caribbean	British West Africa	Cyprus	All birth-places
Total in employment	15,520	1,250	21,940	19,180	4,760	7,900	1,568,290
% self-employed	2·4	5·6	0·7	0·7	0·2	8·4	3·1
% all employees	97·6	94·4	99·3	99·3	99·8	91·6	96·9
Managerial, foremen, and supervisors	5·9	4·0	1·0	1·5	1·3	1·3	6·0
Apprentices, articled clerks, and formal trainees	1·8	—	3·9	8·0	8·4	1·1	1·9
Professionals	1·9	4·0	—	0·1	0·2	0·1	1·0
Other employees	88·1	86·4	94·3	89·7	89·9	89·1	88·1

(d) Females — West Midlands Conurbation

	India	Jamaica	Rest of Caribbean	All Caribbean	All birth-places
Total in employment	1,230	7,150	1,750	8,930	437,440
% self-employed	2·4	0·7	1·7	0·9	3·1
% all employees	97·6	99·3	98·3	99·1	96·9
Managerial, foremen, and supervisors	3·3	0·6	2·2	0·9	3·9
Apprentices, articled clerks, and formal trainees	2·4	4·1	6·2	4·5	1·6
Professionals	0·8	—	—	—	0·5
Other employees	91·1	94·7	89·9	93·7	91·0

Source: 1966 Census, special tabulations; and figures for 'All birth-places', Table 13, Economic Activity Tables, Part I.

For the groups in positions of authority, that is, managers, fore-men, and supervisors, all the immigrant groups are considerably under-represented in comparison to the total population. Jamai-cans (1 per cent) have the smallest proportion in this category, whilst Indians (8 per cent, as compared with 15 per cent for the total population) are the most well placed. Generally, as far as those in the training category are concerned, the proportion of the selected birth-place groups, except for the two West Indian groups, is comparable to or more than that for the total popula-tion. Similarly, the numbers of Indian, West African, and Pakistani professional employees are comparable to or more than that of the total population. The differences between these groups become clearer when one examines the residual category of 'other employees' into which fall 69·3 per cent of the total population, 69·7 per cent of Cypriots, followed by Indians, Pakis-tanis, West Africans, those born in the rest of the Caribbean, and Jamaicans (95·1 per cent). Another way of expressing these figures would be to say that approximately three out of every ten of the total population do not fall into the residual category, whilst only one in twenty Jamaicans does not fall into this group.

In the West Midlands conurbation (section (b) of Table 3:11) the differences among the selected birth-place groups are smaller, whilst the difference between these groups and the total popula-tion is generally larger than for London. For all four specific categories examined (self-employed, managerial, trainee, and professional), the four selected immigrant groups are under-represented in comparison to the total population. Caution should, however, be exercised in attributing too much to some of these differences as the numbers involved are often fairly small; however, it is significant that in every instance numbers are smaller. However, the difference in numbers falling into the residual category of 'other employees' is significant and it can be seen that whilst only 75·3 per cent of the total population are in this category, 96·9 per cent of Jamaicans and 97 per cent of Pakis-tanis are in this category. Using the concept of climbing out of the ruck, it can, therefore, be said that whilst one in four of the total population has managed this, the Indians have achieved a one in ten ratio, whereas for Jamaicans and Pakistanis, the ratio is only three in one hundred.

The status of females in Greater London is shown in section

(c) of Table 3:11, and certain interesting variants to the male pattern are apparent. Cypriots are again over-represented in the self-employed category and the other groups (except the Pakistanis whose numbers are small) are under-represented compared with the total population. As far as managerial and supervisory jobs are concerned, the Indians have a similar proportion to the total population, whilst the other groups are under-represented. In the trainee category, both West Indian groups, but especially those from the rest of the Caribbean (8 per cent), and the West Africans are over-represented in comparison to the total population. The numbers involved in professional jobs are too small to be of significance. Section (d) of Table 3:11 looks at females in the West Midlands. Because of the numbers involved, the only comparisons that are possible, and then only with caution, are between the West Indians (both groups combined) and the total population. Briefly, the pattern is that there are fewer West Indians who are self-employed and in the managerial, supervisory category, and more in the trainee group.

From this analysis, certain points emerge, the chief of which is that for all the selected birth-place groups of both sexes in both conurbations there was a lower proportion of persons enumerated as managers, foremen, and supervisors than for the total population. This difference was least for the Indians, which is probably due, in part, to the presence of white English Indians, a factor discussed earlier. The very heavy under-representation of West Indians in the managerial and supervisory category is extremely significant and possibly reflects the reported reluctance of employers to promote coloured staff to positions of authority.

One interesting sidelight is a comparison of the two West Indian groups. Whilst the West Indians are generally regarded by the English public as a homogeneous group, certain differences emerge in this analysis. For both sexes and for both areas a proportionately higher number of persons born in the rest of the Caribbean, as opposed to Jamaica, were enumerated in the managerial, supervisory category and the trainee category. It would seem that the employment status of persons born in the rest of the Caribbean was marginally higher than for those born in Jamaica.

The very high proportion of Cypriots who are self-employed is probably due to the large numbers owning small shops, especially in the catering industry, and small factories in the clothing industry. The over-representation of West Indian and African females in the trainee category reflects the large number of student nurses in these two groups. The greater success of the Indians as compared to the other immigrant groups is, in part, accounted for by the presence of the white Indians, especially in Greater London, but is also, in part, indicative of the greater diversity of skills and education within the migration from India.

Even without allowing for the above points, it can be clearly stated that the industrial status of Commonwealth immigrants is much lower in general than that of the total population. They have not to any significant extent reached the positions of decision-making and power in the employment field. It is not possible to assess change between 1961 and 1966 as no comparable data exist, but when one considers the current position of West Indians it is difficult to imagine that their position could have been less advantageous in 1961.

(d) OCCUPATION

The main occupations of the different immigrant groups in the London and West Midlands conurbations are shown in Table 3:12. The occupations examined are those in which 5 per cent or more of any one of the immigrant groups or the total population were enumerated. It should be noted that although the General Register Office classifies 27 different occupational orders; the range of occupations within any one order can be considerable. In this analysis, we shall usually refer only to those occupational orders; in a few cases of particular interest, specific unit groups within those orders will be examined.[1] Due to the size and diversity of occupational groups, large differences in the occupational distribution of different immigrant groups and the total population are often minimized and this should be borne in mind when interpreting the tables of occupational distribution.

The occupational distribution of males in Greater London shows the wide divergence among the different immigrant groups. Both Indians and Pakistanis are heavily represented in professional and clerical jobs, while few are labourers or transport workers. The complete reverse is apparent for Caribbeans. Undoubtedly,

---

[1] The census divides the population into 27 major divisions (occupational orders) and over 200 sub-divisions (unit groups). See General Register Office, *The Classification of Occupations* (London, H.M.S.O., 1960).

TABLE 3:12

OCCUPATIONAL DISTRIBUTION FOR SELECTED BIRTH-PLACE GROUPS BY PERCENTAGE, BY SEX, 1966 CENSUS

(a) Males — Greater London Conurbation							
	India	Pakistan	Jamaica	Rest of Caribbean	All Caribbean	British West Africa	Cyprus	All birth-places
Number economically active	36,530	9,440	33,710	30,240	63,950	8,480	18,700	2,468,300
Selected occupations								
VII Engineering and allied trades workers n.e.c.	13·7	11·0	17·4	15·4	16·4	12·1	9·1	12·6
VIII Wood-workers	2·5	1·9	9·1	7·7	8·4	1·5	3·6	2·7
XI Clothing workers	1·0	8·1	2·0	1·0	1·5	0·6	9·3	1·1
XIV Makers of other products	3·4	5·1	3·7	1·8	2·8	0·7	1·4	1·4
XVIII Labourers n.e.c.	6·0	5·9	20·7	15·1	18·1	7·5	4·7	6·0
XIX Transport and communications workers	7·6	5·8	12·4	18·3	15·2	10·7	3·2	10·1
XX Warehousemen, store-keepers, packers, bottlers	3·8	4·1	3·3	4·9	4·1	7·1	2·6	3·9
XXX Clerical workers	17·9	12·9	1·9	5·6	3·6	21·8	3·3	11·3
XXII Sales workers	5·9	4·8	0·8	1·0	0·9	1·3	5·7	8·9
XXIII Service, sport, and recreation workers	5·1	13·2	3·6	6·5	5·0	6·6	33·9	7·6
XXIV Administrators and managers	3·4	2·0	0·2	0·5	0·3	1·3	1·4	5·7
XXV Professional, technical workers, artists	18·1	12·3	1·6	4·7	3·0	17·5	3·6	11·0

(b) Males — West Midlands Conurbation					
	India	Pakistan	Jamaica	Rest of Caribbean	All Caribbean	All birth-places
Number economically active	12,630	11,470	13,530	3,380	16,910	777,490
Selected occupations						
V Furnace, forge, foundry rolling, mill workers	15·9	5·7	8·6	4·4	7·8	4·3
VII Engineering and allied trades workers n.e.c.	19·2	22·3	25·3	27·5	25·7	28·3
XIV Makers of other products	3·2	0·8	5·6	3·8	5·3	1·9
XVII Drivers of stationary engines, cranes, etc.	3·9	3·2	5·8	5·6	5·7	2·2
XVIII Labourers n.e.c.	26·6	53·1	22·9	20·7	22·7	7·8
110 Engineering and allied trades	9·9	37·4	11·8	12·4	11·9	3·6
XIX Transport and communications workers	4·9	1·1	9·8	12·7	10·3	6·3
XXI Clerical workers	1·7	0·9	0·5	1·5	0·7	5·5
XXII Sales workers	3·6	1·2	0·4	—	0·4	6·7
XXV Professional, technical workers, artists	5·9	1·0	0·8	3·6	1·4	8·0

	India	Jamaica	Rest of Caribbean	All Caribbean	British West Africa	Cyprus	All birth-places
(c) Females — Greater London Conurbation							
Number economically active	16,220	23,510	20,340	43,850	5,170	8,170	1,611,140
Selected occupations							
VII Engineering and allied trades workers n.e.c.	3·2	7·1	5·1	6·2	4·9	1·1	2·7
XI Clothing workers	2·7	15·6	10·8	13·4	7·6	64·5	4·7
XX Warehousemen, store-keepers, packers, bottlers	3·0	6·1	6·2	6·2	11·1	1·2	3·5
XXI Clerical workers	45·5	7·5	13·4	10·2	21·4	8·1	35·7
139 Typists, shorthand writers, secretaries	26·9	4·1	6·5	5·2	7·8	4·9	13·9
140 Clerks, cashiers	16·5	2·9	6·0	4·3	10·3	2·9	18·9
XXII Sales workers	5·7	1·3	1·5	1·4	1·4	3·3	10·0
XXIII Service, sport, and recreation workers	9·9	27·9	22·2	25·3	17·5	13·6	21·4
XXV Professional, technical workers, artists	18·6	13·5	22·0	17·4	19·0	1·8	10·4
183 Nurses	1·0	12·8	14·3	13·5	13·4	0·5	3·9

	Jamaica	All Caribbean	All birth-places
(d) Females — West Midlands Conurbation			
Number economically active	7,720	9,670	447,110
Selected occupations			
VII Engineering and allied trades workers n.e.c.	39·5	37·8	15·0
XXI Clerical workers	2·3	2·5	26·3
139 Typists, shorthand writers, secretaries	1·2	1·4	9·0
140 Clerks, cashiers	1·2	1·0	15·1
XXII Sales workers	0·9	1·2	11·1
XXIII Service, sport, and recreation workers	14·2	14·5	20·4
XXV Professional, technical workers, artists	15·9	16·4	7·4
183 Nurses	15·8	16·3	2·7

Notes:
1. The occupational orders shown in this table are those in which 5 per cent or more of a selected birth-place group or of the total population were enumerated.
2. Figures for the number economically active have been multiplied by 10 as the census was a 10 per cent sample of the population.
3. Unit groups (identified by 3-digit code numbers) are sub-divisions of the occupation orders (identified by roman numerals) directly above them.
4. n.e.c. = not elsewhere classified.
Source 1966 Census, special tabulations; and figures for 'All birth-places' from Table 13, *Economic Activity Tables*, Part 1.

the heavy representation of persons born in India and Pakistan in certain occupations is due in part to the presence of white Indians, but it also represents real differences between the occupational structures of Asians and Caribbeans. These differences can also be seen in the West Midlands where the complicating problem of the white Indians, from the viewpoint of a statistical analysis, is less severe. Here the differences are just as marked, but instead of being across the manual/non-manual line as in London, the differences are mainly concentrated within manual occupations.

Both in London and, to a greater extent, in the West Midlands, the occupational distribution of the various immigrant groups differs from that of the total population. An example of this is the virtual absence of Caribbeans in sales jobs and their over-representation as labourers, wood-workers, and transport workers in London. Similarly, Indians in the West Midlands are very much over-represented as furnace workers, and Pakistanis as labourers; and all immigrant groups are almost completely absent in clerical and sales jobs.

Similar patterns of differing occupational structure are to be seen for females in the two conurbations. It should be noted, however, that the highest concentration of all is shown by a non-coloured group, the Cypriots, of whom nearly two-thirds of females in London are clothing workers. No other group, male or female, exhibits such a phenomenally high occupational concentration.

The occupational data can also be analysed in terms of the percentage of each group in those occupations which are generally considered more desirable. In Table 3:13, we examine the population of each group in white-collar jobs. It will be seen that for males in London, Indians and West Africans are more likely to be in white-collar jobs than the total population. However, Caribbeans do far worse than the total population, and within this group, the Jamaicans do extremely badly. Thus, while less than one Jamaican in twenty has a white-collar job, more than one in three of the total population have white-collar jobs. In the West Midlands, all the immigrant groups are badly under-represented in white-collar jobs, and the representation of Pakistanis and Caribbeans is minimal.

In our examination of similar jobs for females, i.e. the 'white-blouse' occupations, we have excluded all nurses from the birth-place groups in order to spotlight more clearly the difference in 'white-blouse' occupations. As for men, Indian-born women do better than the total population, and Caribbeans, especially Jamaicans, do worse. In the West Midlands, the differences between Caribbean women and the total population are even

4*

more extreme: whereas 42·6 per cent of the total population are in 'white-blouse' jobs, a mere 3·8 per cent of Caribbean women have jobs in this category.

TABLE 3:13

DISTRIBUTION IN MAIN 'WHITE-COLLAR' OCCUPATIONS OF SELECTED BIRTH-PLACE GROUPS, BY PERCENTAGE, BY SEX, 1966 CENSUS

(a) *Males — Greater London Conurbation*

Occupation	All birth-places	India	Pakistan	Jamaica	Rest of Caribbean	All Caribbean	British West Africa	Cyprus
XXI Clerical workers	11·3	17·9	12·9	1·9	5·6	3·6	21·8	3·3
XXII Sales workers	8·9	5·9	4·8	0·8	1·0	0·9	1·3	5·7
XXIV Administrators and managers	5·7	3·4	2·0	0·2	0·5	0·3	1·3	1·4
XXV Professionals, etc.	11·0	18·1	12·3	1·6	4·7	3·0	17·5	3·6
Total % of economically active in above occupations	36·9	45·3	32·0	4·5	11·8	7·8	41·9	14·0

(b) *Males — West Midlands Conurbation*

Occupation	All birth-places	India	Pakistan	Jamaica	All Caribbean
XXI Clerical workers	5·5	1·7	0·9	0·5	0·7
XXII Sales workers	6·7	3·6	1·2	0·4	0·4
XXIV Administrators and managers	4·6	0·9	0·1	—	0·1
XXV Professionals, etc.	8·0	5·9	1·0	0·8	1·4
Total % of economically active in above occupations	24·8	12·1	3·2	1·7	2·6

(c) *Females — Greater London Conurbation*

Occupation	All birth-places	India	Jamaica	Rest of Caribbean	All Caribbean	British West Africa	Cyprus
XXI Clerical workers	35·7	45·5	7·5	13·4	10·2	21·4	8·1
XXII Sales workers	10·0	5·7	1·3	1·5	1·4	1·4	3·3
XXIV Administrators or managers	1·1	1·2	0·2	0·1	0·1	0·8	0·4
XXV Professionals, etc. (excluding nurses)	6·6	17·6	0·7	7·7	3·9	5·6	1·3
Total % of economically active in above occupations	53·4	70·0	9·7	22·7	15·6	29·2	13·1

(d) *Females — West Midlands Conurbation*

Occupation	Jamaica	All Caribbean	All birth-places
XXI Clerical workers	2·3	2·5	26·3
XXII Sales workers	0·9	1·2	11·1
XXIV Administrators or managers	—	—	0·5
XXV Professionals, etc. (excluding nurses)	0·1	0·1	4·7
Total % of economically active in above occupations	3·3	3·8	42·6

Source: 1966 Census.

TABLE 3:14

CHANGE IN THE PERCENTAGE OF THE ECONOMICALLY ACTIVE OF DIFFERENT BIRTH-PLACE GROUPS IN SELECTED OCCUPATIONS IN THE GREATER LONDON CONURBATION BETWEEN 1961 AND 1966, BY SEX

(a) *Males*

India			*Pakistan*		
Occupation	*1961*	*1966*	*Occupation*	*1961*	*1966*
XXI Clerical workers	21·7	17·9	XVIII Labourers n.e.c.	16·6	5·9
XXV Professionals, technical			XXIII Service, sport, and		
workers, artists	17·2	18·1	recreation workers	14·4	13·2
VII Engineering and allied			XXI Clerical workers	13·6	12·9
trades workers n.e.c.	14·3	13·7	XXV Professionals, technical		
			workers, artists	12·3	12·3
			VII Engineering and allied		
			trades workers n.e.c.	7·1	11·0
Total	53·2	49·7	Total	64·0	55·3

Jamaica			*Rest of Caribbean*		
Occupation	*1961*	*1966*	*Occupation*	*1961*	*1966*
XVIII Labourers n.e.c.	22·1	20·7	XVIII Labourers n.e.c.	19·0	15·1
VII Engineering and allied			XIX Transport and		
trades workers n.e.c.	14·8	17·4	communications workers	15·9	18·3
XIX Transport and			VII Engineering and allied		
communications workers	10·5	12·4	trades workers n.e.c.	13·1	15·4
VIII Wood-workers	8·7	9·1	VIII Wood-workers	6·7	7·7
Total	56·1	59·6	Total	54·7	56·5

All Caribbean		
Occupation	*1961*	*1966*
XVIII Labourers n.e.c.	20·7	18·1
VII Engineering and allied		
trades workers n.e.c.	14·0	16·4
XIX Transport and		
communications workers	12·9	15·2
VIII Wood-workers	7·8	8·4
Total	55·4	58·1

(b) *Females*

India			*Pakistan*		
Occupation	*1961*	*1966*	*Occupation*	*1961*	*1966*
XXI Clerical workers	51·1	45·5	XXIII Service, sport, and		
XXV Professionals, technical			recreation workers	22·9	27·9
workers, artists	18·7	18·6	XI Clothing workers	17·1	15·6
			183 Nurses	14·9	12·8
Total	69·8	64·1	Total	54·9	56·3

Rest of Caribbean			*All Caribbean*		
Occupation	*1961*	*1966*	*Occupation*	*1961*	*1966*
XXIII Service, sport, and			XXIII Service, sport, and		
recreation workers	24·1	22·2	recreation workers	23·4	25·3
183 Nurses	17·0	14·3	183 Nurses	15·1	13·5
XI Clothing workers	12·2	10·8	XI Clothing workers	15·1	13·4
Total	53·3	47·3	Total	54·3	52·2

Source: 1961 Census, England and Wales, *Commonwealth Immigrants in the Conurbations*; and special tabulations, 1966 Census.

Before discussing the significance of these occupational distributions, we shall attempt to assess the changes that have occurred in the occupational distribution of the different immigrant groups between 1961 and 1966 in Greater London. Table 3:14 shows those occupations in which high concentrations of immigrant workers were located at both dates. Both Indians and Pakistanis showed a decrease in their occupational concentration between 1961 and 1966. As the number of Pakistanis in London in 1961 was extremely small, it is possible that the effects of compiling error may be greater than any real change that has occurred, and the reliability of the data is extremely doubtful. For Indians, the changes are probably a function of the continued growth of the Indian-born population and the relative proportional decrease of the white Indian element in that population. Both Caribbean male groups showed no sign of decreasing concentrations; they showed, if anything (although this could be due to compiling error), a slight reverse tendency to increasing concentration. Among females, the Jamaicans showed a similar tendency to that of the Caribbean males, but those born in the rest of the Caribbean showed a decrease in their occupational concentration.

The proportion of all male immigrant groups in white-collar jobs decreased (in most cases marginally) between 1961 and 1966 (see Table 3:15). This trend for immigrant groups is in the opposite direction to that of the total population, which has shown

TABLE 3:15

COMPARISON OF PERCENTAGE OF
ECONOMICALLY ACTIVE IN WHITE-COLLAR
OCCUPATIONS IN THE GREATER LONDON CONURBATION,
1961 AND 1966, FOR SELECTED BIRTH-PLACE GROUPS
AND THE TOTAL POPULATION*

	Males		*Females*	
	1961	*1966*	*1961*	*1966*
India	50·2	45·3	66·8	70·0
Pakistan	34·5	32·0	—	—
Jamaica	4·8	4·5	7·5	9·7
Rest of Caribbean	11·9	11·8	15·1	22·7
All Caribbean	8·0	7·8	10·6	15·6
Total population	35·8	36·9	51·1	53·4

* See Table 3:13 for definition of white-collar occupations.
Source: 1961 and 1966 censuses.

an increase in the proportion in white-collar jobs. All female immigrant groups showed an increase, but the Jamaicans who were the worst represented in those occupations in 1961 made less progress than any other group, including the total population.

Certain general conclusions can be drawn from the analysis of the occupational distribution of immigrant groups. Firstly, this distribution differs from that of the total population and also it differs among the different immigrant groups. Secondly, it can, in general terms, be stated that the occupational distribution of immigrant groups is less favourable than that of the total population. Thirdly, the occupational distribution of each immigrant group is less favourable in the West Midlands conurbation than it is in the Greater London conurbation. Finally, there has been no indication that during the five-year period from 1961 to 1966 there has been an improvement in the occupational position of the immigrant groups.

The causes for these four conclusions are complex and it is difficult to separate out the weight which should be given to each particular cause. Assessments of skill levels of immigrant workers either in their countries of origin or in Great Britain are notoriously unreliable, but it is probable that, in part, the different occupational distributions are due to different skill levels. Another contributing factor may be the different aspirations within each immigrant group. These aspirations are fashioned by both the social and cultural context of the society that the immigrants have come from and also by the realities of the British labour market. Another factor in assessing occupational distributions is the reactions of British employers and workers to the employment of immigrants. It is not possible here to discuss the causes for these reactions other than to say that in effect they are often discriminatory.

In considering all the factors above, it is possible to indicate certain pointers to some of the effects, but it is unlikely that it is possible to quantify the relative weights of these effects. Of considerable interest, in showing the difficulties of isolating out certain effects, are the differences between the positions of immigrants in London and in the West Midlands. The two areas have different industrial and occupational structures; but even allowing for this, the occupational position of immigrants in the West Midlands is far less favourable. The question that must then be asked is whether there are differences between the enumerated immigrant populations of the West Midlands and of London or whether there are differences in the reactions of British employers and workers in the two areas. The probable answer is that both these alternatives are partly correct and that each, in part, explains the situation. It is probable that the London conurbation has attracted a greater proportion of highly skilled and educated immigrants than has the West Midlands. There are various reasons for this, including such factors as the size and facilities of a great, cosmopolitan city, the location of educational and training institutes, the greater diversity of the capital city, and the location of agencies of the country of origin of immigrants. However, it would seem that above and beyond these differences in the qualities of immigrants in particular areas, there is also the factor of local reaction. It is possible that many of the factors that make London a greater magnet for skilled immigrants are also factors which affect the reactions of the local population. Over time one can expect that the reactions of the local population will select out by feedback mechanism the types of immigrant who remain in certain areas. Thus, in areas where immigrants are less favourably received, a proportion of the most able amongst them will move to areas where they can hope for a better reception.

We have discussed these factors in very general terms and it may be useful to examine the position of Caribbean women in 'white-blouse' jobs in order to throw some light on this discussion. From Table 3:14 it will be seen that Caribbean women in both conurbations are very heavily over-represented in nursing. As a generalization it would seem fair to state that the skills, educational levels, and application required in nursing are no less, and are often more, than those required by most 'white-blouse' occupations. Bearing this in mind, it should be noted that in London, the ratio of Caribbean women in 'white-blouse' occupations to those in nursing is approximately 1:1. In the West Midlands, however, the ratio for Caribbean women is approximately 1:4. For the total population, however, the ratio of 'white-blouse' workers to nurses in London is 13:1, and in the West Midlands, 16:1. The reasons for these gross differences would seem to lie as much in the reactions of the local population as they do in terms of skill and aspirations. Obviously, the unwillingness of the local British population to accept coloured immigrants has played a considerable part in diverting skilled and educated Caribbean women away from many 'white-blouse' occupations and into nursing. It would also seem that this channelling effect has been much greater in the West Midlands than in London. From the position of Caribbean women, it is also possible to comment on the position of males. There is little reason to suspect that there are gross differences in the skill and educational levels of males and females coming from the same societies and the same type of home background. It would, therefore, seem that there are a considerable number of Caribbean males who are capable of white-collar jobs who are not employed in those jobs.

Similar considerations probably apply to the Indian and Pakistani immigrants, especially in the West Midlands conurbation. While their concentration as unskilled labourers and as labourers in unpleasant, semi-skilled jobs such as foundry work, is explicable in terms of their previous industrial experience and poor command of the English language, these factors are insufficient to account for their very poor representation in white-collar jobs in the West Midlands. Factors above and beyond those of skill, education, and facility of English would seem also to be operating in determining their access to what are generally considered more desirable occupations.

The conclusion that little or no change occurred between 1961 and 1966, has disturbing implications for the future. If the high concentrations of immigrant workers in unskilled jobs and their absence in the better jobs continue, then there is a very strong possibility that there will be firmly implanted a socio-economic pattern which will take generations to remove.

Part II
The Process of Racial Discrimination

CHAPTER 4

Housing

ELIZABETH BURNEY

1. *Introduction*

How effective are measures against racial discrimination in housing? It may be possible to answer this question in Britain in ten years' time. As previous articles have shown, the British situation is a new one, and legislation to combat discrimination in the housing field very new indeed. The target is complicated by the fact that the racial situation is still very largely associated with immigration, itself a source of many of the disadvantages clearly suffered by non-white people in competing for house-space. Moreover, this population is mainly one of parents and children (about one-third is under the age of 15), and children of any colour constitute a handicap in the eyes of private landlords on whom newcomers must depend in the big cities and conurbations. Discrimination on racial grounds must be seen against this background, and also against the background of a housing market in which social and economic discrimination of many kinds is taken for granted by people who control access to that market.

The housing condition of the coloured population in Britain, in so far as it can be traced through the imperfect medium of the census (which records birth-place, not race), is strikingly different in many respects from that of the population as a whole. Discrimination is one, but only one, of the reasons. More important is the character of the neighbourhoods to which, as newcomers filling gaps in the labour market, coloured people have come in the first stages of their settlement. Here, especially in London, they share cramped, ill-equipped, and relatively expensive housing with others who have neither the money to buy better private accommodation, or the residential or other status to claim a share of the growing public sector (which now covers 27 per cent of all households in England and Wales).

Table 4:1 illustrates their condition according to two measures: crowding and sharing of accommodation. Compared with 1961, the crowding index has improved, while sharing has actually increased. But the main point is that, as the table shows, the coloured immigrant population is very much worse off than the native English population, and even the Irish immigrants. Fifty-four per cent of coloured immigrants are covered by the figures for the London and West Midlands conurbations; the selected London boroughs and Midlands wards are chosen to cover particular areas of coloured concentration.

TABLE 4:1

HOUSING OF COLOURED IMMIGRANTS,
1966 SAMPLE CENSUS

	Coloured immigrants	Irish	English
Persons per room			
London Conurbation	1·05	n.a.*	0·57
West Midlands Conurbation	1·10	n.a.	0·58
Selected London boroughs	1·19	0·93	0·62
Selected Midlands wards	1·14	0·92	0·56
% sharing households			
London Conurbation	70·1	n.a.	31·2
West Midlands Conurbation	40·9	n.a.	4·2
Selected London boroughs	83·9	60·3	39·2
Selected Midlands wards	44·0	25·9	6·6

* Not available.

Source: Rose and associates, *Colour and Citizenship: A Report on British Race Relations* (London, Oxford University Press, for Institute of Race Relations, 1969).

Racial discrimination does make matters worse, in the sense that coloured families often have to pay more, and have an even narrower choice, than white families of equivalent social and economic status. But its true sting is more likely to be felt when a coloured household seeks to move into better quality housing in a more suburban setting. In the London area, price may anyway make this impossible. But the effect is seen more clearly in the Midlands and the North, where housing is cheaper. Old housing is cheap too, so that coloured families have often been able to satisfy a desire for owner-occupation—or accepted it as the only alternative—in terms of shabby dwellings in parts of the inner city already undesirable to most white families except possibly as an interim solution. The crunch comes when the Indian or West

TABLE 4:2

HOUSING TENURE, 1966 SAMPLE CENSUS

	Owner-occupiers		Renting from local authority		Renting privately, unfurnished		Renting privately, furnished	
	Coloured immigrants	English	Coloured immigrants	English	Coloured immigrants	English	Coloured immigrants	English
London Conurbation	32·6	43·5	4·2	22·2	18·1	28·3	43·6	2·6
West Midlands Conurbation	60·1	42·3	8·2	39·1	10·0	14·6	21·4	1·3
Selected London boroughs	22·2	14·0	5·2	33·3	23·5	44·1	48·2	6·2
Remainder of London	36·4	46·4	3·9	21·1	16·1	26·8	41·9	2·2
Selected Midlands wards	55·7	29·9	8·1	35·9	10·3	26·5	22·9	4·0
Remainder of West Midlands	73·9	45·4	6·2	40·0	6·8	11·5	16·7	0·6

Source: Rose and associates, op. cit.

Indian family seeks to follow the general trend towards newer suburban-type housing: here the factor of racial discrimination can be seen more clearly in operation. It is significant that the first case to get as far as the courts under the 1968 Race Relations Act concerned a housing developer in Leeds who admitted he had refused to sell a new house to a man from Aden on grounds of race.

The mechanics of the housing market, and, therefore, of discrimination within it, differ according to tenure. It is best, therefore, to examine the problem under three heads: private rentals, owner-occupation, and local authority rented housing. Within these tenure categories can be seen some of the most obvious differences between the immigrant coloured, and the native English, populations. The Institute of Race Relations' 'Survey of Race Relations in Britain' has produced the breakdowns for the London and West Midlands conurbations (see Table 4:2).

2. *Private Rental*

In England and Wales as a whole, the total rented private sector—furnished and unfurnished—declined between 1961 and 1966 from 32 per cent to 24 per cent of all households. The second half of the table shows how very much more dependent coloured immigrant households were on this diminishing supply, most strikingly in the furnished rented market in London. The capital is unique in the size of its furnished rented sector, and so is the position of the coloured population within it. Though this is less overwhelmingly true than it was in 1961, it is still more true of Commonwealth coloured households than of other immigrant groups (except, perhaps, short-stay Australians). This reflects the fact that, outside local authority housing, young working-class families with jobs which tie them to inner London can seldom hope to find anything better than a furnished room or rooms for their permanent home. This means high cost and low security and amenity. Increasingly, landlords turn to the furnished sector where returns are higher and control laxer than in the unfurnished sector. Because of the demand, they can pick and choose tenants. A survey of London housing carried out in 1964 noted that out of a sample of landlords' advertisements, 27 per cent specifically excluded coloured people. The 'Sorry no coloured' or 'Europeans

only' type of small ad, until recently taken for granted, was
an easy target in the early months of the new Race Relations Act.
Newspaper editors and shopkeepers do not as a rule want to be
out of line with the law.

It is, of course, rather harder for the law to pin-point whether
a particular applicant for a room or flat has been turned down on
grounds of race. In real cases, there is not always the kind of
evidence which can show up racial discrimination in a test situation.
The seriousness of the problem was summed up in the tests conducted on behalf of the Race Relations Board by Political and
Economic Planning whose report led to the 1968 legislation.[1]
English, Hungarian, and West Indian applicants sought accommodation; in two-thirds of the cases where the first two groups
were encouraged, the West Indian was either turned down
outright or offered stiffer terms.

The most important step is to prevent estate agents co-
operating with discriminatory landlords, which many will continue to do, possibly becoming more sophisticated in their methods,
unless or until the law manages to pin-point one or two clear-cut
cases. Many small private lettings do not, of course, go through
agents at all; but then small landlords who live on the premises
and share facilities with a maximum number of tenants are
exempt under the 1968 Act. A 1964 London survey[2] showed that
nearly two-fifths of landlords lived in the same house as their
tenants, a tendency that is increasing as commercial landlords
diminish and more owner-occupiers finance house purchase this
way. A large number of these rentals, though not of course all,
would be exempt from anti-discrimination law.

Partly because of discrimination, but also because of other
aspects of immigrant and ethnic experience, coloured householders
are much more likely to be landlords, and coloured tenants more
likely to live with their landlords, than most landlords and most
tenants. As long as this situation persists, many will anyway be
outside the scope of the law, at the same time as being more than
usually exposed to the tensions which can mount up when
accommodation is shared between owner and tenant, especially

---

[1] See Political and Economic Planning and Research Services Ltd., *Racial Discrimination* (London, P.E.P., 1967).

[2] *Report of the Committee on Housing in Greater London* (the Milner Holland Report)
(Cmnd. 2605) (London, H.M.S.O., 1965).

when different ethnic groups are concerned. Many allegations of racial discrimination in fact concern grievances for which the proper remedy is the law of landlord and tenant, or the 'harassment' provision of the 1965 Rent Act (this enables local authorities to prosecute a landlord who ill-treats tenants). Even so, the conciliation procedure built into the Race Relations Act has already been found to have a bonus value, whether or not there is cause for complaint under the Act. The mere fact of investigation by a conciliation officer may bring out explanations which help to soothe feelings and cause a reappraisal of conduct.

The fact remains, however, that until coloured people in Britain are able, with the help of the law and by other means, to compete equally for economic status and for the secure housing that goes with it, they will continue to be over-exposed to crowded and ill-run accommodation which breeds stress and suspicion among the occupants. They will also be subject to the constant threat of disturbance through the action of the public health laws. Local authorities have a duty to prevent overcrowding and powers to impose standards of amenity and density on dwellings shared by more than one family. They vary in their enthusiasm for carrying out these powers and duties; but some have come in the last few years to regard it almost as a mission to prevent the spread of shared dwellings (known as 'multiple occupation'), which they see as a disease specifically associated with coloured occupancy. They are, of course, right that sharing predominates among coloured households, and they cannot shut their eyes to bad conditions. But the consequence in towns like Birmingham has been the persecution of coloured landlords and the continual disruption of the homes of coloured tenants, without any positive efforts being made to help them solve their housing problems.[1]

3. *Owner-occupation*

To turn again to Table 4:2, one of the most striking features of all is how far, in comparison with the English population of the London and Midlands conurbations, the coloured Commonwealth

---

[1] See John Rex and Robert Moore, *Race, Community, and Conflict: A Study of Sparkbrook* (London, Oxford University Press, for Institute of Race Relations, 1967); and Elizabeth Burney, *Housing on Trial: A Study of Immigrants and Local Government* (London, Oxford University Press, for Institute of Race Relations, 1967).

immigrants actually own their own houses. Owner-occupation is on the rapid increase in the country as a whole and now exists in over half of all households in England and Wales. In 1966, the proportion was 49 per cent. But in the West Midlands, no fewer than 60 per cent of all coloured immigrant householders were owner-occupiers, compared with 42 per cent of English households, although in London the proportion was much lower, 32 per cent. This needs some explanation. The West Midlands, and indeed most industrial areas outside London, contain many neighbourhoods of comparatively inexpensive, low quality, terraced housing which can be bought, if not dirt cheap, at least on terms which compare favourably with those for a furnished room. While an English family of equivalent income and occupation might consider first of all the possibility of a council tenancy, this might not occur to a Commonwealth immigrant. Or, for reasons which will be explained later, a council tenancy may not be available to him. In any case, he may want to acquire property. But how he does so, and where, may make the result less attractive than the statistics might suggest.

House purchase, in fact, is a prime example of a situation in which a coloured person in Britain may be at a disadvantage as an immigrant, as a low-wage earner, or as a person in a low-status job, and specifically on the grounds of his race. In the first instance, as a newcomer, perhaps with poor English, he is open to all kinds of exploitation. His general ignorance of the market may limit his own awareness of what is available, and it may be natural to him to look first in the run-down locality where he has already been living in lodgings and has formed some connections, rather than seeking straight away the newer suburban housing to which is attached better finance and value for money.

To be effective, therefore, measures against racial discrimination in the purchase of this type of property must distinguish between the existing economic and social types of discrimination of the market. Old houses in poor areas are not considered good 'risks' by conventional lending institutions, nor are working-class wage earners with growing families. Moreover, building societies are concerned to keep up the value of properties on which they lend. All these things influence their attitude to borrowers. And, of course, when money is scarce, only the best 'risks' will be helped anyway.

These attitudes have, however, led on to the assumption of many building societies, or their individual officials, that coloured purchasers, and 'coloured property', are in themselves bad risks. Some have long been in the habit of refusing to lend, or lending on more stringent terms, to borrowers of alien origin. Some big societies changed 'nationality' to 'birth-place' on their application form when they began to get applications from Commonwealth immigrants. Many automatically demanded higher deposits or stricter terms from the immigrants. Some denied mortgages to coloured people in 'respectable' areas where they were already lending on property, for fear of reducing house values. Conversely, building societies lending in established immigrant areas, who, in fact, may have adopted a more liberal attitude than others, sometimes have been known to ration their lending to coloured people so as to avoid becoming known to investors as 'Black' building societies. In some areas the effect of this discrimination has in practice been mitigated by the willingness of local authorities to give mortgages on old property (a facility which almost disappeared during the recent financial stringency). But the local authorities themselves are not always free from racial bias in this field.

Until recently, although discriminatory practices might not be carried out openly, in private conversation building society officials saw no need to defend their actions, other than to explain that in their view such actions were necessary for commercial reasons. They claimed the faster depreciation of property occupied by non-white people—and by this view creating to some extent a self-fulfilling prophecy, since 'black' property thereupon became harder to borrow on and harder, therefore, to sell. At least the existence of law will now cause a reappraisal of attitudes; and since the societies do not, on the whole, wish to tarnish their traditional philanthropic image, their top management is likely to take pains to see that they do not gain a reputation for racial discrimination. Against this must be weighed the fact that especially since the Race Relations Board cannot demand to see office records, it is not at all easy to prove that a borrower has been turned down on racial grounds unless he is a blue-chip risk— in which case he would probably have been accepted anyway. The same sort of status judgements are made by estate agents when they are faced with a coloured buyer: he may be offered

only a certain type of property because he is poor and working-
class, and/or because he is coloured. Some agents also have a
vested interest in confining coloured immigrants to certain areas,
where their demand creates a market for property which might
otherwise be almost unsaleable. In order to make it saleable there
has to be a loan. Hence the alliance with high interest money-
lenders who may charge as much as 20 per cent interest, and may
do so on hire-purchase terms which give the buyer no security of
tenure should he fail to keep up payments.

In this situation, the coloured purchaser is no better or worse
off than many low-income, low-status white buyers. But discrimination really begins to show when he is denied access to
anything better on racial grounds. The attitude of building
societies has already been discussed. The attitude of the vendor is,
of course, crucial. Discrimination is much easier to pin down in
the case of developers selling brand new houses. Prior to the Race
Relations Act, there were several well-publicized incidents of
builders openly declaring that certain estates were not available
to coloured purchasers. Others, rather more chary of their liberal
reputations, merely instructed their salesmen privately to 'go
easy' with selling to coloured people in the early stages of marketing an estate for fear of scaring off white buyers. It is those who
have been most forthright about their discrimination in the past
who must now most obviously alter their ways; the more subtle,
or shamefaced, types of discrimination will as usual be harder to
detect and prove. Moreover, a liberal policy formally declared at
the top of a firm will not necessarily be carried through to the
bottom. It is not enough merely to convert the board (a principle
which, of course, applies still more strongly in matters of employment). As the sales director of a large Midlands building firm
put it to the author in 1966:

We built some cheap houses and our agent reported an influx of
inquiries from blacks—what should he do? I thought we should refuse
them and said so to the Board, but they did not want to go on record
as racialists. So the policy is 'sell to blacks'. I say to our agent: 'You're
not supposed to refuse blacks but use your discretion. . . . ' They say
to the site salesman: 'Be careful how many blacks you sell to.' We
certainly didn't broadcast the official policy or we'd never have sold to
any English people at all.[1]

[1] Burney, op. cit., p. 45.

At least the existence of the law now makes it rather harder to use commercial expediency as a justification for discrimination, even though the market facts may take a good deal longer to change.

The other source of discrimination in house purchase is, of course, the individual vendor selling his owner-occupied house. British law spares no one, except in those instances of purely private sales which do not come on the market in any sense. Estate agents in the past have sometimes pleaded vendor's instructions when charged with a colour bar. The vendor in turn may plead pressure from neighbours, or at least a friendly anxiety not to reduce the value of their property. The law should now help people who would like to resist this kind of pressure, although it may take some time for them to realize it is on their side. It is also now unlawful for neighbours to incite a vendor to discriminate, although it would be hard to prevent them approaching him to arrange a private sale before he had put his house on the market at all.

Again, the extent to which people persist in such practices once they feel the law, or its spirit, is against them, presumably must depend upon how strongly they feel. As far as can be judged, the most determined resistance to coloured house purchase has come from neighbourhoods which are just on the verge of areas into which coloured families have already moved: some of the keenest resisters may have moved out themselves for that reason. Prejudice cannot be eradicated by law. But at least if the professional element in the market—the mortgagees and the agents— stop behaving as though they believed that black faces spell depreciation, then it is less likely to be true.

If it is untrue (and the best available research suggests that the opposite is often the case),[1] then there is no basis of self-justification for the discriminators. The new law may be just what is needed to tip the wheel in the right direction.

4. Local Authorities

Meanwhile, what of the third arm in the housing field, the subsidized public housing which is supposed to be supplied to people 'in housing need'—as so many coloured people in Britain so patently are? Why has it so far done so little to help them? The

[1] For example, see Valerie Karn, 'Property Values Amongst Indians and Pakistanis in a Yorkshire Town', *Race* (Vol. X, No. 3, January 1969).

tenure table (4:2) shows the low percentages scored in this sector by Commonwealth immigrants compared with the native English population. Evidence that this small share is increasing somewhat is tempered by the knowledge that in many areas this is due merely to the fact that local authorities have taken over areas of old housing prior to demolition. There is no sure statistical means of telling how far coloured families are finding their way into ordinary council housing estates, most of which are found in the suburbs or near suburbs rather than the heart of the old cities. Observation suggests that the numbers are still very small, although individual councils here and there can prove some progress. Why it should be so slow, and why council housing as a whole appears to repeat the discriminatory processes of the private sector, rather than counteract them, requires some understanding of how the local authority housing system in Britain works. The essence of the system is discrimination: that is to say, limited resources have to be allocated to people who by various criteria are judged to be more 'deserving' than others. In the course of operating these criteria, local authorities can cause situations which have the appearance of racial discrimination. Very rarely is this their formal motive, and nearly always some other feature of the system can be shown to be responsible. But at the same time, there can be shown to be a considerable degree of racial bias, often unconscious, in the treatment of coloured tenants or applicants by local authorities.

For example, most local authorities maintain waiting lists of people who want to become council tenants. Admission to the waiting list may not be open to everybody, and once on it, priorities are usually determined by various measures which are supposed to indicate the degree of 'housing need' or other factors considered to be important. Each local council devises its own rules, and it is commonplace that the mere factor of long residence in the area, or a long time on the list, often takes a major part in determining priorities at various stages. A few councils exclude, or give lower preference to, non-British subjects or even people 'born overseas' (a provision found in Wolverhampton but later modified to conform with the law). The Race Relations Act can attack the few formal systems which specifically discriminate against people by their nationality or birth-place, but it can do nothing against the prevalence of residential qualifications which

are far more damaging to immigrants of all types—even 'immigrants' from one city to another—and which, incidentally, harm
the housing prospects of most coloured people, in their role as newcomers. Fortunately, there is a continual tendency, now gathering
momentum through central Government pressure, to do away
with these and other arbitrary distinctions which have little to do
with helping those with the real housing problems (who are
indeed more likely to be 'immigrants').

Similar local autonomy governs the duty of local councils to
rehouse people displaced by slum clearance and redevelopment.
The duty placed on them by Act of Parliament is slight; the most
that is required, and this does not apply to every type of urban
renewal, is to rehouse people for whom 'suitable alternative
accommodation . . . does not already exist'. Under this umbrella,
local councils variously exclude from rehousing furnished tenants,
owner-occupiers, lodgers, or single people. They are also free to
exclude people who have only moved into the area since the
redevelopment scheme was first mooted. Quite obviously, there is
a strong bias against newcomers and against the precise tenure
categories in which the coloured population mainly lives. So the
mere fact that redevelopment is now biting deep into many areas
of Afro-Asian settlement does not necessarily mean that there will
be a commensurate increase in the number of black and brown
people on council housing estates. But there will be, and is, some
increase, which sometimes appears larger than in it is because of
its visibility and may arouse opposition.

These factors, plus the ignorance of the Commonwealth
immigrants of the council house system and their possible rights
within it, allied to their natural distrust of authority and the too-
ready assumption of officials that 'anyway they don't want to be
council tenants', all go to explain why there are so few coloured
council tenants as yet. Direct racial discrimination has played
very little part in this process.

There is more obvious racial bias, however, in the manner in
which coloured families are treated once they do have dealings
with the local housing department. Once again 'discrimination'
is the essence of the system. The tradition of housing management
is based on Victorian values of public health and paternalism.
It is seen as the duty of officials to 'grade' applicants according to
their needs—and their deserts. As the author has written elsewhere:

The principle is simple: a clean person gets a clean house and a dirty person gets a dirty house. In between are all kinds of subtle gradings which are the everyday material of housing management. Quiet, clean, steady-earning families with not more than three children are highly prized because they make life easier for management and their neighbours. They are usually repaid by being put near other 'good' families in better houses. The most unsatisfactory tenants may only get old terraced property awaiting demolition, or rehabilitated as part of the council's permanent stock; or simply one of the shabbier inter-war houses. These are also the cheaper as well as the larger properties, so that the worse-off tenants and big families . . . may also be housed there. Those of a lower standard both economically and socially are therefore segregated in public sector housing in much the same way as they would be on the private market.[1]

Coloured immigrants tend to have large families and may have low incomes: but they also suffer a subtle 'downgrading' in the process of interview by housing officials. The author has sat in on many of these interviews, where it became obvious that the crude assumption 'Black equals dirty' was a conscious or unconscious influence in the mind of the official. Misunderstandings or misrepresentations abound, the coloured interviewee being the victim of his own ignorance of the system and of the possible desire of the interviewer to influence him towards the type of accommodation which will be hard to let to other people. The upshot is that coloured council tenants predominate in 'dirty' property or in terraced houses acquired by the council in run-down districts remote from their purpose-built estates.

The law is no safeguard against anything but the crudest manifestation of this type of bias. But it can, and is, doing two important things. First of all, primarily in self-defence against direct charges of discrimination, housing authorities are beginning to maintain records of the race of their tenants and applicants. The idea that records of race are in themselves discriminatory is hard to overcome, especially as many authorities have been in the habit of surreptitiously marking cards to distinguish 'coloured' applicants for reasons which they would not always like to defend. Nevertheless, the positive use of records as an anti-discrimination weapon is beginning to be appreciated, and the more progressive authorities are beginning to realize that this is the only way of

[1] Burney, op. cit., p. 71.

checking their own administration against the kind of bias described in the previous paragraph. If they know themselves that the
'normal' process of administration is resulting in 90 per cent of
their West Indian tenants going into bottom quality property,
then they can check the validity of their own processes. Otherwise,
even the best intentions at the top may not be carried through by
minor officials.

Secondly, central Government are now becoming more
concerned to prevent discrimination in council housing. The
Government have never assumed the power of telling local
authorities how to allocate their houses (as they do tell them how
to build them). But one direct consequence of the Race Relations
Act, and of the earlier publication of research studies (such as that
of the present author), was to cause the Ministry of Housing and
Local Government to set up the Cullingworth committee to
examine the whole basis of council house allocation, so that it
could then try to advise or persuade the councils to reform their
practices. The housing of coloured immigrants was only one
aspect of this study,[1] but an important one. It included an
examination of whether, and the extent to which, there should be
an effort to use the council house sector to disperse coloured people
from areas which already bear the marks of incipient ghettos.
(The Race Relations Act would act as a brake on doing this too
rigidly, or against the wishes of those concerned.)

Thus the question of council house allocation, which for
some time has caused concern through its apparent failure to
give priority to many of the most needy groups of people, is one
which has been brought out into the open through the specific
examination of its effects on coloured people, and by the prospect
of local authorities coming up against the law in the form of the
Race Relations Act. This is a very good example of how measures
and methods aimed in the first place against racial discrimination
can end up working against other kinds of socially harmful
discrimination. There are many other contexts in which similar
results can be expected, thus lending practical force to the view
that it is not the minority but the majority—or the sum of
minorities—whose problems in our society must be solved.

---

[1] Ministry of Housing and Local Government, *Council Housing: Purposes, Priorities, and Procedures* (London, H.M.S.O., 1969).

CHAPTER 5

Education

JULIA McNEAL

1. *Introduction*

Discrimination in education has not been regarded by administrators as a problem facing coloured children or immigrant children in British schools. On the contrary, the framework of reference for decisions has often been the burden placed upon the schools by the children of immigrants, particularly non-English speaking children. Even when race relations has come into the debate about policy measures, the bogy has been not discrimination—less favourable treatment—but concentration. This has been condemned not so much because it might lead to less favourable treatment, but often because it was seen as the development of foreign enclaves within British culture and society. More recently, there has been some talk of 'ghetto schools', the assumption being that the blacker a school is, the worse it is. Officials have often drawn on issues from the situations in South Africa and the American South, and have condemned segregation. Other forms of discrimination have not, on the whole, been discussed.

Immigrant children began to arrive in British schools in large numbers only after 1962. The education system has, therefore, been dealing with the present generation of immigrant pupils for less than ten years. If the attainment of these children is relatively low, this can be, and is frequently, put down to the fact that they are immigrants, and have not had the supposed good grounding of a British primary education. There is evidence that the performance of immigrant children in London schools does improve with length of education in Britain. Thus, the education system has no history of failure to provide for ethnic minorities and no burden of guilt; and few teachers or administrators believe that the system has discriminated against immigrant or coloured children. Nor is there any feeling that the system is morally obliged to compensate for historic discriminations against the

5

forbears of these children—under slavery or the British colonial empire.

The policies which are described below were not intended, therefore, as *anti-discrimination* measures. Racial discrimination would seem to most people at the time of writing an inappropriate frame of reference for policy-making in the education field—and at best marginal to the real problems. Policies have, however, sometimes been justified in terms of an ethic of fairness—fairness both to immigrants and native-born pupils. (The idea has not been used in a 'second-generation' context.) This has sometimes meant, as in the case of the dispersal policy (discussed below), that administrative action must seem to provide simultaneous advantages to both groups. In the absence of special measures, 'fairness' has meant balancing the claims of each group to the teacher's attention. But the most important factor in policy-making so far has probably been the sheer pressure on class teachers who are unable to cope with sudden arrival of immigrant —especially the non-English speaking—pupils. Only recently have educators been freed from the fevered atmosphere of that particular crisis.

In this chapter, I shall try to outline the relevant facts about the coloured minority in the schools and the policies adopted in Britain in relation to them. I shall not discuss any measures taken to educate white children for a multi-racial society, because there has been no attempt to do this above the level of the individual school. There are voluntary organizations who are eager to make progress in this field, but nothing resembling a national or local policy has yet emerged. It is necessary to make one further qualification before launching into the subject: research into the position of coloured pupils in schools has been uneven. Most major research has been concerned with non-English speaking pupils. The only large comparative study of attainment has been based on London primary school pupils, and most of the minority children in it were relatively recent arrivals to Britain. It is, therefore, difficult to generalize about the situation in schools over the country as a whole.

2. *Statistics*

No nationwide statistics about the numbers and distribution of immigrant pupils were collected before 1966. After the Commonwealth Immigrants Act 1962, children entering the country as dependants were recorded in the Home Office immigration statistics, but their destination in the United Kingdom was not; thus, the figures were of little use to the Local Education Authorities. Some authorities started to keep their own statistics. The Department of Education and Science began its national census of 'immigrant pupils' in January 1966. Its definition was to include children of Commonwealth immigrants who were themselves immigrants, and those born in Britain to parents who had arrived within the previous ten years: thus, the count at January 1966 would include children born to parents who had arrived since January 1956; the count at January 1967, children born in Britain to parents who had arrived since January 1957, and so on. As the years go by, therefore, more and more parents will have been in Britain for ten years, and an increasing number of children of immigrant parents will fail to qualify as 'immigrant pupils'. Indeed, since most of the West Indian migrants arrived before control was introduced, on the present definition we may predict that by 1972 very few pupils of West Indian parentage will be recorded. The ten-year rule was inevitably an arbitrary line, intended perhaps to divide pupils who presented a problem from those who did not, at a time when problems were believed to be due to cultural conflicts, i.e. linguistic or social. Under the rule, most of the coloured pupils in, for instance, Liverpool schools, who are second- or third-generation English, are not recorded, and the Department's figures cannot be used to discover, for example, the concentration of coloured pupils, or to measure the participation of coloured British groups in different activities. At the time when the record first began, however, it would have been interpreted as discriminatory to have introduced statistics of race. We have to remember that the atmosphere in which decisions were being made was generally hostile to immigrants: they were seen as creators of problems. In contrast, the liberal position in Britain still includes resistance to the singling out of immigrant groups as different from the general population. To single out a coloured group seemed, and still seems to many, in itself discriminatory. The decision to collect figures was not being made as part of a drive against discrimination. On the contrary, 1965 was the year in which the large-scale immigration of Commonwealth workers was for the first time halted, under the White Paper of August

TABLE 5:1

NUMBERS OF MEN, WOMEN, AND CHILDREN FROM SELECTED COMMONWEALTH COUNTRIES COMING FOR SETTLEMENT UNDER THE 1962 COMMONWEALTH IMMIGRANTS ACT, 1 JULY 1962 TO 31 DECEMBER 1967

	West Indies			India			Pakistan			Cyprus		
	Men	Women	Children	Men	Women	Children	Men	Women	Children	Men	Women	Children
1962*	1,241	3,119	2,644	724	1,005	1,127	409	311	386	163	372	398
1963	1,593	4,244	5,281	8,444	3,289	3,750	13,648	1,339	2,104	513	688	639
1964	2,111	4,738	8,769	3,849	4,196	4,988	3,500	2,146	4,876	495	838	1,096
1965	2,342	3,739	9,025	4,009	5,921	7,201	2,696	2,748	3,957	271	698	575
1966	561	1,600	8,827	3,347	5,508	7,853	919	3,041	6,285	110	335	340
1967	662	1,356	10,406	3,963	5,982	9,122	1,121	4,706	12,817	111	313	280
Total	8,510	18,796	44,952	24,336	25,901	34,041	22,293	14,281	30,425	1,663	3,244	3,328

* 1 July to 31 December.

Source: Race Relations Board, *Report of the Race Relations Board for 1966–7* (London, H.M.S.O., 1967).

TABLE 5:2

CHILDREN IN COLOURED COMMONWEALTH HOUSEHOLDS BORN IN ENGLAND AND WALES* AS A PROPORTION OF ALL CHILDREN IN HOUSEHOLDS

| | Children in households and percentage of those born in England and Wales | | | | | | Children 0–14 years born in England and Wales | | |
| | 0–4 | | 5–9 | | 10–14 | | Total | Proportion to all children in households | |
Birth-place (of parents)	No.	%	No.	%	No.	%	No.	No.	%
India†	38,776	88·6	24,176	60·0	22,878	35·2	85,830	56,886	66·3
Pakistan‡	7,863	73·3	5,186	32·5	4,148	0·1	17,197	7,427	43·2
Jamaica	47,775	98·1	26,999	80·2	13,032	20·7	87,806	71,218	81·1
Rest of Caribbean	34,686	96·7	17,704	66·0	9,495	12·0	62,885	47,364	75·3
West Africa	6,363	86·5	2,343	33·4	993	25·4	9,699	6,632	68·4
Cyprus	11,894	93·5	10,391	62·9	7,488	38·1	29,773	20,431	68·6
Total		100		100		100			100

* These estimates do not include children who were under-enumerated.

† Children of white Indians are included (estimated by 'Survey of Race Relations in Britain' to number 9,000).

‡ Children of white Pakistanis are included.

Source : D. Eversley and F. Sukdeo, *The Dependants of the Coloured Commonwealth Population of England and Wales* (London, Institute of Race Relations Special Series, 1969), Table 27.

that year. This move was preceded and accompanied by much publicity about the immigrants as a problem group. If statistics are neutral, there was certainly no reason for the average man to suppose that the authorities wanted these data in order to help minorities. In this and, as we shall see, other fields, the decision taken by the Department could only be a temporary one. The Department decided to identify 'immigrant pupils', not coloured pupils; thus, its definition could remain valid only so long as it was possible to class coloured children as an *immigrant* minority. The inclusion of some pupils born in Britain can be regarded as a decision that recently arrived immigrant parents will bring their children up in the language and culture of the country of origin; or it can be regarded as a way of finding out about concentrations of *coloured* children at that time, without acknowledging that this was the intention. Instead of recording only birth-place of persons, the 1971 general census did record the birth-place of parents, and it is possible that the Department will follow suit in its collection of statistics on children of immigrants. The Department is worried about its statistics, as is clear from its evidence

to the House of Commons Committee on Race Relations and
Immigration in 1969. Table 5:4 shows the variety of countries of origin from which the immigrant pupils came. Unlike the
full statistics, it does not show the great differences in the particular 'mix' between different L.E.A.s, and between different
schools in the same area.

TABLE 5:3

IMMIGRANT PUPILS IN BRITISH SCHOOLS
(ENGLAND AND WALES)

	Immigrants	All pupils	% Immigrants
January 1967			
All schools	183,776	7,328,110	2·5
Schools with			
over 10 immigrants	164,725*	1,209,828	13·6
January 1968			
All schools	220,212		
Schools with			
over 10 immigrants	200,742†		

* Includes 36,295 pupils from Europe, North America, and Australasia.
† Includes 38,414 pupils from Europe, North America, and Australasia. (An
additional 20,000 were in schools with less than 10 immigrant pupils.)

TABLE 5:4

IMMIGRANT PUPILS BY ORIGIN, IN SCHOOLS
WITH 10 OR MORE IMMIGRANT PUPILS,
JANUARY 1967

Country	Boys	Girls	Total
Africa	3,150	2,489	5,639
Cyprus (Greek)	4,955	4,871	9,826
Cyprus (Turkey)	2,060	1,949	4,009
India	18,761	14,361	33,121
Italy	5,422	5,263	10,685
Malta	506	482	988
Pakistan	7,982	3,880	11,862
Poland	1,499	1,379	2,878
Spain	650	639	1,289
West Indies	35,147	38,458	73,605
Others	5,684	5,138	10,822

Source: Statistics of Education (London, H.M.S.O., 1967).

TABLE 5:5

PERCENTAGE OF IMMIGRANT PUPILS IN
MAINTAINED PRIMARY AND SECONDARY SCHOOLS
(IN EXCESS OF 2 PER CENT) IN BOROUGHS WITH
A POPULATION OF 50,000 OR MORE

| | January 1968 | | | January 1968 | |
	Primary schools	Secondary schools		Primary schools	Secondary schools
Inner London boroughs			*County boroughs*		
Hammersmith	18·7	12·5	Bath	2·7	1·3
Kensington and			Birmingham	9·6	8·0
Chelsea	18·7	16·8	Blackburn	6·9	4·9
Camden	19·2	15·4	Bolton	4·7	5·2
Westminster	20·6	12·4	Bradford	7·5	9·2
Islington	25·5	20·0	Bristol	3·9	2·8
Hackney	26·2	19·6	Burton-upon-Trent	3·2	2·5
Tower Hamlets and			Coventry	5·7	7·8
City of London	10·7	7·1	Derby	11·4	8·2
Greenwich	4·4	3·9	Dewsbury	4·2	5·3
Lewisham	14·8	8·5	Dudley	2·8	2·6
Southwark	13·7	11·3	Gloucester	4·8	3·3
Lambeth	22·0	16·4	Huddersfield	11·4	7·6
Wandsworth	17·6	12·0	Ipswich	4·0	2·7
			Leeds	4·4	3·8
			Leicester	10·1	9·7
Outer London boroughs			Luton	7·3	6·2
Barnet	7·6	4·8	Manchester	5·2	4·0
Brent	27·2	21·4	Northampton	3·8	2·2
Bromley	2·0	2·0	Nottingham	8·5	5·7
Croydon	7·9	6·6	Oldham	2·1	2·4
Ealing	17·3	14·6	Oxford	6·8	4·8
Enfield	6·4	4·7	Preston	7·7	6·7
Haringey	30·8	21·1	Reading	6·8	5·2
Harrow	3·5	2·6	Rochdale	4·4	4·2
Hillingdon	2·5	2·2	Sheffield	2·6	1·9
Hounslow	8·0	7·7	Southampton	2·5	1·6
Merton	6·9	3·6	Walsall	6·2	6·7
Newham	13·1	10·0	Warley	9·7	9·3
Redbridge	4·3	3·7	West Bromwich	5·6	4·9
Richmond-upon-			Wolverhampton	17·9	9·7
Thames	3·3	2·6			
Waltham Forest	9·8	7·2			

Source: Evidence to the Select Committee on Immigration and Race Relations by the Department of Education and Science (13 February 1969), cited in *Colour and Immigration in the United Kingdom 1969*, Institute of Race Relations Facts Paper (London, Institute of Race Relations, 1969).

TABLE 5:6

DISTRIBUTION OF IMMIGRANT PUPILS,
JANUARY 1967

No. of schools	% immigrants
19,688	0
4,335	under 2
2,757	2–10
557	10–15
362	15–20
861	over 20*

* 516 of these schools had 20–33⅓ per cent immigrant pupils, and 345 had more than 33⅓ per cent.
Source: Statistics of Education (London, H.M.S.O., 1967).

TABLE 5:7

IMMIGRANT PUPILS IN MAINTAINED PRIMARY
AND SECONDARY SCHOOLS* IN ENGLAND AND
WALES, BY AGE GROUPS

	1967	1968
Under 5	5,539	6,138
5	22,114	27,520
6	19,565	23,814
7	16,951	20,162
8	15,090	17,506
9	13,774	16,222
10	11,636	14,865
11	11,808	14,367
12	11,636	14,192
13	11,285	14,265
14	11,192	14,030
15	7,964	10,365
16+	5,390	7,296
All ages	164,725	200,742†

* The figures relate to schools having 10 or more immigrant pupils. In addition, there are about 20,000 immigrant pupils in schools where they number less than 10. (No figures are available for immigrant pupils in other types of maintained school or independent or direct grant schools.)

† This total includes 38,414 pupils from Europe, North America, and Australasia. The corresponding figure for 1967 was 36,295.

Note: The decrease in the numbers of immigrant pupils as the ages rise in the above table can be explained in part by the fact that children cease to be counted as immigrants when their parents have lived here for ten years.

Source: Department of Education and Science, evidence to the Select Committee on Race Relations and Immigration, Minutes of Evidence, 13 February 1969 (London, H.M.S.O., 1969).

3. *The Structure of the Education Service in Britain*

Before describing the various policies adopted in relation to the education of the children of immigrants, it is necessary to say something about which institutions are responsible for forming these policies. Decision-making in the British education system is extremely decentralized. The Department of Education and Science is primarily responsible for planning the allocation of resources 'within the framework of the Government's economic and social policy', i.e. it approves or negatives all major school building plans. It also controls the number of teacher-training places available and, through the quota system of allocation, the maximum number of trained teachers going to each Local Education Authority (L.E.A.). H.M. Inspectorate, a separate and parallel institution, is responsible for seeing that standards are maintained in educational institutions and in the different subjects taught in schools. It is, however, the L.E.A.s which are responsible for employing teachers, allocating them among schools, maintaining schools and colleges of education, and organizing educational services in each area. Head teachers determine their own curricula and choose their textbooks (under the influence, in secondary schools, of the examination system prevailing in their L.E.A.). Indeed, individual teachers have the right to use their own methods and books and there is not necessarily any common school programme. The larger L.E.A.s have developed their own local inspectorate which acts as a link between the authority and the individual schools. In teacher training, the local colleges of education, grouped under their academic guardians—the Institutes of Education in universities— are autonomous institutions. Since 1964, curriculum development has been the responsibility of a new body, the Schools Council, which is independent of the Department and financed predominantly by the L.E.A.s, although the Department contributes and the Council is staffed from the Department. Again, any materials developed by the Council must be sold to schools in competition with other commercially developed materials.

There are certain ambiguities in the structure. The 1944 Education Act appears to give the Secretary of State greater powers in fact than he has exercised in practice. The Labour Governments of 1964 and 1966 determined from the centre that

5*

there should be comprehensive schools (i.e. schools not segregated by ability) and called on L.E.A.s to produce their own detailed plans within this broad framework. In response to the recalcitrant L.E.A.s, they began to plan a new education statute dealing with this among other topics. In relation to immigrants and race relations, however, while the Department has adopted a view, it has confined itself to an advice-giving, hortatory, role.

At the time when the policies to be advocated or adopted to deal with the immigrant pupils were being devised, three major reports had described, among other things, the unequal opportunities for education within the British system. These were the Crowther report on secondary and further education (1959), the Newsom report on secondary education for non-academic pupils (1963), and the Robbins report on higher education (1963). The Newsom report has produced particularly vivid descriptions of pupils in schools in socially disadvantaged areas, and Robbins and Crowther showed how, irrespective of ability, children of manual workers do relatively badly in the system compared with children from middle-class homes. It was also found that girls had fewer opportunities than boys. The very detailed work in the Robbins report, in particular about what could well be termed class discrimination, contrasts strikingly with the confused debate about racial integration of immigrant pupils in the various reports, circulars, and white papers of 1963 onwards. In 1967, the Plowden report on primary schools was published. Its most noted recommendation was the adoption of 'education priority areas' into which extra resources would be pumped: positive discrimination to compensate for enormous disadvantages. One of the criteria for the selection of these areas was to be the proportion of children needing special English teaching. Although the Government discarded the precise criteria outlined in the Plowden report, spending on immigrant areas and spending on poor English areas have, since this time, tended to be uneasily amalgamated. Officially, there has been a shift from total disregard of inequalities in the British system, to discussion of the problems of immigrant children solely in the context of social and economic disadvantages shared with English children. The shift certainly represents a gain. It would do so even more if there was some likelihood that the full Plowden compensatory programme would be implemented. But there has been no sharpening of the analysis of the specific handicaps of children of immigrants. The race factor in education has been scarcely discussed. Description of the handicaps of children of immigrants is usually in the form of a list, and argument about particular policies, in the form of 'on the one hand, or the other hand'. There has been no consideration of the pessimistic findings on 'compensatory' measures in the United States.

4. *Central Government Policies*

Two major policies are identifiable. The first, which took the form of a recommendation to L.E.A.s, dealt with the placement of immigrant pupils (undefined, at the time the policy was initiated). This was the so-called dispersal policy—a commitment to the view that the proportion of immigrants in any school or class should not rise above one-third, that the catchment areas of schools might be adjusted to ensure this, and that 'bussing' immigrants to schools out of their neighbourhood might be similarly used. This commitment to a minority quota, and to one-way bussing, has existed since 1964; but in 1969, there seems to have been some retreat from it. In evidence to the House of Commons Select Committee on Race Relations, a spokesman for the Department of Education and Science said the Department would not now be so dogmatic in endorsing dispersal. At the hearing of the Committee, there was discussion of the counter-advantages of neighbourhood schooling in making children feel secure. There was no evidence that dispersal had helped with language learning in the boroughs where it had been adopted. It was also made clear that there had been no 'scientific basis' for the choice of one-third as the maximum quota.

In Section 5, we give a more detailed analysis of the policy, its history, and rationale.

The second arm of central Government policy consisted of support to boroughs with high proportions of immigrant pupils. The policy began in a piecemeal and undirected way: teacher quotas were raised for those authorities having many non-English speaking pupils. While helpful to those areas that found it easy to attract teachers, the extra allowance made little difference in some of the less attractive authorities since they could not get the staff. By 1969, however, some 2,000 teachers above the standard quota were employed by 51 L.E.A.s.[1] Financial support was also forthcoming. Under Section 11 of the Local Government Act, local authorities were able to claim a support grant of half the cost of extra staff or of the extra work burden on existing staff which could be attributed to the presence of immigrants in the borough. One and a half million pounds was paid out from the central Government to local authorities for the first year, the largest claims being for the education service. From April 1969, the central Government contribution was raised to 75 per cent. Plowden recommended a salary addition of £120 for teachers in priority areas, and in 1968, the Burnham committee (which determines teachers' pay) agreed to an addition of £75 for qualified teachers in schools recognized by the Secretary of State as 'schools of exceptional difficulty'. The initial requests far exceeded the possible number of grants, given the limit of about £400,000 p.a. allocated for increments. By January 1969, however, the grants were being made and about 500 schools had been recognized in this category. One of four criteria governing recognition is the proportion of children with serious linguistic difficulties.

After the publication of the Plowden report on primary schools in 1967, there was, for a short time, a shift towards greater central decision-making about priorities, based on the whole 'priority area' approach. Under the Government's Urban Programme, announced in the spring of 1968, £3 millions was to be spent in the first year on the expansion of nursery schools in poorer areas. Again, one of the criteria under which grants are made is the size of the immigrant school population of a borough. A further £20 millions has still to be allocated over the next three years. Under Phase 2 of the Programme, the Home Secretary has approved expenditure of £4·5 millions on 500 projects in eighty-nine boroughs. Just under £2 millions of this has gone to various kinds of pre-school facilities. However, this time local authorities have been invited to submit any projects which they think would tackle social deprivation, so that the previous element of central determination of priorities, based on an analysis of the problems, seems to have been abandoned. One of the curiosities of the Urban Programme is that the money is not *just* going to projects

[1] Department of Education and Science, evidence to the Select Committee on Race Relations and Immigration, op. cit.

concerning race relations, or boroughs with immigrants, and an interdepartmental committee has responsibility for the Programme. But the Home Office—the department traditionally dealing with immigration policies and execution—is co-ordinating the Programme.[1]

5. *The Origins and Rationale of the Dispersal Policy*

The dispersal policy was advocated from the end of 1963 onwards for a number of different reasons. The idea of limiting the proportion of immigrant children in a school goes back to the second report of the Commonwealth Immigration Advisory Council (C.I.A.C.), a voluntary committee set up by the Conservative Government to advise the Home Secretary on matters related to the 'welfare and integration' of immigrants. Paragraphs 25 and 26 of this report, published early in 1964, exemplify the beliefs and the kind of arguments advanced in favour of a quota dispersal policy. The underlying assumptions were held even by those who did not advocate the dispersal policy, and are still held by many officials, teachers, and politicians.

The presence of a high proportion of immigrant children in one class slows down the general routine of working and hampers the work of the whole class, especially where the immigrants do not speak or write English fluently. This is clearly in itself undesirable and unfair to all the children in the class. There is a further danger that educational backwardness which, in fact, is due to environment, language, or a different culture may increasingly be supposed to arise from some inherent or genetic inferiority.

But something more than academic progress is involved. Schools want to give their immigrant pupils as good an introduction to life in Britain as possible. The evidence we have received strongly suggests that if a school has more than a certain percentage of immigrant children among its pupils the whole character and ethos of the school is altered. Immigrant pupils in such a school will not get as good an introduction to British life as they would get in a normal school, and we think that their education in the widest sense must suffer as a result. . . . We were concerned by the evidence we received that there

[1] For some detailed criticism of this see E. J. B. Rose and associates, *Colour and Citizenship: A Report on British Race Relations* (London, Oxford University Press, for Institute of Race Relations, 1969); and also Nicholas Deakin, *Whitehall and Integration: An Unauthorised Programme* (London, Institute of Race Relations Briefing Paper, July 1968).

were schools in certain parts of the country containing an extremely high proportion of immigrant children, moreover the evidence from one or two areas showed something a good deal more disturbing than a rise in the proportion of immigrant children in certain schools: it showed a tendency towards the creation of predominantly immigrant schools, partly because of the increase in the numbers of immigrant children in certain neighbourhoods, but also partly because some parents tend to take native-born children away from school when the proportion of immigrant pupils exceeds a level which suggests to them that the school is becoming an immigrant school.

Thus, the main reasons advanced for keeping children of immigrants in a minority in schools were (i) that, it was assumed, these pupils lowered general standards, and (ii) that high proportions hindered cultural assimilation of the individual pupils.

In an earlier paragraph, it was noted that 'a national system [of education] cannot be expected to perpetuate the different values of immigrant groups'. The idea of predominantly immigrant schools was by this standard intolerable.

The Department's own championship of the policy was precipitated by a crisis in Southall, one of the western suburbs of London, at the beginning of the school year in the autumn of 1963. Southall had seen the build-up of its Indian, mainly Sikh, population in the late 1950s. Before control was introduced in 1962, many of the Indian workers had brought over their wives and children from India. In the early sixties, the children began to enter schools in greater numbers, and because of residential concentration, one or two schools began to have large proportions of Indian children. White parents at one school with about 60 per cent Indian pupils, staged a protest calling for separate education of immigrant children. The then Minister of Education, Sir Edward Boyle (a noted liberal Conservative), attended a meeting at the school and refused to countenance the idea of segregated education. Instead, the policy adopted by the L.E.A. was to keep the proportion of immigrant pupils in schools to a maximum of 30 per cent, and to do this, if necessary, by 'bussing' immigrants away from their nearest school. Sir Edward Boyle explained to the House of Commons later: 'If possible, it is desirable on education grounds that no one school should have more than about 30% of immigrants.' It was, he said, 'both politically and legally more or less impossible to compel native parents to send their children to school in an immigrant area if there are places for them in other schools'. (This was a reference to a guarantee of parental choice in the 1944 Education Act.) 'I must regretfully tell the House', Sir Edward went on, 'that one school must be regarded now as irretrievably an immigrant school. The important thing to do is to prevent this happening elsewhere.'

The dispersal policy was endorsed and generalized in departmental circular 7/65, sent out in April 1965, a few months after the Labour Party had been elected. In a section headed 'Spreading the Children', the circular advocated the limitation of the proportion of immigrant pupils to about one-third of a school or class; where this was exceeded, 'every effort should be made to disperse the immigrant children round a greater number of schools and to meet such problems of transport as may arise'. The only italicized paragraph of the circular ran as follows:

It will be helpful if the parents of non-immigrant children can see that practical measures have been taken to deal with the problem of schools, and that the progress of their own children is not being restricted by the undue preoccupation of the teaching staff with linguistic and other problems of immigrant children.

The dispersal policy was included in Part III, 'Integration', of the White Paper on immigration of August 1965. In the White Paper, the 30 per cent quota is recommended as, among other reasons, an aid to the organization of special English language classes for pupils with language difficulties.

Underlying the dispersal policy were a number of assumptions: that assimilation was the ultimate goal of policy; that immigrant pupils were a burden on the schools; that they caused a drop in standards which led white parents to withdraw their children; and, finally, that the resulting concentration and separation were considered bad for immigrants for several reasons: the immigrant children would not learn English; they would not learn the British way of life; and, perhaps, separation conjured up images of apartheid, or segregation in the United States, and, therefore, must be wrong in itself for coloured children in Britain. This mixture of pro- and anti-immigrant explanation in the second report of the C.I.A.C., is typical of most later statements issued by organizations on the question of immigrant pupils in schools. Immigrants are blamed for the schools' problems, and policies are recommended which would keep down their number —but this is also presented as a benefit to immigrant pupils. It is worth quoting at length from a 1968 report prepared by a teachers union group in Wolverhampton, the National Association of Schoolmasters, four years after the C.I.A.C. report. The national union report to which the Wolverhampton one is attached favours dispersal out of deprived areas wherever possible. This is how the Wolverhampton teachers describe the effect of the arrival of immigrant pupils:

... While the total [of coloured children] was less than 5% (i.e. about 2 per class of 40) there was no serious difficulty. As the number approached 10% there was uneasiness and when it soon moved to 15% and then 20% there was definite distress in the school and within the catchment area. With classes of 40 the presence of 8 children in each who demanded special attention caused a drop in standards of attainment and behaviour. By this time many of the more intelligent parents saw what was happening and found some reason to move their children to another school ... the downward spiral accelerated. The 'best' families moved away, coloured immigrants or problem families moved into the vacant place, school standards dropped, teachers became discouraged and some left.

Here, numbers alone, of 'coloured immigrants', are blamed for a school's distress. A little later, however, the teachers write: 'A coloured school can all too easily become synonymous with a low standard school, the place where the authority can "off-load" its problems and society can send its rejects.' And the report goes on to argue that coloured children are 'deprived' because of the *areas* in which their parents have settled; and that they need to break out of their present situation otherwise the vicious circle of low attainment, poor jobs with frustration and low wages, and poor houses, will be established. 'The decaying centres of the U.S.A. give us a clear warning.' Finally the Wolverhampton report places colour discrimination within the context of class discrimination in the British education system.

The association of falling standards of attainment with the arrival of coloured immigrants is widely accepted, but the only large-scale study of attainment published by 1970—a report based on research conducted by the Inner London authority in

1966—showed that English children aged 11 plus in schools having more than 30 per cent of immigrant pupils (coloured and white), had the same distribution of scores in English, verbal reasoning, and mathematics as all children throughout the authority.[1] Two-thirds of the head teachers in the 52 schools surveyed felt there had been some fall in the level of intelligence of their non-immigrant pupils, due to the fact that the more able families had moved. About one-third of the heads felt there was also under-achievement by non-immigrants, i.e. they were not doing as well as they could. The movement of families out of inner city areas cannot be attributed to the arrival of immigrants. It had been going on since the early fifties, and was facilitated by increased housing opportunities to which both public and private housing contributed.[2]

That the composition of some schools was changing in terms of social class and the educational development of pupils, was true: that this inevitably meant falling standards, let alone descent into anarchy, was not. Few reports wrote of the schools in which immigrants constituted the more stable and the brighter element. The Inner London authority's report noted:

In some under-privileged areas many immigrant children are providing a reservoir of ability which is very welcome in the secondary schools. In many primary schools also, children of immigrants, especially when they have had a full primary school education in this country, are contributing both to the intellectual and social quality of the school.

That the presence of immigrant pupils by itself caused the change was not true. That their presence caused the school to become substandard was tantamount to group libel. There was in the rationale of the dispersal policy, a stigmatization of the 'immigrant school' and immigrant pupils, which contributed to the fluctuating white hostility to immigrants and which made it hard to present the policy as a measure of goodwill.

[1] *The Education of Immigrant Pupils in Primary Schools* (London, I.L.E.A., 1967). But more recent research has found these pupils scored below average.

[2] For a more elaborate theory of the way in which immigrants functioned as a 'replacement population' in employment and housing, see Ceri Peach's study, *West Indian Migration to Britain: A Social Geography* (London, Oxford University Press, for Institute of Race Relations, 1968).

(a) THE RATIONALE OF SOME OPPONENTS OF DISPERSAL

It would be wrong to give the impression that most teachers favoured dispersal. The National Association of Schoolmasters (N.A.S.) report did favour it, but an earlier statement by the much larger National Union of Teachers remained non-committal, basically adopting the view (now shared by the Department) that L.E.A.s should decide for themselves in the light of local circumstances. Teachers in Inner London, Haringey, and Brent opposed the dispersal proposal. Brent teachers in particular produced a report (in conjunction with the local Community Relations Council) whose perspective lies at the opposite extreme of the report of Wolverhampton N.A.S. (National Association of Schoolmasters):

We have made a conscious and deliberate attempt in writing this report to avoid terms which have come to have discriminatory meanings and to stress the physical differences between people. Examples of such words are 'race', 'immigrant', 'host', 'coloured', 'black' and 'white'; . . . to see the picture in terms of 'immigrants' or 'skin colour' is wholly misleading. What essentially we have to deal with are deprived areas, and it is in those terms that the problem must be viewed.

. . . as with previous generations of inhabitants of such localities they are generally the victims and not the cause of the problems often attributed to them. The difficulties posed by immigrant children are only in a few respects different from those commonly found in association with children in deprived areas, and these differences have to do with language and educational and cultural background. These factors can affect school organisation but they are not in themselves new to the educational experience of this country.

We would support the C.E.O. [Chief Education Officer] of Brent when he asks ' . . . why shouldn't schools in predominantly immigrant areas be predominantly immigrant?'

The Brent teachers opposed dispersal, reception centres, the collection of statistics of the numbers of immigrant pupils, and the use or development of tests of attainment. Although the report made a number of positive recommendations, the viewpoint which distinguished it was a negative one: opposition to a number of developments which, it argues, had racist origins. The Brent teachers' report represented the views of teachers who were committed to 'neighbourhood' primary (and small secondary) schools, and who deplored the stigmatization of immigrants. It represented rational liberal opposition to the 'scare tactics' of the opponents of immigration.

It is noteworthy that the Brent report, while against the singling out of immigrant or Black pupils, does place them in the context of the deprived neighbourhood.

The tactical difficulty presented by the 'no distinctions' view was how to stress the problems of multi-racial schools enough to get more resources for them, but without stigmatizing them. Interestingly, one of the most bitter attacks on racial and class prejudice, and lack of organization in the present multi-racial schools, came from a West Indian writer after her experience teaching in a number of Brent schools.[1] The Brent Teachers' Association, which had produced the education report, disliked her article.

It is, however, now possible to discern among teachers, particularly language teachers, a view which is anti-dispersal while recognizing that the multi-racial, multi-cultural school is different from the all-English school in some significant respects and involves, if it is to be successful, major changes in organization and orientation. It is a viewpoint which in many cases has arisen directly from trying to run a multi-racial school as though it were an all-English, even all-English 'deprived', school, and finding this an inadequate framework. Dislike of dispersal has in this case rested on the sense of success in handling changes in the school population, the sense of contribution which the school can make to a relatively unstable neighbourhood, and the experience of the contribution of immigrant pupils or children of immigrants in this process.

(b) DISPERSAL IN PRACTICE

The discriminatory tone of the arguments commonly advanced for dispersal, and the hostile climate of opinion in which the policy was announced in 1965, do not exclude the possibility that dispersal might in its practical effect benefit immigrant pupils, or even that it might be essential to an anti-discrimination programme. Unfortunately, there has been no general study of the dispersal schemes in operation or comparative assessment of

[1] Marina Maxwell, 'Violence in the Toilets', *Race Today* (September 1969).

L.E.A.s with and without dispersal policies. The latest statement for the D.E.S. displayed a considerable retreat from the dogmatism of circular 7/65.

Dispersal has not been universally welcomed and is adopted by only about a quarter of authorities which have more than 2% of immigrants on the school roll. Its opponents regard it as discriminatory since in practice only immigrant children are dispersed. The children receive their schooling away from localities where their families live and where they spend their leisure time, the ability to concentrate teachers especially trained in or attuned to the needs of immigrant children is lessened. But equally there are advantages in dispersal, if the alternative would be predominantly immigrant schools in downtown areas, where overcrowded premises and staffing problems might add to the disadvantages of largely segregated education. In the Department's view dispersal is not in all cases appropriate but it can ease the situation in certain circumstances which local authorities are well-planned to judge. A rigid policy applied from the centre would not only be a derogation of authorities' freedom but would be educationally unsound.[1]

The D.E.S. here, for the first time, suggests dispersal as a weapon against environmental deprivation—the kind of discrimination which it was intended to counter in the United States. In this connection it should be noted that prominent among the L.E.A.s that rejected dispersal, are Inner London and Birmingham, areas where particularly acute housing conditions exist—and it is the Caribbean population who, of all ethnic groups, are probably the worst victims of this situation, in terms of the proportion of families affected. Also among the rejecting boroughs were Brent and Haringey, the two outer boroughs with the highest proportions of immigrant pupils (27·2 per cent and 30·8 per cent, respectively, in primary schools at January 1968). Moreover, these four education authorities contain within their boundaries approximately half the total Caribbean population in England and Wales, as enumerated in the 1966 Census. (Haringey is now planning a 'banding' scheme which would involve dispersal for some secondary school children, both immigrant and native; see below.) Of the L.E.A.s which did adopt some form of dispersal, the best known are Ealing (Outer London, incorporating Southall, with a population c. 300,000); Bradford (a northern

---

[1] Select Committee on Race Relations . . . , op. cit.

industrial town with a population *c.* 300,000); and Huddersfield (a northern industrial town with a population *c.* 130,000). In all three boroughs Indian and Pakistani children have been the particular source of attention; and the preoccupation has been the problem of non-English speaking children, and the cultural differences between the Asian and English groups. (Despite many references to cultural differences, no satisfactory definitions have really been provided.) Ealing is the only borough where a published assessment of the dispersal scheme has been made,[1] and much of the comment on the working of dispersal which follows is based on the Ealing experience. The possible advantages of the dispersal scheme, noted by the E.I.F.C. Committee, would be (i) to promote social integration and prevent all-immigrant schools, and (ii) to help Indian children to learn English by seeing that they mixed with their English peers. The report notes that these advantages seemed obvious when the scheme began in 1964: the Indian Workers' Association (I.W.A.), the main immigrant body, at that time supported it; the only opposition came from white parents at one of the receiving schools.

By 1968 when the E.I.F.C. report was published, about 1,000 of Ealing's 7,000 immigrant primary[2] school children were being bussed to schools away from their homes—in 21 coaches and at a cost of about £20,000 p.a. In 1969–70, the central Government contributed 75 per cent of this cost, as part of the Urban Programme. The original 33 per cent quota has been raised to 40 per cent and Ealing has also (vainly) requested neighbouring boroughs to accept some of its immigrant pupils. Under the quota system, 400 secondary school children were travelling by public transport to distant schools. The children dispersed initially entered over 60 special classes in the receiving schools. The E.I.F.C.—and others—found that in some schools immigrant pupils remained in these separate reception classes all or most of the day. At Beaconsfield Road Primary School in Southall, the original 'crisis' school where the proportion of immigrants was held at 60 per cent, the Head put her English children in one class, with some immigrants, and had one wholly

---

[1] Ealing International Friendship Council (E.I.F.C.), Education Committee, *The Education of the Immigrant Child in the London Borough of Ealing: A Report* (London, E.I.F.C., 1968).
[2] That is, 5- to 11-year-olds.

immigrant class, because she believed this was fair for the English children. The reception and travel arrangements for the younger children have been criticized by some observers. Some five-year-olds leave home at 8 a.m., go on a half-hour coach ride, and have to leave school 20 minutes early, which in some schools was in the middle of the 'story time'—the only part of the day spent with English children. After-school events were difficult to provide: in one case immigrant pupils who had practised for the school concert could not participate because of transport difficulties. Contact with parents (described in a report for the Schools Council on infant schools as a vital part of the integration process) was difficult to establish and very few schools had made any effort to do so. In a survey of one Southall ward, many of the Asian parents did not know which school their child attended. The supervision of children on the coaches has not always been adequate: in Bradford and in Ealing there have been cases of non-English speaking primary school children being put off at the wrong stop. The most bitter critics of the scheme, including, recently, some prominent members of the Indian Workers' Association, have described the situation along these lines: five-year-olds are in some cases travelling up to six miles to school to spend the day in a segregated classroom; when they return home they are again an out-group, as local children will play with their schoolmates. Immigrant parents have no opportunity of meeting English parents in the natural school situation; communication between groups, among adults and children, has, in fact, decreased as a result of dispersal.

Apart from the possibility that dispersal could increase the racial/national self-consciousness of the 'bussed' children, the policy necessarily involved a more formal act of discrimination against immigrant parents. Under the 1944 Education Act, a parent has the right to choose the school to which his child goes 'so far as is compatible with the provision of efficient instruction and training and the avoidance of unreasonable public expenditure'. It was because of this that Sir Edward Boyle said in the House of Commons that it was 'legally' impossible to compel native parents to send their children to schools in 'immigrant areas'. (It would seem likely that this is the legal basis for the 'pairing' effect which has been noted in some L.E.A.s, i.e. the proximity of one all-white school and one mixed school within a neighbourhood.) Under the dispersal policy, immigrant parents cannot exercise the same right of choice. According to the E.I.F.C. report, if challenged about this, Ealing L.E.A. argues that under the quota system which has Government backing, no place is available in the nearest school. In practice, the E.I.F.C. report notes, allocation is done without consulting parents. It seems probable that where there is a special need for a child to attend a particular school (e.g. to be with brothers and sisters) or not to attend a distant school (e.g. because of travel sickness), it has, in Ealing and Bradford, been the head teachers who have attended to the children's interests and dealt with the L.E.A. to safeguard them. The E.I.F.C. committee remained divided on the issue of principle—i.e. whether the quota system was desirable —they agreed, however, that the scheme should not be compulsory, but voluntary.

The E.I.F.C. report also suggested that children be selected for dispersal on the basis of English language difficulties, and not on the basis of their being 'immigrant pupils'. The proportion of children with 'defective English', and not the over-all proportion of immigrant children, indicated a problem within a school. In its chapter on immigrant pupils, the Plowden report made the same suggestion. But laudable though the desire to move away from a racial or nationality criterion may have been, the evidence on language learning indicates that until far more teachers have some knowledge of the teaching and learning of English as a second language, dispersal may have done more harm than good. It might, indeed, have been more sensible at the time for E.I.F.C. to have recommended the selection of *English-speaking* children for dispersal, and the concentration of the maximum teaching effort and equipment in the limited number of neighbourhood schools attended by non-English or partial-English speakers.

The Huddersfield dispersal policy is operated on rather different lines. Although no published assessments of the scheme have been made, both the development of local policy before dispersal was started and the principles of the scheme suggest that some of the pitfalls of the Ealing scheme concerning English language learning may have been avoided. From the start, local authority policy in Huddersfield has been geared to the problems of teaching English to Asian and European immigrant pupils. It has been expanded from the development within Spring Grove

Primary School of a special English department to provide expert language tuition for new entrants until they were of a sufficient standard to learn the subjects of the normal class. The Spring Grove experiment has been described in detail by Trevor Burgin, formerly head of the school and now adviser on immigrant pupils for the L.E.A.[1] By the spring of 1963, just over half the pupils were coloured, and two-thirds of the total roll (of 320) were of immigrant origin, mainly from overseas. Conventional standards had not fallen, e.g. as expressed by the number of grammar school places secured. Some native parents continued to send their children to Spring Grove even after moving from the area. At the end of his book on Spring Grove, Trevor Burgin clearly favours a quota system (30 per cent maximum) because of his belief in social integration of immigrants into an English culture. Like the C.I.A.C., he says the school should preserve its English 'ethos'. Under the Huddersfield scheme, all newly arrived pupils go first to a Reception Centre where they stay 2–8 weeks, and are documented, medically examined, and given some elementary lessons in the 'British way of life' and simple oral English. They then move to a school, accompanied by the same teacher who becomes their class teacher. The emphasis on specialized teaching has thus been preserved, although one would expect standards to vary in practice. How successful English language teaching is in the larger number of schools now receiving immigrant pupils, cannot be judged. It is also unclear how many Caribbean pupils are getting the language help they may need.

To sum up:

(i) *Language:* In oral evidence to the Select Committee, the D.E.S. has said that there is no evidence that dispersal helps with language teaching. If it is accepted that expert tuition is the basis of a successful policy here, and that there is still a shortage of teachers qualified to teach English as a Second Language, then dispersal is likely to make language learning more (not less) difficult. These problems might be overcome if dispersal followed major in-service training drives for teachers in the receiving schools, including reception-class teachers and ordinary class teachers.

(ii) *Integration:* Whether dispersal policies do provide immigrant

[1] Trevor Burgin and Patricia Edson, *Spring Grove: The Education of Immigrant Children* (London, Oxford University Press, for Institute of Race Relations, 1967).

pupils with the chance to participate in a 'normal English school' depends on the receiving school's arrangements for language teaching and placement. Immigrant or coloured pupils can remain isolated academically and socially within a mixed school, and some would argue that contact with English peers is diminished by dispersal, because of difficulty of contact after school hours. The singling out of coloured pupils to be bussed must create a sense of their separate identity both within the children themselves and among white children in their neighbourhoods and in the receiving schools. The high cost of the travel arrangements alone raises the question: could not the money be better spent in the schools, or in the pre-school programmes? To the question, does dispersal prevent segregated schools?, one would answer that to a limited extent, it probably does. But in none of the L.E.A.s practising dispersal were more than two or three schools likely to become 'all immigrant', and it is debatable whether this was inevitable even had there not been a dispersal scheme. The major give-away of the dispersal policy was the absence of concern or provision for the receiving schools, and the lack of provision for evaluation of the policy. In this, practice departed from the norm for other consciously adopted curriculum or organizational changes.

6. *The Professional Response: Language Teaching*

In the various official and semi-official pronouncements about immigrant pupils, there is an unexplained blurring, an overlap in references to a general problem (or sometimes the problem of 'strain' or 'social problem') and the problem of non-English speaking pupils. For example, it has never been clear whether dispersal policies are to help arrangements for English teaching or to prevent the formation of Black schools, or both. For administrators and politicians, concentration on language was, perhaps, a way of defusing the issues, of not talking about race relations, nor about intractable problems of poverty. The language problem was, above all, a soluble one and, moreover, one which fitted easily into the framework of skills of those in the education profession. There were some fairly obvious needs and a number of recognizable ways in which these needs could be satisfied by an administrative structure.

This may partly explain why, of the inadequate resources devoted to solutions of problems emerging in many schools with immigrant pupils, most have gone towards language teaching efforts: it makes it surprising, however, that action even on the relatively straightforward language issue was so long in coming.

One obvious explanation for the slow development of language teaching is that, almost without exception, the initiative came from individuals at the base of the system or in its middle rungs: that is, teachers, one or two training college heads or lecturers, one or two members of institutes of education in the universities. The decentralized structure meant that (except for school building) decisions about the use of training and financial resources and, in the case of teacher training, curricula, were taken by L.E.A.s, colleges, and institutes of education. Therefore, even after the D.E.S. statistical department, in its first census (1966), had identified a problem (in terms of language proficiency) numerically, there was no corresponding shift of effort or resources to deal with it. Administratively, the problem was a simple one: a number of immigrant pupils did not speak adequate English and some others were regarded as non-English speaking. On the first estimate by the D.E.S., 25 per cent of all immigrant pupils (by the D.E.S. definition) needed further intensive language teaching. Another quarter needed some help, and about half had no language problems. John Power[1] (and others) has shown that the D.E.S. statistics tended to underestimate the scale of language teaching effort required. Nevertheless, they provided a guide; and since returns were from each school and each authority, the scale of effort per L.E.A. could have been estimated. In providing such effort, L.E.A.s in the early 1960s were faced with the fact that there were no teachers of English as a Second Language working in the schools. Nor were there any published materials or books available for teaching English as a Second Language to children in Britain. (One of the most popular series, especially in the North of England, became the *Peak Series* of readers, designed for Asian children in East Africa. In Smethwick, the Director of Education obtained his English as a Second Language readers from Australia.)

The first response to this shortage situation came from

[1] John Power, *Immigrants in School: A Survey of Administrative Policies* (London, Councils and Education Press, 1967).

voluntary teachers groups, mainly the Associations of Teachers of English to Pupils from Overseas (ATEPO). At first in the West Midlands, then in London, then elsewhere, the ATEPOs provided do-it-yourself training and workshops for teachers who were actively involved in language training. They also sometimes acted as ginger groups in relation to L.E.A.s and training colleges. The ATEPOs are now a national, federal organization.

The trouble with this response was that it affected only those teachers who were professionally committed to solving the problem. What of the rest? In the field of teacher training, the institutes of education—based in the universities and responsible for keeping the colleges of education up to a certain academic standard—remained almost completely passive. (A notable exception was the Institute at York, where Professor Eric Hawkins and Harry Ree have begun to demonstrate what can be done through intensive, and imaginative, use of existing capital resources and student volunteers.) Local colleges of education began to take action after much polite prompting from voluntary groups and officials. By 1967–8, approximately 30 per cent included some instruction in English as a Second Language in their basic courses; by 1968–9, 60 per cent included, or intended to include, this instruction in their curriculum.[1] Two colleges were offering one-term courses for serving teachers, and another one-term course, in London, had been taken over from the Institute of Education by the I.L.E.A. The slow response of the institutions concerned with teacher training meant that at first the organization of pre-service and in-service courses in language training was left to the L.E.A.s. Some of these, in turn, did nothing (particularly if the majority of their immigrant pupils were of West Indian origin), but the coverage of non-English speaking or poor-English speaking children has been gradually extended, due to L.E.A. in-service courses and L.E.A. support of voluntary teachers groups.

A variety of administrative arrangements was made, which may be broadly divided into three categories:

(i) separate reception centres, used on a full-time basis for new arrivals, or part-time for children already placed in their

[1] Ken Millins, Principal of Edge Hill College of Education at Ormskirk. Member of the Education Advisory Committee of the Community Relations Commission.

local schools; the reception centres were first devised to cope with the sudden arrival of teen-age Indian and Pakistani boys after the 1965 White Paper;

(ii) peripatetic language teaching teams, giving part-time instruction in 'withdrawal' groups in local groups; and

(iii) language instruction in the local schools, by their own staff, which in some cases (and increasingly) would include someone trained, and specializing, in the teaching of English as a Second Language.

For any measure of success, all these arrangements depended on adequate numbers of teachers trained in English as a Second Language and, therefore, in most cases, on L.E.A. courses of some sort, whether in-service or pre-service, and L.E.A. help for voluntary training groups. The language centres and the peripatetic teams had a high proportion of expert teachers. One of the difficulties was that where the instruction was part-time, it was often too short—afterwards children would return to normal classes, where the staff had no understanding of their linguistic needs and could not build on the language instruction which had been given. The more experienced language teachers made conscious efforts to involve class teachers. There was tremendous variety in the amount of special teaching that different children got per week, which suggested that lack of resources determined the arrangements, rather than attention to educational needs. The same variety existed—and exists—in the 'withdrawal' classes held by staff members of local schools, who are less likely to have had any training in English as a Second Language. Some L.E.A.s have made a determined effort to provide at least a rudimentary training. The outer London borough of Haringey, for example, which has the highest proportion of immigrant pupils of any L.E.A. (chiefly Cypriots and West Indians), now claims to have one trained teacher of English as a Second Language in each school; and Haringey runs a pre-service two-week training course for its new recruits. But this would not yet be true of most authorities. At the infant level (the 5- to 7-year-olds), expert tuition of English as a Second Language was in 1967–8 practically unknown —and strongly resisted by many infant head teachers opposed to formal instruction for this age group.

One of the problems of the selective language teaching arrangements which has not been faced as yet involves the question: Which children get the special teaching? This is partly a problem of sheer scarcity. For example, by spring 1968 in Birmingham (one of the most energetic of L.E.A.s in language provision), there were 52 full-time and some part-time peripatetic teachers, dealing with some 2,000 children in schools, with another 250 children attending full-time language centres. Beginners were given seven or eight lessons a week, each lasting 40–50 minutes. Four thousand six hundred children in the L.E.A. area were at that time assessed to be in need of special English tuition. The number of language teachers has since increased so that supply has gradually extended to meet *assessed* demand.

But there is also a major problem of assessment, which was illustrated in detail in John Power's able pamphlet.[1] He found that whereas the D.E.S. census of 1966 produced an estimate of 25 per cent of immigrant pupils who required special language tuition, another survey, conducted a few months earlier by the Schools Council, while asking slightly different questions, had estimated that 52 per cent of immigrant pupils had a command of English which was 'inadequate for educational purposes'. The D.E.S. census categorization of language ability had distinguished between written and spoken English, and suggested that a combination of 'reasonably good' spoken English with weak written English could be tackled by the ordinary teacher without special tuition.

In the D.E.S. census of January 1967, teachers were asked to draw the line between (i) pupils whose spoken English is comparable to that of non-immigrant children (even though their written English may be weak) and who do not, therefore, require *special* tuition; and (ii) pupils whose standards of English, whether written or spoken, are so far below those of local non-immigrant children as to demand special tuition.

Here the teachers were being asked to make a diagnosis and an administrative decision, so to speak, in one breath and in a context of scarce resources. John Power argues convincingly that, on the whole, teachers placed their West Indian pupils in the first category.

[1] Power, op. cit.

In most schools, if intensive teaching in English as a Second Language can be made available at all, it is likely to be reserved for the non-English speaking pupils. The West Indians, though they might need some intensive teaching of a kind suited to their own special linguistic needs, would come in second place. Hence, in schools where this was the situation, and they could be a majority, West Indians would not be counted in Form 7i [the D.E.S. Census Form] as offering a statistically ascertainable language difficulty!

The important statistical and educational point which John Power made should be considered together with a number of others: for example, the possibility (referred to in the I.L.E.A. 1967 report) that West Indian pupils are being wrongly, and too often, referred to school for the 'educationally sub-normal' and the fact that the only major project which had by 1970 produced teaching materials in English for immigrants (the Leeds Project) has been exclusively concerned with non-English speaking pupils of Asian and Southern European origin.

In relation to the general problem of language teaching, it is perhaps worth-while noting some of the remarks made by Mrs. Margaret Rogers, Secretary of the ATEPO in 1969–70:

In West Africa and in East Africa I have seen how each year, after the transfer from infant to primary, and even from primary to secondary education, the first year after the transfer has been written off for remedial work. This is a tragedy which I do not want to see happen to the immigrants here. I am not going to talk about children who cannot communicate, nor about children of mixed parentage, nor middle-class children, nor about the very newly arrived, but about the vast bulk of immigrant children in between . . . .

The conditions we have in our multi-racial class are not those of a shared mother tongue, nor those of purely foreign language learners, where at least you can contrast the mother tongue with the second language and grade contrasts according to language difficulty. Immigrant learners are in neither of these two situations so neither approach applies.

Her remarks suggest that however useful the language statistics may be as a rule of thumb, they oversimplify the picture and the nature of the teaching task required.

The first attempt to analyse the problems and policies of L.E.A.s and the actual classroom situation was the survey conducted in 1965–6 for the Schools Council by Miss June

Derrick, then a lecturer at Leeds Institute of Education. A shortened version of her report was published in 1967 (Schools Council Working Paper, number 13). She found that very little expert language training was going on: the best teaching was found in a few schools which had increased their intake of immigrant children, over the years, to quite high proportions and had had to develop new techniques for dealing with their language problems; and a lot of non-integration was going on in classrooms where immigrant pupils with inadequate English were 'passengers' in a class which was numerically 'integrated'. On the strength of her report, the Schools Council financed a three-year programme in Leeds, under June Derrick, to develop language teaching materials for Asians and Southern Europeans. The project functioned from the beginning (in late 1966) as an information centre and a training operation, since the material was tested in a large number of schools. The first 'kit' was available in January 1969. The project also undertook a further survey of language problems and policies in infant schools. Conducted in 1967 by Mrs. Diana Stoker, this survey found that little expert tuition was taking place for this age group. Those teachers (of 'reception' classes in dispersal schemes, for example) who were attempting language teaching usually had no training in the teaching of infants. Apart from these two reports, which provided the only national surveys of practice in the classroom, there have been no further general assessments of the situation of immigrant pupils or the multi-racial schools. On the encouragement of the language teaching team which piloted the scheme, one regional school examination board—the West Midlands—has set an examination in English as a Second Language. This means that there now exist certain standards by which the success or failure of the special tuition can be judged. There has been an expansion of English teaching for immigrants, particularly within L.E.A.s which have had schemes for some time. Full-time courses for serving teachers have not so far succeeded, partly due to the authorities' reluctance to release staff. The production of at least one set of materials by the Schools Council's Leeds Project marked a genuine advance. The D.E.S. has begun a series of one-week in-service 'courses'—more in the nature of conferences—which may help to stimulate new work in schools. On the whole, one can say that the advances have been in the teaching of English to children from non-English speaking homes, and have developed through the teachers' voluntary work, with some support from more vigorous local officials.

It is not known how many non-English speaking children are still not receiving any expert help—indeed, very few are getting any at the infant level. As for the West Indians, almost none of them are getting adequate help to increase their command of standard English, although a Schools Council project to produce language teaching materials for West Indian pupils was to be completed in about mid-1971. For them, the absorption of children in the 'normal' routine of a school often means relegation to lower or remedial streams, and the sad time-lag described by Margaret Rogers.

The conclusions which may be drawn from the two studies of attainment made up to 1968[1] indicate that children who arrived as immigrants from their parents' home-land are not doing as well as their English contemporaries; performance improves with length of time spent in Britain; and children born in Britain of immigrant parents do as well as the English. One of these studies found one school in which these children were doing better than the English. However, the total number of English-born children of immigrants surveyed in the two studies was only about one hundred—all from London and all children of parents who arrived in the mid-fifties. When one reads Diana Stokers's description of the children in infant schools, it seems unlikely that this optimistic conclusion—that length of time in Britain is a vital factor—will remain valid. Preliminary reports of the Schools Council's West Indian project show no difference in performance between British and Caribbean-born children of West Indian parents.

7. *The Haringey 'Banding' Scheme*

The dispute over Haringey's 'banding' scheme illustrates a number of the points already made about policy-makers. The scheme was proposed in the spring of 1969 by a sub-committee of the Education Committee of the borough council—a council recently won from Labour by the Conservative Party, and it was the Party's first response to the situation of the borough's newly

[1] *The Education of Immigrant Pupils in Primary Schools* (London, I.L.E.A., 1967); and Sylvane Wiler, 'Children from Overseas', Parts 1 and 2, Institute of Race Relations *Newsletter* (February and June 1968).

created comprehensive school system. From the beginning, the 'banding' scheme was identified particularly with the vice-chairman of the Education Committee, Alderman Doulton. In his individual capacity, he was head of a large and prestigious private day school. Briefly, the proposal (inaccurately copied from Inner London's scheme, which was applied in a partial, not a wholly, comprehensive system) meant that before leaving primary schools at the age of eleven, children would be assessed and categorized into seven ability 'bands'; these bands would then be reduced to three by the Education Office; and placement in secondary schools would be arranged to achieve a 'balanced' ability intake.

Superficially, the first objective of the scheme was to correct the difference in standards of the eleven comprehensives due to their parent schools (grammar or non-academic secondary modern) or to the kind of neighbourhoods they served. The second objective of the scheme, as presented, was to avoid the development of predominantly 'immigrant' schools, in other words, to promote 'integration'. The ostensible objectives of the scheme might both, therefore, be counted as broadly liberal, although debatable in terms of educational or race relations ideology.

Why, then, was it opposed so bitterly, and primarily from the Left?

Let us take, first of all, the objections on general grounds, which are not concerned with immigrants and race relations. Underlying all of them was the belief that the new education councillors were not committed to the comprehensive reorganization at all. According to the sub-committee report: 'Those who do not favour the comprehensive system ... considered the possibility of "unscrambling" the system.' The report goes on to say that 'upheaval' of this sort could not be justified: 'There was no alternative but to consider ... what steps could be taken to overcome the shortcomings of the present system.' No reference was made to the strong support for the comprehensives from teachers and the generally favourable attitudes of the few parents the committee had seen.

The re-introduction of I.Q. assessments in primary schools was seen as a return to the selective system. Despite the Committee's assurance that children would be continually assessed throughout their primary schools, without a final all-or-nothing examination, this was not believed. In the event, school children were given a written intelligence test in the summer term of 1969.

The teachers (e.g. the local secretary of the National Union of Teachers [N.U.T.], and the Consultative Council of Teachers, representing all borough teachers) argued that it was quite invalid to argue that there was imbalance in the academic ability and standards of the comprehensives, until they had received the full comprehensive intake. The teachers foresaw an expansion of the 'academic' side of schools as they became fully comprehensive.

The banding proposals were accompanied by proposals for the 'rationalization' of sixth form courses, 'so that at all schools we provide instruction in the more usual "A" level subjects but restrict the instruction in some subjects to a limited number of comprehensive schools'. Quite where the axe would fall on Sixth Form development in the less 'academic' schools was not clear. The argument is interesting, however, because of the light it sheds on the Education Committee's earlier proposals. Of particular interest is this statement by the Committee: 'If the number of "high flyers" in our schools were spread around the borough they could not be catered for economically or efficiently in all the subjects they might wish to study. Groups at each school would be too small to provide the stimulus necessary for children of high ability.' This statement casts some doubt on the intention of the Committee, in the future 'banding' scheme, to spread the *top ability* group among the eleven comprehensives. Elsewhere in the document, the Committee proposes to encourage 'streaming' and 'setting' so that children work within their own ability group. The differences in the two methods are not discussed, but taken together with the regretful approach to comprehensives as such and the concern for the 'high flyers' (and a rejected suggestion that a Sixth Form College be established), it would appear that the Committee was concerned to separate the most able children, rather than to integrate them with the less able.

For what reason, then, it might be asked, was the Committee concerned about 'academic imbalance'?

The 'banding' scheme, however, became a *cause célèbre* because of the race relations issues it raised and the manner in which it treated these issues. It was opposed by the Consultative

Council of Teachers, and by the North London West Indian Association, in a pamphlet which was both thoughtful and polemical.

The Committee's report which introduced banding, struck an alarmist tone in dealing with the issue of immigrant pupils: 'we are faced with a problem which, by its magnitude, transcends all the problems outlined earlier in the report'. It quoted the figures for the percentage of immigrant pupils (by the D.E.S. definition) in Haringey, Wolverhampton, and Birmingham. The last two, while they have low percentages compared with many parts of Inner London and the Outer London boroughs, serve as code-words for 'immigrant trouble'. This is particularly true of Wolverhampton, whose problems were so frequently cited in Enoch Powell's speeches of 1968. Haringey, which had hitherto avoided publicity on the 'immigrant problem' theme, had the highest percentage of immigrant pupils of any borough (30·8 per cent of primary school pupils in 1968). 'We already have primary schools in the borough at which no less than 70% of the pupils are immigrant', the report continued; 'we are therefore faced with a situation where, in the 1970's, we shall have comprehensive schools containing over 70% immigrant children.'

The use of the plural here, with no supporting analysis of the actual distribution of immigrant pupils, is interesting. Since many primary schools went to 'feed' a single secondary comprehensive, the Committee's mathematics were faulty. In fact, there was considerable natural residential dispersal of the West Indian population of Haringey (one of the two largest immigrant groups) and their children, who made up half the immigrant pupils (by the D.E.S. definition), were, thus, widely dispersed in the schools. There were some concentrations, at primary level, but these would not necessarily continue into secondary schools. Even assuming there would be some predominantly 'immigrant' schools, why were they viewed with such alarm by the Committee? There was, as we showed earlier, a tendency automatically to reject the 'immigrant' or Black school as bad. But the Haringey report produced a variation on this theme: 'If we do nothing', it argued, 'the probability is that some schools will become in effect ghetto schools with an entirely immigrant population. It seems likely this would attract a larger immigrant population into the locality, and we are seriously concerned with the far reaching social and educational repercussions, including the serious effect this would have on the housing problem.'

Why was it that the Haringey Committee believed that dispersal by ability would produce dispersal of immigrants? It was assumed that instead of having a normal spread of ability, immigrants would be found predominantly in the lowest ability range. This point became brutally clear in an unpublished earlier document signed by Alderman Doulton. Describing the movement of the present primary school pupils into the comprehensives, this private document stated:

On a rough calculation, about half the immigrants will be West Indians at seven of the eleven schools, the significance of this being the general recognition that their I.Q.'s work out below their English contemporaries. Thus academic standards will be lower in schools where they form a large group.

In discussion of the need for Sixth Form rationalization, to produce large enough academic Sixth Forms, the document says:

the evidence indicates that the large number of immigrants, with West Indians in the majority, will result in a lower level of intelligence than average and that this, when added to the size of the schools, will produce small academic Sixths. If, then, able pupils are to be given their fair chance, as equality of opportunity demands that they should be, special arrangements will be required to ensure this; . . . it would be wrong to equate over-all numbers of 'A' level candidates. The biggest imponderable here is the assessment of the intelligence of the immigrant pupils. I venture to doubt whether in ten years' time the academic Sixths in the majority of the schools will be above 80, which brings up the objections raised in 6(b) [on size of viable Sixth Forms], quite apart from the complications of running academic and non-academic Sixths side by side.

It is clear from the public and private documents of the Haringey Education Sub-committee that the source of their 'integration' proposal, i.e. the dispersal of immigrant pupils, is an inferior stereotype of immigrants and particularly of West Indians. Moreover, whether or not the committee realized this, the majority of West Indian and Cypriot children (the main national groups in the area) aged 5–9 were born in the United Kingdom—a group who, the published evidence showed, were doing as well as English children.

The North London West Indian Association made the following comments on the scheme:

No black man or woman is going to believe that his neighbourhood is a 'ghetto' (used in its worst sense) just because he and his black West Indian neighbour who may cluster in the same street or district, are living there. . . . In plain language, knowing what they think about the low I.Q.'s of black West Indian children, the banding scheme simply means spreading and keeping down West Indian children, in the lowest rungs of the school on the spurious ground of their inability. . . . We therefore oppose dispersal absolutely in whatever disguise it may be cloaked. Already black children of West Indian parents are at a disadvantage as far as testing methods are concerned. If there is a majority of black children in any one school it is impossible to believe that all will be 'backward'. By spreading a few in classes all over the schools they can be pigeonholed and ignored, thus reinforcing pre-conceived notions about lower I.Q.'s. . . . We believe that unnecessary obstacles are being placed, for very obscure reasons, in the path of the optimal educational advancement of black West Indian and other immigrant children. We believe that our children are being used as racial scapegoats and as a political ploy to try to put into effect once again the old, or another variation of, the 11-plus system. We also know that there are other obscure motives which only time and our continuing opposition will clearly reveal.

The arguments put forward to justify the banding scheme, confidentially and publicly, brought out into the full light of day the old stigmatization of immigrant groups which had lain in the shadows of previous proposals for dispersal. Ironically, the linking of dispersal of immigrants (or Black children) with dispersal by ability, reinforced the conviction of many immigrants, especially West Indians, that dispersal was a hostile move in a hostile game.

8. Conclusions

I have described the main kinds of action taken—national and local, official and voluntary—within the education system in the wake of the arrival of children of Commonwealth immigrants in British schools. It might be helpful to summarize these actions, together with a rough assessment of the success and limitations of each, within its own framework of reference:

(a) CENTRAL GOVERNMENT

(i) *The Dispersal Recommendation*

About a quarter of L.E.A.s have some dispersal scheme, but there has been no evaluation of these, or any attempt to compare them with alternative measures to improve, among other things, language learning, general attainment, and social contact with white children. The D.E.S. now sees the policy not as essential, but as a possible local option.

(ii) *Resource Help*

Resource help includes building authorization, off-quota teachers, teacher aids, incentive payments for teachers in 'priority areas', and such projects as nursery schools and classes, teachers' centres, etc., under the Urban Programme. Such resource help has been useful to head teachers when they have known how to make use of it, and has, in a number of areas, provided token improvements benefiting small numbers of families. The Urban Programme, and the E.P.A. (Educational Priority Area) programme, should be classified in general as token schemes, poverty pork barrels, not able nor intended to equalize education and other facilities among poor and better-off areas. They have facilitated good work in some schools, where there has been good leadership and administration by the head.

(b) SCHOOLS COUNCIL

(i) *The Leeds Project*

This project producing materials for teaching non-English speaking pupils, was, together with the survey of practice and needs which preceded it, the most important contribution made by any central organization. The project involved a look at educational needs and an attempt to meet them by providing resources; its perspective was not muddled by concern with the school's socializing or assimilating role, or preoccupation with numbers of immigrant pupils as a source of undefined strain. Its chief limitation was that it focused entirely on Asian and Southern European pupils, to the exclusion of West Indians whose problems were assumed to be quite different.

(ii) *The Schools Council's Birmingham Project*
This project is intended to devise teaching techniques and some
materials for teaching English to West Indian pupils with linguistic problems. It was set up in 1967, on a lower budget than the
Leeds project, and is directed to improvement of written English,
initially for primary school children. An account of the research
stage of the project was published in 1970. The project covers the
period 1967–72.

(c) LOCAL AUTHORITIES
Effort was mainly directed to arrangements for some language
teaching for Asian pupils. By 1968–9, such special arrangements
were fairly extensive, although it would be impossible to estimate
the quality of teaching and follow-up: they were only a partial
response to the problems of multi-racial schools. There is no
reason to think that, for example, protests from teachers and
parents about 'standards' and other problems, including racial
conflicts in schools, will stop. One obvious gap in provision of
language teaching is lack of attention to West Indian pupils,
and it seems that many children who would benefit from language
teaching, or simply, understanding, are being misallocated to
remedial teachers who may not recognize their problems; there
is also evidence of over-referral of West Indian pupils to schools
for the educationally sub-normal (an official designation).

(d) TEACHER TRAINING
In 1969, about 60 per cent of colleges of education provided some
kind of course for student teachers in English as a Second Language. About 30 per cent included some course on education in a
multi-racial, multi-cultural society. No evaluation of these
courses had been published by the beginning of 1970. Professor
Eric Hawkins has suggested that the isolation of most student
teachers from the areas where immigrants live, and from urban
problems generally, prevents their making any real contribution
in the multi-racial schools. He has proposed a scheme to link the
colleges with the most difficult areas.

(e) VOLUNTARY AND SCHOOL-BASED ACTION
Apart from the Schools Council's Leeds Project, the most important contribution has come from individuals and voluntary

teachers groups, with all the limitations which that inevitably imposes—i.e. lack of time, lack of finance, and the absence of evaluation.

Three characteristics emerge clearly from the current situation. First, there is the emphasis on language teaching, and the institutionalization of arrangements for non-English speaking pupils, i.e. Asians. The institutionalization is less marked in Inner London than in the Midlands and particularly the North of England. Secondly, there is the lack of evaluation of these institutions by the authorities running them. I do not include here the Leeds materials which were tested throughout; I do include the dispersal schemes in Ealing and Bradford, particularly reception classes, reception centres, and peripatetic language teaching schemes. The largest of the latter—in Birmingham— now has a partial evaluation through the C.S.E. (Certificate of Secondary Education) examination. But a wider assessment of the scheme's contribution to the education problems of the total minority population in Birmingham schools, is needed. The need for evaluation is great because the particular arrangements for teaching English as a Second Language (and for 'dealing' with immigrants) have been devised in a period of high numbers of arrivals of Asian pupils. Thus, while these arrangements may make a valuable contribution now, they may not be appropriate to a situation, fast arriving, where the overwhelming majority of 'immigrant pupils' are English-born. The experience of these children may differ from that of their immigrant older brothers and sisters in ways which affect how they are taught. They will start their educational life in infant schools, and may not be easily or appropriately siphoned off to centres or distant schools. The question is how far the ordinary schools are, and will be, able to educate these pupils, and how far existing institutional arrangements will help the schools to do so. The third characteristic of the present situation is the lack of attention to West Indian pupils, and to the problems beyond that of language provision. For example, in a large multi-racial school, there is likely to be some kind of special tuition for Asian pupils in English language— administered, perhaps, by a visiting teacher or a staff member who has done a short course, or even, possibly, a basic course at a training college. West Indian pupils, whether or not they have identifiable language difficulties, would be unlikely to participate in the English as a Second Language class, but might be put in a remedial class. The language teacher has training, materials, and resource groups to which she can turn, such as ATEPO. The remedial teacher has none of these things in so far as her West Indian pupils have special needs. The head teacher also lacks these resources. The result of this is that while some schools are altering organization and curriculum to meet pupils' needs, in others many West Indian pupils are treated as difficult and/or backward, and are not expected to move out of remedial groups. This is just one example of a school situation. In some schools, teachers with no remedial training are doing remedial work with immigrants; and the issues which are raised in the better multi-racial schools go far beyond that of remedial work and include, for instance, streaming versus all-ability classes, 'integrated studies', race in the curriculum, and multi-racial staffing.

The UNITAR Project is concerned with anti-discrimination measures. It would, perhaps, be interesting, finally, to apply the concept of discrimination to the education field. It is necessary to take into account two distinct but overlapping notions of discrimination.

The first involves provision of inferior educational resources and opportunities which minority pupils share with many majority pupils. It may be objected that this is not racial but class discrimination. There are several answers to this. One is that *class* discrimination, which includes racial minorities among the disadvantaged, may well have dramatic effects upon race relations by its adverse effects on both whites and Blacks. Another answer, for both conservatives and supporters of a class system, is that immigrants may live in disadvantaged areas and suffer from inferior facilities, while being quite mixed in class terms themselves—for example, with the possible exception of the Pakistani community living outside London, immigrant groups have the same proportion of skilled craftsmen as the general population, although their housing is considerably worse than the average.

The second notion involves racial discrimination of various kinds, some but not all of which directly involves inferior education. It is possible to identify the following types of racial discrimination within the education system at present:

(i) Discrimination in placement of children, and denial of the

6*

right of parental choice: This is hard to prove in some areas because parent choice may be limited generally. However, allegations that some heads refuse to take coloured children, or restrict their entry, have been made in London, Birmingham, and Wolverhampton. In Birmingham, it has been alleged that one primary school draws its intake from beyond its legitimate catchment area and at the same time refuses to take many coloured children from within the catchment area. There is some evidence to suggest that concentration of coloured pupils in one school, and their absence from a nearby school, may be caused by this form of discrimination. It may or may not mean that the 'Black' school is inferior.

(ii) Inferior stereotyping of immigrant pupils or West Indian pupils as backward, difficult, of lower intelligence: There is a dual effect here. First, this kind of 'group libel' may be seen as a contribution of educationists to the general race relations situation in the United Kingdom. The presence of immigrants in Britain has been attacked on the ground that immigrant pupils lower the standards in schools. Secondly, it can be argued that, to the extent that a teacher's expectations are self-fulfilling, a pupil's performance will actually be lowered if his teacher *expects* that it will be low. This kind of discrimination is, then, also directly linked to inferior education.

(iii) Misplacement of pupils within schools in 'lower' or 'remedial' streams: This was an almost universal practice in 1966; it is hard to tell how far schools have moved away from this to more appropriate organization of ability groups. Some large multiracial secondary schools, of a kind whose head teachers talk at conferences about reorganization, are moving away from streaming altogether. Reports of discussion groups at a teachers' conference on English-speaking immigrants (held in January 1969) expressed anxiety over 'remedial' class expectation which was usually low and overspecialized, and led to under-achievement. This was, one group reported, 'particularly worrying when the ease with which West Indians make their way into "remedial" classes is considered'. The group was worried by the force of class expectation as a depressive factor and the unsettling effects of streaming in the first year (of secondary school). Another group reported:

We should remain especially alert to the possibility that immigrants are failing to reach their potential attainment simply because of their difficulties with language. It is significant that an apparently undue proportion of immigrants remain in our 'lower streams' and unfortunate that in some schools immigrants are put into remedial classes, without any special encouragement to move out to courses with strong academic ambitions as soon as they have mastered their language difficulties. They may then tend to respond, only at a remedial or backward level.

Interestingly, in a lecture given in 1968, Sir Edward Boyle, former Education Minister under the Conservative Government, proposed the elimination of streaming as part of a programme concerned with equal opportunities for immigrants.[1]

(iv) The dispersal policy itself, as proposed and implemented, has many discriminatory aspects: It is an infringement of the right of parental choice which was guaranteed by the 1944 Education Act; its presentation involved a stigmatization of immigrant groups; it was badly motivated, in that it was concerned to spread the 'burden' and preserve the 'routine' and standards of schools with high numbers of immigrants rather than get the immigrants into schools appropriate to them; it was implemented clumsily, without proper care of the children who were being bussed; and, above all, it gave no attention to policies which should be followed, or resources which would be needed in the receiving schools.

However judged, the measures described have been at best a partial response to the needs of teachers and of pupils—because they have tackled only the most obvious problems, or those capable of straightforward solution through the provision, to a limited extent, of more resources. And even the measures taken to deal with these (for the most part, language) problems cover only some of the pupils who suffer from them. Countless numbers of immigrant pupils have left school in the past ten years without having received instruction which could have helped them, and there seem only a handful of further education institutions as yet trying to fill the gap.

There is, at present, no broadly accepted definition of problems and goals which could serve as a basis for policy and

[1] Sir Edward Boyle, 'Race Relations: The Limits of Voluntary Action', in *Race* (Vol. 9, No. 3, January 1968).

resource development to meet the current and future situation of the multi-racial schools. Some of the more complex problems faced by teachers in multi-racial, multi-cultural schools are now being discussed in a positive way, with a search for solutions through changes in school organization. There are the beginnings of debate among teachers which may produce guide-lines for a general policy. But, just as it was, initially, with the question of language teaching for non-English speakers, this discussion is among a few individuals and has yet to reach a wider or powerful audience.

CHAPTER 6

Employment

BOB HEPPLE

1. *The Significance of Racial Discrimination in Employment in Britain*[1]

The problem of racial discrimination in employment is one of the factors which influences the processes of absorption of immigrants (of all origins and colours) into the receiving society of Britain. It is of particular significance in relation to the status and opportunities of second and later generations of immigrant groups who have retained their ethnic and cultural distinctiveness or dark pigmentation.

In relation mainly to the first generation, empirical research in six areas in 1967[2] confirmed and elaborated the finding of several earlier local studies that there was 'substantial discrimination', largely based on colour, against coloured immigrants applying for jobs. Other, more fundamental, research has isolated several factors influencing the absorption of the first generation, such as the immigrants' educational attainments, employment experience, language ability, cultural background, motivations, and attitudes; the local labour core's economic fears, mild antipathy to all strangers, and stereotyped attitudes about coloured people from former British colonies; the status, personality, and degree of pragmatic 'business sense' of management; and, occasionally, the behaviour of customers and the public at large.

In order to comprehend all these factors, some researchers have made use of S. N. Eisenstadt's theory of absorption,[3] and this is discussed in Chapter 2. In the leading study, Mrs. Sheila Patterson[4] has demonstrated the development of attitudes and

---

[1] That is, England, Wales, and Scotland. The position in Northern Ireland, where Catholic/Protestant discrimination presents a serious problem, is not considered.

[2] Political and Economic Planning and Research Services Ltd., *Racial Discrimination* (London, P.E.P., 1967), p. 81.

[3] S. N. Eisenstadt, *The Absorption of Immigrants* (London, Routledge & Kegan Paul, 1954).

[4] Sheila Patterson, *Immigrants in Industry* (London, Oxford University Press, for Institute of Race Relations, 1969), esp. p. 206, Table 3.

behaviour on the index of absorption from the level of initial contact (where management will not employ immigrants and local labour will not work alongside them) through two phases of accommodation (in which managements try various modes of selection and local labour agrees to accept them subject to such safeguards as quotas and gradually comes to regard each new-comer both as an individual and as 'one of us') to the level of assimilation (in which managements are prepared to promote immigrants and local labour, to accept them in supervisory posts). On the part of immigrants, there are corresponding levels in which, at first, they keep together in groups and later start to mingle and become capable of supervisory work. In another stage (which may be 'final' or may lead on to assimilation) described as 'pluralistic integration', managements use ethnic work-gangs and individual immigrants emerge as leaders of these gangs.

Each of these stages of industrial absorption can be found in British industry—the precise level reached in a particular firm depending on such factors as the size and 'culture' of the enter-prise and the character and adaptability of the particular immi-grant group involved. For example, in her study of Croydon industry (where about 4 per cent of the total labour force is immigrant and there is considerable economic expansion), Mrs. Patterson[1] found that Polish political refugees and exiles were well on the way to industrial assimilation, while the younger, British-educated workers of Polish origin were fully assimilated in a wide range of firms; at the other extreme, West Indians (the largest and most recently arrived group) were for the most part mainly in semi-skilled and unskilled work in the earlier or later phases of accommodation. Most of the West Indian second generation were still at school, and it remained to be seen whether the first-generation immigrants would have established themselves sufficiently as part of the working community to be able to sponsor their locally educated children by the time the latter entered the job market.

The majority of coloured youngsters seeking jobs in 1968 spent most of their lives in their native lands; they were less likely than their British-born contemporaries to have had gram-mar or technical school education, less likely to have been apprenticed or in training for skilled jobs. There is now some

[1] op. cit., pp. 173–204.

weight of evidence, however, to suggest that coloured school leavers have higher job expectations than whites.[1] These aspirations may be the product of the cultural alienness of children of immigrants for whom the normal process of socialization—which is said to limit aspiration to a 'realistic' level—does not work. In part at least, the higher aspirations may reflect an understanding by coloured school leavers that they must aim higher and have better qualifications than their white counterparts. To some extent these young people are creating unfavourable stereotypes, thereby affecting the chances of the 'true' second generation of those born or mainly educated in Britain.

Little is known about this second generation, but as long ago as 1947 a study in Cardiff[2] showed that few of the coloured children who grew up and sought employment there could break through the 'closed circle' created by discrimination, and they quickly lost any ambitions they may have had. Apart from racial discrimination, it is clear from another study of Moslem communities in Tyneside and Cardiff,[3] undertaken in 1949–51, that the assimilation of coloured children may be retarded by the strong controls of the young person's own culture.

Racial discrimination, then, cuts across the generations but is of primary importance only in the second.

2. An Analytical Model for Studying the Effectiveness of Measures Against Racial Discrimination in Employment

There are two principal ways in which this problem can be studied.

The first is to examine the generalized attitudes and behaviour of those persons who are in a position to discriminate, and the measures taken to alter them. A great deal of research has been devoted to this approach.[4] For example, James H. Robb,

---

[1] D. Beetham, *Immigrant School Leavers and the Youth Employment Service in Birmingham* (London, Institute of Race Relations Special Series, 1967); Peter Figueroa, 'School Leavers and Colour Barrier', thesis in preparation.

[2] K. Little, *Negroes in Britain: A Study of Racial Relations in English Society* (London, Kegan Paul, 1947).

[3] S. F. Collins, 'The British-Born Colonial', *Sociological Review* (N.S.) (Vol. 3, No. 1, 1955), p. 77.

[4] A survey of this research will be found in my paper 'Ethnic Minorities at Work: Research and Its Translation into Action in Britain', *Race* (Vol. X, No. 1, July 1968).

in his study of anti-Semitism in a working-class London borough,[1] and Anthony H. Richmond, in his study of West Indian workers in Liverpool,[2] both used psychological models and were chiefly concerned with the way personal insecurity underlies the expression of prejudiced attitudes, although they did recognize the role of social factors (e.g. the fear of unemployment) in creating insecurity. Michael Banton,[3] who was more concerned with discrimination than prejudice, described discrimination in Britain as 'a form of avoidance of strangers', as a result of his survey of six areas, four of which had a settlement of recent coloured immigrants. He found that Britons were more likely to accept coloured people in work relationships than in intimate personal ones. In his pioneering study in Cardiff, where coloured people have lived for generations, Kenneth Little[4] demonstrated that British people tend to identify those who are coloured with the lowest social class.

The second approach, which will be pursued here,[5] is to relate the question of racial discrimination to the system of industrial relations as a whole. This approach has several advantages. It allows full account to be taken of structural and institutional factors, such as managerial decisions, trade union rules, collective agreements, social conventions, law, and accepted customs and practice. Instead of studying race relations in industry from the standpoint of one or two disciplines (e.g. psychology or social anthropology), it becomes possible to offer an integrated view of the whole complex of factors which influence the position of ethnic minorities at work. By concentrating on particular aspects, the separate disciplines present a partial view, accurate and valuable within limits, but of necessity distorted. Moreover, by constructing a general analytical model of an industrial relations system, a basis will be provided for a comparative study of the

[1] *Working-class Anti-Semite: A Psychological Study in a London Borough* (London, Tavistock, 1954).

[2] *Colour Prejudice in Britain: A Study of West Indian Workers in Liverpool, 1942–51* (London, Routledge, 1954).

[3] *White and Coloured: The Behaviour of British People Towards Coloured Immigrants* (London, Cape, 1959).

[4] Op. cit.; see also K. Little, *The Race Question in Modern Science* (Paris, UNESCO, 1956), p. 165.

[5] I have drawn heavily on my publication *Race, Jobs, and the Law in Britain*, 2nd edn. (Harmondsworth, Penguin, 1970), in which this approach is implicit, although central attention was focused there on the relation between legal and voluntary measures.

problem in several countries. Needless to say, however, there is not a great deal of value, except by way of contrast, in direct comparisons between countries with established racial patterns (e.g. the United States) and those in which these patterns are fluid (e.g. Britain).

The general model which will be used here is that of Dunlop,[1] who describes a system of industrial relations as a system of rules. 'Rules' is used as a generic term to describe all the means by which jobs are regulated. These rules are established by the actors in the system, namely, a hierarchy of managers and supervisors, a hierarchy of workers and their spokesmen, specialized government agencies and private agencies set up by the actors (e.g. trade unions, employers' bodies, and immigrant organizations). They make these rules in certain contexts which involve three determinants: (i) the technological characteristics of the work place and the work community; (ii) the market or budgetary constraints which impinge on the actors; and (iii) the locus and distribution of power in the larger society. This analytical system is completed by an ideology (or 'shared understanding'), that is, a set of beliefs and ideas commonly held by the actors which helps to bind or integrate the system as an entity (e.g. in Britain, the importance attached to voluntarism).

It must be emphasized that such an industrial relations system is logically an abstraction. It is not designed to describe in factual terms the real world of time and space. It is useful simply as a tool of analysis which focuses attention on certain critical variables. This framework of theoretical analysis, although rudimentary, may help researchers to set the right questions for inquiry and statistical testing and to arrive at general propositions. It must also be made clear that this chapter is solely concerned with the way in which the inner structure of the industrial relations system affects ethnic minorities and the way in which their presence affects the system. But it must be remembered that an industrial relations system is no more than a sub-system of the whole social system.

The actors in the British system of industrial relations (e.g. the numbers, occupations, and status of the immigrant and 'native' work forces) have already been described in Chapter 3.

---

[1] John T. Dunlop, *Industrial Relations Systems* (New York, Holt, Rinehart and Winston, 1959), esp. pp. 7-18.

In this chapter, an attempt will be made to consider, in the light of existing research: (i) the contexts of the industrial relations system; (ii) its rules; and (iii) its ideology.

3. *The Contexts of the Industrial Relations System as They Impinge on Ethnic Minorities*

(a) THE TECHNOLOGICAL CHARACTERISTICS OF THE WORK PLACE AND THE WORK COMMUNITY

The type of work, the skill and educational levels which it requires, the degree of contact with customers that it necessitates, and the locality of the work place are among the technical contexts of the system. Clearly, these and similar matters have an important bearing on rule-making as it affects ethnic minorities in the work force.

For example, it has for long been an untested assumption that the employment of immigrant labour is associated with old, under-capitalized industries unable or unwilling to invest in new machinery. However, recent research by Brian Cohen in the wool industry in the West Riding of Yorkshire,[1] discovered that it was the new investment in high-cost machinery which led to the employment of Pakistani males. This was because the machinery required intensive working to become profitable and these men, without family commitments in England, were prepared to do night-shifts and were anxious to work long hours of overtime so as to accumulate savings. The semi-skilled nature of the work and the length of time for which it had to be undertaken determined the source of labour supply in the absence of local male labour. Day-shifts for this type of work tended to remain the prerogative of local female labour, where this was available. A change in the job content and hours of operation served to change the rule of the work place, i.e. that local female labour was normally employed. This change resulted in further rule changes about overtime and wage-fixing. Technical changes, therefore, are a dynamic element leading to changes in the complex of rules.

The contact of workers with customers affords another illustration of the impact of the technical environment on rules, and is one that is particularly significant to ethnic minorities.

---

[1] Brian Cohen and Peter Jenner, 'The Employment of Immigrants: A Case Study Within the Wool Industry', *Race* (Vol. X, No. 1, July 1968), pp. 41–56.

Just as rules are fashioned to impose special standards (e.g. of dress and appearance) on workers who must have direct contact with customers, so too management takes account of the real or supposed objections of customers and the public to members of different ethnic groups. At one point this may lead to the employment of only Chinese waiters in a 'Chinese-style' restaurant; at another point, it may result in discrimination against coloured people in respect of certain 'contact' jobs. In her study of Croydon industry, Mrs. Patterson[1] found that the acceptance or non-acceptance of coloured immigrants in particular roles depended on the whole context and scope of each role, the extent to which it was regular or intermittent, intimate or distant. For example, very few objections are heard about coloured immigrants in the role of doctors, nurses, and hospital staff due to the kind of services they render, the abnormal circumstances imposed by illness and need, and the depersonalized nature of hospital relationship. The public may be less willing to accept coloured immigrants as teachers because their role is more personalized, longer sustained, and overlaps into the informal social sphere. At lower status levels, coloured immigrants were most 'acceptable' where they were identifiable by means of a uniform or badge or where the performance of their role takes place in a circumscribed area (e.g. in public) over a limited period. Examples are railway-men, busmen, postmen, sportsmen, and entertainers. The greater degree of intimacy involved in relationships with shop assistants and waitresses makes these somewhat less acceptable roles. Most unacceptable of all are those roles which involve intrusions into the Englishman's 'castle-home', e.g. meter-readers, repairmen. The role of policemen, as guardians of public order and social norms, has made police authorities reluctant (particularly in the early years of coloured immigration) to appoint coloured police-men. In all these situations, public reaction—direct or indirect, real or imagined—affects rules.

The geographical location of the enterprise also affects its rules. In the West Riding study,[2] one of the firms not employing coloured immigrant labour was sited near a new housing estate and had an adequate supply of local labour. In Croydon, Mrs. Patterson[3] found that the difficulty which coloured immigrants had in obtaining residential accommodation in the more 'select'

[1] op. cit., pp. 275-80.   [2] Cohen and Jenner, op. cit.   [3] op. cit., p. 231.

suburbs, limited the number of immigrant workers in employment in those areas. (Incidentally, it ought to be noted that the rules of the industrial relations system, in turn, have their effect on the housing of immigrants in 'twilight areas' or 'zones of transition': for example, the widespread operation of informal quotas in Croydon industry unintentionally regulated the build-up of immigrants in these areas; contrast this with the rapid concentration of Asians in certain areas where they are employed in local factories in ethnic work-gangs.)

These illustrations show the impact of the technical context on the substance of rules as they affect ethnic minorities. It must not be forgotten that this context also affects the hierarchies of workers and management. For example, the nature of the work may determine whether management uses an English-speaking 'go-between' to supervise Asian workers. The similarity of work done by workers in an enterprise, coupled with their strategic position, may induce a degree of solidarity which cuts across ethnic divisions. The character of the enterprise (e.g. nationalized railways as compared with municipal or private road transport) may determine the degree of State involvement in establishing fair labour practices.

(b) MARKET OR BUDGETARY CONSTRAINTS

The competitive structure of an industry or firm, its specialized market conditions, general economic conditions, and the state of the market for labour services, all have a vital bearing on rule-making as it affects ethnic minorities.

Research into these matters is virtually non-existent. Cohen[1] showed that in the competitive labour-intensive wool industry (consisting of many small units) the employment of immigrant labour was the almost inevitable choice of management since higher wage-rates to attract internal migrants would have made night-shifts uneconomic and would have raised prices, with some firms going out of business in the process. Increased capital investment of a labour-substitution nature has been hampered by money shortages (in turn traceable to imperfections in the money market) and bottle-necks in the production of investment goods. The rules which evolved were, accordingly, ones which favoured the employment of immigrant labour at relatively low wage-rates.

[1] Cohen and Jenner, op. cit.

Comparative research in an industry with a different wage and competitive structure, e.g. engineering, might be expected to yield a different set of rules, possibly discriminating against the employment of immigrant labour.

A striking example of the way in which specialized market conditions affect rule-making is the shipping industry. Here economic circumstances favoured the employment of lascars (sailors who are natives of India) on British ships because of their relative cheapness per head and their apparent suitability for work in the tropics. This led to racial differentiations between seamen employed on British ships, which were embodied in legislation since the early nineteenth century. This legislative discrimination persisted until its repeal in 1970. However, much customary segregation and discrimination on British merchant ships is specifically excepted from the provisions of the Race Relations Act 1968.[1]

General economic conditions have an important bearing on rule-making. The higher proportions of male and female immigrants (as a percentage of those economically active) out of employment in comparison with the corresponding proportion of the total population out of employment, as revealed by census figures, not only reflects the jobs that immigrants do but may also be due, in part, to redundancy rules which discriminate against recent immigrants ('last in, first out') or 'foreign' labour. In turn, these rules are seen by local labour as necessary protective devices against the threat of unemployment. To the extent that other rules—usually the result of national policies such as redundancy payments schemes and job security measures—cushion local labour from the effects of economic recession, ethnic minorities are indirectly protected as well.

Both the technical and market contexts determine the size of the work force in particular enterprises and this affects the rules relating to ethnic minorities. For example, large, efficient, rapidly expanding mass-production plants in the light engineering sector in Croydon[2] had developed increasingly satisfactory techniques for the selection, induction, training, and industrial integration of West Indians and other coloured workers, and, unlike some smaller firms, showed little evidence of 'favoured

[1] Hepple, op. cit., Chapters 3 and 6.
[2] Patterson, op. cit., pp. 70-4.

nation' policies which discriminate against some but not all ethnic minorities.

Thus far I have discussed the 'market' contexts in purely economic terms. But perhaps the most important 'market' is that for labour services; and it is in this connection that students of industrial relations recognize that the ethnic characteristics of the work force and the racial prejudices or antipathies of workers and managements, complicate the substance of rule-making. For example, racial myths about the 'dirty' habits of Asians may lead local English workers to demand separate toilets; objections to the wearing of beards and turbans by Sikhs may involve the managers of municipal transport departments in disputes about the interpretation of rules which require certain standards of dress or appearance; and language differences may result in the maintenance of ethnic work-units.

The 'immigrant' character of the work force, too, has significant effects on rules relating to training and discipline. For example, in his study of coloured workers in the North and Midlands, Dr. Peter Wright has shown how special demonstration techniques were evolved for immigrants and how, in some instances, complex jobs were modified.[1]

(c) THE LOCUS AND DISTRIBUTION OF POWER IN THE LARGER
    SOCIETY

The power context is crucial in defining the status of managers, local labour core, ethnic minorities, and Government and private agencies.

For example, where a trade union exists and is active on behalf of all its members, jobs and promotion may be secured for those who allege discrimination. On the other hand, if the union is inactive or allies itself with management discrimination, advancement will be denied. Where no union exists, immigrant-based groups tend to lack the power or status to negotiate with management. Attempts to create such a power-base by forming 'immigrant' factory groups or separate unions of coloured workers have been opposed by trade unions as divisive and have not met with any noticeable response from coloured workers themselves. In fact, the policy of most immigrant and sponsor

---

[1] Peter Wright, *The Coloured Worker in British Industry* (London, Oxford University Press, for Institute of Race Relations, 1968), pp. 105–9.

organizations has been to encourage membership in the general trade union movement. The belief of these groups is that active union participation will provide the only feasible power-base for anti-discriminatory activities. This attitude may be contrasted with the formation of separate occupational organizations by Polish immigrants which for a time reduced the frequency of contacts between Poles and British people but at the same time helped the Poles find jobs and sheltered them from discrimination.[1]

The relation of trade unions to their own members is no less important in determining the context and application of rules. For example, in a study of a strike involving 600 Punjabi workers at a Southall factory,[2] Peter Marsh found that poor communications between the administrative wing of the Transport and General Workers' Union and its members were accentuated by the fact that most of the strikers were not articulate in English or in the subtleties of local union practice. A protracted dispute between the strikers and certain officials arose over a question of the interpretation of ambiguous union rules concerning 'official support' for strike action.

The status of local managements in relation to national hierarchies of management is another feature of the power context. For example, the initiative of the Engineering Employers' Federation in negotiating with the unions a special agreement relating to racial discrimination in employment, resulted in the establishment of committees of local employers and unions to consider complaints of discrimination. These procedures, in turn, were adopted by some non-federated employers, such as Fords.[3] Weak national bodies, on the other hand, are incapable of influencing the situation in this way.

Finally, Government agencies define rules. For example, the employment services of the Department of Employment and Productivity claim to have seen encouraging results in the course of persuading employers to consider job applicants on

---

[1] J. Zubrzycki, *Polish Immigrants in Britain* (The Hague, Martinus Nijhoff, 1956), pp. 108, 115, 119.

[2] Peter Marsh, *Anatomy of a Strike: Unions, Employers and Punjabi Workers in a Southall Factory* (London, Institute of Race Relations Special Series, 1967), esp. pp. 87–90.

[3] This agreement was later abandoned, however, because the Confederation of Shipbuilding and Engineering Unions was not prepared to accept the system of appeals from the voluntary bodies to the Race Relations Board, provided for in the Race Relations Act of 1968.

merit alone. On the other hand, the Department's ability to affect the situation is hampered by other general rules; for example, it is not compulsory for employers to notify the Department of vacancies, and the Department faces competition from private fee-charging agencies which, prior to 1968, were free to practise discrimination. In the future, other independent agencies (created by Parliament), such as the Race Relations Board and its local conciliation committees and the Community Relations Commission and its local groups, may play a significant part in the rule-making that directly relates to ethnic minorities. It is, as yet, too early to gauge the impact of these agencies.

4. *The Rules and Ideology of the Industrial Relations System as They Affect Ethnic Minorities*

In *Race, Jobs, and the Law in Britain*, I have described the substantive rules of industrial relations which affect persons differently on grounds of race,[1] and in the preceding discussion I have mentioned some of these by way of example.

The main point that needs to be emphasized here is that these rules are of two kinds. First there are those which form part of the *internal* system of job regulation within particular enterprises. On the other hand, there are a number of rules of an *external* nature in that they depend upon the participation and consent of persons outside the enterprise.

Examples of internal rules are: shop-floor 'understandings' about the proportion of 'foreign' or coloured workers to English or white workers to be employed in the establishment or in certain occupations; barriers against promotion; formal and informal arrangements about the sharing of overtime work; the establishment of ethnic work-units; the separation of toilet or canteen facilities; special redundancy rules. These all share the characteristic that they are settled autonomously within each enterprise.

Examples of external rules are: the policy of the Department of Employment and Productivity about discriminatory job referrals; collective labour agreements restricting or protecting foreign or coloured labour; the intervention of union officials either for or against discriminatory conduct within an enterprise;

[1] See especially Chapters 5 and 6.

the admissions policy of trade unions and, in particular, the existence of closed shops and craft barriers; special vocational training schemes for immigrants; legal rules; the activities of bodies outside industry such as community relations groups and immigrant organizations.

In order to understand the effectiveness of measures against racial discrimination in employment, it is essential to analyse the ways in which the technical, market, and power contexts influence the development of the internal and external rules respectively. At present, the main feature of the internal rules is their discriminatory content. Indeed, discrimination (through quotas, 'favoured nation' policies, and ethnic segregation) has been used spontaneously in order to accommodate ethnic minorities. These rules are the product of such factors as the type of work involved, the degree of contact with customers required, geographical location, the economics of labour-intensive industries and general economic conditions, as well as personal psychological tensions, fear of strangers, and colour/status consciousness.

These rules will not change in themselves unless there is some fundamental change in the actors, the contexts, or the ideology. As Dunlop points out, 'industrial relations systems show considerable tenacity and persistence'.[1] The very notion of an industrial relations system implies an internal balance which is likely to be restored if that balance is temporarily displaced. For example, the temporary organization of immigrant workers (as in the Southall strike) will have no long-term effect on the rules. But a major organizational change, such as the recognition by management of a powerful shop-floor organization dedicated to racial equality or a change in personnel management, is likely to result in rule changes. Present indications are that such changes are unlikely. Indeed, such events as the London dockers' and meat porters' marches in support of Enoch Powell's anti-immigrant speech are reminders of the strong internal resistance to change. Moreover, although a limited study has shown fairly active participation by coloured workers in trade unions, these workers are not themselves at the centre of deliberations for change.

It is not easy to predict what effect likely changes in the

[1] Dunlop, op. cit., p. 27.
[2] B. Radin, 'Coloured Workers and British Trade Unions', *Race* (Vol. VIII, No. 2, 1966), p. 157.

technical and market contexts will have on rules affecting ethnic minorities. But it seems improbable that automation (labour-substitution investment) will in itself favour minorities. As long as other pressures exist for racial discrimination, coloured minorities are bound to be excluded in the main from the new skilled and white-collar job opportunities which automation promises; instead they are likely to be relegated to the declining activity of manual labour.

The present direction of the internal rules, then, appears to be increasingly discriminatory.

The external rules, on the other hand, are moving in an anti-discriminatory direction. The principal feature of the traditional system of job regulation as it affected ethnic minorities, as I have said elsewhere, 'is that the competition of the labour market was restricted by rules aimed at limiting the supply of labour and the terms on which competition could take place'.[1] This was usually done on the basis of nationality (e.g. against 'foreign' workers) rather than on grounds of colour. This traditional system rested upon a set of values appropriate to the colonial era, with all its notions of national superiority.

A very significant feature of these external rules is that they were achieved almost exclusively through voluntary processes, that is they rested on social sanctions and, above all, the threat of strikes or dismissals. Apart from the shipping industry, the law played no role except in the limited form of restrictions on the right of aliens to seek and change employment, more recently extended to certain Commonwealth citizens.

The changes which are now taking place rest on the changing ideology of the system, a new set of 'shared understandings' as yet indefinite and in the process of formation. The ideas of racial equality and 'integration', rooted in the post-colonial world and strongly influenced by world-wide movements against racial oppression and *apartheid*, are now in conflict with the older *laissez-faire* philosophy of 'freedom to discriminate' and 'freedom of contract'. At the same time, the response of successive British Governments to economic difficulties and industrial unrest is bringing about a new climate of opinion in which voluntarism and corporate autonomy, twin pillars of the traditional system, are under growing attack.

[1] Hepple, op. cit., p. 156.

The major changes at present taking place are:
(i) legislation which makes racial discrimination in employment illegal;
(ii) joint policy decisions by trade unions and employers' organizations;
(iii) the evolution of voluntary procedures to deal with complaints of racial discrimination in employment;
(iv) increasing anti-discriminatory activity by bodies and individuals outside industry; and
(v) Government action.

(a) LEGISLATION

The political aspects of the Race Relations Acts will be described by Louis Kushnick in Chapter 9. Here two points of major significance must be emphasized: (i) the use of legal means was strenuously opposed by the Trades Union Congress (representing 8·75 millions of Britain's 10 millions organized workers) and the Confederation of British Industries (the major employers' body); (ii) the Bill which emerged from discussions with these bodies was broadly 'acceptable' to them. This 'acceptability' was achieved by means of a series of compromises in relation to the employment provisions of the Bill. The conclusion to be drawn is that the changes in the legal rules, important as they are, were achieved without any fundamental or structural change in the system of industrial relations itself. The anti-discrimination law was structured to meet the requirements of the industrial relations system, and not the other way around.

The common opposition of some, but not all, unions and employers to legal means was in part the result of their adherence to the principles of autonomy (the priority accorded to collective bargaining over other methods of job regulation) and voluntarism (the practice of leaving it to employers and workers to settle their own differences). In addition, the preoccupation of the British industrial relations system with procedural rather than substantive rules of collective bargaining (rules regulating conflict, rather than codified rules about wages and conditions), helps to explain why employers and unions, despite frequent declarations against discrimination, have left discriminatory practices undisturbed for so long. 'Peace' has been considered more important than justice for individual victims of discrimination.

The Act keeps these principles virtually intact. Complaints relating to employment must go first to the Department of Employment and Productivity. If the Department is satisfied that there is a suitable voluntary body to consider the complaint, it must give that body four weeks to do so (exceptionally, this period may be extended). If that body fails, or if there is no suitable voluntary machinery, the Department must refer the complaint to the Race Relations Board. The other compromises are con- cessions to the discriminatory measures used in the past to accommodate ethnic minorities. In particular, discrimination 'in good faith for the purpose of preserving or securing a balance of different racial groups employed in the undertaking which is reasonable in all the circumstances' (i.e. racial quotas), is legalized in respect of immigrants not wholly or mainly educated in Britain, as are all the common forms of racial discrimination in the shipping industry.

On the one hand, the enforcement of the Act may not result in major changes in the position of ethnic minorities in industry because: (i) employers and unions may be more interested in a peaceful 'settlement' than an adequate assurance against future discrimination; (ii) the exceptions make it possible to continue, with legal blessing, certain important forms of discrimination; (iii) members of ethnic minorities may lack faith in the law and fail to complain because of its lengthy and complex procedures; (iv) by its very nature, the law is concerned with individual cases and not primarily with established patterns of job inequality.

On the other hand, the provisions of the Bill may: (i) encourage the growth of voluntary procedures to combat discrimination, a desirable development because of the traditional importance of group solidarity and autonomy in the British industrial relations system (so helping to avert a 'backlash' on the part of local labour); (ii) create a climate of opinion in which change is possible; (iii) open certain 'middle-class' jobs previously closed to members of ethnic minorities; (iv) protect employers against the real or fancied reactions of customers, employees, and trade competitors; (v) back union officials who want to educate their rank-and-file; (vi) give members of ethnic minorities a sense of justice, thus easing the processes of absorption.

(b) JOINT POLICY DECISIONS

The most significant effect of the threat of legislation was that it prompted trade unions and employers to formulate policies for dealing with racial discrimination. For some years the Trades Union Congress has publicly condemned discrimination, and it has regarded as legitimate action to improve the training and language ability of immigrants. But it has opposed special treatment which might savour of 'privilege'. Some large unions, however, have gone much further, for example, by sponsoring recruitment drives among immigrants, appointing special officials, and questioning union officers about their attitudes on racial matters. A significant feature of decisions currently being taken in this field is their joint nature: that is, they are a product of discussions between unions and management, and a common set of 'understandings' on questions of racial discrimination is being evolved.

(c) VOLUNTARY PROCEDURES TO DEAL WITH RACIAL DISCRIMINATION

Most important of these joint decisions are the special collective labour agreements on the procedures for dealing with complaints of racial discrimination negotiated at national level.

The main defects of existing procedures for the settlement of industrial disputes as applied to questions of racial discrimination are that: (i) about 5 millions of Britain's 23 millions workers are not subject to any form of collective bargaining or wage-fixing machinery, and it is precisely in those industries that are non-unionized that immigrant labour is most often found; (ii) the most frequent form of discrimination is in respect of engagement and this falls outside existing procedures, being regarded, in general, as a management prerogative; and (iii) in most cases there will be no 'dispute' in the usual sense of that term since an individual worker, and not a section of workers, will be aggrieved.

After the passing of the 1968 Race Relations Act, a number of joint negotiating bodies (which exist on a voluntary basis to settle industrial disputes) expressed an interest in setting up special machinery to deal with individual complaints of racial discrimination. In most cases employers and unions were prepared, after discussion, to bring this machinery in line with the criteria laid down by the Department of Employment and Productivity. The approved procedures all provide for semi-independent investigation of the complaint by persons not directly involved at the work place where the alleged act took place. As pointed out earlier, it is only if such machinery fails that the complaint will be referred to the Race Relations Board. Where no such machinery exists (as is the case in most industries), complaints are dealt with immediately by the Board or one of its local committees.

(d) ACTIVITIES OF BODIES OUTSIDE INDUSTRY

A survey of the activities of the voluntary community relations groups in regard to specific complaints of racial discrimination in employment (conducted by the writer in November 1967) revealed that by and large these bodies were unsuited to the task of handling individual complaints and that their 'official' image (reflecting participation by the local authority and other representatives of the local 'establishment') had robbed them of some potential immigrant support. They do, however, exert some influence on unions, employers, and local authorities.

The fragmented organizations of coloured immigrants also appear to have had little impact in the settlement of individual complaints of discrimination. Their main role has been to collect evidence to support the campaign for legislation. In this they may be contrasted with the Trades Advisory Council of the Board of Deputies of British Jews which for twenty-eight years has enjoyed considerable success in settling complaints of discrimination against Jews. The relative success of the latter body seems to rest on the widespread belief that it is 'unwise' to be seen discriminating against Jews because of their supposed economic power; coloured immigrants, on the other hand, lack this apparent economic strength and do not have effective organization.

(e) GOVERNMENT ACTION

There has been little direct implementation of the policy of 'equal opportunity' within the realm of Government employment. Although no colour bar exists in the Civil Service, there is a Nationality Rule which sometimes operates disadvantageously to second-generation immigrants (particularly if their parents were aliens). A proposal, first made in 1966, that Government contracts with suppliers should include an anti-discrimination clause was not implemented until late 1969. The clause is likely to be ineffective because no specific procedures have been laid down for ensuring that contractors observe this contractual obligation. There have been incidents of discrimination in nationalized industries (e.g. railways) without subsequent Government intervention. The Army was said to operate a 'colour' quota of about 4 per cent for most units, and most local police authorities were reluctant to attempt recruitment. The practices of local authorities (e.g. municipal transport services) are by no means uniform; in some cases coloured workers have been welcomed and successfully absorbed, while in others there have been difficulties about recruitment, the wearing of turbans, and promotion.

On the other hand, one of the most significant developments since the passing of the 1968 Act has been the growing concern of the Department of Employment and Productivity with problems of race relations. There is now a specialist headquarters staff dealing with these matters; local officers likely to deal with immigrants are given special training; and research is being initiated.

This concern has not permeated all official thinking on industrial relations. The important *Report of the Royal Commission on Trade Unions and Employers' Associations*, published in June 1968, paid absolutely no attention to the implications for race relations of its proposals for the reform of collective bargaining. Nor did the Government, in its White Paper on industrial relations published in January 1969, consider the problems of race relations. There is no indication that the Commission for Industrial Relations, set up by the Government to encourage the growth of effective plant procedures, will attempt to ensure that factory and company agreements contain effective safeguards for members of ethnic minorities.

5. *Summary and Conclusions*

Racial discrimination in employment is one of the factors influencing the absorption of minorities. It is of primary importance in relation to the status and opportunities of second and later generations of immigrant groups, but its significance in relation to the first generation must not be underestimated.

The question of racial discrimination can be related to the system of industrial relations as a whole by using as a tool of analysis a well-known model of such a system of rules. According to this, the actors regulate jobs in contexts which involve three determinants: (i) the technological characteristics of the work place and the work community; (ii) the market or budgetary constraints which impinge on the actors; (iii) the locus and distribution of power in the larger society. This system is completed by an ideology or set of 'shared understandings' which bind the system together.

The impact of each of these contexts on rule-making as it affects ethnic minorities was illustrated and the substantive rules were seen to be of two kinds, internal and external. Many of the internal rules are discriminatory, and the technical, market, and power contexts make it more than likely that they will continue to be discriminatory. The external rules, by contrast, show signs of rapid, albeit uneven, change against racial discrimination. These changes reflect the nascent ideology of racial equality and the simultaneous erosion of traditional principles of autonomy and voluntarism.

The limits of change are those imposed by the dogged persistence of the traditional system and the common reluctance to make fundamental changes in the system itself. Traditional conservatism entrenches those technical, market, and power forces which favour patterns of inequality. The major question which hangs over the next decade is whether national antidiscriminatory policies and norms can ensure that the growth of work-place bargaining and the spread of automation do not lead to worsening discrimination against ethnic minorities.

CHAPTER 7

Racial Discrimination and White-collar Workers in Britain

ROGER JOWELL AND
PATRICIA PRESCOTT-CLARKE

In this chapter, we outline the aims, methods, and results of a study[1] carried out during the spring and summer of 1969 to test the degree of job discrimination in white-collar employment within four areas of high immigrant concentration:

The areas studied were:

> Nottingham/Derby/Leicester;
> Reading/Windsor/Slough;
> Birmingham/Wolverhampton;
> Greater London

The piloting for the study was carried out during January and February 1969; and the main research spanned the period from April to August.

The study was carried out on a fairly small scale and was also regarded as a methodological pilot of a hitherto untested research technique in this area. As will be seen from the body of this chapter, the technique proved to be extremely successful and promises to provide a valid and economical method of discrimination testing, not only in employment, but in a variety of possible contexts.

1. *Basic Approach*

The aim of the study was to investigate any differences in treatment accorded to limited samples of immigrant and white British applicants for jobs.

Our first approach to the brief was to use the established and tested method of measuring discrimination, i.e. sending a series of matched coloured and white 'actors' to job interviews. The

---

[1] Prepared and carried out by S.C.P.R. in consultation with the Institute of Race Relations.

P.E.P. study employed this method successfully and, despite certain inherent drawbacks of the technique, it is still widely used in the United States. It is, of course, almost the only feasible method of testing discrimination in manual employment. We were, however, concerned with white-collar jobs—for which postal applications were possible and, in many cases, necessary—so that we were in a position to evaluate and decide on three possible approaches:

(i) A sample survey to find out the actual employment situation of a group of white and coloured employees (or aspiring employees): This was ruled out on several grounds, the most important being that it would contribute little in the way of concrete evidence. It is, of course, true that this technique would have revealed the extent to which comparable groups of British whites and immigrants were managing to find employment; the relative status structures of their employment situations; the extent to which they were holding 'preferred' jobs or 'forced choice' positions; and so on. But all this information—however relevant it may have been to the many human problems involved—would have avoided the basic question contained in our research objective: to what extent are white and coloured applicants treated differently when applying for the same jobs and with the same appropriate qualifications? No amount of scrutiny of the present employment or unemployment situation (or of attitudes towards it) could answer this question. Nor could any answer have been *inferred* if the results had shown both groups to be equally active economically and equally satisfied with their present respective positions. As has been pointed out, the same finding could well emerge from a similar survey in South Africa.

(ii) The P.E.P. approach of sending 'actor applicants' to prospective employers: This was ruled out, after serious consideration, for various technical reasons. Firstly, it is an extremely expensive technique and—because of budgetary limitations—would have meant a large reduction in the coverage of our survey. Secondly, the inherent drawbacks of the technique are simply not capable of validation and therefore impossible to allow for in the analysis of the results.

An important problem related to the question of motivation. It has been suggested that there could well be a conscious or unconscious motivation on the part of coloured actors to *prove* discrimination, and that this would bias the results. This is, of course, an extremely tenuous argument. It is equally likely (and equally unprovable) that there would be a conscious or unconscious motivation on the part of white actors to *disprove* discrimination. Nevertheless, the strength of the criticism lies precisely in the fact that both arguments *are* unprovable, because it is virtually impossible to measure, or control for, differing levels of motivation. The problem was simply that a fairly important and relevant consideration could not adequately be allowed for in the research design and analysis, unless the scale of the operation had been large enough for these factors to have cancelled themselves out.

Precisely the same argument applied to personality differences among the actors. This encompasses a whole range of relevant variables: e.g. how plausible or credible they are; how (appropriately) modest they are; how fluent they prove to be in answering questions; how well they sell themselves; and so on. There is no reason to expect that these positive characteristics would not be randomly distributed between white and coloured actors, *provided* that the sample of actors and jobs was large enough to counteract biases in either direction. But our sample—within the budget—could not have been large enough. This meant again that discrimination could have been either exaggerated or underrated in our findings, simply because of uncontrollable and unquantifiable personality biases.

Arising from these drawbacks, the most important reason for rejecting the job interview was the need for reliable base-line information which could be used for purposes of *monitoring* levels of discrimination over time. This is, of course, much more important now, in view of the extension of the Race Relations Act to cover employment. We felt that, for monitoring purposes, it was essential to control all possible variables which could conceivably affect the results differently between one study and the next. If levels of discrimination were to be measured at regular intervals, the changes (if any) had to be accountable for by real shifts in practice, and not be blurred by possible alterations in the research input. In other words, we were concerned that budgets for monitoring would—in practice—rarely be large enough to allow motivational and personality variations to be randomized out. So we needed a technique which could successfully neutralize them as relevant variables.

It was these objections—in addition to the desirability of exploring new techniques—which finally persuaded us to adopt the third approach, described below.

(iii) A postal approach of sending matched written applications in reply to advertised vacancies: By opting for written applications, we were able effectively to eradicate the two major 'unknowns' of the job interview approach. On the other hand, we were also opting for a very different measurement from that tested in the P.E.P. study. The test variable with which we were concerned was more fundamental and more decisive: it was the extent to which differences in treatment occurred in the granting of job *interviews*. In other words, we were assessing the propensity of different types of employer to *consider* different types of applicant for different types of job. The study was insufficient in scale to draw any generalized national conclusions from the results. Its chief aims were to test the levels of discrimination found within the areas we surveyed; to test the feasibility of the postal technique; and to develop the technique as an economical and accurate tool of measurement.

In comparing our findings with previous studies, it is important to remember several major differences both in the content and context of the research. Firstly, we were measuring a different stage of possible discrimination: i.e. it can reasonably be assumed that discrimination in the granting of interviews would be lower than (and probably different from) any discrimination found in the allocation of jobs. The decision to interview an applicant is clearly much less conclusive than the decision to employ one.

Secondly, we were concerned only with white-collar jobs. In 'inventing' suitable applicants with equal qualifications for the advertised vacancies, we were, in effect, creating a group of immigrant applicants who—in terms of both qualifications and job experience—were probably far in advance of the great majority of their 'real' counterparts in Britain today. There must, for example, be very few Pakistani area sales managers with ten years' experience in leading manufacturing firms all over Britain; and very few Indian advertising executives with the pedigree of having managed several large British offices, dealing with a variety of clients and products.

If these types of applicant were not invited for interview

(while their white counterparts were), this would indeed be discrimination at a debilitating level. We do not take the view that we should have restricted ourselves to a more 'realistic' range of jobs, i.e. those for which the bulk of immigrants are currently applying. What we were trying to assess was the extent to which immigrants with equal qualifications would (or do) suffer in relation to their British-born, white counterparts. While it is doubtless true that the immigrants' qualifications may have been regarded as suspect by potential employers, this would, of course, still apply to 'real' immigrants in 'real' situations. The result, in both cases, would be discrimination against the immigrant, regardless of the reason or even the justification. What we were measuring was the degree of discrimination, not the extent of prejudice or the rationale behind it: how much do immigrants with equal qualifications get accorded equal treatment? No more and no less.

Thirdly, the passage of the Race Relations Act will probably have made inroads into the levels of discrimination since the period of the last major study conducted by P.E.P. We cannot, of course, know the extent or types of change that the Act has promoted. What we do know is that the context in which this research was conducted is different from that in which previous work has been undertaken.

2. Research Method

We decided early on to restrict the letters of application to actual vacancies, rather than trying to apply 'blind' to a series of unsuspecting firms. In this way, we were able substantially to reduce wastage: the firms were intending to make an appointment and, provided that our two matched applicants were at least as good as any others who applied, they were *both* likely to be invited for an interview or sent an application form. Had we applied 'blind', we would probably have encountered a large (and wasted) number of negative responses to both our applicants.

We restricted the scope of the study to four job categories in four different areas of the country. The job types selected were: (i) sales and marketing; (ii) accountancy and office management; (iii) electrical engineering; and (iv) secretarial. The areas were:

Greater London; Birmingham/Wolverhampton; Nottingham/ Derby/Leicester; and Reading/Windsor/ Slough.

In all, 128 jobs were applied for by 256 applicants (i.e. two matched applicants per job—one British-born white and one immigrant). The 128 jobs were spread evenly between the four job types *and* the four areas; thus, within each area and each job type, thirty-two job applications were made:

8 from West Indians matched against British-born whites
8 from Asians matched against British-born whites (i.e. 4 Sikh Indians and 4 Pakistanis)
8 from Australians matched against British-born whites
8 from Cypriots matched against British-born whites

The notion of choosing four different types of immigrant was to ensure that variables both of country of origin and mother tongue were included. Our four groups could, therefore, be described respectively as: (i) coloured English-speaking; (ii) coloured non-English-speaking; (iii) white English-speaking; and (iv) white non-English-speaking. Nevertheless, these descriptions related only to the applicants' *likely* mother tongue, not to their relative fluency in English. All letters of application—from British-born whites and immigrants alike—were of a comparable standard of literacy; and all immigrant applicants had received their higher or further education in Britain. (In fact, one-half of the sample had also received their secondary schooling in Britain.)

The typical sequence of events, from the appearance of the advertisement to the result of the application, was as follows:

TABLE 7:1

Advertisement appears in, say, Wolverhampton paper	(Day 1)
Paper arrives at S.C.P.R. offices; advertisement extracted; and letters of application formulated	(Day 2)
Letters of application hand-written by two 'hand-writers' (the same two for the whole study); and letters posted to the two Wolverhampton posters (the same two for the whole study)	(Day 3)
Letters posted from the two Wolverhampton addresses	(Day 4)
Letters arrive at firm	(Day 5)
Replies arrive at the two Wolverhampton addresses and posted to S.C.P.R. offices (on day of arrival)	(up to 3 weeks later)
Replies arrive at offices; booked-in; and 'scored'; successful applicants' letters sent off declining offer of interview	(1 day later)

The 'scoring' was naturally very straightforward. We were not looking for possible reasons or justifications for differences in treatment, but merely recording the results of each application:

A score of 0   signified that both applicants were treated equally, i.e. both asked for interview, both sent application forms, or both refused.

A score of — 1   signified that the immigrant applicant received an unfavourable response in relation to his white counterpart.

A score of + 1   signified that the immigrant applicant received a more favourable response than his white counterpart.

In order to allocate scores of this kind, we had to be sure that all exogenous variables (which could have influenced the responses received) were accounted for in the research design. Our applicants had to be identically matched in terms of all possible relevant variables so that the crucial factors of colour and country of origin could be isolated and tested.

This is, of course, an impossible task to achieve on two individual applicants. Handwritings would necessarily be different; the two postal addresses might be perceived in different terms; letter styles had to be different enough for them not to be spotted as 'fakes'; and so on. What we were concerned with, however, was that these exogenous factors were neutralized *over the sample as a whole*, and that only certain selected and controlled factors were *identical* for any two matched applicants. Ideally, of course, all pairs of applicants would have been identically matched; but from the point of view of authenticity, there had to be minor variations. Five 'profile variables' were therefore neutralized between matched applicants in the following way:

(i) *Age:* The two applicants for each job were always given ages which were within one year of each other.

(ii) *Marital status:* The two matched applicants were always given the same marital status; and they did not differ—in terms of number of children—by more than one child.

(iii) *Present and previous employers:* No applicant's *present* employer was ever named, but was described broadly as a 'large' or 'leading' firm in the relevant field; *previous* employers—which were named— were always a group of companies, so that references could not be taken up without further information from the applicant.

(iv) *Salary:* No details of present salary were ever provided by any of the applicants; where 'present salary' was demanded in the job advertisement, the job was excluded from the universe. (This was done on the basis of our pilot results, which showed that marginal salary differences often seemed to have a very major influence on whether or not a candidate was invited for interview. Since it did not warrant inclusion in the research design, we felt it better to exclude it completely from the range of relevant influences.)

(v) *Date of sending applications:* All matched applications were always made to arrive on the same day; and this was never in excess of one week after the advertisement had appeared. On several occasions, the time span from appearance of the advertisements to despatch of letters was less than three days.

Two other variables could equally have been neutralized, but we preferred to include them as 'test variables' so that we could isolate and test their relevance. These were:

(i) *Country of schooling:* All our immigrant applicants received their *primary* schooling in their country of origin; however, one-half of them (spread equally among all types) received their secondary schooling in Britain and the other half reported having arrived in Britain immediately after secondary school.

(ii) *Level of qualification and experience:* Each pair of matched applicants was allocated a minimum of six 'O' levels; beyond that the qualifications were matched to specific job requirements so that—for one-half of all immigrants (spread equally among all types)—the immigrant was given a *higher* qualification or greater length of appropriate experience than his British-born counterpart; and for the other half, their qualifications were identically matched. (A higher qualification always meant either one [more] 'A' level, in the case of junior posts, or two [extra] years of experience, in the case of senior posts.)

Finally, there were three further variables which—in the very nature of the study—had to be 'test variables':

(iii) *Country of origin:* The 128 British-born white applicants were matched (with equal frequency) against four different groups of immigrant applicants—West Indians, Asians, Australians, and Cypriots. These groups were identified by their names (in the case of Asians and Cypriots) *and* by mention in their letter of application of when they had arrived in Britain. All immigrants stated in their letters that they were now permanently resident here.

The names allocated to all applicants were standardized, so that one male name and one female name were used throughout the study for each national group, e.g. the British-born applicant was always John Robinson or Mary Robinson; the Cypriot was always George Demetriades or Helen Demetriades.

(iv) *Job type:* Similarly, the 128 jobs were divided equally among four job categories—sales and marketing, accountancy and office management, electrical engineering, and secretarial. Each job type was applied for with equal frequency in each of the four areas and was included on the basis of an advertisement appearing in either local or national press, or, in a few cases, specialist professional journals. Once a vacancy had been found (in one of the four job categories), it was always included in our sample, unless it specified that salary must be mentioned in the application or unless the firm had already been selected for another vacancy.

(v) *Letter of application:* As we have mentioned, each pair of letters had, of course, to differ in style, so that the authenticity of the two applicants was retained. This stylistic difference could have been a biasing factor (equivalent to 'personality' in a personal interview context) unless it was capable of randomizing out. Similarly, handwriting and home address (which had to differ for two matched applicants) had to be neutralized over the sample as a whole. Two *standard* letters were therefore devised and used throughout the study. Style A was always written in handwriting X and posted from address number 1 in each area; Style B was always written in handwriting Y and posted from address 2 in each area. This was, therefore, a composite variable, incorporating and neutralizing three possible biasing factors. The two letters were naturally identical in content, in degree of motivation, in literacy, etc. But they varied in style and ordering sufficiently to appear to have been authored by two different applicants. Space was left appropriately in each letter for the insertion of relevant qualifications, experience, background, etc., all of which were obtained from 'experts' in the four relevant job categories. The two basic letter-types were, of course, allocated with equal frequency to each different type of applicant.

Thus, the research method was an experimental design,

7*

comprising five interlaced variables: country of origin, job type, country of schooling, level of qualification, and letter of application. This enabled an analysis of variance to be carried out on the scores, so that mean differences among the five variables could be identified and their significance tested. For *each* of the four *job types*, for example, the following design balance was achieved:

TABLE 7:2

DESIGN OF RESEARCH

		Country of origin	Qualifications*	Schooling†	Letter style‡
Immigrant	1	West Indian	Higher	Abroad	A
	2	,,	,,	,,	B
	3	,,	,,	U.K.	A
	4	,,	,,	,,	B
	5	,,	Equal	Abroad	A
	6	,,	,,	,,	B
	7	,,	,,	U.K.	A
	8	,,	,,	,,	B
	9	Asian	Higher	Abroad	A
	10	,,	,,	,,	B
	11	,,	,,	U.K.	A
	12	,,	,,	,,	B
	13	,,	Equal	Abroad	A
	14	,,	,,	,,	B
	15	,,	,,	U.K.	A
	16	,,	,,	,,	B
	17	Australian	Higher	Abroad	A
	18	,,	,,	,,	B
	19	,,	,,	U.K.	A
	20	,,	,,	,,	B
	21	,,	Equal	Abroad	A
	22	,,	,,	,,	B
	23	,,	,,	U.K.	A
	24	,,	,,	,,	B
	25	Cypriot	Higher	Abroad	A
	26	,,	,,	,,	B
	27	,,	,,	U.K.	A
	28	,,	,,	,,	B
	29	,,	Equal	Abroad	A
	30	,,	,,	,,	B
	31	,,	,,	U.K.	A
	32	,,	,,	,,	B

* A higher qualification relative to the British counterpart.

† Schooling abroad relates to secondary schooling. All British counterparts were schooled in the United Kingdom.

‡ In each case, the British applicant was allocated the alternative style of letter.

3. *Results*

As we have mentioned, all *pairs* of applications were allocated one of three possible scores: 0 = no discrimination; — 1 = discrimination against immigrant (whatever his country of origin); and + 1 = discrimination in favour of immigrant. Table 7:3 shows the distribution of the actual scores.

TABLE 7:3

DISTRIBUTION OF SCORES

			Total	%
Score	0	Both applicants invited for interview	51	40
		Both received application forms	26	20
		Both received acknowledgements only	3	2
		Both received no reply	5	4
		Both refused interviews	16	13
		One refused, one no reply	1	1
		No discrimination	102	80
Score	—1	Briton interview, immigrant refused	12	9
		Briton interview, immigrant no reply	5	4
		Briton interview, immigrant application form	1	1
		Briton application form, immigrant refused	3	2
		Briton application form, immigrant no reply	2	2
		Discrimination against immigrant	23	18
Score	+1	Immigrant interview, Briton refused	1	1
		Immigrant application form, Briton no reply	2	1
		Discrimination in favour of immigrant	3	2
		TOTAL	128	100

The null hypothesis was that the aggregate score would not differ significantly from zero. It could, of course, be argued that our null hypothesis should have been a *positive score*, since one-half of the immigrants were given higher qualifications for the jobs than their British-born counterparts. Nevertheless, the basis of the design was such as to neutralize the differences among candidates to an extent that any variations in the granting of an interview should have been ruled out. Stated unscientifically, it might have been fairer to say that the aggregate score over the sample as a whole should have been *at least* zero.

In the event, the aggregate score was — 20, a statistically significant difference from zero (at the 99 per cent level). This aggregate score predictably concealed the fact that different immigrant groups received very different treatments, i.e. the figures in Table 7:3 only show the total refusals for all immigrants and, therefore, do not yet reveal the effect of the race factor for coloured, as opposed to white, immigrants.

Taking first a broad view of the results, it can be seen that the success rate (being invited for interview or sent an application form) of the *British-born whites* was very high. Of the 128 applicants, 100 were successful, i.e. 78 per cent.

Australians were just as successful, 78 per cent of them being granted an interview or sent an application form.

West Indians and *Cypriots* were less successful, with identical results: 69 per cent of both groups received a positive response to their applications.

Asians were, by far, the least successful: just under 35 per cent of them were invited for interview or sent an application form.

Immigrants with higher qualifications than their white counterparts and immigrants who had received their secondary schooling in the United Kingdom received only *slightly* more favourable treatment than other immigrants, but the differences were not significant.[1]

		Success Rate
Immigrants with:	higher qualifications	69%
	equal qualifications	56%
Immigrants with:	secondary schooling in the United Kingdom	70%
	secondary schooling abroad	58%

Since we had taken four immigrant groups to examine variations between colour and language, we can now assess these as independent variables. Taking language as a variable first, we tested two 'English-speaking' immigrant groups and two 'non-English-speaking' groups. (The language variable was, of course,

[1] Where references are made (here and later) to differences being 'not significant', they imply that the result could have occurred by chance in more than 5 cases out of 100.

in terms of imputed mother-tongue differences only, since *all* letters indicated clearly a complete fluency in English.) The results were as follows:

		Success Rate
English-speaking:	Australians	78%
	West Indians	69%
Non-English-speaking:	Cypriots	69%
	Asians	35%

In each case, the white group was more successful than the coloured group; and in the case of the non-English-speaking groups, the difference was statistically significant (at the 99 per cent level).

It is interesting to note that there was no discrimination against Australians in relation to their British-born counterparts. (Both groups achieved a success rate of 78 per cent.) This would imply that 'foreignness', in itself, may be insufficient grounds for discrimination by British employers, i.e. the 'xenophobia argument' as a cause of discrimination is not borne out by these results. Additional 'disabilities' of either colour or mother-tongue differences (and preferably both) are apparently necessary to induce the onset of active discrimination at this level.

Using colour as an independent variable, we found substantial differences between the success rates of white and coloured immigrants (accounted for by the high Australian and low Asian success rates):

	Success Rate
White immigrants (Australians/Cypriots)	74%
Coloured immigrants (West Indians/Asians)	52%

There were virtually no differences in the degree of discrimination between either the four areas or the four job types covered in the study. Nor were there any differences between the two groups of Asians which we covered, i.e. half were Indian Sikhs (identified by country of schooling and surnames) and half were Pakistanis.

An analysis of variance, carried out on the full sample of jobs, is shown below. As will be seen, only 'country of origin' emerged as a significant variable (out of the five variables tested).

TABLE 7:4

ANALYSIS OF VARIANCE

Variation between	Degrees of freedom	Sum of squares	Mean square	F ratio
Letter type	I	·026	·026	·15
Job type	3	·188	·063	·37
Country of origin	3	2·750	·917	*5·36
Qualifications	I	·125	·125	·73
Schooling	I	·278	·278	1·63
	9	3·367		
Letter/job interaction	3	·536	·179	1·05
Letter/country interaction	3	·099	·033	·19
Letter/qualification interaction	I	·287	·287	1·68
Letter/schooling interaction	I	·009	·009	·05
Job/country interaction	9	1·437	·160	·94
Job/qualification interaction	3	·062	·021	·12
Job/schooling interaction	3	·159	·053	·31
Country/qualification interaction	3	1·000	·333	1·95
Country/schooling interaction	3	·847	·282	1·65
Qualification/schooling interaction	I	·035	·035	·20
	30	4·471		
Residual	88	15·037	·171	
TOTAL VARIATION	127	22·875		

* Significant at the 99 per cent level.

In examining 'country of origin' further, we found that the difference between British-born and West Indian *or* Cypriot success rates was *not* significant at the 10 per cent level. However, the difference between British-born and Asian success rates was *significant* at the 1 per cent level, i.e. this result would have occurred by *chance* in only one out of one hundred similar tests.

None of the cases of discrimination found would have been even remotely apparent to the disadvantaged applicant. We list here some of the typical replies for each of the four job types:

(i) *Reply to British applicant:*

Dear Miss Robinson,

Thank you for your letter of the 9th inst., in answer to our advertisement for a secretary. I should be glad to see you, if you would kindly telephone me to arrange an interview. I enclose a copy of our catalogue and also a form for you to complete and bring with you to the interview.

Yours sincerely,

Reply to Indian applicant:

Dear Miss Kaur,

Thank you very much for your answer to my advertisement for a secretary. The standard of all applications was excellent, but I have chosen someone with more experience in publishing.

Yours sincerely,

N.B. Miss Robinson's secretarial experience had been in chemical manufacturing and metal manufacturing.

Miss Kaur's secretarial experience had been with a transport firm and a *publishing* firm.

In all other respects, the two applicants were identical.

(ii) *Reply to British applicant:*

Dear Mr. Robinson,

Thank you for your application dated 4th July for the post of Cost Accountant.

Would you please telephone the writer to arrange a convenient time for you to come to this office for interview.

Yours sincerely,

Reply to Indian applicant:

Dear Mr. Singh,

Thank you very much for your letter of 4th July. I am very sorry to have to advise you that other applicants appear to fit the job description better and I am therefore unable to take your application any further.

Yours sincerely,

N.B. Mr. Singh had both longer and more relevant experience than *Mr. Robinson*. The two letters above were written on the same day.

(iii) *Reply to British applicant:*

Dear Mr. Robinson,

Thank you for your letter dated 1st August 1969 regarding our vacancy for a Sales Representative.

We have pleasure in enclosing an application form ... and will be in further contact with you as soon as possible after receipt, when an interview will be arranged.

Yours sincerely,

Reply to West Indian applicant:

Dear Mr. Gardiner,

We thank you for your application for the position of representative with this company, but regret to advise you that we will not be proceeding further with this appointment due to internal re-organization.

Thanking you for your interest, we remain,

Yours sincerely,

N.B. The two letters arrived within a week of each other.

(iv) *Reply to British applicant:*

Dear Mr. Robinson,

Thank you for your letter of 31st July in response to our advertisement for an electronics engineer.

We should like you to attend for interview so that we can discuss the position further, and would ask you to telephone ... as soon as possible so that we can arrange this. ...

Yours sincerely,

Reply to Indian
applicant:

Dear Mr. Singh,

Thank you very much for your letter of 31st July in connection with an advertisement for an electronics engineer.

There was a big response to this advertisement and we have studied all letters carefully before making our final short list of candidates. It seemed to us that you were really a little too well-qualified for the type of job we were offering and therefore regret to inform you that we decided against including your name on the short list.

We would like to wish you every success in obtaining the type of position for which your qualifications fit you.

Once again, our thanks for your interest.

Yours sincerely,

N.B. Mr. Robinson and Mr. Singh had identical qualifications.

4. *Conclusions*

To our knowledge, this was the first study to be carried out in Britain on the propensity of employers to discriminate at this level of staff selection. It is a peculiarly decisive and absolute form of discrimination: the employer is (deliberately) denying himself the opportunity of even considering an applicant whose qualifications appear to be suitable; and the disadvantaged applicant is denied the chance even of competing with other applicants, whether or not his qualifications are better than theirs.

The results of the study show Asian immigrants to be the chief sufferers from this form of discrimination; West Indians and Cypriots in our sample were also disadvantaged, but not at a statistically significant level; Australians suffered no discrimination in relation to their British counterparts. These findings differ from those of the P.E.P. report in that—in the present study —Asians, rather than West Indians, appear to be the main target for discrimination. But we were measuring a different kind of disadvantage and were looking at white-collar jobs only. It is probably true that Asian immigrants are more frequent applicants for the type of job covered in our study. It seems certain that they are more frequently denied the chance of an interview. There was some suggestion that West Indian applicants would have suffered more discrimination had they, in fact, been less 'unique' in terms of their qualifications. As we have said earlier, some of the qualifications and levels of experience reported may have been regarded as suspect, simply because they were so unusual. In this sense, some applicants may have been invited for interview out of curiosity value alone, and with no real prospect of employment. Three or four letters from employers to West Indians certainly implied that this was the case. If this were true to any marked degree (and it cannot be validated), then the extent of discrimination against West Indians, in particular, will have been under-represented by our survey.

The scale of the study was necessarily small and it was inevitably in some senses a pilot project. As such, it has proved extremely successful. It has shown, firstly, the relative economy, flexibility, and precision of a postal approach to discrimination-testing; and, secondly, the way in which measurements arising from such studies can be used for monitoring changes in the level of discrimination. The methods outlined in this report could be applied to a wide range of testing situations, e.g. holiday camps, hotels or boarding houses, new housing estates, and many others. Although the scale needs to be larger if generalized national conclusions are to be drawn, the basic methodology can be applied with good effect, even in very limited and specific situations.

The findings of the study give little cause for encouragement: immigrants who completed all their secondary schooling (and further or higher education) in Britain did not encounter significantly less discrimination than more recent arrivals; those immigrants who had higher qualifications than their white counterparts were not treated (significantly) differently from those with equal qualifications; and, most important, in none of the cases of discrimination found, could a complaint feasibly have been made under the Race Relations Act by the disadvantaged applicant: he or she would simply never have known that discrimination was taking place. All refusals were (predictably) polite, benevolent, and often charming: for example, 'We would like to wish you every success in obtaining the type of position for which your qualifications fit you.' No doubt Asian immigrants, in particular, will have to face the fact that their country of origin is frequently the only significant qualification taken into account.

CHAPTER 8

Minority Group Leaders

DR. R. MANDERSON-JONES
AND JYOTHI KAMATH

Chapter 1 of this report stressed the importance of testing the perceptions of minority group members within the social process of discrimination. This chapter, therefore, includes an analysis of interviews with minority group leaders drawn from the larger non-white immigrant groups. These interviews were carried out in 1968, after the Race Relations Act of 1965 had been in operation for three years and during the widely publicized debates on the passage of the 1968 Race Relations Act.

1. West Indian Leaders
by Dr. R. Manderson-Jones

(a) INTRODUCTION

This attitudinal study of West Indian immigrant leadership in Britain is based on detailed unstructured interviews with twenty-one popularly selected leaders.[1] The sample of leaders was composed from the individual preferences of a larger number of West Indian immigrants. This method of selection was favoured in view of the notion of leadership found to be prevalent within the West Indian community in Britain, and the dubious validity of analysis based on such conventional sociological concepts as 'institutional' and 'model' leaders[2] in a community which showed very few of either, while hardly accepting individuals in the traditional professional and political élitist framework as models at all. In terms of country of origin, the leaders comprised eight Jamaicans, four Trinidadians, two Barbadians, two Grenadians, two Guyanese, one Dominican, one St. Lucian, and one St. Vincentian. Their average age was 36·5 years, with one person above 50, one aged 49, fourteen in the age group of 30–45 inclusive,

---

[1] Nineteen in London and two in a Midlands town.
[2] S. Collins, *Coloured Minorities in Britain* (London, Lutterworth, 1957).

and five between 25 and 29 years. Residence in Britain of 12·7 years was the average, with 37 years being the longest period and 5 years the shortest. The leaders included politicians, social workers, writers, journalists, clerks, students, businessmen, members of the legal, medical, and theological professions, a postman, and an architect. In duration, the interviews varied from one to one and three-quarters hours, and were principally concerned with ascertaining both specific and general attitudes on race relations and discrimination in Britain.[1]

TABLE 8:1

THE WEST INDIAN LEADERS

Age	Country of origin	Years in United Kingdom	Occupation
30	Guyana	10	Architect
35	Guyana	13	Lawyer
40	Trinidad and Tobago	7	Publisher/writer
49	St. Vincent	10	Community Relations Officer
44	Jamaica	20	Postman
25	Jamaica	6	Barrister-at-Law
34	Grenada	25	Medical practitioner
34*	Dominica	10*	Councillor (C.)
34*	Trinidad and Tobago	10*	Teacher
42	Jamaica	14	Businessman
40	Jamaica	10	Businessman
26	St. Lucia	18	Political activist
35*	Jamaica	12	Councillor (C.)
27	Jamaica	6	Student
26	Trinidad and Tobago	5*	Student
36	Barbados	12	Clerk (British Rail)
36*	Barbados	10*	Minister of religion
40*	Jamaica	12*	Mechanical engineer
40*	Grenada†	12*	Clerk
27	Jamaica†	8*	Journalist
68	Trinidad and Tobago	37	Writer/journalist

* Estimated.
† Probable country of origin.
Note: With one exception, all interviewed were male.

(b) WEST INDIAN IMMIGRANT LEADERSHIP AND ORGANIZATION: THE PROBLEM OF DEFINITION

The initial reaction of most persons interviewed was retreat from the term leader. Many were somewhat surprised that it

[1] For examples of the types of questions behind the interviews, see the schedule in Appendix 2.

should have been assumed that West Indians in Britain necessarily have leaders. The common view was that West Indians tend to move on a broad front, each individual jealously clinging to his individuality and refusing to place it at the disposal of any so-called leader. It was held that the greater number of the so-called leaders of the West Indian community in Britain are largely fictitious creations of the communications media, or simply 'local spokesmen' who as easily slip ahead of the broad line of West Indians as they slip again behind it. A few West Indians inter-viewed went so far as to suggest that the concept of leader was essentially alien to the Black man and was by and large a 'Euro-pean concept'. A fairly typical response was: 'If there are any leaders, then you are a leader, I am a leader, everybody is a leader'.

Apart from the question of 'leader', issue was taken in some quarters over reference to 'West Indian immigrant'. One objection raised was that the majority of so-called 'West Indian immigrants' in the United Kingdom are in fact British, bearing British pass-ports. If it were necessary to distinguish between Black British of sometime West Indian descent or connection and white or other British, then, it was suggested in a few cases, preference should be given to the term 'Afro-Saxon'. But the problem did not end there, rather it became more complex. Reference to 'West Indians' in Britain was contested on other grounds, particularly in relation to the assumption that they were joined together in such ways that a common leadership might justifiably be expected to 'umbrella' them. Might not the whole notion of West Indian leadership in Britain simply be an indication of the grave misconceptions of those who seek it? One person analysed the issue accordingly:

The breakdown of federation [of the West Indies] meant quite a lot in terms of West Indian organizations in Britain. It meant that while the independent and separate countries now have their own national political institutions, this is really a *sub rosa* phenomenon in the sense that British society still regards them as *West Indian*. Insular conscious-ness revives among West Indians but the society as such is unaware of the phenomenon. In effect you can have no real West Indian leader-ship for at least another generation until they are Afro-West Indians (or Afro-West-Indian-British, or Afro-Saxon, the Black British, what you may). Nevertheless, the society sees West Indian leaders and a unity of West Indians which are both nonexistent in fact. Hence, there is a constant contradiction between 'West Indians' in Britain and white British natives. The depth and strength of the insular consciousness among the 'West Indians' is the primary factor in the entire situation, yet it is precisely this which is ignored. Even the colour problem *per se* is not enough to overcome the insularity in favour of any substantial degree of unity. . . . The wave of immigration has meant that the first comers have reached the conclusion that *their destiny is here.* . . .

It is difficult to assess exactly what this means in terms of 'West Indians'—as they become more and more aware that they are cut off from the West Indies and are living in an island in a 'white sea'. This will very likely lead to a breakdown of West Indian insularity here and the growth of the Afro-West-Indian-British.

and again, on leadership:

What is a leader?! A leader is obviously a man who elects himself by virtue of the fact that he thinks a certain situation demands a certain change which he elects to do, and who validates himself among a small group of people to bring about change. But this is only a small group. In short, he is no more than a 'spokesman' among 'spokesmen'.

The pattern of organization with which the leaders interviewed associate themselves, tends to support the general observations on the difficulty of practically defining West Indian leadership and, particularly, any genuinely representative leadership. Chief among the various organizations investigated were: the West Indian Standing Conference, the West Indian Students Union, the Derby West Indian Association, B.C.A. (the British-Caribbean Association), CARD (Campaign Against Racial Discrimination), RAAS (The Racial Adjustment Action Society), U.C.P.A. (Universal Coloured Peoples' Association), U.C.P.A.A. (Universal Coloured Peoples' and Arab Association), and the Lambethian Party. Of these, only the first three are exclusively West Indian in membership. Besides the larger organizations mentioned, there are the strictly national organizations—such as the Jamaican Association U.K., the Jamaica National Organization, the Trinidad & Tobago Society, and the Trinidad & Tobago Association. Leaders from the Clapham and St. John's Inter-racial Clubs were also interviewed.

All the organizations referred to are either formally or semi-formally constituted, if not without strict constitutions at least with functional executives distinguishable from the main body of membership. These groups have varying degrees of preoccupation with the racial question and differing modes of operation. The Lambethians, for instance, are really a local political party with wide-ranging interests relating to the area of Lambeth, and differ, as such, from the others mentioned. The interracial clubs naturally have much to do with race relations, but their activities are generally conducted within the broader context of social work. The B.C.A., the Derby West Indian Association, and the various national organizations, all have a wider frame of reference, relating generally to the activities of West Indians in Britain and to developments in the West Indian countries, thereby leaving only the West Indian Standing Conference, the West Indian Students Union, CARD, RAAS, the U.C.P.A., and the U.C.P.A.A. as the significant organizations centring on the race question. There are no reliable figures for the membership of any or all of these groups, but even at the most generous estimate it is unlikely that their total membership would constitute any significant fraction of the West Indian population in the United Kingdom, or even in London. This leads to the point that a considerable amount of the main current of West Indian dialogue—not only the interchange of ideas but practical organization and planning for action—occurs outside the major formal and semi-formal structures and within small, completely informal groups, either locally-based or drawing together people with common interests from widely separated areas. This is as valid for purely political activity as it is for intellectual, artistic, or general cultural communion. Such groups generally have no fixed base and might move from house to house as they see fit. In practice, therefore, the general problems of West Indian organization—that is, formal or semi-formal organizations varying in size but not specifically or even mainly West Indian in membership; strictly national groups, splinter groups, invisible groups; and the vast majority of West Indians remaining aloof—place grave reservations on even the most reasoned generalizations on West Indian leadership in Britain.

(c) SELF-REGARDING ATTITUDES: THE QUALITY AND DIRECTION OF
    LEADERSHIP

Among the most significant revelations here were the general pessimism concerning the quality and direction of West Indian leadership, based on many of the points raised above; and the almost rigid division between, and mutual disdain of, conservative-moderate leadership and radical-militant leadership. It must be emphasized, however, that this categorization is based solely on divergencies over the strategy to be employed in dealing with discrimination and on the ultimate end sought; and 'labels' are reluctantly used only to facilitate the analysis within this paper.[1]

On the first issue, the quality and direction of leadership, the following are some of the comments made:

The leadership very much reflects the organizations themselves and on the whole, the public leadership is very weak, there being not many people of outstanding organizational abilities and public status. . . . Moreover, the present leadership does not fit race into the broader picture of what kind of society they would like to see. . . .

We have good leaders but too many and too fragmented. Each fellow who has some initiative and time holds himself in a small conclave, working for himself, for what end he doesn't know. Some of them do more social welfare work, give dances; others are more concerned with housing, etc. There are too many West Indian groups proliferated all over the place, and they won't come together under one umbrella.

West Indian leadership is sad in the sense that it is extremely fragmented. The organizations are formed on an insular basis. Even where organizations are brought together there is a clash of personalities which is detrimental to their development. Each West Indian group wants to strive not only for a national identity, but a sense of preservation of what belongs to the territory of that group. . . . The break-up of the Federation [of the West Indies] had to some extent increased the pre-existing insularity and shattered the one chance of developing a truly West Indian identity—of being West Indian. . . . Within the Establishment there is a knowledge that we are fragmented, and divided, and there is an attempt to exploit division towards the end of saying that the people who speak on behalf of West Indians do not really have the backing of the West Indians who are divided. . . . West Indians tend to be interested in their dances, in the fact that they have a house, that they have a job, etc., so only the politically conscious West Indian originally joined [this organization] and the ordinary West Indian only comes when he needs protection after a confrontation with race. . . .

[1] Moreover, any conclusive spectrum analysis would carry with it the reservations imposed by differentiation between privately and publicly held attitudes and by their relative weight in influencing the individual's general behaviour. This chapter is often concerned with privately held attitudes revealed in the interviews.

Leadership of West Indians is a crying shame. A few good chaps around but unfortunately they don't go forward for leadership. . . . Ideally the movement should produce a leader, but so far 'leaders' have imposed themselves on the movement.

. . . as long as you are on proper terms and popular with the news-papers, which in any case like to make fools of West Indians, then you are considered a leader.

This is the decisive moment for leadership. One of our problems in getting real leadership in the past is that the intellectuals are reluctant to come in and play an active part in community affairs.

The concept of leadership in this particular field [race] is quite foreign to the West Indian. It was not necessary in the West Indies. The more educated West Indians have been withdrawing themselves from their Black brothers and trying like hell to join white society. Few middle-class West Indians who have joined groups did so out of anything but paternalism and in order to feather themselves and increase their prestige so that they might get increased accessibility into white society. Consequently, the leadership of West Indian organi-zations has fallen primarily into the hands of the ordinary [working-class] West Indian: the man who was really facing the problems—can't get a room or a job, together with having to face up to personal abuse. Thus, a sort of instinctive leadership has developed among the West Indians. The original form of organization was a kind of tea party until now; however, West Indians realize that this is not the only thing they are to get together for. Present West Indian leadership definitely lacks perception and this is due to the fact of the new type of leadership demanded for a situation which did not exist and to a 'colonial complex'.

A lot of organizations that are being formed are being formed within the concepts of white men's organizations. We have tried this and found that they failed. No doubt others will find the same thing too. An organization based on the concept of the system cannot possibly undermine the abuses of the system, for *inter alia* such organizations are too easily penetrable. Many of the organizations are puppet organized conferences, Government subsidized, looking for personal recognition inside the echelons of Government—then what happens, they get a contact, get a better job, more money, and the whole scene for Black people is over. Valuable contributions? How can any organization which recognizes the legal system make valuable contributions—valuable contributions to what?

These comments fully illustrate the nature of the criticisms about West Indian leadership and organization along the entire attitudinal spectrum. While the criticisms vary little on specific points—such as 'fragmentation', 'insularity', or lack of sufficient intellectual participation—it is interesting to note that the last comment condemns organization on the 'European' model. This may be taken as the beginning of a major divergence over strategy.

(d) STRATEGY

Attitudes concerning the strategy for overcoming racial prejudice and discrimination are intricately interrelated to the very complex issue of identity fulfilment which the West Indian faces. What this section hopes to do is to sketch a very general picture of the significant features of the cognitive and emotive structures underlying the two main types of attitude relating to strategy. All the leaders interviewed were either born or brought up in the West Indies, and in the analysis which follows, this fact is of especial importance. Consequently, it is not intended that our general conclusions be taken as applying with equal force to whatever leadership might ultimately emerge in Britain without such immediate and direct links to the West Indies; one must also bear in mind that the countries of the West Indies themselves undergo constant change.

The militant-radical leader finds his identity in Blackness which is supranational and conceptually embraces a universal 'Black brotherhood'. While some degree of similar identification with Blackness is accepted by conservative-moderate leaders, these have not jettisoned their need for nationality. They fully subordinate Blackness to the requirement of a national identity and acceptance in Britain, as the country which they have adopted. As a consequence, the conservative-moderates tend to be preoccupied with the problem of race at the British level, while the radical-militants have far more of an international perspective. The radical-militant's basic national identification lies in the prefix 'Afro', relating to Africa and being for him the 'national' translation of an ethnic-cultural identity as well as the 'original' country of origin.[1]

Among the conservative-moderates, 'Afro' identification is

---

[1] Africa is seen as a unity of the Black man, with any national boundaries being merely artificial creations of European imperialism.

hardly existent and where so, it is only in latent form. Rather, there is a visible 'Euro' identification, if the expression may be pardoned by virtue of the usefulness of the analogy. The roots of the 'Afro' and 'Euro' division are found in the ambivalent historical influences to which the West Indians have been subjected. These have mainly been African and European. The ambivalent historical, cultural, and psychological orientation of the West Indian has over recent years been increasingly aggravated by a variety of factors; chief among these are quite rigid socio-economic class delineations within the countries of the West Indies, 'colour' problems within these countries, and race problems outside, as well as the post-independence search for national identities.

In most West Indian countries, the class structure from bottom to top corresponds with an increasing lightness in shade, complexion, or 'colour', with the lower (working) class and the middle class being 'dark', while the upper-middle class and the tiny upper class are 'light'. The inference has been not only that if you are 'white'[1] you are at the top but that if you are at the top you are white. This thus engages the lower- or middle-class man who may be black with the possibility of 'becoming white' by moving up in the social scale. If he succeeds, it is only too likely that he will effectively repress the 'Afro' inclinations of his dual personality in favour of the European identifications of the upper echelons. If he fails, then the contrary impulse might be expressed on account of the rigidity of the class systems and the virtual non-acceptance and non-identification of the upper-middle and upper classes with the rest of the population. The tendency of these classes to separate themselves from or reject the lower class leads to a kind of social schizophrenia whereby the rejected lower classes are forced towards an identification based on colour and conjuring up 'Afro' sentiments, while the upper classes, who perceive themselves white and who refuse to identify with the lower classes, follow a neo-colonial European orientation. The issue is complicated by the problem of a national identity and national unity. This problem tends to unshroud the fundamental division and to force an issue, namely, 'Are we "Euro" or "Afro" or both, and is being both undesirable?' The question is still in the

---

[1] Used to mean any of a number of non-black complexions, including brown-skin, red-skin, 'red-ibbo', 'dundus', off-white.

process of finding a suitable answer. Yet the putting of the question merely accelerates alignment, while the 'Afro' disposition daily receives more sophistication and legitimacy from the intellectuals who have found 'consciousness' and from the politicians who want votes and, perhaps, unity. By the same token, the predicament of the 'white', 'Euro-oriented' West Indian becomes more unbearable. Most of the West Indians who have emigrated to Britain come from the lower or lower-middle classes in the West Indian countries. In the majority of cases, they are industrious people who hoped to take good advantage of the economic opportunities presented here and denied them in their home country. But in their attempt to exploit the opportunities here for increased income, their psychological motivation remained attuned to the situation in the West Indies. Thus they saw in emigrating to the United Kingdom the opportunity for not only increased income but also increased status in the West Indies sense of 'becoming white'. This has often been misinterpreted as an over-anxiety to assimilate in Britain. Actually, the focus and the standards—the reference group—remain within the West Indies, and the immigrant is not so much trying to become a bowler-hatted Englishman, but symbolically an upper-middle class West Indian domiciled in Britain, able to return 'home' for sunny vacations at Christmas.

The problem arises when the immigrant is confronted with the racial situation here. Perhaps the most significant feature of the colour problem in Britain, in terms of impact on the West Indian, is that it completely denies his assumption of 'colour transformation' carried from the West Indies. In the words of one of the leaders interviewed: 'If you are Black that's it, you can never be white—all the Jaguars notwithstanding.' There are commonly two simple reactions to this dramatic confrontation: (i) further rationalization that one is not trying to be 'white', while at the same time cementing the conviction that one can be; or to put it another way, acknowledging the fact that one is black-skinned but not really 'Black'; or (ii) complete acceptance of the fact that one is Black and being proud of it, which in effect requires reversing all the introjected notions of 'white superiority'. While many West Indians in Britain vacillate between the two options, many have pronounced in favour of continuing 'Euro' orientation, while others have become 'Afro'. The implications of this forced identification are profound in terms of the strategy of combating discrimination.

The conservative-moderate side of the spectrum of leadership accepts in varying degrees the 'Euro' orientation: the radical-militant is committed to the 'Afro'. Both would like to see a society free of prejudice in which the Black man has full equality with the white man, in terms of opportunities and freedoms, rights and duties. But they have different approaches which lead to somewhat differing ends.

The radical-militant embarks on a safari for Blackness. In his hunt he recognizes that he must shed whatever 'whiteness' is stamped on his personality. The search for Blackness, although basically an all-consuming attempt to find an identity, represents for many a search for Utopia; it is as well a very sophisticated line of ego-defence and protection. Notwithstanding his preoccupation with Blackness, the radical-militant does not believe that true Black men cannot live side by side with white men. According to his dialectic, however, before an equal society of men can be attained, it is necessary that men feel equal to one another. This requires the removal of false assumptions of inferiority and superiority among both Blacks and whites. The development of Blackness is supposed to achieve this by giving the Black man the security of a true identity and by denouncing 'white superiority'. Blackness involves total rejection of 'white civilization'—not white men, but white men's concepts, institutions, organizations, morals, the lot—which is seen to have made the world an uninhabitable place for all men—although, confessedly, Black men in particular. 'White civilization' must be replaced by a more 'humane' order allowing full scope for free individual development of the personality and placing greatest emphasis on the individual as a person, on equality, and on liberty. Ultimately, the liberated Black man would not only have accepted that he is Black and have come to recognize his equality with the white man, but, above all, he would have made his white 'brother' love him as a man, through having forced him to see him as a Black man and not as an inferior man. Accordingly, the radical-militant ultimately believes in a multi-racial society. What he rejects is a multi-racial personality which nourishes Black inferiority feelings and presumptuous white overlordship.

The conservative-moderate also recognizes the necessity of

divesting himself of his inferiority feelings *vis-à-vis* the white man. But the conservative-moderate would accomplish this by proving himself within the framework of the introjected norms of the existing system. Rather than discard the 'Euro' values with which he has grown, in favour of a completely 'Afro' orientation, he believes that by fully displaying them he will eventually be accepted by the white man as an equal. Since the British way of life—in language, law, morality, politico-economic and social forms—is substantially the same as that in the West Indies, the conservative-moderate feels that in being West Indian he is in fact being basically British with just a little difference, which he is publicly prepared to play down in the hope that his prior familiarity with British forms will win his acceptance by the British. Accordingly, while the radical-militant is at great pains to demonstrate that he is Black and equal—by not cutting hair on head or chin, by wearing woollen ski caps and, perhaps, multi-coloured long-flowing garments which he associates with Africa, as well as by speaking in an affected American accent—the conservative-moderate who is equally concerned with the image of the Black man as equal to the white, engages himself in being 'respectable', 'decent', and in 'setting a good example'—all in the sense of the 'Euro' system. Small wonder the one is apt to see the other as 'stooge', 'colonial', and 'Uncle Tom', while the other sees him as 'fanatic', 'extremist', 'rabble-rouser', and 'anarchist', who is 'letting down the side'. Where one would purge the existing system of its prejudice, the other sees it so filled with prejudice against the Black man that the system has to go. Thus the salient difference between the radical-militant and the conservative-moderate is that while the former would do away with the existing system in favour of a new one, the latter accepts the system while seeking to eliminate its most offensive racist features. On the subject of change, total or in part, both sides express a preference for peaceful means, while demonstrating an increasing pessimism about the utility of such methods and the possibility of completely ruling out violence. Neither, however, in 1968, professed any intent to resort to violence unless in return for violence. Yet the difference in perception of the system leads to a further divergence here: for while the conservative-moderate tends to view violence in the restricted sense of a direct physical aggression against the Black man, the radical-militant is prone to perceive 'an inherent violence' in the system in so far as it is prejudiced against the Black man.

(e) LEGISLATION

Two main attitudes were revealed concerning legislation against discrimination. In general these were:

(i) Legislation itself, while necessary and desirable as a framework of legitimacy for the development of interracial harmony, is but a means of curing discrimination; it should never be regarded as an end in itself.

(ii) Legislation drawn up without the direct participation of those discriminated against, is useless, if not detrimental to the course of integration. This attitude was less commonly held by the leaders.

As far as the experience of anti-discriminatory legislation in Britain was concerned, namely, the Race Relations Act of 1965, the consensus was that this piece of legislation was worth-while mainly to the extent that legislation *per se* is at all useful.

An elucidation of the first attitude maintained that:

What the law does is to rally all the forces into [coloured peoples'] hands. The law creates and is itself the norm. Consequently the racists of the society are placed outside the law, which therefore tends to weaken their support and legitimacy. On the other hand, the law strengthens those working for the cause but who are weak. The law also gives voluntary bodies an objective to work towards—all they have to do is to make the law effective.

Another person put it this way: 'I regard legislation as a sort of framework in which society can operate. This is the benefit of legislation—in other words, it is the leadership given by Government to public opinion for change.'

Subscribers to this view generally agreed that efforts towards combating discrimination were unlikely to succeed without the explicit support of the law in the background. It was, however, appreciated that having the law behind even the best efforts was by no means a guarantee of their success. An argument generally made is that the existing legislation has at least one good point, deriving from its mere existence: it testifies to a racial 'problem'. Until the passage of legislation, the British had gone far towards convincing themselves that there was no 'racial problem'.

The second attitude carefully distinguishes between physical and psychological freedom, seeing both as indispensable for overcoming discrimination. The significant feature of racial conflict is considered to be the historical presumption of superiority by whites and an introjected feeling of inferiority among Blacks. Both feed on the other. Thus, the elimination of racialism primarily involves removing the false psychological positions based on pigmentation. The first step must be to get the Black to shed his inferiority feelings *vis-à-vis* the white. Legislation framed without the direct participation of those discriminated against, it is feared, tends to overlook the psychological question. This is regarded as having been borne out historically. Such legislation might simply offer nominal physical freedom while in fact seeking to perpetuate a situation of psychological slavery to a system built on the very premises which must be destroyed, and an inherently racialist system. The corollary, therefore, is that legislation is secondary to the imperative of total destruction of the existing social, economic, and political system and its replacement by a new system affording direct participation of the subjects of discrimination in the legislative processes. Accordingly:

To recognize the legal system one must play an active part in framing it. If one goes into history and examines what happened post-emancipation [of slaves], one will find that the slaves were not freed at all. In fact, slavery was perfected, and though the slaves were physically free in the sense that their chains had been removed, they remained in mental slavery perfected by a bunch of economists. As the system stands now it is impossible to construct any successful way of getting to change the legal system—proof is the Race Relations Bill and 'Asian legislation'. One is therefore forced to move into a stage of fighting for one's freedom—as freedom is something you just can't hand to a man and say 'you are free'—so the system must be destroyed, and it is an absolute necessity that it must. The destruction of the system then is the prerequisite to any form of meaningful change.

It is, of course, quite clear that while the first attitude relates to legislation *per se*; the second refers to a particular type of legislation, qualified with respect to its formulation, namely, legislation arrived at without the direct participation of those discriminated against. This difference, together with the criticisms levelled at the effectiveness of existing legislation by those subscribing to the first attitude, considerably narrows the apparent divergence

8

between the two attitudes. This is supported by the general view that the existing legislation is racist and acts against the Black man. From a broad familiarity with the terms of the Race Relations Act of 1965, as well as its practical operation, and bearing in mind, as one person put it, that 'legislation can mean one hundred and one things including ineffectual legislation', the following are the specific criticisms most frequently voiced:

Scope of the legislation

(i) Housing, employment, advertising, insurance, the vital areas of discrimination, are not covered: instead the legislation only extends to a few places of 'public resort', etc., which are hardly affected by the racial problems.

(ii) The failure of the legislation to cover the Crown, Ministers of Government, and the police.

(iii) The inclusion of the clause 'incitement to racial hatred' without any explicit definition accompanying it.

This is seen as a 'whip' to be used against the back of the Black man. Its application and non-application in cases brought before the courts have justified the very worst suspicions that this clause was meant to be applied mainly to the Black man and, perhaps, a single 'Nazi' to whom the Establishment long wanted to teach a lesson, as his views were no doubt as much a threat to the Establishment as to Blacks. The clause's conspiracy against the Black man is seen more in relation to its non-implementation against white extremist racists who are part and parcel of the Establishment and direct their hostilities solely at the coloured population of the United Kingdom.

(iv) The limited scope of the legislation (see *(i)* above) is interpreted as condoning by implication discrimination in areas not included. For this reason, the legislation is further considered racist.

Machinery

(i) The impotence of the Race Relations Board, with respect to subpoena of witnesses, enforcement of decisions, and inspection of documents of various kinds.

'Just being able to conciliate is not enough. It must be able to go beyond this, when and if their "conciliation" does not work, to actual enforcement—commanding the party to act in the right way.'

(ii) The 'undemocratic' and 'unrepresentative' nature of appointment and constitution of the Race Relations Board.

There should be some provision for the election of its officers by the immigrant organizations, as without that there is no guarantee that the Black members of the Board might not simply be puppets and stooges of the Establishment.

Redress

(i) There ought to be greater damages for humiliation and degradation suffered by people who are discriminated against.

(ii) The fundamental right of the individual to seek redress before the courts is contravened by the stipulation that the victim of alleged discrimination cannot do so once the Race Relations Board has turned down his petition.

Attitudes towards legislation have been influenced by the Commonwealth Immigrants Act 1968 (Kenya Asian legislation) and its predecessor of 1962. While the first was seen as being principally directed against the 'coloured Commonwealth', the 1968 Act is unanimously regarded as 'blatant racism' indicating a tendency towards more explicit racist legislation and policies by the Government. The invariable response of 'See, I knew it all along', is accompanied by most pessimistic prognostications. Some of these related to the 1968 Race Relations Bill which, on enactment, was expected to be even more disadvantageous to the Black man than its fore-runner. With reference to the proposed 'balance and quota' clause which is widely disliked, one person summed up the matter thus: 'When an Act says "a racial balance should be permissible" or where it requires that a pattern of discrimination has to be established, one can only see the tendency towards increasingly more explicit racialism in the legislation.' The view has been expressed that more attention might be given to the lessons of the American legislative experience in connection with its racial problem. Stated simply these are: legislate before it is too late; token legislation is not good enough; and once you have legislation you must have adequate enforcement machinery. 'The American experience shows that good law enacted early can work. But it also shows that it is possible to legislate too little and too late.' In the context of their legislation, the British Labour Government were viewed, at best, as having been forced into an increasingly compromising position by the pressure of the Opposition and the majority of the public who are overtly racists; and, at worst, as being racist themselves. One complaint against the Government related to their failure to sponsor an aggressive campaign to whip up public support for the so-called anti-discriminatory legislation:

. . . the measures are not being *sold* to the public. If they had been sold in a similar rush campaign to that accompanying the 'Asian legislation', then they would have won much more acceptance from the public. Above all, the [forthcoming] Race Relations Act should have been brought out at the very same time as the 'Asian Act'. Callaghan should have said, 'We can't have the economy overrun by the Blacks, etc., etc., hence we have put through this forbidding ['Asian'] legislation. But it is necessary for us at the same time to insist on this [new] Race Relations Act in order to ensure against discrimination encouraged by any misinterpretation of our motives.'

In the circumstances, the common view was that in putting forward a new Race Relations Bill the Government were doing little more than saving face and engaging in ritual hand-washing. There was little confidence that the Government could be relied upon to put forward the type of legislation most needed by the immigrant community—particularly in relation to housing, employment, and insurance. The moderate hope and optimism initially held out in anticipation of the Labour Government's policies on racial discrimination were felt to have been completely frustrated in the light of the actual body of legislation passed, which, 'apart from clearing the conscience of the Establishment, has no earthly use'. There was thought to be no justification at all for continuing to look to the Government or to their timid legislative measures for assistance in the solution of the racial problems.

(f) OTHER MEASURES
This question concerning the utility of voluntary non-Governmental measures in combating discrimination—such as the individual employer's efforts to increase the ratio of coloured people working for his business—provoked the most divergent responses. For a very few people, such measures were considered very important:

If you hope to attain an integrated society, coloured people have to be presented for contact at all levels of the society. Hence the need for *positive discrimination*. Positive discrimination means *deliberately* finding Black people and placing them in certain positions. But there is no need for rushing into publicity, as when a Black man becomes a policeman; it is simply that the process must be deliberately done.

Others might call this 'tokenism' or 'show-case' integration and consider it both unbecoming and undesirable:

It depends what putting the clerk in the front counter means. It is tokenism or, perhaps, a hypocritical maintenance of the 'racial balance', so that when you have enough clerks in the front of the store who are Black, then you are under no obligation to employ any more Blacks. Or does it mean that if a man has the qualifications he will get the job irrespective of colour?

One person felt not only that such measures are 'a good thing', but that at present the process 'is going as fast as it can go, on the basis of supply and demand'.

But the prevailing temper was one of suspicion:

The big danger is that the Black man is being associated with particular jobs—messengers, porters, sweepers, packers, etc. . . . Some of the firms are sincere in their efforts to facilitate Black employment, but they still can't avoid the very simple equation of identification of the coloured person with a particular type of job, and in any case they do not want to upset their staff and they will only be prepared to do so when the Black man begins to upset them.

Finally, there was the view that: 'these measures should be natural and not forced, and should not at all be publicized. The employer must give a *man* a *job* and not give a *coloured* man a *break*.'

(g) ROLE

The idea of a multi-racial society is, quite understandably, generally conceded to be desirable. All further agreed that the form of integration within the multi-racial society should not be assimilation towards the creation of a 'stereotype Englishman', Black or white, but should be akin to 'a grapefruit with various segments, and with acceptance of different customs being an important feature of the multi-racial society'. Nevertheless, discussion of multi-racial society was thought to be premature and there was full agreement that both an increasing and more overt display of racial prejudice by the white British population has now placed the realization of the ideal well beyond sight. It did emerge from the discussion, however, that there were differing responses and conceptions of role in relation to the dismal picture with which the leaders saw themselves confronted. All recognized the need for more 'militant' organization among the West Indians, in the sense of a firmer stand against racial intolerance and abuse. While, however, the conservative-moderates were inclined to interpret 'militancy' and 'firmness' in the context of non-violence, this tendency was less apparent among the radical-militants whose conception of role was more clear-cut and may be useful as a gauge in estimating the probable increase in militancy. While conservative-moderate leaders generally viewed their role as one of aiding in the solution of a problem affecting West Indians in Britain, and, more often, even on a smaller local scale—in the county, city, or borough—the radical-militant invariably presented himself as servant and instrument of the most important international cause. The following is an illustration of the latter's attitude in relation to 'militancy' and role:

Since the system is based on violence, it can only be violence that can destroy the system, as the only return to violence is violence. We are freedom fighters. We are only going to use violence in return for violence used against us. Black people are not searching for physical and visual independence; what we want is Black Nationalism and economic independence. The movement for the liberation of the Black man is world-wide and, therefore, our approach is international. It so happens that we have a greater part of the struggle in England and in the United States in so far as they represent the head of the heart of the Octopus. While our Brothers are banging away at the tentacles, we have to cope with the head and the heart, the only places that can be damaged enough to kill it.

The conservative-moderate leaders were always restrained and hesitant in defining any future *modus operandi*. Perhaps one can attribute this to a temporary confusion in face of a rapidly deteriorating situation. The confusion manifests itself in the form of a conflict between a basic dislike of violent action and the recognition that it may be necessary to employ such action. As one leader rather ruefully put it: 'It may be that counter-violence is the answer, and certainly this seems to be the developing trend.' According to another conservative-moderate:

The whole discussion of militancy and violence is an abstraction, because when large masses of people decide to be militant it is not because they desire militancy for militancy's sake, but because they believe that this is the only way to achieve what they want. Here we are in a situation, and if people say we are going to lose our freedom we say 'No!' If they want to call that militancy, then they may do so.

Also influencing the attitude of the conservative-moderate is a fundamentally pragmatic predisposition to, and confidence in, an *ad hoc* approach. Here the observations of another conservative-moderate are very appropriate:

The U.S. situation has acted as a source of ideas to West Indians in Britain as to what is and what is not practicable. Up to 1967 . . . people thought that integration was a practical reality. Since then they have lost faith that society here would naturally give way to integration. The West Indians here feel that they gave their hand, but that the clasp was refused and so they have to withdraw it. There is a radical political sensibility among West Indian leaders, even though they work within welfare organizations, etc. But it is a sensibility which does not necessarily accept what extremists predicate as a programme. It is much more of a pragmatic approach generally, and they will more or less find their way rather than jump to extremist doctrines.

The decisive, explicit point of agreement among the conservative-moderates is that the time has come for unity and maximum self-help by West Indians.

(h) SELF-HELP
Self-help is seen as a new stage. Until recently, it has been pointed out, West Indians had not only 'held out their hand', but had sought to tackle the racial problem primarily on the basis of a joint-approach with 'white liberal helpers' of the host community. The worsening racial situation in society at large, and the frictions between 'white liberals' and West Indians within West Indian organizations, are taken as adequate testimony of the failure of this approach. The implication, however, is not that 'white liberal' help will be rejected or that there is no room for such help, but that it will be accepted only on West Indian terms. It is interesting that the radical-militant, for all his concern with Blackness, is in fundamental agreement with this and himself does not simply rule out 'white' help. Both the radical-militant and the conservative-moderate are nevertheless increasingly suspicious about 'white

liberals' and fear possible internal subversion of their organizations. Above all, experience is felt to have taught both that only the Black man really knows his troubles and he alone can really solve them. There is no divergence on that score. What follows is a radical-militant's analogy of 'white liberal' help, and his conclusions:

If I am sitting on a stove that is throwing out 500° C., the white liberal will say: 'It's O.K., you can sit on the stove and I will turn it down to 250° C.'—while what I want is that he turn the whole damn thing off completely. So the only function the white liberal has got as far as we are concerned, is that if he is so damn willing to help that he helps on our terms which are quite simple: namely, you do what we tell you to do when we tell you to do it—none of these half-measures buying time for the system, for we don't have that kind of time.

A conservative-moderate said much the same thing in his own way:

Let's be realistic. Racial discrimination is a disease of *white* society. In the final analysis it is the *white* society that has to rid itself of it, therefore, in that way *white* people can play a major part. The trouble is that white liberals only see themselves in the leadership roles, and in paternalistically and patronizingly helping the Black man. Accordingly, co-operation is 'unequal' and must be unsatisfactory to the Black man. . . . What is required is sufficient understanding by both sides of what each can do, and [white liberals] must stop thinking that they can make a contribution for you.

According to another conservative-moderate:

What I see as a drawback is not the presence of white liberals—there is a place for white liberals—but what was a drawback is that the white liberals tried to dominate. That was the source of the crisis. The Black man's struggle must be fought and *led* by the Black man. He must evolve his own philosophy and cannot take other people's theories. What we want for example is a Black Marx or a Black Chairman Mao. The role of the white liberal is a supportive one.

Thus, for both sides of the leadership spectrum, the parting of the ways has been reached and passed. The prevailing attitude is 'you watch your problems while I take care of my own'.

The concept of self-help is all-embracing. But the most emphasized areas are political and economic organization. It was fully agreed that it is imperative that West Indians organize themselves under a few good leaders for meeting the difficulties ahead. No spelling out of the type of organization was given, but there was recognition of the need to overcome apathy and disunity among West Indians, as well as their purely national orientations. Similarly, in the economic sphere, there was much talk of the need for finding a firm foothold in the economic structure— particularly in such areas as financing loans and mortgages, insurance, and marketing—but there was a conspicuous absence of definite planning. There was only one case of a leader whose organization had made any significant start in this direction. He gave full expression to his view that:

As far as I am concerned these lads [the other leaders]—the lot, without exception—are wasting a lot of time. I feel very strongly that it is only through economic parity with the host community that we can really demand respect and that the host community can really see us as we are. They must stop believing that we are here to prey on them. We have helped the situation 80 per cent in Britain.

It is interesting to find that this leader, along with a few others, refers to the desirability of West Indians emulating the approach of the Jewish community in Britain and aspiring, as a group, towards similar economic status. This is understandable in the light of the fact that the countries of the West Indies are relatively free from any significant or obtruding degree of anti-Semitism; added to this is the fact that while there are some indications of an undercurrent of controversy as to whether economic or political independence is the prerequisite of full independence of the Black man, none would dispute the immense importance of group economic independence. Whatever the case, the Jewish community is a forceful example.

The Jews, for instance, because of their economic status in the society have a lot of control. It would hurt the country as a whole if the Jews were to withdraw their financial backing, and, therefore, the Jews can't be touched. This should prove to us how powerful it is when one is in a really powerful position. The Jewish community has to be consulted before Parliament can pass laws. That, in due course, will be the case with us if we move towards economic independence.

But self-help extends well beyond the economic and the political to a spiritual-educational revival: the need to help the West Indian to see himself in relation to fellow West Indians and

8*

to the rest of British society. Once he has developed a proper group identification, he will be in a proper position to place his resources at the service of the group in a collective endeavour. Yet this sentiment rings the old familiar note of identity fulfilment; and in a changing situation—with West Indians in Britain losing direct contact with the West Indies and having British children for whom the West Indies is at once unfamiliar and irrelevant to their immediate needs—there remains one constant factor: white against Black in Britain and, some would say, in the world. In such circumstances, could not colour become the most prevalent, if not the sole, form of identification for the next generation of leaders? If so, is not, perhaps, theoretical distinction between conservative-moderate and radical-militant leaders of today— necessary though it may be for critique—a vanishing posture?

(i) CONCLUSION

The interviews with the West Indian immigrant leaders leave no doubt about their conviction that the racial situation in Britain is rapidly deteriorating as much in degree and kind as in the expression of racial prejudice. Equally clear is their impression that legislative measures have been quite inadequate for dealing with racial discrimination and for reducing the socio-economic disadvantages of the coloured minorities in Britain. With Government suspect, law and justice uncertain, the police persecutory, and white society becoming overtly and uncompromisingly prejudiced, the leaders see themselves as having to rely almost exclusively on self-help in the ever-widening racial rift. Their forecast is grim.

Outside of self-help, thoughts for improving the situation bear primarily upon changing the attitudes of the white community, which are seen to be shrouded in an unfathomable ignorance concerning the relative humanity and equality of the Blacks and whites of mankind. The leaders often stressed the fact that racial prejudice, while alien to the behaviour of the Black man, is the engrained historical attitude of the white. The fundamental ingredient of any improvement in race relations is generally held to be a large-scale, profound re-education of white people—a re-education freed from the prejudice, myth, and narrowness of the existing system which is posited on the superiority of white people and their civilizations, which seldom glances

beyond European national horizons—and does so only to perpetuate the self-satisfying fiction of the white man's burden. It is
cautioned that while realistic anti-discriminatory legislation can
provide the framework for mass re-education, legislation itself
is no substitute for that indispensable task. Consistently enough,
it is assumed that with legislators and educators themselves
submerged in the mire of historical ignorance and prejudice, useful
developments in both fields will long be awaited, and re-education
will have to be largely experiential, proceeding mainly through
interracial contact at all social levels. In the meantime, the
necessity for effective self-help commands the Black man to
organize.

2. *Asian Leaders*
by Jyothi Kamath

One of the characteristic ways in which Indian and Pakistani
immigrants express their views is through their leaders in the
community. The object of this survey was to investigate the views
and attitudes of 25 leaders of the Indian and Pakistani communities in England, regarding racial discrimination and the effectiveness of measures taken against discrimination in this country.

(a) THE LEADERS
(i) *Basis of leadership*
A total of twenty-five Indian and Pakistani leaders were interviewed. The sample for interview was chosen from two areas, one
in London and one a Midlands town. The purpose in concentrating on these two areas was to get a contrasting picture of the
problem and to compare the viewpoints of people living under
somewhat different social conditions. The sample was established
by listing persons recognized by the local communities as being
prominent in the religious, cultural, and political fields. Whom do
we then call a leader? Collins,[1] for example, has defined two kinds
of immigrant leadership: the 'model' and the 'institutional'. As
will be seen, nearly all the 'leaders' here interviewed were
'institutional', with their leadership based on a recognized
position of importance within a community organization. For
various reasons, model leadership was not apparently relevant.

[1] S. Collins, *Coloured Minorities in Britain: Studies in British Race Relations based on
African, West Indian and Asiatic Immigrants* (London, Lutterworth, 1957).

TABLE 8:2

ASIAN LEADERS*

Age	Country/region of origin	Years in United Kingdom	Occupation
thirties	Punjab state, India	5	Teacher
38	Punjab state, India	4½	Factory worker
mid-thirties	Punjab state, India	6	Factory worker
early forties	Punjab state, India	8	Medical practitioner
35	Punjab state, India	2	Factory worker
33	Punjab state, India	6½	Factory worker
36	Punjab state, India	7½	Assistant N.C.C.I. Liaison Officer
29	Uganda	12	Business consultant
42	Punjab state, India	6½	Aircraft electronic engineer
48	Pakistan	10	With B.O.A.C.
forties	India	11	Bus conductor (and aspiring journalist)
37	Pakistan	10	Grocery shopkeeper
36	Punjab state, India	7	Insurance agent
38	Punjab state, India	3½	Teacher
late fifties	South India	8	Journalist
forties	Pakistan	11	Restaurant owner
33	Pakistan	10	Semi-skilled worker
mid-forties	Punjab state, India	2	Landlord of Punjabis
50	Pakistan	4	Education Welfare Officer
35	Punjab state, India	11	Press operator
28	Punjab state, India	4½	Civil servant

* Data not available for four leaders. With one exception, all interviewed were male.

According to Indian and Pakistani conceptions, a leader is a person who works for the welfare of the people without any self-interest, and who is capable of influencing the attitude and action of at least a part of the community. This is, of course, an ideal concept. Very few community leaders in this country work without any self-interest and have a stronghold over what their community thinks and does. Yet in so far as they are accepted as leaders by their own respective groups, they fulfil the general function of leadership and qualify as spokesmen. Leadership, in this sense, has been attributed on the basis of either religious, socio-cultural, or political status. In this survey, 17 per cent of people were found to be religious leaders, mainly Sikhs. A General Secretary of a Sikh 'Gurudwara' (temple) was interviewed; he holds command in his community because of his religious activities. The Sikh Church owns the temple building (allegedly worth £26,000) and has a following of 500 members. Of course, the religious activity also has strong social connotations. This Church provides free food and accommodation for people who need them. This type of socio-religious feeling is very deep among Indians and Pakistanis. Many Hindu leaders also undertake social activities for their own community people.

Another basis of leadership is political activity. Of the total number of people interviewed, 25 per cent fall under this category. Some of them participate directly in local political activities. For example, in the London area, there is an Indian councillor who commands great respect from his community. The other leaders who do not themselves directly engage in political activities, run associations like workers' unions which deal with the political problems concerning the immigrants. The Indian Workers' Association (which, incidentally, also helps Pakistanis) has a large following. They own the building where their offices are situated and a cinema. They help their members to achieve fair wages and better working conditions. The union has a very strong hold in the local area.

The third type of leadership is cultural in character. Some communities run arts and literature societies whose main aim is to keep Indian art and culture, and their concomitant values, alive. Of the total number of leaders interviewed, 37 per cent were found to be socio-cultural leaders.

The level of formal education, in conjunction with the above-mentioned qualification, is an additional factor helping one to emerge as a leader. Initially, such a person advises people on the problems of acquiring mortgage facilities, renewing their passports, or applying for jobs. In the process, he acquires peoples' faith and eventually emerges as a leader. This is the type of leadership which cannot strictly be classified as cultural, political, or religious. It is social in character but associated with one's level of formal education and ability to speak and write good English.

The types of leadership defined above are not necessarily restricted to only one kind of activity. Most of the leaders, though mainly engaged in one type of activity, take some interest in most other activities as well. Almost all the organizations, whether religious or cultural, participate in some political activities relating to immigrants. A leader in the areas can be found helping people with their passport and employment problems, conducting cultural programmes, and trying to create centres for all types of social and religious activities. Leadership is, therefore, of a mixed nature, rather than strictly social, cultural, or religious. Thus, in most cases, the leadership is more of a comprehensive type, though initially it usually originates from one of the bases described.

Leadership springing from economic prosperity was not found to be common among the communities. This is because most of the people living in Britain enjoy a similar economic status. The people in the lowest income group are also economically independent and enjoy a 'reasonable' standard of living. Mere economic prosperity, therefore, does not qualify a person to be a leader. Economic prosperity together with other qualities may help initially, but leadership is only maintained in so far as there is an understanding and concern for the common problems of the immigrant community.

Similarly, there was not enough evidence to suggest that leadership emerged among the people belonging to superior caste. Surprisingly, very few people were found to be conscious of their own caste. This is not because most of them had progressive ideas; it is probably because in the new social situation they were all classified as 'immigrants' irrespective of their caste or creed. This new social classification has, therefore, temporarily helped them to forget their inner social differences.

(ii) Homeland Background of Leaders

The backgrounds of the leaders varied widely. They all came from different areas and followed different careers. Except for Mr. S., who worked for a trade union, and Mr. G., who had strong political views, most of them had a passive social and political life and almost all of them said that they had come to Britain mainly for their own economic betterment. In general, they were ordinary workers and would not have regarded themselves, or have been regarded, as leaders in the areas from which they had come. The real community leaders in their homelands do not usually emigrate to other countries as they feel that their presence is important in their own countries. The leaders interviewed agreed that only those Asians who had no special social or economic status to cling to, and who were enterprising, came to this country. Leadership in this country, therefore, has little relevance to social status in the home country. It is by and large the product of their natural abilities and responses to circumstances in Britain.

Among the Asian community in Britain, there were those who sought to identify themselves with the host community and, also, to retain their cultural and social heritage, starting social, cultural, or religious activities; and these people eventually emerged as leaders. Political leadership is comparatively of more recent origin. The Commonwealth Immigrants Act of 1968, refusing entry to Kenya Asians holding British passports, and other developments increasing the tension between the host and immigrant communities aroused the spirit of some of the immigrants to take action against the deteriorating race relations situation. Political leadership was thus the direct result of the recent political situation concerning the immigrant community in this country. Thus, some of the Asian leaders fought local elections to attain a seat on the local councils.

(c) THE ATTITUDES OF THE LEADERS

This survey of the values and attitudes of 25 Indian and Pakistani leaders was carried out through personal interviews. They were asked to express their views on a number of questions.[1] The summary of the findings is given below:

(i) *Racial Discrimination*

Most of those interviewed expressed very strong feelings against the racial discrimination in this country. Acknowledging the existence of racial discrimination, Mr. C. said: 'there is a total awareness among the immigrant communities about it'. Some of those who had been in this country for a long time said they could clearly see a change taking place for the worse. The problem, they thought, was of recent origin. According to them, discrimination exists in almost all fields of life.

The respondents claimed that discrimination operated in employment and that there were certain areas in which coloured immigrants could not find jobs easily. When they did find jobs, they were restricted to certain departments only. They were often discriminated against in cases of promotion. The situation was even worse for well-qualified people. It was very seldom that they got jobs according to their qualifications. The employers always

[1] See Appendix 3 for interview schedule.

found an excuse to turn down the application of a coloured immigrant (on the grounds that the immigrant applicant did not have either a recognized British degree, or local experience). Even if one had acquired a British degree, one was asked if one had local experience. Mr. B. said: 'I would like to secure a good position according to my qualifications, but I cannot get it. Although I am educated, my children will think I am an ordinary factory worker.'

In the field of housing and mortgages, the immigrants' house hunt did not end until they had found a coloured landlord. It was a dream for a coloured man to get a council flat. If an immigrant wanted to buy a house, the mortgage conditions were undoubtedly stricter for him than for white people. It was mentioned in the Midlands town that coloured people had to pay deposits of 50–70 per cent of purchase price, against the 10 per cent requirements for white people.

It was claimed that the policemen were unnecessarily rude to coloured people. Mr. L. related an incident where an Indian got involved in a hot discussion with an Englishman in a restaurant. The argument got so heated that the police were called. As soon as the policeman appeared on the scene, his first sentence to the Indian was: 'Why don't you go back to your country?'

The same theme reappears in descriptions of hospitals. Mr. S. quoted a relevant incident. In the Midlands town, a coloured patient refused to go to the hospital in spite of his critical ill health. The reason, as found out later, was that he was treated very badly by the staff on an earlier occasion. He was bitterly abused for 'bringing germs to this country and spreading them among the local population'. The husband of a patient (Mr. S. continued) went to the doctor to collect the report of his wife's health. The doctor told him: 'She is an idiot. She cannot speak a single word of English. Even the dogs are better than her.'

Even the school children claimed that they felt segregated. White children often insulted them by asking them to go back to their countries. In certain towns like this Midlands town, there were still some public places where Indians or Pakistanis were not allowed. They were treated as second-class citizens and looked down upon socially.

The respondents thought that this type of racial attitude appeared to be prevalent mainly among people in the low-income group. Most of the coloured immigrants were themselves illiterate and looked for lower-type jobs, for which they directly competed with the local working class, which, consequently, directed feelings of hatred towards the coloured immigrant. After his well-publicized speech, Mr. Enoch Powell received his most widespread support from the local labouring-class people.

There were three respondents whose views on this point were different from others. Mr. B. thought there was no racial discrimination in this country. His views were limited to his own experiences. According to him, those who were able and efficient found no difficulty in getting jobs, mortgages, or other facilities. 'English people have no dislike for colour. What they probably do not like is certain bad habits of the coloured people.'

Mrs. A. said there was no problem for Christian Asians in this country. It was true, she continued, that racial discrimination existed for Indians, Pakistanis, and West Indians, but this was their own fault. Their living conditions were poor and their way of life was not civilized.

A third person replied that although racial discrimination no doubt existed in this country, it did not exist to the degree usually described. It was the fault of the immigrants in many instances that they expected too much too soon; they exaggerated the degree of discrimination.

(ii) Reasons for Prejudice

The interviewees were asked their opinions of the basis of the alleged racial attitudes. In their replies they claimed that there were different factors which had contributed to the development of racial prejudice.

Some of the respondents thought that these prejudices derived from the historical British sense of superiority. Another reason given was inherent dislike of the hosts for coloured people themselves. The third and basic reason was the failure of Britain's economic policy. The Government had failed to sustain an increasing rate of economic growth, which resulted in inadequate employment opportunities, inadequate housing facilities, and an unsatisfactory rise in real income. The immigrants had, therefore, been made the scapegoats of economic frustrations. The British were also partly jealous of foreigners who came and enjoyed a better life in this country than they did in their home countries.

(iii) *Are Indians and Pakistanis Responsible?*

An argument put forward by many British people is that racial prejudice is due to the immigrants themselves. Their living conditions are poor; their way of life is uncivilized; they show hardly any manners; they tend to create immigrant ghettos; they are too rigid to give up their turbans and beards; they are not law-abiding and adopt illegal practices in order to enter this country. The interviewees were asked to express their views on these points. Their answers often refuted these points, denying the responsibility of immigrants for the prejudices levelled against them.

Mr. L. argued that a community's way of life depended on its cultural and traditional heritage. The Indian and Moslem cultures and traditional heritage are entirely different from the European or British cultures. The immigrant's way of life, therefore, had to be different. 'It is true that sometimes there is overcrowding in our houses. If my brother comes to England, naturally he will come to me, and I would want him to come and live with me. We are hospitable; we do not count shillings and pennies. That is our culture.'

It was also true, the respondents said, that some (but not all) immigrants' living conditions were very poor and unhygienic, but British people had prejudices against those immigrants with a better standard of living as well. Moreover, even English society has a similar poorer class, living in London's East End and other similar places.

Regarding turbans and beards, the leaders presented different arguments. Mr. B. said:

'Be Romans in Rome' is a phrase applicable only in the restricted sense. It should be applied only in the case of certain social etiquette and certainly not to one's culture and religion. If British people really believed in the principle of local convention, why did not every Englishman in India at the time of the British rule become Hindu and wear dhotis?

Mr. M. shouted: 'What is wrong with turbans and beards? If we could fight the war with turbans and beards, why cannot we efficiently drive a bus with a turban on?' Mr. B. argued on the rational ground: 'If we do not expect this much freedom in a democratic country like this, where else can we look for it?'

Mr. P. considered it to be too minor a problem to make such a big issue of. Mr. H. thought it was only a short-run problem as the next generation was not going to wear turbans and beards anyway.

(iv) *The Caste System*

Selected leaders were asked to compare the Indian caste system with racial discrimination in this country. They thought that such a comparison was irrelevant since no evil could be justified on the basis of another evil. Moreover, the caste system was a centuries-old institution which was dying out fast. It was now illegal in India to discriminate against a person on the basis of caste. Racial discrimination, on the contrary, was of recent origin and political in character. The recent Commonwealth Immigrants Act, and particularly the section restricting the entry of Kenyans with British passports, echoed the discrimination. It was an irony that such racialism should emerge in the very country which promoted the basic principles of democracy and fraternity.

They claimed there were no caste differences among the Indians and Pakistanis living in this country that could reasonably be equated with racial discrimination. The basis of the caste system, they claimed, was occupational classification. No such classification existed among the immigrant community[1] in Britain as most immigrants enjoyed an equal economic status.

Mr. G. summed up the comparison of the caste system and discrimination by saying: 'The point is that both are evils. If I cannot justify the caste system, that does not necessarily mean I have to accept racial discrimination. It is the duty of every individual to eradicate such evils from the society.'

(v) *Government Policy*

The leaders were asked to express their views on the British Government's policy on the question of racial discrimination. Most of them had a very poor opinion of the Government's policy. Some of them even doubted the honest intentions of the Government to eradicate racial discrimination in this country. Mr. L. said: 'If I don't want to see you, I am worse than a blind man. The Government is just like that; it does not want to see the

---

[1] The use of the term 'immigrant community' should usually be taken to refer only to the Asian 'community'—here the Indian and Pakistani communities. It does not include West Indians and others.

problem of racial discrimination.' Mr. E. said: 'the Government acts like a stepmother towards the coloured immigrant community. It gets an equal amount of tax from them and yet gives very little in return.'

Mr. H. argued that one could not trust the Government's intentions when, on the one hand, they presented the Race Relations Bill and, on the other, hurriedly passed the Commonwealth Immigrants Act of 1968 to stop the entrance of stateless Kenya Asians! In his words: the 'Commonwealth Immigrants Act stinks of racialism'. On the same matter, Mr. L. said: 'Mr. Callaghan as a finance minister first devalued the pound and then as Home Secretary devalued the British passports.' Kenya Asians were talented, civilized people, and had money of their own; yet they were refused entry because 'they were coloured, a bit more tanned'.

The Race Relations Bill received various types of comments. Some thought it was a good start but was certainly not the end. Mr. H. said: 'A law disciplines people's minds but does not change people's hearts.' According to Mr. F., the Government, by passing a Bill that did not cover the most important fields of employment, religion, and mortgages,[1] among others, were spreading hypocrisy. Contrary to these views, Mr. M. thought that the Race Relations Act was 'nonsense'. With this law, people would become more conscious of the coloured people in society. By passing such a Bill, the Government were making fun of all the coloured immigrants.

The Race Relations Board, according to most of the interviewees, had only a symbolic status. In fact, it had no investigatory powers to follow up any case. Most of them thought it must be given legal powers to enforce the Act properly.

The National Committee for Commonwealth Immigrants was virtually unknown to the interviewees. Those who knew of it, saw little hope in such a body; and a few of them, while appreciating the ideas that led to its creation, criticized its practical functioning. They thought that the National Committee did not achieve the real representation of the immigrant community, since the representatives were selected by Government officers and not elected by the community. Moreover, the Government officers appointed to the voluntary committees had neither

[1] This is a misconception since the 1968 Act covers employment and mortgages.

sympathy for the immigrants' problems nor knowledge of their cultural background. In the committees, the immigrant views were either suppressed or neglected. Mr. B. said: 'Such committees are useless as they do not directly come into contact with the local working class who have the highest degree of prejudices.'

What the Government should do, according to Mr. C., was to create equal opportunities for all the immigrants in society. Training centres must be run to educate the local working-class people. In his view, the Government should also run training centres for immigrants in order to facilitate the process of adjustment at work and in social life. In the beginning, the immigrants always remained under strain due to their new social surroundings. At this critical time, they should be given some sympathetic treatment before their ability was judged. With a little encouragement, they could, perhaps, bring out the best of their abilities.

Mr. P. strongly suggested the dispersion of the immigrant community. He thought that the real problem was that too many people were concentrated in a few towns. There were no racial prejudices in Devon or Cornwall, as there were not many immigrants there. If, therefore, the Government were to spread the immigrants all over the country, they would not be noticed much. Holland had a similar problem at the start, which they solved by dispersal: 'If Holland could do it, why not Britain?'

Mr. Q. had two suggestions to make. Firstly, the Government must give equal representation to the coloured community in Parliament. If there were a great many immigrants in the London urban area, they should have one coloured M.P., elected by themselves.

According to Mr. B., the solution lay in some sort of arrangement between the British Government and the countries concerned. The Government, he said, should fix the number of immigrants that could be absorbed in the economy in a year. The Governments of India and Pakistan should then allow only that number, and no more, to emigrate to Britain. Once they arrived, they should be given all the basic facilities and equal opportunities in all fields. In other words, immigration must be treated like an exportable commodity, transacted internationally.

All the interviewees, on the other hand, stressed that the immigrant community should make certain efforts to ease the tension. Mr. M. summarized the general view:

Indians and Pakistanis as a community can contribute a lot towards the solution of the problem. Firstly, they must participate in all kinds of local activities and thereby try to mix with the host community. Secondly, they must be dynamic in their approach, and should accept certain good points of English society. Thirdly, they must try and learn English, which is a most useful means to bring two communities closer.

The leaders thought they had a special role in this context: i.e. that of educating the immigrant community to improve their living conditions and change their orthodox outlook.

However, there was not enough awareness among the immigrant leaders of the need for a united effort among immigrants of every race. Mr. F. strongly recommended the united efforts not only of the Indians or Pakistanis, but of all the coloured immigrants; however, the rest of the interviewees were found to be indifferent in their attitudes to West Indians. They did not show any eagerness to join hands with West Indians in a common fight against racialism. Some thought the problems of West Indians were different and that they would be the losers if they joined forces. Some were not even convinced of any specific benefits in co-operating with West Indians. Some said West Indians would look after their own interests—why should they worry about them? Others said that the West Indians had a better position in this society as their way of life was similar to that of the English; they had a common language and religion—why, then, should Indians or Pakistanis worry about West Indians?

Not one of the Asian leaders interviewed suggested violent means of fighting against racialism in this country. Rather, they would try appeals to authority, increasing pressure, peacefully and democratically, until their demands were satisfied. Violence, they said, was never a proper answer to any problem. They, therefore, heavily condemned what they considered the underlying thinking of Black Power as another extreme and irrational concept. Mr. F. said: 'if racialism is bad, [Black] racialism is bad too . . . it is nothing but an absolute way to destruction'. Their own basic approach ought to be on non-violent lines. The future of the problem then depended, they thought, on what course of action the Government decided to follow. If the Government did not take quick and effective steps, racialism would spread rapidly throughout society. Then there would not be much hope for the immigrants. An Indian who had lived in this country for the last thirty years, said: 'I never considered myself as an immigrant in this country. But now the time has come when I feel like going home.'

(d) CONCLUSIONS

Except for a few educated leaders, the Indians and Pakistanis interviewed seemed to have an emotional approach towards the problems discussed, expressing complaints rather than analytical views. Very few could suggest any alternative measures to the Government actions. This was perhaps because these were for the most part people uneducated in the tradition of analytical reasoning applied to the problems of social affairs, their emphasis being on criticisms rather than constructive suggestions.

The immigrant in general, and the group leaders in particular, did not at this stage have a well-defined, consistent policy. Their different viewpoints had not been rationalized into any kind of united thinking. Leadership was dispersed among the leaders of individual groups who seemed to await some sort of central leadership. All these leaders (except for one or two exceptional persons) have a very small following. They conduct cultural or social activities on a community basis. The recent trend to the formation of community organizations—such as the Punjabi cultural association, Gujarati Sabha, or Maharashtra Mandal—catering for particular communities, takes people away from the spirit of unity and integration and reasserts the caste spirit in a different form.

Part III
The Prevention of Racial Discrimination

CHAPTER 9

British Anti-discrimination Legislation[1]

LOUIS KUSHNICK

1. *The Government and Race Issues*

The British Government have twice legislated against racial discrimination, in 1965 and in 1968. These Acts have been the most dramatic indications of Britain's new position as a multi-racial state. The path towards the acceptance of the implications of this new situation has not been smooth. There has been a marked reluctance on the part of many political leaders, as well as large portions of the population, to come to terms with the requirements imposed by this situation. These attitudes and expectations, as well as the political situation, have shaped the legislation, as they have shaped the nature of other Governmental actions designed to deal with the problems related to the influx of large numbers of coloured people.

The initial response of most public officials to the large-scale immigration, which began in the mid-1950s, was basically, as Sheila Patterson has described, *laissez-faire*. They assumed that whatever problems emerged from this entry would largely solve themselves and, therefore, that no special Government activity was needed. This approach continued until the early 1960s when it was partially eroded. It was replaced by a Conservative Party commitment to immigration control, culminating in the Commonwealth Immigrants Act of 1962. But this element of Governmental interference was not accompanied by any comparable commitment to positive Government action to deal with the social or racial problems associated with immigration. There has been more emphasis in recent years—mainly from the Labour Party, but also from some Conservatives—on more positive Governmental

---

[1] This chapter is based on research made possible by grants from the Nuffield Small Grants Scheme for the Social Sciences and from the University of Manchester. The author wishes to thank them and all those who allowed themselves to be interviewed and consulted. The final responsibility for all interpretations, of course, rests solely with the author.

activity, including the passage of anti-discrimination legislation. It is important to note, however, that the basic assumptions underlying the Labour Government's commitment have led to the view that the level of activity needed was not very great.

They have assumed that the problem was a small and easily manageable one, because of the size of the coloured population, the relative recency of their arrival, and the fact that the British people are basically law-abiding. There is an element of truth in each of these assumptions, but they are not completely accurate and the real advantages they bring are temporary. The fact that the coloured population of about one million is roughly only 2 per cent of the total population, is less significant than the fact that they are concentrated in certain areas. These areas are characterized by high job opportunities, but are also, unfortunately, noted for overcrowded housing and inadequate social services. Patterns of discrimination have formed despite the recency of the problem, as outlined in Chapters 4 to 7, and the extent to which the British people are naturally law-abiding, can be overplayed. It is important to note that to a significant extent people obey the law because their value of so doing is not outweighed by a countervailing value. When it is, they will obey the law to the extent that the consequences of not doing so are both unattractive and likely. It is, therefore, important not only that legislation be passed to act as a guide-line for the population, but that such legislation be enforceable and enforced, if it is to be effective.

In a strange way, the relative newness of the problem made possible the passage of anti-discrimination legislation while militating against the passage of effective legislation. The newness meant that the opposition to any legislation at all was less intense than has been found, for example, in a country like the United States with its long history of racial conflict and its centuries of white vested interest in Negro suppression. This was reinforced by the nature of the British political system which limits the opportunities available to those who want to block completely Government legislation.

Both factors, however, worked the other way as well when it came to ensuring effective legislation. The newness of the problem and its seemingly small size made it possible for political leaders to cling to their assumptions about the ease with which it could be dealt. They saw the role of the Government as largely declaratory. James Callaghan, who had responsibility for shepherding the 1968 Race Relations Bill through Parliament, expressed this point of view in his first interview as Home Secretary on 28 January 1968. The following statement is interesting not only because it was the basis on which he acted with regard to the 1968 Bill, but also because it had been made after the failure of previous Government declarations to stem the tide of discrimination, and after both the P.E.P. and Street reports, and was, therefore, seemingly immune to the large body of evidence about the nature of the problem and the required solutions. Mr. Callaghan said in that interview:

The race problem is as much a question of education as of legislation. I think the law can give comfort and protection to a lot of people who do not wish to discriminate but who might otherwise be forced by the intolerant opinions of their neighbours to discriminate. *Any legislation introduced, I think, will have less emphasis on the enforcement side than on the declaratory nature of the Act itself, which must show where we stand as a nation on this issue of principle.*[1]

These assumptions, as we shall see, were largely responsible for the weaknesses in the 1968 Bill, as they were for those in the Race Relations Act 1965. Another factor which influenced the outcome of these legislative battles, and which affected the nature and extent of other Governmental activity, was the political situation facing the Labour Government. As shown by Smethwick and Leyton in 1964, and the public reaction to Enoch Powell's race speech in 1968, there were few, if any, votes to be won by Labour taking a clearly liberal line on this issue. In 1964, the Government, with a majority of only three, had to be especially conscious of this fact and in 1968, despite their large majority, they felt it necessary to avoid Conservative opposition at Third Reading. These factors strengthened their reluctance to get far in advance of public opinion, which was based on their basic assumptions about the nature of the problem. It resulted in limiting positive Government action and Governmental leadership, and in weakening the enforcement side of the 1968 Bill.

This combination of forces has militated against a broad programme of positive Governmental measures against prejudice

---

[1] *The Sunday Times* (28 January 1968). Italics added.

and discrimination. To be effective, anti-discrimination legislation cannot operate in a vacuum. It must be accompanied by positive Governmental programmes designed to eliminate the social problems which cause and exacerbate racial prejudice, which, in turn, justifies discrimination. This prejudice must also be countered by vigorous leadership from the political leaders of the land. Without these activities, the coloured population will continue to be a ready scapegoat for whatever social and economic pressures, inadequacies, and frustrations are felt by the host population. If this happens, or is allowed to continue, then the assumed willingness to obey anti-discrimination laws upon which the Government has been counting, will not be present; and the law will not be able to control and eliminate discrimination effectively.

Despite this, and despite the availability of information about the nature of the social problems and prejudices of the white population, little in the way of positive programmes has been forthcoming until very recently. There has been a marked reluctance to provide special assistance to areas with special problems—assistance which would have benefited not only the coloured inhabitants but also the white residents who have suffered for decades because of the low priority successive Governments have given to social programmes. It would have been politically risky to be seen giving special help to coloured people when 'our people' were in need. If political leaders were to risk this and educate the population about the truth of the situation, i.e. that the coloured immigrants did not cause the social problems of overcrowded and inadequate housing, schools, and hospitals, they would have had to admit their responsibility for these shortcomings.

The Local Government Act of 1966 made a tentative start in the direction of helping local authorities with special problems by authorizing, in Section 11, the Home Secretary to pay a proportion of the extra expenditure incurred by those local authorities who are required to make special provisions because of substantial numbers of Commonwealth immigrants—but only in respect of the employment of staff. During his Second Reading speech on the 1968 Race Relations Bill, the Home Secretary said that £3 millions had been spent in the 57 local authorities which had especially large concentrations of immigrants. This was hardly a magnificent sum and was hardly likely to make a significant impact on the problem. On 22 July 1968, the Home Secretary announced that subject to legislation in the forthcoming session of Parliament, the Government would provide a further £20 to £25 millions over the next four years. He indicated that priority would be given to nursery education and child care. While this is to be welcomed as an important step in the right direction, one may query whether the sum will be sufficient to make a major impact and whether housing might not have been a more important place to start. The Government have hitherto been reluctant to use the powers at their disposal to force local housing authorities to stop discriminating in the allocation of council housing. The consequence of this failure has been the development, and hardening, of inner-city incipient ghettos. This is a problem which should receive the highest priority, if the worst consequences of the American racial conflict are to be avoided.

There similarly must be a high degree of public education led by the political leaders of the country to counter prejudice and discrimination. The Government have been content by and large to leave this to the National Committee for Commonwealth Immigrants—a body which, incidentally, has received more money for its activities than has the Race Relations Board to enforce the anti-discrimination legislation. One would have expected, if the problem had the priority it deserved, that the political leaders of the country would have acted more expeditiously and courageously than they did to oppose Enoch Powell's race speech on 20 April 1968. Much of the public reaction to it was so frighteningly favourable that Britain can no longer go back to believing that racialism is not a major factor in British life. Despite this, Government leaders were remarkably slow in mounting a counter-attack, and their leadership was very restrained, often accepting the legitimacy of some of Powell's points, for example, the relevance of voluntary repatriation. It took the Prime Minister two weeks to speak out and he did not follow it up with any further speeches. In a major television appearance, the Home Secretary talked in terms of 'our people' and 'them', and argued that it was unfair to accuse the Government of not having a programme of voluntary repatriation by pointing to such a programme administered by the Ministry of Social Security. He did not, interestingly enough, challenge the relevance of such a programme for most immigrants and did not point out the dangers inherent in making repatriation a legitimate alternative to solving the problems of prejudice and discrimination in Britain.

In this situation, it is perhaps understandable that the political leaders did not give this problem the priority that it deserved and that was essential if their over-all programme in this area was to be fully effective. For reasons of both attitudes and politics, they were reluctant to admit that this problem needed a major commitment of Government time, energy, and money, and that it needed solutions that would seem to be almost revolutionary, in that they were entirely new and far in advance of anything that had been done before. They were reluctant to admit the relevance of much of the North American experience in this area. Here lies one of the most important aspects of the British experience in the fight against discrimination. If the political leaders are unwilling to be responsive to the stimuli provided by information about the lessons of other countries' experiences, the availability of this information will not be sufficient to ensure that the same mistake will not be made again.

The British Government have dealt with this problem, as indeed, to be fair, they deal with most problems, in a piecemeal fashion. Each additional piece of Government action is an important increment in the fight against discrimination. But each increment is not as effective as was anticipated, for at each stage the problem becomes more difficult to deal with. Therefore, action which might have had a dramatic impact if taken in 1965 will tend to have a more marginal impact when taken in 1968 because patterns of behaviour have hardened in the intervening period.

The following discussion of the passage of the Race Relations Acts of 1965 and 1968 will highlight many of these points.

2. *The Race Relations Act 1965*

(a) THE HISTORY OF THE 1965 ACT

The origins of the Race Relations Act 1965 can be found, in part, both in an ideological commitment to the principle of brotherhood and in political considerations. There always has been a strong ideological section of the Labour Party who felt that discrimination was morally wrong and that it should be outlawed by the Government. There were a number of attempts to implement this view in the 1950s, starting with a Bill introduced by Reginald (now Lord) Sorenson in 1950 to make discrimination in public places a criminal offence. This attempt failed to obtain the support of the Labour Government of the day, but was continued throughout the rest of the decade by Sorenson's long-time colleague Fenner (now Lord) Brockway, who introduced the first of his nine private member's Bills on the subject in 1956. The Brockway Bills kept the criminal aspect and provided that anyone found guilty of discriminating on the grounds of 'colour, race or religion' would be liable to a maximum fine of £25 and withdrawal of his licenses and registration, if any. The legislation was to apply to keepers of inns, lodging-houses, restaurants, public houses, and dance halls, as well as to employers of more than fifty people, as regards hiring and firing. This exemption of employers of fewer than fifty employees was withdrawn from the 1958 Bill, and the whole field of employment was dropped in 1960, at the behest of trade union M.P.s. This was one of the first indications of trade union attitudes towards legislation in this field, and the emphasis of the 1968 Bill on voluntary machinery was in part the price that had to be paid for Trades Union Congress (T.U.C.) support—or at least neutrality, as Bob Hepple has indicated in Chapter 6.

The Brockway Bills never achieved a Second Reading despite the fact that each successive Bill was supported by a wider spectrum of opinion, not only within the Labour Party, but from the other parties as well. The National Executive Committee of the Labour Party pledged in 1958 to 'introduce legislation to stop discrimination in public places', and Harold Wilson promised, both in the Commons debate on the Expiring Laws Continuance Bill (on 27 November 1963) and at a Trafalgar Square meeting (on 17 March 1963), that if Parliament persisted in rejecting Fenner Brockway's private member's Bill, 'when we have a Labour majority we will enact it as a Government measure'.

This commitment to enact anti-discrimination legislation became even more important in terms of maintaining party unity when Labour came to power in 1964. Having experienced the Smethwick, Eton and Slough, and Leyton defeats on the race issue, the Government decided to diffuse the race issue by strengthening the 1962 Commonwealth Immigrants Act despite their intense opposition to that measure when it was debated in Parliament in

9

1962. This strengthening, formalized in the White Paper of 1965 on *Immigration from the Commonwealth*, eliminated the 'C' vouchers, limited the number of Commonwealth immigrants to be admitted each year to 8,500 (with 1,000 reserved for Malta), limited the classes of dependants to be allowed free entry, and tightened controls on Commonwealth immigrants. It was bound to create a storm of opposition within the Labour Party. Given its tiny majority of three in the House of Commons, the Government had to ensure party unity and this made the introduction of an anti-discrimination bill even more important.

This commitment did not, however, involve the details of legislation, which were built around the Brockway formula of making discrimination a criminal offence. There was little consideration of the problem of discrimination outside public places or of the actual details of enforcement. The Labour Party appointed two committees to look into the question of detail in early 1964. One, chaired by Sir Frank Soskice, was made up of three members of the Shadow Cabinet (Soskice, Douglas Houghton, and Gilbert Mitchison). The other, set up by the Society of Labour Lawyers, was chaired by Andrew Martin. The Soskice Committee was much more restrictive in its approach, as was the Government; and while basically accepting the Brockway approach, limited it by excluding discriminatory leases, the right of the complainant to bring civil suit, and Brockway's proposal that the discriminator should also be liable to the loss of licence or registration, if any. They emphasized the difficulties of enforcement as justification for these omissions—an argument which runs throughout the history of legislation in this area. The Martin Committee, which accepted the applicability of criminal penalties for discrimination in public places, went further than the Soskice Committee in wanting to include all places of public resort run by local authorities and by indicating that discrimination in other areas was more important and that, with reference to them, other methods might be more applicable—such as the American administrative machinery based on conciliation.

Another group of outsiders who saw the importance of widening the scope of anti-discrimination legislation and of creating an administrative agency based on the conciliation process, was one led by Anthony Lester, a barrister familiar with the American experience. His group argued that the areas of employment, housing, credit and insurance, and Government departments were of more importance than the restricted list of places of public resort which the Government were considering and that a statutory commission, which had full powers of investigations and subpoena and authority to enforce its decisions through the courts, should be created. This commission could attempt to settle the complaint by conciliation in the first instance, but if that failed they would then use their statutory powers. The Lester group won over the Campaign Against Racial Discrimination (CARD), and other interested groups, and lobbied extensively on behalf of their proposals. They won over most of the interested Labour M.P.s—who, unfortunately for the success of their attempt to get effective legislation, were all back-benchers and, therefore, not in a position to make the crucial decisions about the shape of the legislation.

Before moving on to a discussion of the legislation introduced by the Government, it might be of interest to note that the Lester group talked of conciliation as merely one method of obtaining compliance. If it failed, the commission would use other methods. Unfortunately, in the debate both within Parliament and outside that followed Soskice's criminally based Bill, conciliation came to be seen as an end in itself, as the counterpoise to criminal sanctions, and almost, indeed, as the alternative to sanctions themselves. This misconception of the meaning of conciliation unfortunately continued and, as we shall see, was partly responsible for the weaknesses in the enforcement machinery of the 1968 Bill.

Unfortunately, the Lester group and their allies were not able to convince the Government, and on 7 April 1965 Soskice introduced the Race Relations Bill 1965 which was restrictive in its scope, based on criminal penalties, and required the authorization of the Director of Public Prosecutions for legal action. In two other sections, it made illegal the incitement to race hatred in speech or writing and extended the scope of the Public Order Act. These later provisions are extraneous to the real purpose of the Bill, but were urged very strongly by such groups as the Jewish community who feared the revival of fascism and were part of the background to the Bill. This fear was related to the formation of Colin Jordan's National Socialist Movement and its slogan, 'Free Britain from Jewish Control'. The Jewish Defence Committees of the Board of Deputies of British Jews began its 1962 report with this revealing sentence: '1962 was without doubt one of the busiest years for the Jewish Defence Committee since its formation, and the events of the latter months of the years were, in many respects, reminiscent of the situation provoked by the fascist activities of the late 1930's.' The Board, in co-operation with the Association of Jewish Ex-Servicemen and Women, the National Council for Civil Liberties, and the newly formed Yellow Star Movement, collected over 430,000 signatures on a national petition calling for legislation against racial incitement. In addition, a deputation led by the Chief Rabbi and the President of the Board met the Home Secretary, Mr. Henry Brooke, to ask for such legislation. While these efforts were unsuccessful in obtaining such legislation from the Conservative Government, they did strengthen the Labour Party's resolve to link legislation against racial incitement with legislation against racial discrimination.

The Bill was attacked both by those who wanted no legislation and by those who wanted effective legislation. As happened again in 1968, this tended to lead the Government to assume that since they were being attacked from both 'extremes', they must be correct. The Bill's criminal penalties drew most of the fire of those opposed to legislation and enabled them to appear to be in favour of more moderate legislation based on conciliation. *The Times* attacked the Bill's criminal provisions in the following terms:

The trouble with the clause making a criminal offence out of discrimination in places of public resort is that there is a risk of hardening attitudes and exacerbating prejudice in the few places where race relations are explosive, in return for some acceleration of full integration where things are proceeding in that direction anyway. Surely it would be better to try the effect of local machinery for conciliation and adjustment before dragging in the law.[1]

But those who were against legislation in this field were not the only ones to criticize the criminal penalties. It was argued that the North American experience clearly showed that few, if any, prosecutions would be brought and that it would be very difficult to prove beyond a reasonable doubt before a jury that discrimination had taken place. Also, as Louis Blum-Cooper

---

[1] *The Times* (8 April 1969).

argued: 'The criminal law is aimed at punishing the wrongdoer, it does nothing to correct the harm done to the victim.'[1] (This, incidentally, is a criticism which has been validly levelled against the 1968 Bill, i.e. that the Bill does not correct the harm done to the victim.)

Those opposed to legislation also centred their fire on the idea of a specially protected class, an attack which has continued throughout the years in which this problem has been discussed. This theme appeared in most of the leaders which opposed the Bill.[2] It also provided a large part of the Conservative opposition's arguments against the Bill in the Second Reading debate. Henry Brooke, former Conservative Home Secretary, stated:

I said in the House two years ago that I had no desire to be the Home Secretary who first introduced into our law the concept that some of my fellow citizens are to be singled out for special protection or distinction from others because of the race to which they belong. My successor appears to have committed this act of unwisdom.[3]

C. M. Woodhouse went even further, seeing such legislation as the beginning of the descent down the slippery slope of *apartheid*:

However benevolent the original intention, once a dominant race starts deciding that it knows best what is needed for the well-being of other races living in the same geographical boundaries, it is only a matter of time before a still more paternalistic attitude creeps in, and then a big-brotherly attitude, and, finally, *apartheid*. The lesson of this is, to my mind, simple, namely, that racial discrimination is just as bad when it is discrimination against minority and other races.[4]

Those who wanted effective legislation criticized not only the Bill's reliance on criminal penalties but also its narrow scope. They argued that the principles underlying this legislation were equally and more importantly applicable to those central areas of life excluded from the purview of the proposed law. David Ennals spoke for the critics when he argued this case:

I believe that the Bill is too limited. The net is not thrown wide enough. Clause 1 tackles the problem of theatres, cinemas, dance halls, and

---

[1] *Jewish Chronicle* (16 April 1965).

[2] See, for example, *Glasgow Herald* (8 April 1965); *Birmingham Evening Mail* (8 April 1965); *Daily Telegraph* (26 May 1965).

[3] House of Commons, Vol. 711, 3 May 1965, cols. 967–8.

[4] Ibid., col. 1021.

other places of public resort, but it does not deal with the problem of employment which is the most serious one. It does not deal with the problem of local authority and private housing. It does not deal with insurance ... with the granting of credit facilities. Admittedly, humiliation from exclusion in respect of restaurants and other public places is wounding and provocative, but in the long run, if we want to achieve equality, the right to fair employment practices is the most important right of all. It is a matter in which conciliation is more suitable than prosecution. Successful conciliation needs the force of law behind it. This is why I believe that we need the Bill, and a statutory commission.[1]

Aware of their lonely position supporting criminal penalties, the Government changed their mind in the month that elapsed between the publication of the Bill and its Second Reading. Indeed, Soskice began his speech with the significant phrase: 'We shall take note of what is proposed in that regard [about conciliation procedures] in argument in this debate.'[2] This was a sure indication of the Government's intention to withdraw, especially when taken with the following statement:

We will listen most closely to the arguments advanced in favour of the introduction of a conciliation process. If we feel that it is practicable and in the public interest, we will, either before or during the Committee stage, amend the Bill to give such effect as we feel able to the general wish of the House.[3]

The narrowness of the Government's legislative majority played a part in this decision.

The Government's intentions *vis-à-vis* the Bill were very narrow, as can be seen in this quote from Soskice's speech: 'Basically, the Bill is concerned with public order.' This was true despite the wider problems of employment, housing, and education:

The Bill had, designedly, the more limited objectives which I have described. It is intended to implement the specific statement in the Labour manifesto of our intention to legislate with regard to discrimination in public places and to incitement.[4]

[1] House of Commons, Vol. 711, 3 May 1965, col. 990.
[2] Ibid., col. 928.
[3] Ibid., col. 929.
[4] Ibid., col. 948.

The Conservatives, led by Peter Thorneycroft, exploited the Government's confusion to the hilt. They were able to play a number of different lines at the same time. They could criticize the criminal penalties, emphasize conciliation, and challenge the Government for the narrowness of the Bill's scope, while at the same time questioning whether there really was as much discrimination as the Government assumed there was and, thereby, questioning the necessity of such legislation. In 1965, they were not averse to using the North American experience in support of their arguments in favour of the conciliation process, something they shyed away from later at the Committee stage and in 1968. Thorneycroft argued that:

We have rather a good test case there, because some of the States have applied the criminal solution and others have adopted the conciliation method. Where they have adopted conciliation, it has, on the whole, worked not too badly; where they have tried the criminal approach, it has not worked at all, or practically not at all.

Taking a position from which the Conservatives backed away in practice, he then went on to state:

He [Soskice] must choose between the two; either conciliation— supplied, if he thinks it necessary, with teeth through the civil pro- ceedings, as has been attempted in a number of States in the United States of America—or the criminal law.[1]

The Government won the day at Second Reading, with Liberal support, and Soskice introduced, as an amendment, a rewritten enforcement section, substituting conciliation machinery for criminal penalties. This machinery was based on a Race Relations Board in London which would create local conciliation committees around the country; these committees would receive and investigate complaints of discrimination on the grounds of race, colour, or ethnic or national origins, and if the complaints were found to be justified, the committees would attempt to conciliate. If they failed, the cases were to be sent to the Board who could merely decide whether conciliation had, in fact, failed and whether a course of conduct was likely to continue. If they decided both in the affirmative, they would then send the cases to the Attorney-General. Only the Attorney-General would be

[1] Ibid., col. 950.

allowed to authorize court action. The local committees were not given any powers of subpoena and the Board was to be merely a post box once it had created the local committees.

And so the Bill remained limited in scope. The critics who wanted a stronger Bill were thus faced with the worst of both worlds: a Bill based on criminal penalties necessitated tight and narrow definition of its scope; and a Bill based on conciliation machinery did nothing to widen its scope.

This confusion was the basis of the first of the four main attempts to strengthen the Bill made by the seven Labour back-bench critics—Donald Chapman, Ivor Richard, Paul Rose, David Ennals, Reginald Freeson, Shirley Williams, and Dr. Maurice Miller—supported by Norman St. John Stevas and John Hunt from the Conservative side. This was an attempt to make the definition of places of public resort inclusive and, thus, to widen the scope of the Bill. However, the seven Labour back-benchers, including Chapman, who had moved the amendment, abstained on the vote. Presumably, they did so out of a desire not to embarrass the Government and in the hope of finding the Home Secretary amenable to some of their proposed amendments. They were to be disappointed in this hope and were themselves embarrassed by the spectacle of only the two Conservatives, Stevas and Hunt, voting for an amendment proposed by a Labour critic. After this debacle and after they realized that Soskice was not going to accept their amendments, the Labour critics joined Stevas and Hunt in voting against the Government. The Government were able to beat off such attacks because of the consistent support provided by the rest of the Conservatives, who were similarly opposed to strengthening the Bill in any way. This alliance defeated attempts to include shops as places of public resort; to allow the Board to use the local conciliation committees for work on problems not actually outlined in the Bill; and to allow the complainant to bring civil actions in those cases in which the Attorney-General refused to act.

The Committee stage was marked by the Government's unwillingness to go beyond the Bill in any meaningful way. It was also marked by the unwillingness of the Conservative front benches to see to it that the conciliation machinery was backed up by the teeth Thorneycroft had suggested at Second Reading. The level of argument used by the Government to justify their unwillingness to move beyond the Bill can only be explained by their basic assumption that the Bill was intended more to provide a lead than to be enforced and that one could not go too far, as this was new legislation. This alone could account for the argument used by Soskice against Chapman's amendment to include shops within the terms of the Act. Soskice argued that shops were different from places of public resort because the latter are places where 'broadly speaking, a person goes to stay for a time and enjoy all the amenities which are provided in that place' and that, therefore, discrimination in those places is more 'injurious and wounding to the feelings' than discrimination in shops. Secondly, he argued that the amendment would greatly enlarge the scope of the Bill. In opposing the amendment, he incorrectly assumed that it would include employment in shops and very revealingly used the sort of argument that many Conservatives were later to use against the 1968 Bill:

There is also an enormous variety of offices. Many of them have almost the private quality which a club has. It is not quite the same but nevertheless an office is a place where people work closely together in the performance of a common task and in the carrying out of an enterprise whether of a business or other nature.[1]

He then went on to raise the spectre of the adverse consequences following from a Bill that could not be enforced, using as his example the proposed wording of the amendment which included the phrase 'Neglects to afford him access . . . or facilities', and suggesting that a person who had been kept waiting in a crowded store could conceivably make a complaint. This, incidentally, was a technique used by the Government in 1968 in defending their refusal to budge from their previously announced position.

The Labour critics were so disillusioned and angry as a result of the Government's intransigence at Committee stage that the Government made a concession in the form of a sentence in Soskice's concluding speech at the Third Reading to ensure their support. Soskice promised that 'the Government will most certainly consider carefully what emerges in the coming months and years and will take such steps as may be dictated to suit the needs of the developing situation'.[2]

[1] House of Commons, Sixth Sitting, Vol. 714, 23 June 1965, col. 258.
[2] House of Commons, Vol. 716, 16 July 1965, col. 1056.

9*

The shape of the Race Relations Act 1965, with its limited and very inadequate scope and its weak enforcement procedures, was a consequence of the Government's minimalist expectations about the role of such legislation and of their very limited knowledge about the requirements of effective anti-discrimination legislation. There was a marked reluctance on the part of the Government to take any cognizance of the relevant North American experience. Such use as was made of this experience by most Conservatives, and certainly by the Conservative leadership, was only of a temporary tactical nature. Only those critics—both within and, mainly, outside Parliament—who wanted effective legislation understood and made use of this experience. But information by itself is not the most important variable in political decision-making. Without the will to act effectively, Governments will not be receptive to the information, or they will use only that part of it which supports their limited measures.

(b) THE CONTENTS OF THE 1965 ACT

The Act, passed on 8 November 1965, makes it unlawful for the proprietor or manager of a specified 'place of public resort' to practise discrimination on the grounds of colour, race, or ethnic or national origins against persons seeking access to facilities or services at that place. The Act does not cover discrimination on religious grounds. It gives an exclusive and, therefore, restrictive definition of places of public resort. The Act covers public hotels, restaurants, cafés, public houses, theatres, cinemas, dance halls, and scheduled transportation services; but it does *not* cover private hotels, shops, offices, night-clubs, holiday camps, chartered transportation facilities, and, most importantly, the Crown. This leads to many anomalies: e.g. discrimination by a hairdresser may be unlawful if his premises are inside a hotel, but not if they are outside it; discrimination in an off-licence is not against the law, but discrimination in a pub is unlawful.

The Act establishes the Race Relations Board to obtain compliance with the law. The Board is required to create local conciliation committees which must receive and consider complaints of discrimination, make any necessary inquiries about the facts alleged in such complaints, and use their best endeavours to settle any differences between the parties and to obtain satisfactory assurances against further unlawful discrimination. One weakness in the law is that neither the Board nor the local conciliation committees are granted powers of subpoena and, thus, respondents can refuse to talk to members or staff of the Board's machinery. If a local committee is unable to secure such a settlement and assurance or if it appears to the committee that any such assurance is not being complied with, the committee must report to the Board to that effect. If the Board agrees that, on the basis of that report, a 'course of conduct' has taken place and is likely to continue, it must refer the matter to the Attorney-General. The Act empowers the Attorney-General, and only the Attorney-General, to bring civil proceedings in the county court to enjoin the defendant from practising unlawful discrimination. No other proceedings, whether civil or criminal, may be brought in respect of unlawful discrimination under the Act.

3. *The Race Relations Act 1968*

(a) THE HISTORY OF THE 1968 ACT

The fight for wide and effective anti-discrimination legislation did not end with the passage of the token Act of 1965. In fact, soon after the enactment of that inadequate measure, it began anew with the replacement of Soskice (who was elevated to the House of Lords as Lord Stowhill) as Home Secretary by Roy Jenkins. Seeing himself as a reformist Home Secretary, Jenkins had fewer compunctions about State action in the sphere than had his predecessor, and appointed Mark Bonham Carter as Chairman of the Race Relations Board. Bonham Carter, a long-time personal friend and intellectual colleague of Jenkins, was determined to get a better law, seeing the present Act as considerably inadequate; and there was a mutual understanding that this was a desirable goal. The Board, including Sir Learie Constantine and Alderman Bernard Langton, established this goal as its highest priority and devoted much of its time to building up the case for extended legislation.

Following the 1966 General Election, Jenkins began the process of public education necessary to make extension a legitimate exercise of Government power and to ensure it a place in the Government's legislation time-table. On 23 May 1966, in a speech before the National Co-ordinating Conference of Voluntary Liaison Committees, he defined integration 'not as a flattening process of assimilation but as equal opportunity accompanied by cultural diversity, in an atmosphere of mutual tolerance'. About the 1965 Act and the need for new legislation, he said:

Some of you, I know, will think we have a better Race Relations Board than we have a Race Relations Act. I would say two things on this. First, I think a lot can be done under the present Act, and secondly, *as I have told the Board*, my mind is far from being closed about future changes to the Act. . . . By far the best way to get a wider Act is to work this one effectively and to show that this is a field in which legislation can help.

Many, I know, take the view that discrimination in employment and, indeed, in housing, should be covered by legislation. For the moment, I reserve judgement on the legislation point but I am in no doubt that the employment aspect of the matter in particular is rapidly becoming central to the whole future success of our integration policy. The problem is now developing with almost every month which goes by, because we are beginning to move from the era of the first generation immigrant to those [*sic*] of the second generation immigrant.[1]

In a major speech before the Institute of Race Relations on 10 October 1966, he went even further and indicated one of the main strategies of those in favour of extending the legislation to the important areas of employment, housing, and credit and insurance, i.e. making the case that discrimination was widespread. This involved the sponsoring of an objective study to show the extent of discrimination (the P.E.P. report), alongside the Board's building up of a record of complaints outside the scope of the 1965 Act. Jenkins stated:

It is not surprising that one should find what might be called mechanical faults in a wholly new type of legislation. I understand that the Board and the local committee are finding some. They find, for example, that the very process of conciliation—which is central to the whole idea—is hindered by the lack of power to compel alleged discriminators even to talk to the local committees. It then becomes very difficult in certain circumstances to investigate complaints, much less to settle them by conciliation. The Board is finding other mechanical difficulties too, and I certainly do not exclude the possibility of the Government amending the Act in due course to take account of experience.[2]

[1] Italics added.
[2] In an address by the Home Secretary to the Institute of Race Relations, published in *Race* (Vol. VIII, No. 3, January 1967), pp. 216–21.

Before moving on to the Home Secretary's discussion of the possibility of widening the scope of the Act, it is interesting to note that this very essential power of compelling alleged discriminators to talk to the local committees was central in the Board's own recommendation in its first annual report, published in April 1967. The Board declared that:

In some cases, persons against whom discrimination has been alleged have refused to meet representatives of the conciliation committee. This hampers their investigation and could, in certain circumstances, render them impossible. It should be considered whether, with appropriate safeguards, there should be power to compel attendance before the committee, or the disclosure of information to it.[1]

Despite the virtual unanimity of those experienced in administering the 1965 Act and those outside the Government with knowledge of the North American experience, including the Street Committee, this provision was not included in the 1968 Bill through Parliament; James Callaghan, as we shall see, steadfastly refused to accept any such power for the Board, largely because of his assumptions about the nature of such legislation, which differed dramatically from those of his predecessor, and because of his misconception of the Board's role as 'conciliatory'. As indicated above, there has been a misconception of the meaning of the word conciliation, which sees it as an end in itself rather than as merely one method among many designed to achieve compliance with the law, which, to succeed, has to be supported by the force of law. In Mr. Callaghan's eyes, giving the Board powers of subpoena would conflict with its role as a conciliator. One may hypothesize that had Mr. Jenkins not changed positions with Mr. Callaghan during the crucial phase of drafting the 1968 Bill, its enforcement provisions would have been very different.

In his speech to the Institute of Race Relations, Mr. Jenkins went on to declare:

When it came to amendment, the Government will of course also consider matters of substance. We welcome the fact that, jointly with the National Committee for Commonwealth Immigrants, the Board is sponsoring an enquiry into the extent of racial discrimination in the

---

[1] Race Relations Board, *Report of the Race Relations Board 1966–7* (London, H.M.S.O., 1967), p. 13.

fields of housing, employment, financial facilities and places of public resort not already covered by the Act [the P.E.P. study]. This enquiry will report early next year. Along with this, the Board and the National Committee are sponsoring a study of legal restraints on discrimination in other countries and their relevance to our own situation [the Street Committee study]. I look forward to reading these reports and *needless to say, the Government will not ignore them in considering any amendments to the Act*.[1]

During this period, outside groups were equally active in their attempts to keep the issue before the public and to build up an overwhelming case in favour of extending the 1965 Act. The Race Relations Committee of the Society of Labour Lawyers published its third report in November 1966, which criticized the 1965 Act and made a case for new legislation, including detailed recommendations about the new Act. The Fabian Society held a conference on Policies for Racial Equality in November 1966, which was attended by Maurice Foley, then the member of the Government with special responsibility for Commonwealth immigrants. This conference published papers in July 1967 in the Fabian Research Series (No. 262); edited by Anthony Lester and Nicholas Deakin, these papers made a very strong case for new legislation. During the period, CARD was active in encouraging victims of discrimination to send complaints to the Race Relations Board even, perhaps especially, if the cases were outside the Board's present jurisdiction. To keep up the pressure, Maurice Orbach, M.P., introduced, as a private member's Bill in December 1966, a Bill to amend the 1965 Act and to extend its scope and strengthen its enforcement machinery. Drafted by CARD lawyers, led by Anthony Lester and Roger Warren Evans, and with the assistance of Nicholas Deakin, this Bill had no chance of obtaining a Second Reading, but was designed to keep the pressure on the Government and to continue making the case for such legislation. Mr. Foley gave a lukewarm indication of the possible Government attitude towards the findings of the P.E.P. report, but added: 'Clearly, the extent of the comprehensiveness of the survey and the extent to which it can clearly demonstrate fields in which much needs to be done will have a decisive effect on the Government in terms of their future attitude.'[2]

[1] Italics added.
[2] House of Commons, Vol. 738, No. 119, 16 December 1966, col. 938.

This build-up reached its peak in April 1967 when the P.E.P. report on *Racial Discrimination* in England was published.[1] While its findings and conclusions were not a surprise either to the coloured community or to those activists who had been working for better legislation, they did have a dramatic impact on the mass media and on public opinion. There was enormous coverage of the report and newspaper leaders gave an overwhelming degree of support for new legislation. *The Times* shifted its position on the role of law as a result of the report, and *The Sunday Times* cogently declared:

The first and indispensable step towards the provision of equal opportunities for all men is the enshrinement of equality in the statute book. . . . The message implicit in every line of the report was this: If the law does not guarantee a coloured immigrant's right to a job for which he is qualified and a home for which he can pay no one else will. The gradualist myth was exploded by the facts. Left to the insidious guidance of their own fears and suspicions, too many employers, union leaders, landlords, estate agents and credit merchants do not and will not regard a coloured man as the equal of a white. As promoters of spontaneous integration they are simply not to be trusted.[2]

This report was followed by the publication of the Board's first annual report which reported that 238 of the 327 complaints received by the Board were outside the scope of the Act, with the largest single group of complaints (101) involving employment and with housing accounting for another 37 complaints. The Board recommended that the Act be amended to cover housing, employment, financial facilities, and places of public resort. It also recommended that certain mechanical deficiencies in the Act be improved: for example, a single act of discrimination should be sufficient to justify action, rather than the required 'course of conduct'; the Committee should have some form of subpoena power; the Act should bind the Crown; only communications made during the conciliation process should be exempted from admission in later proceedings; and, finally, the Attorney-General should be removed from the operation of the Act. It is interesting to note that except for the last of these enforcement recommendations, only those regarding scope were adopted by

[1] Political and Economic Planning and Research Services Ltd., *Racial Discrimination* (London, P.E.P., 1967).
[2] *The Sunday Times* (23 April 1967).

the Government. Within a week of the publication of the P.E.P. report, 106 Labour M.P.s signed a motion calling on the Government to extend the Act to cover housing and employment.

The latter was to prove the major stumbling-block. Despite the Conference on Equality in Employment sponsored by the National Committee for Commonwealth Immigrants in February 1967, the T.U.C. and the Confederation of British Industry (C.B.I.) remained adamantly opposed to legislation in this area. They argued that there was at most only a minor problem and that it could best be dealt with by the traditional industrial machinery. The battle was fought with the Government as well, with Ray Gunter and the Ministry of Labour taking a similar line. In order to carry the T.U.C. and C.B.I. along, the legislation was drafted to include voluntary machinery to be established by the unions and the employees, who would have first crack at complaints of discrimination in the employment field. This procedure has been criticized on the grounds that it is too cumbersome and time-consuming and that it is not directly under the Board. There is, as well, the danger of cosy arrangements to the detriment of the complainant. As *The Times* pointed out in an excellent leader:

What is wrong here is not that the voluntary machinery is given the first opportunity but that a Government department is to become involved at all. In principle it would be better to keep the Government right out of the whole conciliation procedure ... it would be more reassuring for coloured people to feel that one independent body was in charge, even if it delegated its powers in certain fields to other bodies. It would be better for this new Department of Employment and Productivity which will have quite enough to do as it is, to be spared involvement in an area where discussions are very delicate and where it has little or no specialized experience. Above all, it would be advisable for industry's own arrangements to come under the scrutiny of a body that is dealing full-time with race relations—otherwise there is the very real danger that voluntary machinery could conceal a cosy agreement between management and workers to keep on discriminating.[1]

On 26 July 1967, the Home Secretary announced in the House of Commons that the Government were going to extend the coverage of the Race Relations Act to include employment and housing. While many newspapers welcomed this announce-

[1] *The Times* (10 April 1968).

ment,[1] as did those groups outside Parliament that had been working so long and continuously for this announcement, there were many groups that continued their opposition unabated. The *Yorkshire Post* typified this latter group when it declared its opposition to the Home Secretary's announcement:

The latest dose of well meaning foolishness from the Home Office would extend the Act to deal with discrimination on grounds of colour, race or ethnic or national origins in employment, housing, insurance and credit facilities. Discrimination on those grounds alone in any of these fields is wicked and uncivilised but we doubt whether it happens as much as people are being led to imagine it does. The trouble is that immigrants are being encouraged to believe that the factors which discriminate against sections of the native population (such as lack of qualifications for the job, the absence of guarantees for credit facilities or housing, and the high fire risk in overcrowded houses) do not apply to them. They are being encouraged to believe that if they are asked to leave a first-class railway seat when they have only a second-class ticket it is because of their colour. Some immigrants may even take advantage of anti-racialism laws to get through subtle intimidation what they would not get through merit, or would not get, everything else being equal, if they were white.[2]

The details of the legislation had yet to be worked out, and the last part of the *scenario* in building up the case for legislation, and most particularly effective legislation, was yet to come: this was the Street report, published on 2 November 1967.[3] The report not only recommended the extension of legislation to include those important areas of life excluded from the 1965 Act, but also made detailed recommendations about the nature of the enforcement machinery required for effective legislation. Unfortunately, most of the Street Committee's valid proposals—based on a perceptive analysis of the successes and failures of the North American agencies and made relevant for the British situation—were ignored. The Board's recommendations and those of Equal Rights, the lobby group set up by those persons who in previous years had actively worked for new legislation, were similarly ignored.

[1] Including *The Times* (27 July 1967).

[2] *Yorkshire Post* (27 July 1967).

[3] Harry Street, Geoffrey Howe, and Geoffrey Bindman, *Report on Anti-Discrimination Legislation* (London, Political and Economic Planning, 1967).

The Bill introduced by the Home Secretary on 23 April 1968 was a courageous step forward in terms of its scope. The Bill included all the areas previously mentioned plus the field of education and closed the loop-holes in the 1965 Act. Yet its enforcement provisions seemed far too weak to ensure effective implementation of the legislation and apparently included a number of thoroughly obnoxious and dangerous loop-holes. One loop-hole exempted the merchant navy in instances where shared sleeping accommodation would be required. Another loop-hole would have exempted 'anything which is done in good faith for the benefit of a particular section of the public and which has the effect of promoting the integration of members of that section of the public into the community'. There was no definition of 'good faith', and this exemption could presumably have allowed separate but equal treatment, justifying the maintenance of segregated facilities on the grounds that it was being done in good faith for long-term integration.

The most important and controversial exemption is that for acts which are done 'in good faith' and designed to secure or preserve a 'racial balance' which is 'reasonable in all circum-stances'. This allows discrimination against individuals if it is in the interests of 'racial balance'. Besides the obvious weaknesses of this exemption—it neither defines 'good faith' nor does it state what constitutes a 'reasonable' racial balance—there is an over-whelming objection in principle. This exemption violates the basic principles underlying the legislation, in that it authorizes unequal treatment of individuals based on racial characteristics. In addition, there is the danger that once a pattern of discriminatory treatment of coloured people has become legitimized, it will be that much more difficult to combat later when the second generation of coloured British youngsters—who are to be treated as white British youngsters as long as they were educated 'wholly or mainly' in Great Britain—is applying for jobs. There is also the danger of a disproportionate concentration of coloured employees in low-level dead-end jobs, without adequate oppor-tunities for promotion or training for new skills. This will establish a vested interest on the part of white employees in the maintenance of such a situation and will be infinitely more difficult to deal with at a later date. This provision was presumably put in to satisfy the T.U.C. and C.B.I., to prevent the development of firms or departments with all-coloured work forces and to protect employers who wish to take action to prevent this happening.

The Bill's weaknesses in the enforcement sections spring from the two basic misconceptions outlined above: namely, the declaratory nature of the Bill, which is assigned greater importance than its enforcement procedure, and the meaning of 'conciliation'. The Government elevated conciliation to an end in itself and, consequently, opposed giving to the conciliating body the powers of either enforcement or subpoena. This ignored the Street report, the Board's own recommendations, and the lessons of the North American experience, all of which warned of the dangers of powerless enforcement agencies. Consequently, the Board was not given the power to subpoena witnesses or documents; there would conceivably be those occasions when the Board would have to face the choice of sending inadequately investigated cases to the courts and risking their dismissal, or not sending those cases that had not been fully investigated, which is likely to be most of the cases.

The operation of the legislation also embodied a basic misconception of the role of the complainant. He has been denied the right to go to court if he is dissatisfied with the Board's handling of the complaint; he has also been denied any meaningful appeal procedure within the terms of the Bill. He has been denied any satisfactory remedy because the courts, and, therefore, the Board, are not empowered to make positive orders requiring the provision of the job or accommodation in question or the next available ones. The only remedy provided is the payment of damages—of provable loss and of loss of opportunity, the latter being an entirely new concept which is likely to lead to a great deal of litigation and unlikely to be very relevant to the complainant. As the Home Secretary indicated in his speech at Second Reading: 'I do not expect that the amount of damages involved would normally be very large but there may be cases in which a claimant can demonstrate substantial loss as a result of discrimination, and I think that this should be payable in full if the case can be proved.' [1] The first part of the statement is likely to be the most relevant.

These weaknesses went against the Street Committee's conclusion that the aims of the implementing machinery were

[1] House of Commons, Vol. 763, No. 102, 23 April 1968, col. 62.

'to secure a satisfactory settlement when there appears to be discrimination and to provide adequate enforcement against discriminators when conciliation has not been achieved'. The machinery certainly did not satisfy their three criteria of 'fairness, speed and effectiveness'.[1] These weaknesses did, however, bring the Bill closer to the Conservative leadership and, most particularly, Quintin Hogg's view of the role of such legislation. Under Hogg, their front-bench Home Affairs spokesman, the Conservatives had moved away from the outright opposition to legislation that had been their position under Peter Thorneycroft. But despite the general support for the principle of legislation, the detailed positions taken by Mr. Hogg were to weaken the Bill's enforcement provision and widen the exemptions, including the total exemption of financial facilities—which would have the effect of largely negating the inclusion of housing, for most people would be unable to purchase a house without a mortgage or a loan. Hogg's position was based on the view that such legislation was intended for the public good, not for the benefit of any particular individual; and he was, therefore, unsympathetic to arguments urging more satisfactory individual remedies.

For internal party reasons, the Conservative leadership decided to table a reasoned amendment at the Second Reading. This decision was opposed by a group of liberal Conservatives led by Sir Edward Boyle who ostentatiously abstained on the division. The Conservative leaders were hard put to justify this decision intellectually, but the fear of a three-way split in the party, especially in the light of Enoch Powell's race speech on 20 April, won the day.

But following on from that vote, at Committee stage and at Third Reading, there was a determination on the part of both the Government and the Conservative leadership to avoid Conservative opposition at Third Reading. This determination helped, in part, to define the nature of the Committee stage and shape the outcome of most of the divisions in the Committee. Of importance, too, was the tendency of the Home Secretary to see himself as the representative of common sense and the average Britisher, and to assume that because he was being attacked by 'extremists' on both sides, his middle course was of necessity the correct one. And, as the representative of the

[1] Street *et al.*, op. cit., p. 92.

middle course, the Home Secretary was determined not to go too far ahead of public opinion. There was, in addition, the Government's great reluctance to back down from a position to which they had publicly committed themselves—a factor that was also found in the Government's reaction to amendments to the 1965 Bill offered by Labour back-benchers. Both times there was an impatience with criticism, an almost contemptuous dismissal of detailed points about the enforcement machinery as 'lawyer's points', and, therefore, either irrelevant or damaging.

This was a marked characteristic of the entire legislative history of this Bill. The critics were predominantly lawyers, organized in Equal Rights; and they prepared briefing material and draft amendments for sympathetic Labour back-benchers and their Liberal and Conservative allies. Their campaign was hindered by their isolation both from the coloured community, which was either unorganized or involved in militant organization not particularly concerned with anti-discrimination legislation, and from a largely uninterested white community. This is not to say that they did not have any support in these communities, but such support as they did have, was not immediately or easily transferable to political action and, therefore, was not an important variable in the decision-making process. The critics were labelled as extremists by the Government, who had successfully occupied the middle ground, arguing that they had introduced courageous and advanced legislation and yet some groups were still not satisfied and wanted even more. Additionally, there was an almost total lack of both trade union or business support for the critics' amendments or pressure from sympathetic community and civic groups—a very different situation from that found in the various American communities which have adopted such legislation. The legislative battles there were marked by a great deal of trade union activity and leadership on behalf of such legislation and political support provided by religious and civic groups.

The campaign, finally, was weakened by the decision of the Race Relations Board not to engage in public lobbying for a stronger Bill, despite the fact that virtually all its recommendations about the enforcement machinery needed for effective legislation, had been ignored. This decision seemed to follow from a number of factors, including the Board's fear that public lobbying would endanger its public position as a neutral, umpire-like, conciliation body. In addition, the split in the Conservative ranks complicated the issue from the Board's point of view, for it was essential not to be seen to be interfering in internal Conservative Party affairs and the Board felt, as did the Government, great concern lest the Government go too far out ahead of public opinion. It relied on contact and communication within the Government, but was not as successful as it, perhaps, hoped to be. This was very largely due to the fact that the Board and its Chairman did not have the same, unusually close, ties that it had with Jenkins. In addition, the other factors mentioned above were obviously too strongly felt by the Home Secretary and the Government to be challenged by the representations of the Board.

These factors led to an alliance of sorts between the two front benches, supported by most of the Conservative back-benchers on Standing Committee B and a handful of largely silent Labour back-benchers. Arrayed against them were most of the Labour back-benchers (ten out of fifteen), two Tories—Sir George Sinclair and Nicholas Scott—who showed extraordinary political courage in consistently voting against the rest of their colleagues, and the Liberal M.P. for Cheadle, Dr. Michael Winstanley. The latter group wanted to strengthen the Bill's enforcement procedures, to close the loop-holes, and to limit the exemptions. The Conservatives, except for Sinclair and Scott, wanted to restrict the scope of the Bill to the larger employers and landlords, to provide greater exemptions in the fields of private housing and employment; and to exclude financial facilities altogether. The Government were willing to make concessions on questions of scope, though they would not go as far as the Conservatives wanted. They were joined with their Conservative allies in a determination to resist attempts to strengthen the Bill's enforcement procedures.

This alliance was strong enough to dominate the Committee's voting on the enforcement provisions of the Bill, and the last weeks of the Committee's deliberations were marked by an increasing sense of frustration and despondency on the part of the Bill's critics, as amendment after amendment was voted down. This was despite the fact that, objectively, the critics had the better of the argument because they were following the logic of the reasoning behind such legislation in attempting to ensure that it was effective and inclusive. The Government were forced to fall back on very naïve and low-level arguments, knowing all the while that they had the votes to win the divisions. One such argument was used by the Government against Nicholas Scott's motion that the courts be empowered to make positive orders so as to provide meaningful remedies for those who had been aggrieved. Speaking for the Government, David Ennals declared that that would not be desirable because it would be wrong to fire the innocent man who was hired. This, surely, is not the point, for in a large operation men are being hired continuously and a suitable remedy would be to promise to offer the complainant the next available job for which he was qualified. The shocking aspect of this situation is that such a low-level argument could have been used at that late a date and after the Government had had so much evidence about the North American experience.

The Government's unwillingness to make concessions did not apply to Conservative attempts to limit the scope of the Bill and to increase the range of exemptions. In the early stages of the discussions, the Government made a number of such concessions to the Conservatives: e.g. to increase the exemptions for small boarding-houses, lodging-houses, and hotels; to stagger the application of the Bill's housing provisions; to increase the size of firms to be granted exemptions for the first two years from those with 10 employees to those with 25, and in the second two years from 5 to 10; and to accept the so-called 'Colorado clause', which provided for the exemption of owner-occupiers who sell their houses privately and who do not use either an estate agent or public advertising. When the Conservatives wanted to go further, however, to exempt credit and insurance facilities from the Bill altogether, or to re-establish the 1965 Act's strict requirement of a course of conduct rather than the 1968 Bill's more liberal provision authorizing action in the event of a single act of discrimination, or to remove damages from the Bill—which would have left the complainant with virtually no redress at all—the Government, joined by the critics who wanted a stronger Bill, defeated the Conservatives. The concessions that were made, however, were sufficient to ensure Conservative abstention at Third Reading, especially when linked to the coalition's success in defeating attempts to strengthen the Bill.

After the critics' one major victory, the deletion of Clause 2, Subsection 3—the 'separate but equal' clause—the Government and Conservatives voted together to defeat all other attempts to strengthen the Bill: the Government not only refused to remove the exemptions involving shared sleeping accommodations in the merchant navy—which represented defeat for the critics—but widened these exemptions to apply to discrimination on passenger ships and the shared mess and other common-room facilities on merchant ships. The critics' major defeat came over the racial balance clause when they failed, by a vote of 14–10, in their attempt to have it deleted. The critics who feared that in the absence of any criteria as to what constitutes a reasonable racial balance, employers who wanted to say 'no more coloureds' would be given the cover to legitimacy, seemed to have these fears confirmed when Eldon Griffiths, speaking for the C.B.I., said that it should be up to the employers and shop stewards to decide what constitutes a proper balance in their plants and departments.

When the Committee began its discussion of Part II of the Bill, dealing with the enforcement procedures, the differences in approach between the Government and their critics became most apparent. The Home Secretary's position on the declaratory effect of the law and on the Board's role as a conciliator, linked with his need to avoid antagonizing the Conservatives lest they vote against the Bill at Third Reading, meant that he and the Government were not receptive to arguments pointing out the need for a law with teeth and for an administrative agency with adequate powers to carry out its function. He, therefore, responded negatively to an amendment moved by Nicholas Scott that would have empowered the Board to go to the county court to obtain the right to summon witnesses and order the production of documents. This was an attempt to get around the Government's opposition to giving the Board that power directly—in spite of the Street report and the Board's own recommendations. It was widely assumed that the Government would accept this compromise formula. But both Hogg and Callaghan felt that even this indirect power would interfere with the Board's performance of its conciliation function, and that, in any case, it was unnecessary; and both feared that such powers might violate the respondent's constitutional rights. This was a hard blow to the critics, which was only slightly softened by the Government's concession empowering the Board to take a case to court on the basis of having 'formed an opinion' rather than having to 'determine' that discrimination had taken place.

The amendment designed to give the courts the power to make positive orders, which would provide satisfaction for the complainant and bring about changes in patterns of behaviour, was opposed and defeated by the Government-Conservative coalition. As the Bill now stands, therefore, the courts can only make a negative order or a restraining injunction, or order the payment of damages. The courts cannot order the affirmative action which has been found essential in North America.

These defeats helped to ensure Conservative abstention at Third Reading—despite the last minute revolt of a small group of right-wing Tories. From that point of view, one may characterize the Government's strategy as a success.

The Bill completed its Parliamentary passage on 24 October and came into effect on 27 November.

(b) THE CONTENTS OF THE 1968 ACT

The Act extends the areas in which discrimination on the grounds of colour, race, or ethnic or national origins is made unlawful, to include employment, housing, credit and insurance facilities, education, and all places of public resort including shops and offices. The Crown is specifically included in the Act. The Act exempts discrimination in employment where such discrimination is done in good faith to maintain a racial balance that is reasonable in all the circumstances, but non-whites born in this country are not so exempted. It also exempts employment in private households and on merchant ships where the sharing of sleeping or mess facilities would follow from the ending of discrimination. It exempts for the first two years employers of 25 or fewer employees; in the second two years, employers of 10 or fewer employees will be exempted, after which time the Act will cover all employers except for those exempted by the provisions mentioned above.

In the housing field, there is an exemption for the private sale of property by the owner-occupier without the use of either estate agents or public advertising. In addition, there will be a phased implementation of the housing provisions, with shared accommodation involving fewer than 12 persons in addition to the landlord and his family being exempt for the first two years, and with a permanent exemption for shared accommodation involving six or fewer persons thereafter.

The size of the Race Relations Board is to be expanded to twelve persons and it will be empowered to initiate investigations where it has reason to suspect that discrimination has occurred. This is an improvement over the limited powers of the Board under the 1965 Act, but it is not matched by the granting of subpoena powers to the Board—these have still been denied to the Board and its committees. There is a special procedure for the handling of employment cases involving the referral of all complaints to the Department of Employment and Productivity which will decide whether suitable voluntary machinery exists in the industry concerned. If it does, the Department will refer the case to that machinery for an initial period of four weeks, which is extendable. If the voluntary machinery is unable to settle the case satisfactorily, or if the settlement reached is unacceptable to the Department, advised by the Board, the case will go to the Board for investigation, but only if one of the parties informs the Board that he is aggrieved by the settlement. If the Board finds that discrimination has occurred they will attempt to obtain a settlement by means of conciliation. If they fail, they may take the case to one of the specially designated county courts to obtain injunctive relief (the Attorney-General has, thus, been removed from the proceedings completely). The courts can only issue negative orders—i.e. an injunction restraining the defendant from engaging in such conduct in the future—but cannot order the hiring of the complainant or the provision of the next available accommodation, or the filing of compliance reports with the Board. It can order the payment of special damages, i.e. out-of-pocket expenses and damages for loss of opportunity.

4. *Conclusions*

Britain has legislated against discrimination much more quickly than most people in Britain could have predicted and more quickly than did any American community at a comparable period of the development of its racial problems. Britain's political leaders deserve credit for this. But when one looks at how they legislated and at the nature of the laws passed, it is hard to avoid the conclusion that they have not benefited from the availability of a great deal of information about the experience of various North American government bodies in enacting and enforcing similar laws. This meant that they had available information which, at the least, should have warned them about certain pitfalls. One of the most dramatic of these pitfalls has been the passage of unenforceable legislation, which not only fails to improve the situation but actually worsens it because both the discriminator and the victim come to have little or no confidence in the law and in the agency administering it. Another pitfall is that of overemphasizing 'conciliation' as an end in itself rather than seeing it as part of compliance machinery, whose objective is 'compliance' not 'conciliation'. Kenneth MacDonald, Chairman of the Washington State Board Against Discrimination, addressed himself to this subject in a speech to the 1967 Conference of Commissions for Human Rights, a conference, incidentally, which was attended by the Minister with Special Responsibility for Commonwealth Immigrants, the Chairman of the Race Relations Board, and a number of senior staff officials. MacDonald said:

Statements by politicians, commissioners and staff members, and by enthusiasts for the legislation extolled the conciliative, educational and persuasive aspects of the law. For a long time the new agencies struggled to change attitudes, not regulate behaviour, and so not much was said then or now by public officers about the need to use 'law enforcement' or the 'coercive power' of the state to exert pressure for improving race relations. Thus words such as 'voluntarism', 'education', 'persuasion', 'conciliation', 'the necessity to change the hearts and minds of men' remained for years part of the jargon and litany under these new laws.

The North American experience also warns against weak enforcement agencies, with minimalist views of their role. As George Schwerner, a noted American practitioner, put it: 'A position of neutral, umpire-like disinterest by a commission has been demonstrated as only slightly more effective than no commission at all. A commission must make itself felt.'

Yet when we look at the legislation passed, so quickly in terms of the development of the problem, we find little or no awareness of these lessons. The 1965 Act seemed almost to be a result of an ignorance of the evidence. While unsatisfactory, it is somewhat understandable given the newness of the problem and of the assumptions with which Government officials and political leaders approached it. That the 1968 Bill should have similarly evidenced a failure to take cognizance of the relevant experience of other societies, can only be deplored as wrong-headed. There is no immutable law which requires every country to make the same mistakes as others. Given the ease of communications and, especially in this case, the availability of information, one could have expected a greater awareness of the problems that have to be solved and the methods for their solution. This highlights the difficulties faced by those individuals and groups who are concerned about a problem and who are aware of relevant experience elsewhere. The political leaders must be receptive to the stimuli of this information. If they are not, then they may make the same mistakes as the pioneers who did not have this relevant experience to guide them.

It is, therefore, of great importance to see how Britain's anti-discrimination law will work in practice. The 1965 Act, with its restricted and largely irrelevant jurisdiction, does not provide a meaningful guide as to how this new law, dealing with important areas of life, is likely to be greeted by potential discriminators and their victims, and how effective it will be. In their first two years of operation, the Board, and its local conciliation committees, received a very small number of complaints, as was to be expected given its limited jurisdiction. In its first year of operation, the Board received 327 complaints, of which 89 were within the scope of the Act; and the corresponding figures for the second year were 690 and 108.

The actual case-handling of the small number of complaints falling within the Board's terms of reference again may not prove a very useful guide for the future. First of all, the new Act by-passes the local committee in the all-important area of employment and the voluntary machinery is likely to prove to be a delaying factor. This is something to be closely watched, given the absolute centrality of speed in handling complaints. Secondly, the Board's handling of many of the complaints was not as expeditious as it should have been, nor was the level of expertise and efficiency totally satisfactory. A number of obvious factors account for much of this, e.g. the inexperience of everyone concerned, inadequate staffing arrangements, and office procedure. There were also the Board's own priorities which placed working for new legislation as the top priority, followed by staffing the local committees and then actual case-handling. In terms of long-term improvement of race relations in Britain, this was in all probability the correct evaluation of priorities. We, therefore, cannot predict very accurately how well the Board will handle the increased and more complicated case-load that will follow from the 1968 Act, although the Board has built up a body of good staff, committees, and Board members. This is of absolutely crucial importance, for the attitudes and experience of the agency personnel have accounted for a great deal of the success (or failure) of the North American laws. This will be even more important in Britain, given the inadequate enforcement aspects of the 1968 law. These shortcomings will make the Board's inescapably taxing job that much more difficult because it lacks powers of subpoena; because it is necessary to use voluntary machinery; because it is impossible to issue positive orders; and, perhaps, because of the racial balance clause. Much will depend on the determination, skill, and ingenuity of the Board's personnel. They cannot operate in a vacuum, however, and much will also depend on other Government programmes, such as major expenditures to remove the social problems in the twilight areas of the central cities which cause and exacerbate prejudice. Much will depend on the willingness of political leaders to provide leadership on this issue and on their willingness to use Government resources to combat discrimination. Since 1966, the Government have been giving urgent consideration to the question of including a non-discrimination clause in all Government contracts. Such a clause, if properly enforced, would strengthen the hand of the Board and would also foster the development of meaningful affirmative action programmes, for as the Street Committee concluded:

The Government are such huge customers of industry that they have a unique opportunity through the medium of their contracts to control racial discrimination. . . . We believe that through the medium of government contracts the opportunity should be taken of controlling discrimination by methods which would not at present be feasible in other areas of employment.[1]

Whether these programmes will be forthcoming, and whether such weaknesses as emerge in the operation of the 1968 law will be

[1] Street *et al.*, op. cit., p. 130.

removed, only time will tell. On 22 October 1969, the Government announced the introduction of a non-discrimination clause in all Government contracts. The enforcement provisions, however, looked so weak that it is doubtful whether it will have much impact. One would have been more optimistic about the outcome and effectiveness of anti-discrimination legislation had there been a greater willingness to learn from the North American experience. Perhaps the British experience will demonstrate to the political leaders of other nations, the importance of receptivity to such information.

CHAPTER 10

The Race Relations Board

BRIAN COHEN AND MARNA GLYN

1. *The Work of the Board*
by Brian Cohen

The Race Relations Board was constituted in February 1966, according to the provisions of the Race Relations Act 1965. The duties of the Board were, in the words of the Act, 'securing compliance with the provisions of Section 1 of this Act and the resolution of difficulties arising out of those provisions'. Section 1 of the Act made it unlawful to practise discrimination on the grounds of colour, race, or ethnic or national origins in specified places of public resort. The Act laid down the administrative structure and the operating procedures by which the Board should secure compliance to the Act. It was the Board's duty to form local committees to receive and consider complaints of unlawful discrimination. These committees, known as local conciliation committees, were empowered to investigate complaints, achieve a settlement between the parties concerned, and receive, where appropriate, assurances as to future behaviour.

The Race Relations Board faced a considerable number of difficulties at the time of its formation, not the least of which was the Race Relations Act 1965. The field of relevance for the Board was severely limited to specified places of public resort, which mainly meant public houses. Potentially, an even more serious weakness was that the Board had no express powers to investigate complaints or undertake conciliation to achieve a settlement. These powers were held by the local conciliation committees. However, if a local conciliation committee failed to achieve a settlement, it had to report this to the Board who had then to decide whether to refer the case to the Attorney-General for possible prosecution. Despite this, the Board was severely limited in its powers and its major functions with respect to the 1965 Act were limited to appointing conciliation committees and staffing them with conciliation officers. As discussed in the last chapter, the first priority seen by the Board was, in fact, the extension of the 1965 Act to cover a wider field, especially housing and employment. We will, however, consider this aspect of the Board's activities after discussing the implementation of the 1965 Act.

As the 1965 Act envisaged a considerable devolution of power and independence to local conciliation committees, their selection was a matter of great importance. The Board proceeded fairly cautiously and the first two conciliation committees for Greater London and the North-West were not appointed until July 1966. Further committees were appointed for the West Midlands and Yorkshire during 1966. In the following year, committees were constituted for the East Midlands, Berkshire, Buckinghamshire, Oxfordshire, and Scotland. During 1968, committees were appointed in Wales and the North of England. At the beginning of 1969, the Board decided to spread more evenly the case-load in the south-east of England and formed three conciliation committees (the North, South, and West Metropolitan) to replace the former Greater London, Berkshire, Buckinghamshire, and Oxfordshire committees. The Board also abandoned its idea of forming a separate committee for the south-west of England and decided to have a single committee for Wales and the South-West.

Under the 1965 Act, six to nine members were appointed to each conciliation committee. Members of conciliation committees are initially appointed for one year and then subsequently for two-year terms (three years under the 1968 Act). In his evidence to the Parliamentary Select Committee on Race Relations and Immigration in December 1968, Mr. Mark Bonham Carter, the Chairman of the Race Relations Board, explained the procedure:

Our conciliation committees . . . are appointed on a regional basis and the way we select them is this: a large number of names have been submitted to us by various bodies ranging from the A.M.C.[1]. . . . to various Government departments, to local authorities, to industry and bodies of one sort and another. Before setting up a committee or when strengthening a committee which is what we are doing at the moment, I or one of my colleagues always visits the area in question, goes to the main towns in question, sees the leading politicians, the officials, the chief of police, and discusses the problems of the area and some of the names which have been put up. They will also probably give us other

---

[1] Association of Municipal Corporations.

names. The ideal way in which to do it is then to find a chairman or chairwoman and, when you have found this person, you can in collaboration with him construct a committee. These committees, we think, should not be more than 14 people and they have to satisfy a number of different criteria. One would like them to have a geographical balance within the region in which they are; one would like them to contain people who come into contact with the problems of race relations in their daily lives; one would like these people to be of some standing in the locality; one wants to have on most committees somebody with knowledge of industry on the management side and the union side, someone with knowledge of local authority housing and private housing, someone with knowledge of social work, for example; one wants members of the immigrant community; and one wants whatever is meant by a reasonable proportion of women, who may double any of these roles. So the selection of the committees is done on this basis. It generally takes five to six visits to any place before you really get a committee off the ground.[1]

Prior to the 1968 Act, there had been less need for some of the balancing factors discussed above and to some extent, less weight was placed on industrial experience, although most committees had one or two members with such experience. With the new Act, the Board has started to reorganize the composition of the conciliation committees, which will entail an increase in the membership of the committees which will now include persons with specialist experience, especially in the fields of industry and housing. Most conciliation committees established under the 1965 Act, had one or two immigrant members, and it is unlikely that this number will increase greatly, as the Board has experienced some difficulty in finding immigrants with the required experience in industry and housing. Essentially, the composition of conciliation committees has shifted from a committee of generalists with a bias towards social work and some legal background, to more specialist committees with a weighting of industrial experience.

It should also be noted that the Board has attempted to select conciliation committees which would have some standing in terms of prestige within their local areas. This has meant that some of the members selected have little experience of race relations and, thus, their knowledge of the subject is not always

[1] House of Commons, Select Committee on Race Relations and Immigration, *Minutes of Evidence*, 19 December 1968.

as extensive as might be hoped. The Board has, however, avoided to some extent the pitfalls suffered by many voluntary liaison committees (now community relations councils which selected certain members by virtue of their local prestige, but who seemed to most observers not wholly committed to the objectives of the committees. In selecting members of conciliation committees, the Board has been able to exercise greater choice than the National Committee did in its selection of liaison committees (due to the larger population areas served), and it has succeeded in making membership of one of its committees a matter of prestige. The Board has also made it a priority to educate the members of conciliation committees and to keep them well informed of current events. The methods by which uniform standards are established nationally and the system of communication between the centre and the periphery, were explained by the Chairman of the Race Relations Board:

A member of our headquarters staff generally, and in future always, I would say, would attend their meetings. We have an annual conference of all members of conciliation committees which lasts for a weekend. We have two to three meetings of chairmen of conciliation committees in London for one day two or three times a year and we issue them with background documents of one sort and another. We also hope we have devised a system of communication whereby we can tell fairly accurately what is going on in any particular committee.[1]

The fact that the number of conciliation committees is small, has been an undoubted asset in ensuring good communication between the Board and its committees. However, it remains to be seen whether the methods of communication developed from 1966 onwards will prove as effective with the greater number of conciliation committee members and the larger flow of work under the new Act.

Of even more importance for good communication has been the fact that all conciliation officers are directly employed by the Board whether they are based at the London headquarters or serving a local conciliation committee. The Board holds monthly one-day meetings of all conciliation officers to discuss policy, planning, and any problems that have arisen. An additional check is that the Board keeps a copy of all enquiries and decisions

[1] Select Committee on Race Relations . . . , 19 December 1968, op. cit., p. 48.

made by conciliation committees and their officers and, thus, is aware of how its policy is being implemented.

The selection and training of the Board's staff are obviously crucial factors in its success in implementing its duties. In one respect, the Board has been extremely fortunate: exceptionally large numbers of people have been applying for posts. This has allowed the Board to be selective, as well as enabling it to choose officers of high calibre. The newness of the Board and the need to create specialist skills have presented major difficulties. In general, the Board has opted for applicants who already hold specialist skills in one of the major areas, such as industrial relations. Training is mainly on the job, but conciliation officers usually spend their first month at the London headquarters, sitting in with the conciliation officers attached to the London headquarters and to the various London conciliation committees. Usually, they are then attached to experienced workers in the regions for a further short period. The monthly meetings at which information is exchanged, are another medium of training.

The size of the Board staff slowly increased in 1966 and 1967, but in 1968 with the new Act, it rapidly increased. Table 10:1 shows the size and distribution of the staff of the Race Relations Board and spotlights the very great increase following the 1968 Act. It is also of interest to note the emphasis, in terms of staff, towards information and research. Within what is a fairly small organization, at least three employees in 1968 and five in 1969

TABLE 10:1

STAFF OF THE RACE RELATIONS BOARD

	Conciliation Officers	Headquarters Others (non-clerical)*	Clerical, etc.	Total	Conciliation Committees Conciliation Officers	Clerical, etc.	Total
March 1967	1	2†	5	8	3	3	6
April 1968	1	4†	7	12	7	7	14
April 1969	7	6	17	30	17	12	29

* In 1969, this category consisted of the secretary to the Board, principal information officer, information officer, temporary information officer, research officer, and research assistant.

† Denotes one part-time employee.

Note: Additionally, a part-time legal adviser was employed by the Board throughout the period.

Source: Race Relations Board, *Report of the Race Relations Board for 1966–7* (London, H.M.S.O., 1967). Also reports for the years 1967–8 and 1968–9.

were wholly occupied in these activities. This, in fact, understates the publicity effort of the Board, as the Chairman of the Board, the Chief Conciliation Officer, and, since the end of 1968, the Principal Conciliation Officers have devoted considerable effort to this work.

As already noted, from its inception in 1966, the Board's major effort was articulating the case for extending the 1965 Act. Within the context of this aim, the Board's activities in the field of information and research are understandable. The implementation of the 1965 Act was seen to be of secondary importance, and this, together with the organizational dangers of too hurriedly appointing conciliation committees, already discussed, determined the Board's course of action until mid-1968. After an interregnum while the 1968 Act was passing through Parliament, the direction of information services shifted to publicity to encourage compliance with the Act plus a small separate element which can best be described as similar in nature, if not in scale, to the Bnai Brith Anti-Defamation League in the United States.

It can be effectively argued that the single most important action of the Board in the pre-1968 period was its co-sponsorship with the National Committee for Commonwealth Immigrants of the P.E.P. report.[1] As the agency most concerned with the question of discrimination and the need for legislation in the fields of employment, housing, and financial services, the Board was extremely active in preparing and seeing through the work. Much of its information and publicity effort was geared to the P.E.P. report as the central driving force and to the follow-up of the report. In its first annual report,[2] whose publication roughly coincided with that of the P.E.P. report, the Board set out the case for further legislation: it stressed the deficiencies within the Race Relations Act and recommended that the Act be extended.[3] In its report for 1967–8,[4] the Board welcomed the proposed Bill and stressed once more the need for a strong Act.

One very useful piece of ammunition that the Board adopted

[1] Political and Economic Planning and Research Services Ltd., *Racial Discrimination* (London, P.E.P., 1967); also W. W. Daniel, *Racial Discrimination in England* (Harmondsworth, Penguin, 1968), based on the P.E.P. report.
[2] Race Relations Board, *Report . . . 1966–7*, op. cit.
[3] Ibid., p. 22.
[4] Race Relations Board, *Report of the Race Relations Board for 1967–8* (London, H.M.S.O., 1968).

was the collection of statistics of complaints made to them outside the provisions of the 1965 Act. Thus, throughout the 1965-8 period, all complaints, whether inside or outside the Act, were recorded; and in all its press releases and in the statistics of complaints published in its annual reports, the Board listed, and commented upon, the number and category of complaints outside the scope of the Act. Thus in the report for 1966-7, it was stated that 70 per cent of complaints fell outside the scope of the Act, and in the report for 1967-8 the figure rose to 83 per cent. By categorizing these complaints, the Board was able to reinforce the P.E.P. report and to show that employment and housing were areas in which discrimination aroused strong resentments. Additionally, the behaviour of the police was subject to considerable complaint. Throughout this period, the Board did nothing to discourage complaints in fields outside the scope of the Act and in certain instances was willing to take informal action on these complaints. Within this context, the activities of such organizations as CARD in testing discrimination and sending in complaints about such subjects as employment, were helpful to the Board's aims.

As has already been discussed by Louis Kushnick in Chapter 9, a part of the Board's information activities was directed to the ways in which methods of enforcement could be improved. The centre-piece of this effort was, as in the case of the P.E.P. report, a research project co-sponsored by the Board and the N.C.C.I.—the Street Report on anti-discrimination legislation.[1] Possibly due to the fact that the content of the Street Report was thought to be less newsworthy than that of the P.E.P. report, its impact was less and, as Kushnick has shown, the Board was less successful in getting its recommendations incorporated into the 1968 Act—and this despite the fact that in attempting to work the 1965 Act, the Board had found certain difficulties. A large section of its first annual report was devoted to these deficiencies, and eleven separate points were listed,[2] including the following:

(i) the confusion between a single act of discrimination and a 'course of conduct' as a requirement for further action by the Board under the terms of the Act;

---

[1] Harry Street, Geoffrey Howe, and Geoffrey Bindman, *Report on Anti-Discrimination Legislation* (London, Political and Economic Planning, 1967).

[2] Race Relations Board, *Report . . . 1966-7*, op. cit., pp. 12-15.

(ii) the Board's inability to deal with certain types of discriminator who refuse to give assurances as to future conduct;

(iii) the ambiguous status of certain groups such as Jews, Sikhs, and gipsies;

(iv) the refusal of certain persons against whom complaints had been made, to meet representatives of conciliation committees;

(v) anomalies arising from the defined places where discrimination is and is not illegal;

(vi) the long delays inherent in a process whereby only the Attorney-General is empowered to bring court proceedings; and

(vii) the exclusion of any evidence of communication received by the Board or conciliation committees from subsequent court proceedings, thereby hampering any future court cases.

In the months that followed, the Street Report added weight to these criticisms and recommended a more coherent procedure for the implementation of the new Act. In the report for 1967–8, the Board further developed the case:

But we would like to repeat the conclusions we reached at the end of our first year's work, namely that conciliation would have been virtually impossible were it not for the sanctions provided by the Act. Simple, speedy and credible enforcement procedures are the prerequisite of successful conciliations. . . . While much of the work of the Board . . . will be concerned with . . . conciliation . . . *it is a mistake to regard the Board as an essentially conciliatory body*.[1]

The report further argued that the role of the Attorney-General be assigned to the Board and that it be empowered to institute proceedings in the courts. Drawing on past experience, the report continued:

. . . neither the conciliation committees nor the Board will be credible unless they have the necessary powers to discharge their functions. The Board has already had the experience of respondents bluntly refusing even to talk to officers of the Board and members of conciliation committees. In certain circumstances this can make it virtually impossible to decide whether discrimination occurred. . . . It is, therefore, important that, in making enquiries under provisions of the new Act, the Board should have the power, with suitable safeguards, to see all relevant papers and to interview witnesses.[2]

[1] Race Relations Board, *Report . . . 1967–8*, op. cit., pp. 13–14. Italics added.
[2] Ibid., pp. 14–15.

The Board also stated the case for permitting individuals to bring their own cases to the courts and for giving the courts the power to make positive orders. The reports from the individual conciliation committees, appended to the main report, supported many of the points in the main report. The East Midlands Conciliation Committee showed disquiet over one particular case:

Two cases, both racial discrimination of the same licensed premises, were referred to the Race Relations Board. The Board passed them on to the Attorney-General, in accordance with the procedure laid down by the Act. The committee understands that both these complaints are still under consideration by the Attorney-General. The committee feels obliged to express its concern at the delay in bringing these cases to a satisfactory conclusion. The present procedure is fatal to the speedy settlement of complaints which the committee feels to be an essential part of the process of conciliation.[1]

Additionally, the West Midlands and the Yorkshire Conciliation committees both suggested that the Board be allowed to initiate complaints, and the West Midlands Committee was also critical of delays and the problems arising from the working of the Act with respect to a 'course of conduct'.

A reading of the reports of the conciliation committees gives a general impression of considerable frustration with the 1965 Act. Firstly, all commented adversely on the limited scope of the Act and on the fact that the majority of complaints were outside the Act. The Greater London Committee expressed the feeling as pungently as any:

The Committee has been gravely embarrassed by the number of cases of discrimination brought to its notice but lying outside the scope of the Act. This circumstance is, of course, well known to the Board, but it must be emphasised at the beginning of this report how acutely the Committee has felt the falsity of its position and how seriously it fears that its powers for good will be fatally compromised if it continues much longer in this state of impotence.[2]

However, despite these limitations, it is interesting to note that six of the seven conciliation committees reported taking some sort of action on certain complaints outside the scope of the Act. Thus, the Greater London Committee:

[1] Ibid., p. 30.
[2] Ibid., p. 25.

has sometimes been able to do something for particular complainants by informal means and some useful work may have been done in these areas. But it is clearly on the merest margin of the problem and no substitute for methodical statutory activity.[1]

And in the West Midlands:

There have been 79 complaints outside the Act. . . . Wherever possible the Committee, besides forwarding the complaint to the Race Relations Board, has encouraged its Conciliation Officer to take any other appropriate steps which may ease the position.[2]

Secondly, nearly all the conciliation committees criticized the procedures of the 1965 Act. The constraints laid down by the Act were felt to have an inhibiting influence on securing compliance. The Act was considered unwieldy and slow, and most committees expressed the need for speedier disposal and settlement of complaints. The difficulties in obtaining evidence and the extremely cumbersome procedure for dealing with recalcitrant discriminators, were highly criticized. The official reports of those who actually worked the 1965 Act, point to a single conclusion: that the Act was the work of thoroughly inept Parliamentary draftsmen.

There was, however, one optimistic note that ran through the reports of conciliation committees and this is their belief in the success of the Act in diminishing racial discrimination in public houses. In the period from 1966, when the Board came into operation, until November 1968, when the new Act came into force, 171 out of the total of 269 complaints within the scope of the 1965 Act, referred to public houses. The singling-out of public houses as the main target of the 1965 Act was in many ways an artefact of the legislation, as they were by far the most important area covered by the Act. It is difficult to see on what evidence the conciliation committees could base their judgement of success other than their negotiations with breweries, the Licensed Victuallers' Association, and others. After negotiations, all these organizations co-operated with the Board and the conciliation committees, and advised publicans on the provisions of the Act. What is probable, is that the Act did, in its two and a half years, control the most overt forms of discrimination, but whether these were replaced by more sophisticated forms of discrimination is

[1] Race Relations Board, *Report . . . 1967–8*, op. cit., p. 25.
[2] Ibid., p. 26.

not certain. Even in its first year of operation, the Board was aware of the dangers of this, for it said in its first annual report:

The Board have noted three general types of discrimination. First, there is the overt discrimination of, say, the hotel proprietor who puts a total ban on all coloured people. Secondly, there is the form of discrimination which amounts to segregation, for example, where a publican will serve coloured people only in the public bar, or alternatively, everywhere except in the lounge bar. Thirdly, there is the less open form of discrimination characterised by overcharging coloured customers or keeping them waiting for service in order to discourage them from coming again.[1]

There is no clear-cut evidence of a decrease in all forms of discrimination, the overt and the more subtle types. There was no sign of a fall in the rate of complaints about public houses during the last six months of the old Act. As, however, the rate of complaints is determined often to a greater extent by the willingness of people to complain and by their knowledge of their right to complain, than by the incidence of discrimination, this cannot be a very satisfactory guide for any short period.

One unexpected effect of the 1965 Act involved gipsies. The Board received a substantial number of complaints about public houses discriminating against gipsies and about signs saying 'No Gipsies'. After some delay, the Board decided on legal advice that gipsies could be considered to be covered by the terms of the 1965 Act. The signs in themselves were not, however, unlawful, but the Board reported some (but not total) success in having them removed.

With the passing of the 1968 Act, the whole emphasis of the Board's work has changed. Racial discrimination in public houses, however insulting and humiliating, is peripheral in comparison with racial discrimination in employment and housing. The test of the Board's effectiveness lies in the new areas covered by legislation, especially those most central to economic and social competition. In many ways, the 1965-8 period was analogous to the early sixties in the United States, the period of the lunch-counter sit-ins; through the struggle over basically non-essential issues, there developed the organizational sinews of the Black minority of the United States. Similarly, the years 1965-8 can be seen as a period during which the Board developed its

---

[1] Race Relations Board, *Report . . . 1966-7*, op. cit., p. 8.

10*

organizational skills, trained a cadre of committed members and staff, and helped to extend its powers to cover the central issues that determine life-style and life-chances.

2. *Analysis of Complaints*
by Marna Glyn

This review covers two periods of the Board's work: the first, under the Race Relations Act of 1965, from the time the Board was constituted, in February 1966, to 26 November 1968, when the second Act came into force; and the second, from that date to the middle of November 1969.

The figures collected were intended, firstly, as management statistics, that is, as a measure of the Board's activity and a guide to forward planning; and secondly, as a source of information about the field of race relations in which the Board operates, identifying, where possible, areas covered effectively, and areas in which it may not yet be working usefully.

The Board and its conciliation committees have statutory obligations to receive and investigate complaints of unlawful discrimination referred to them. Since 1968, the Board has also had powers under Section 17 of the Act to initiate investigations, without an actual complaint, where it has reason to suspect discrimination as defined for the purposes of the 1968 Act. The records are, therefore, an indication of the extent to which those most at risk (a) are aware of machinery to redress their grievances; (b) are prepared to use this machinery; and (c) understand the implications of the term 'unlawful discrimination'. They are not a reliable index of the extent of racial discrimination.

It would indeed be encouraging to be able to accept that the total of 3,040 complaints received up to 19 November 1969 was a true measure of racial grievance among a coloured population estimated to be 1,254,000 in 1968.[1] Furthermore, one has to remember that this total includes not only complaints from 'multiple complainants' (one complainant had signed a total of 25 complaint forms by early 1970), but also cases where more than one investigation arises from one complaint (e.g. advertisement cases under Section 6 of the 1968 Act where two respondents may be registered, the advertiser and the publisher).

[1] Race Relations Board, *Report . . . 1968–9*, op. cit., p. 57.

It should, at the same time, be remembered that in many cases one finding of unlawful discrimination may affect many people throughout a large enterprise or entire industry. Equally, an opinion of 'no discrimination' may approximate more to 'not proven', and the work done by conciliation officers in the course of investigation and conciliation may have considerable practical effect in discouraging discrimination.

The distribution of complaints in different areas has been an important factor in the siting of regional offices, recruitment and distribution of conciliation staff, and changes in the boundaries of areas covered by regional committees. These boundary changes make exact comparisons between regional figures over time impossible, but the totals attributed to different regional committees, are given below together with indications of the percentage of total coloured immigrants in selected conurbations according to the 1966 census.

TABLE 10:2

COMPLAINTS RECEIVED, 1966–1969

| | | 1965 Act | 1968 Act | | % of total U.K. coloured immigrant population** |
| | | | April 1968 to | Nov. 1968 to | |
Region	1966–7	1967–8	26 Nov. 1968	March 1969	
Northern	1	5	7	7	Tyneside: 0·5
Yorkshire	22	92	47	34	West Yorks.: 5·5
North-West	50	74	39	42	South-east Lancs.: 4·1
West Midlands	36	82	47	74	West Midlands: 13·4
East Midlands	12	40	25	25	
Eastern	5	20	—	—	
Berks., Bucks., and Oxon.	8	21	20	19	
Hants., Sussex, and Surrey	11	19			
Kent	17	39	249*	283*	Greater London: 43·2
Greater London	152	259			
South-West	5	9	6	11	
Wales	4	13	13	7	
Scotland	4	9	8	5	Clydeside: 0·9
Total	327	682	461	507	

* Amalgamated for Hants., Sussex, and Surrey; Kent; and Greater London. From March 1969, these areas were amalgamated with Berks., Bucks., and Oxon.

** Figures refer to conurbations of Great Britain at 1966 Census.

Variations between regions reflect many factors: the vigour of interested local groups, the efficiency of local information services, the extent to which local immigrant groups form self-sufficient communities effectively insulating them from the effects of discrimination. But, predictably, complaints tend to concentrate where there are concentrations of immigrants.

DETAILS OF THE COMPLAINTS 1966–1970

Similarly, the areas of greatest contact, first employment and then housing, have been the subjects of the majority of complaints falling both within and outside the scope of the 1965 and 1968 Acts. Of the 1,478 complaints received under the 1965 Act, 539 concerned employment and 143 housing, all falling outside the scope of the Act. During the first year of the operation of the second Act, under which the powers of the Board were widened, the distribution of complaints by region was as follows:

TABLE 10:3

EMPLOYMENT COMPLAINTS RECEIVED

Region	Employment	All other
Yorkshire and North-East	63	69
North-West	70	56
West Midlands	129	87
East Midlands	50	27
London and South-East	414	510
Wales and South-West	30	32
Scotland	10	15
Total	766	796

* First year of the 1968 Act, 26 November 1968 to 19 November 1969.

The Board's experience of this preponderance of employment complaints is reflected in two ways: first, in management terms, the recruitment of specialists to the conciliation staff and the setting up of a Board Employment Committee (certain types of complaint, e.g. those against the Crown, are reserved to the Board's committees rather than delegated to its regional committees); secondly and more widely, the number of cases falling outside the 1965 Act formed the basis on which the Act of 1968 was framed. The table below shows the breakdown of such cases by type:

TABLE 10:4

COMPLAINTS OUTSIDE THE 1965 ACT

Type	1966–7	1967–8	April 1968 to 26 Nov. 1968
Employment	101	254	184
Publications	24	19	11
Housing	37	61	45
Financial facilities	12	21	15
Police	14	74	40
Shops	7	9	8
Other	43	86	72
Total	238	524	375

The breakdown of complaints received in detail which did fall within the 1965 Act is as follows:

TABLE 10:5

COMPLAINTS WITHIN 1965 ACT

Subject of complaint	1966–7	1967–8	April 1968 to 26 Nov. 1968	Total
Public houses	54	78	39	171
Hotels	12	—	2	14
Cafés	7	10	8	25
Clubs	11	5	15	31
Hospitals	—	1	1	
Public transport	—	7	4	
Places of public entertainment	—	1	3	28
Other	5	6	—	28
Total	89	108	72	269

Of the valid causes for complaint in this period the most common was treatment in public houses. In the course of the year 1967–8, the Board reached an agreement with the Brewers Society whereby when a complaint is being investigated, the brewery concerned will, if requested, make clear to the publican its policy against discrimination.

A detailed analysis of complaints received under the 1968 Act is given at the end of this section, but the following is a brief tabulation of complaints, other than those related to employment, for comparison with the above table. This covers the whole of the first year of the 1968 Act from 26 November 1968 to 19 November 1969 and, therefore, overlaps with the data in the penultimate column in Table 10:5.

TABLE 10:6

COMPLAINTS OTHER THAN EMPLOYMENT, BY TYPE,
26 NOVEMBER 1968–19 NOVEMBER 1969

Type	Total received	Outside scope
Section 2		
Public resort	59	6
Hotels and pubs	80	6
Goods, facilities, and services	152	38
Insurance	21	1
Education	32	4
Police	64	62
Other	66	27
Section 5		
Housing	160	24
Section 6		
Advertisements and notices	153	6
Section 12		
Incitement to commit an unlawful act of discrimination	9	6
Total	796	180

It will be seen that the only major source of complaint which remains largely outside the scope of the Board is complaints against the police. These are only subject to investigation by the Board in very limited circumstances, namely, when the police offer a service to the public (e.g. information services at police stations), but not when the police are discharging their operational roles.

Another constant factor throughout both periods is the high proportion of investigations which resulted in a finding of 'no unlawful discrimination'. The significance of this is not clear. It may, perhaps, show that there is still no real understanding of the functions and powers of the Board. As with many social services offered to the public, those most in need of it may be unaware of its existence. The employment complaints suggest that much friction arises from inadequate communication. Practices which are generally harsh or unfair (but not based on race, etc.) also lead to friction. For example, the reasons given for hiring and firing are rarely properly understood by the immigrant worker; although the white worker suffers in the same way, the coloured man interprets the situation as racial exploitation.

The Board is now undertaking more detailed analysis of the complaints it receives. It will, in future, be possible to know considerably more about the kind of person who complains, against whom he complains, and the situations most prone to produce friction. But in general, the records kept by the Board[1] simply tend to reinforce what common sense and previous surveys have indicated: namely, that most substantial complaints will arise where immigrant communities are concentrated, and that the largest number of complaints refer to the matters of greatest importance to the immigrant—i.e. his work and his home.

[1] For further detail, see Appendices 4 and 5.

CHAPTER 11

The National Committee for Commonwealth Immigrants, the Community Relations Commission

SIMON ABBOTT

In this chapter, the intent is to analyse the effectiveness of the National Committee for Commonwealth Immigrants (N.C.C.I.), re-formed under the Race Relations Act 1968 as the Community Relations Commission (C.R.C.). The succeeding chapter in this book considers the voluntary liaison committees (later called the community relations councils); therefore, the emphasis here is placed on the central, national body, and on its relations with the local committees, the immigrant communities, and the national Government.

Following a brief review of the historical origins of the N.C.C.I. in section 1, we attempt, in section 2, to provide a reasonably comprehensive survey of the work undertaken, and the services provided, by the N.C.C.I. This is immediately followed by a discussion of previous evaluations of the work of the N.C.C.I. in section 3. It is not surprising that there have been several such evaluations: the total resources of the race relations agencies in this country have been small, and the N.C.C.I. has, therefore, loomed correspondingly large in the race relations field; the N.C.C.I. early attracted many of the minute number of articulate, educated, and moderately experienced people, and, understandably, several of them have put forward their own ideas; also, as the social work cum community relations agency, the N.C.C.I. fell heir to a wide potential field of activity which invited discussion as to the precise and most necessary roles that should be adopted. These evaluations, moreover, are obviously relevant in discussing the N.C.C.I./C.R.C. as an effective measure against racial discrimination. The final section of this chapter (4) is concerned with the evaluation of the preceding sections in the light of the discussion in Chapter 1 of this book.

Since the N.C.C.I./C.R.C. has been set very much in a community relations role, it might well be asked what relationship there is between the N.C.C.I./C.R.C. and racial discrimination. A first answer is that the N.C.C.I./C.R.C. is not primarily concerned with racial discrimination as defined under the 1965 or 1968 Race Relations Acts. A comment on the C.R.C. coming from the Race Relations Board, was that the Commission was:

basically, . . . as its title indicates, concerned with community relations at its grass roots level, assisting the harmonious integration of communities. If a person comes along to their liaison officer and says 'Look, I was refused a job here or a house there and I think it was because of the colour of my skin' their liaison officer is not trained to deal with this particular kind of complaint and the right thing for that liaison officer [sic] to say is 'If you think you have been discriminated against on these grounds, the right way to deal with this is to send it to the Race Relations Board'.[1]

A further and more full answer would recognize that the C.R.C. is, or at least should be, vitally concerned with the question of race discrimination. Even if precluded from participation in the legal and administrative processes operated by the Board, local community relations officers in practice find they are repeatedly approached for advice and at least preliminary assistance over alleged incidents of discrimination, some of which may in any case fall outside the scope of the legislation. But community relations is basically concerned with the general discriminatory situations that surround and extend beyond the simple act of discrimination. This wider relationship was discussed in Chapter 1, where the discriminatory act was set against such related factors as the positions of in- and out-groups, their relationship to society as a whole, and the issues of second-order discrimination (for example, discrimination arising in part from migration and longer-term historical factors). It is, therefore, reasonable to discuss the N.C.C.I./C.R.C. in relation to effectiveness and racial discrimination.

1. *Historical Origins*

The Government initiative and action, in respect of non-white people in Britain, has functioned mainly on two fronts: firstly,

[1] House of Commons Select Committee on Race Relations and Immigration, *Minutes of Evidence*, 19 December 1968 (London, H.M.S.O., 1968), p. 41.

to control immigration; secondly, to promote integration. Thus the 1965 White Paper declared:

This policy has two aspects: one relating to control on the entry of immigrants so that it does not outrun Britain's capacity to absorb them; the other relating to positive measures designed to secure for the immigrants and their children their rightful place in our society, and to assist local authorities and other bodies in areas of high immigration in dealing with certain problems which have arisen.[1]

The 1965 National Committee for Commonwealth Immigrants was the first major attempt by the Government to take action in the direction of integration. But from the beginning of any analysis of the N.C.C.I. and its successor, it is important to note four conditioning factors: that the themes of immigration control and integration were firmly linked together; that the N.C.C.I. was considered largely as a voluntary body, and so in a sense non-Governmental ('its main stimulus must come from the harnessing of voluntary effort');[2] conversely, that the N.C.C.I. in its creation and financing was the creature of Government; and, finally, that the tasks of local work and national advice, when linked, proved unhappy partners.

The N.C.C.I. was not, of course, the first national body in the field. With the passing by the Conservative Government of the Commonwealth Immigrants Act 1962, came also the appointment of the non-statutory Commonwealth Immigrants Advisory Council (C.I.A.C.). This body, which was to advise the then Home Secretary Mr. R. A. Butler, had certain specific tasks:

(i) to examine the arrangements made by local authorities in whose areas substantial numbers of Commonwealth immigrants have settled, to assist immigrants to adapt themselves to British habits and customs, and to report on the adequacy of the efforts made;
(ii) to examine whether the powers of local authorities to deal with matters affecting the welfare of immigrants are sufficient, and whether any further action can usefully be taken to stimulate action by local authorities; and
(iii) to examine the relationship between action by local offices of Government Departments and local authorities on the one hand, and

---

[1] The Prime Minister, *Immigration from the Commonwealth*, White Paper, Cmnd. 2739 (London, H.M.S.O., August 1965), p. 2.
[2] Ibid., p. 17.

the efforts of voluntary bodies on the other, in furthering the welfare of immigrants.[1]

During its nearly three years of existence, the C.I.A.C. produced four reports: the first (Cmnd. 2119, July 1963) dealt with housing, and argued against special measures for immigrants; the second (Cmnd. 2266, February 1964) mainly considered education, and recommended a degree of dispersal; the third (Cmnd. 2458, September 1964) examined the problems of immigrant school-leavers; and the final report (Cmnd. 2796, October 1965) again dealt with housing. In its operation, the C.I.A.C. was, therefore, a non-Governmental and voluntary body set up by the Government to offer advice to the Government. It is difficult to gauge the effectiveness of this organization: Sheila Patterson considered that: 'Over these years, the Council accumulated and rediffused a substantial body of knowledge and expertise which was to provide a valuable basis and a positive climate of opinion for the more centralized work of integration that was to follow.'[2] While it cannot be pretended that the actual conditions of the immigrants, or the extent of discrimination against them, can have been significantly affected by the existence of the C.I.A.C., it can be argued that a foundation was laid for the successor body, and that the C.I.A.C. participated in and assisted with the élitist group interested in race relations. In these limited but not unimportant terms, it can be regarded as effective.

In its second report, the C.I.A.C. had recommended the appointment of a full-time officer 'concerned with practical problems arising from the presence of Commonwealth immigrants in Britain'.[3] This Advisory Officer, Miss Nadine Peppard, was appointed in April 1964 on a grant from the Government; she was, however, responsible to the National Committee for Commonwealth Immigrants formed in the same month.[4] This first N.C.C.I. was again, like the C.I.A.C., a small voluntary committee. The main task of the Committee and of Miss Peppard was to co-ordinate the activities of the various local groups later

---

[1] Quoted in Sheila Patterson, *Immigration and Race Relations in Britain, 1960–1967* (London, Oxford University Press, for Institute of Race Relations, 1969), p. 115.

[2] Ibid., p. 116.

[3] Ibid.

[4] The Committee Chairman was Philip Mason, then Director of the Institute of Race Relations. This ten-man Committee was initially known as the National Advisory Committee for Commonwealth Immigrants.

known as 'voluntary liaison committees'. This work was supported by a Government grant of £6,000 for the first year and £9,000 for the second.

A review of the growth of these committees is given in the following chapter, but it can here be noted that the first local committees had been formed in the mid-1950s: some, such as the Committee for the Welfare of Colonial Workers in Bristol, have been judged 'overtly paternalistic';[1] others, such as the Nottingham Commonwealth Citizens Consultative Committee, aimed to involve the immigrants themselves in a joint effort to improve relations.

From a hotch-potch of fifteen committees in April 1964, there was created a coherent network of thirty-one committees, thirteen staffed by full-time officers and financed either by the local authority or the Council of Social Service. In April 1965, there took place the first centrally organized conference of such local committees.[2]

This would appear to be no mean achievement.

Thus the 1965 White Paper, which heralded the restriction of Commonwealth immigrant workers to not more than seven and a half thousand a year, saw also a considerable extension of Government action in the field of integration. The uniting of the advisory functions of the C.I.A.C. and the local committee co-ordination of the N.C.C.I., created in August 1965 the new National Committee for Commonwealth Immigrants. Although it is probably the case that most observers felt the co-ordination of the local committees to be the main aim of the N.C.C.I., to a considerable extent the advisory role was to dominate over the next three years.

2. Work

(a) TERMS OF REFERENCE

The 1965 Government White Paper succinctly defined the tasks of the old N.C.C.I. in this way: 'The work of the National Committee consists largely in providing advice and information. It also has an important function in assisting in the formation of

---

[1] E. J. B. Rose and associates, *Colour and Citizenship: A Report on British Race Relations* (London, Oxford University Press, for Institute of Race Relations, 1969), p. 383.

[2] Patterson, op. cit., p. 117; but 31 is contradicted by the N.C.C.I. in *The First Six Months: A Report of the National Committee for Commonwealth Immigrants* (London, N.C.C.I., 1966), p. 8, which gives the number as 27.

local liaison committees and regional organisations.'[1] It went on to emphasize that, for the new N.C.C.I., 'Its finances and staff will be such that it will be able to expand existing services to the voluntary liaison committees and the regional organizations', and that:

it is important that the new National Committee should be able to build up a comprehensive body of doctrine which can be flexibly applied to a variety of local situations, extend the range of existing information work, organise conferences of workers in the field, arrange training courses, stimulate research and the examination by experts of particular problems, and generally promote and co-ordinate effort on a national basis.[2]

These, then, were the initial Governmental guide-lines, and they contained the two main functions of giving advice and information, and of co-ordinating the voluntary liaison committees.

The 'terms of reference' were in 1966 defined as follows:

The National Committee for Commonwealth Immigrants shall be required to promote and co-ordinate on a national basis efforts directed towards the integration of Commonwealth immigrants into the community. In particular the Committee shall be required to:

(a) Promote and co-ordinate the activities of voluntary liaison committees and advise them on their work

(b) Where necessary, assist in the recruitment and training of suitable men or women to serve these committees as full-time officials

(c) Provide a central information service

(d) Organise conferences, arrange training courses and stimulate research

(e) Advise on those questions which are referred to them by Government or which they consider should be brought to the attention of Government.[3]

In 1969, the general guide-lines were re-expressed in terms of the recently granted statutory rights and obligations:

1. The statutory responsibilities of the Community Relations Commission are set out in Section 25 and Schedule 4 of the Race Relations Act 1968. Under the Act it is the duty of the Commission:
(a) to encourage the establishment of, and assist others to take steps to secure the establishment of, harmonious community relations and to

---

[1] *Immigration from the Commonwealth*, op. cit., p. 16.
[2] Ibid., p. 17.
[3] National Committee for Commonwealth Immigrants, *Report for 1966* (London, N.C.C.I., 1967), p. 24.

co-ordinate on a national basis the measures adopted for that purpose by others;

(b) to advise the Home Secretary on any matter referred to the Commission by him and to make recommendations to him on any matter which the Commission consider should be brought to his attention.

2. For the purpose of (a) above the Commission are empowered:

(a) to establish services for giving advice on community relations to local authorities and other local organisations concerned therewith and for collecting information with respect to community relations;

(b) to provide courses of training in connection with community relations;

(c) to arrange or promote the holding of conferences on matters connected with community relations.

3. The Commission are also empowered to give financial assistance to any local organisations appearing to the Commission to be concerned with community relations and, with the approval of the Home Secretary, to appoint advisory committees for the purpose of such of their functions as the Commission think fit. Financial assistance given to local organisations from public funds requires the approval of the Home Secretary and the consent of the Treasury. The Commission are also required to make annual reports to the Home Secretary with respect to the exercising of their functions.[1]

The terms of reference remained on the same lines, but the advisory functions at the national level had been refined and somewhat diminished, and the co-ordination of the local effort somewhat extended and strengthened. For whereas the N.C.C.I. could and did treat directly with the Prime Minister, the C.R.C.'s ultimate Government contact was the Home Secretary. His approval was required for appointing certain advisory committees, and the C.R.C. became subject to closer financial control from the Treasury. Also, the advice-giving panels, whose work is later described, were not continued in their previous form. On the other hand, the community relations concept did imply a widened role for the local committees.

(b) RESOURCES AVAILABLE

What were the means and materials available to the National Committee and its successor? Table 11:1 shows sources of income and expenditure:

[1] House of Commons Select Committee on Race Relations and Immigration, *Minutes of Evidence*, 23 January 1969 (London, H.M.S.O., January 1969), pp. 55–6.

TABLE 11:1
N.C.C.I./C.R.C. £ INCOME AND EXPENDITURE
1965–1970

	Income	Expenditure*				
	Government grants	Secretariat	Conferences, etc.	Grants to voluntary liaison committees	Information services	Total
1965–6†	70,000	17,914	620	1,603	—	20,137
1966–7	120,000	47,376	10,310	10,867	8,976	77,528
1967–8	170,000	74,246	10,854	37,084	9,551	131,735
1968–9‡	200,000	60,940	9,011	42,288	3,762	186,000
1969–70	300,000	127,280	7,136	134,915	15,077	284,408
1970–1	395,000					

* This expenditure excludes 'the Special Fund', which was set up with a grant of £50,000 from the Calouste Gulbenkian Foundation (Lisbon). The N.C.C.I. *Report for 1967* (London, N.C.C.I., 1968), pp. 23–5, shows grants from this Fund, of £24,192 to Fair Housing Groups, £20,362 to multi-racial play-groups, and £2,571 to summer programmes.

† For six months, from October to March only, others being for financial year April to March.

‡ Expenditure for January–November 1968 only, except that the total expenditure is the approximate expenditure for the whole financial year 1968–9.

Source: Annual reports of the N.C.C.I. and C.R.C.

Figure 11:1 illustrates the structure of the National Committee as it was in early 1968:

FIGURE 11:1
THE N.C.C.I. 1968

National Committee *
Chairman
Deputy Chairman
18 other members

Administrative Staff of the Committee (later Secretariat) †	*Advisory Panels* *
Administration	Children's (11 members)
Education	Community Relations (18)
Fieldwork (later Development Officers)	Education (17)
Industrial Relations	Employment (9)
Information	Health and Welfare (7)
Publications	Housing (9)
Research	Information (10)
Social Development	Legal and Civil Affairs (6)
Training	Training (11)

* All voluntary, part-time, and unpaid.
† Including General Secretary and 31 other staff.
Source: N.C.C.I., *Report for 1967*, op. cit.

The organization of the Secretariat, or Administrative Staff, is shown below in more detail.

FIGURE 11:2

THE N.C.C.I. SECRETARIAT, LATE 1968

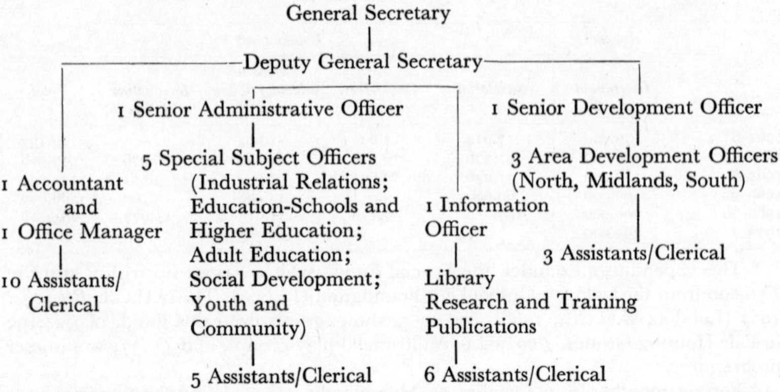

General Secretary

Deputy General Secretary

1 Senior Administrative Officer

1 Senior Development Officer

1 Accountant
and
1 Office Manager

10 Assistants/
Clerical

5 Special Subject Officers
(Industrial Relations;
Education-Schools and
Higher Education;
Adult Education;
Social Development;
Youth and
Community)

5 Assistants/Clerical

3 Area Development Officers
(North, Midlands, South)

1 Information
Officer

3 Assistants/Clerical

Library
Research and Training
Publications

6 Assistants/Clerical

Source: Evidence submitted by the C.R.C. to the Select Committee on Race Relations and Immigration, 'Annex III', simplified.

By the end of 1970, the general arrangement and staffing of the Commission had changed very little, but the nine Advisory Panels had been replaced by only three Advisory Committees.

FIGURE 11:3

THE C.R.C. STRUCTURE, EARLY 1970

The Commission

Chairman
2 Deputy Chairmen
9 Members

Administrative Staff

General Secretary
1 Assistant
Deputy General Secretary
Press and Information Officer
2 Assistants
Senior Development Officer
4 Development Officers
2 Assistants
Special Subjects Officer (vacant)
5 Special Subjects Officers (1 vacant)
1 Assistant
Office Manager
Accountant

Advisory Committees *

Education (18 Members,
2 'Special Advisers', 1 Department of
Education and Science 'Observer',
1 Education Department 'Assessor')

Employment (7 Members)

* The Housing Committee did not meet until October 1970.
Source: Community Relations Commission, *Report of the Community Relations Commission for 1969/70* (London, H.M.S.O., 1970).

The intended number within the Secretariat does not seem to have been reached. Between 1966 and 1969 the situation would seem to have been as follows:

TABLE 11:2

N.C.C.I./C.R.C. SECRETARIAT 1966–1969

	Senior staff*	Other	Total
1966†	8	7	15
1967	12	11	23
1968 March	17	15	32
1969 March	18	19	37

* For example, in early 1967: General Secretary, Deputy General Secretary, Assistant Secretaries, Assistants, etc.

† These dates are, approximately, for March or earlier of each year.

Source: N.C.C.I., *The First Six Months*, op. cit.; annual reports for 1966 and 1967; and information received from the C.R.C.

For the purpose of further analysing the work of the N.C.C.I./ C.R.C., it is proposed to consider the activities of the three main constituent parts: the main Committee, the panels, and the permanent Administrative Staff or Secretariat.

(c) THE MAIN COMMITTEE

The National Committee, in the sense of the voluntary, controlling council, exercised one unique function: namely, direct converse, at a high level, with the Government (although, it is true, the panels also exercised this function, but usually at a lower level).

Soon after its formation, on 1 December 1965, a deputation was led by the Chairman[1] to the Prime Minister, to dispute the part of the 1965 White Paper referring to immigration, particularly on procedures of admission and the right of appeal. Not long after, on 15 December, a further deputation to the Home Secretary on behalf of the voluntary liaison committees, queried cases of refusals of admission.

At the time of the Commonwealth Immigrants Act in early 1968, there were deputations to the Home Secretary (on 27 February), the Prime Minister (on 14 March), and an exchange of letters between the Committee and the Prime Minister, largely

[1] The Archbishop of Canterbury was Chairman throughout the life of the N.C.C.I., and Sir James Robertson was Deputy Chairman.

on the position of the Kenya Asians and the potential effectiveness
of the then forthcoming Race Relations Bill 1968. These were
supplemented by a public statement issued on 1 April 1968, and
by the publication of the above correspondence in the Committee's *Report for 1967*. The Committee, undaunted, has continued its 'opposition to Section 1 of the Commonwealth
Immigrants Act, 1968', and has remained 'much concerned
about the need to include in it [the Race Relations Bill] really
effective enforcement procedures'. In its concluding statements, it
maintained that: 'It [the N.C.C.I.] is of course an independent
body and it will continue to submit for the consideration of the
Government whatever advice it feels will be most helpful in
achieving its aim. . . . '[1]

However, this high-level exchange, of course, formed a very
small part of the total work of the N.C.C.I. It has already been
pointed out that it could not continue, at least direct with the
Prime Minister, under the C.R.C. It would also seem reasonable
to believe that the task of advising the Government over, for
example, the immigration issue, was in effect abandoned: 'You
will be glad to know that the members of my Commission and
those with whom we are dealing have understood the difference
between . . . us and the question of the immigration policy of the
country; that is determined by you people, in a political
judgement.'[2] In effect, the Commission of twelve members was
ceasing to operate publicly as a monitor or pressure group against
the Government. However, the Commission did express to the
Home Secretary their 'concern' about the projected South
African cricket tour.

(d) THE ADVISORY PANELS
Seven panels had been formed by the end of the first six months,
in April 1966, and their number had increased to nine by the time
of the metamorphosis to the C.R.C., on 25 November 1968; on
this date the panels in their existing form were abandoned. The
panels had been serviced by members of the Administrative
Staff; therefore, this account also covers part of the work of the
Secretariat.

[1] Letter of 29 March 1968 printed on p. vii of insert in the N.C.C.I.'s *Report for 1967*,
op. cit.
[2] Select Committee on Race Relations . . ., 23 January 1969, op. cit., p. 75.

The Education Panel was one of the most successful.[1] In 1966, there was a series of N.C.C.I. fact-finding conferences with Chief Education Officers and teachers; this was followed by week-end conferences in colleges of further education and discussions with inspectors from the Department of Education and Science. This discussion pin-pointed such needs as booklets designed to enable teachers to understand the cultural and psychological problems of immigrants; improved training of teachers and in-service training; the education of all pupils (and parents) on racial and immigration questions.[2] As a result, pamphlets were produced and conferences held (for example, in the West Midlands in May–June 1966; at the University of York on 22–24 July 1966). Another initiative was in the direction of the Teacher Training Colleges. Responses to a questionnaire sent to the colleges, revealed specific needs. Consequently, two national conferences were held (at Edge Hill in January 1967 and at Leicester in 1967), and the Chairman 'wrote a personal letter to all chief education officers describing what some LEAs had been able to do, and giving a comprehensive catalogue of imaginative and forward-looking initiatives'.[3] Later, a further questionnaire was sent to all training colleges. Other conferences were held: in March 1967, in association with the Society of Friends, a four-day meeting was held on Education in a Multi-racial Britain; and in April 1967, at Nottingham University, a conference discussed the possibilities of including race relations within liberal and social studies courses. How often did the Education Panel meet? In 1967, for example, the main panel met ten times and, additionally, twice with other panels. This panel also issued a public statement concerning the Government's dispersal policy for immigrants in schools.

The work of the Housing Panel was also significant. Following a study in 1966 of the general and particular problems facing immigrants in the housing field, *The Housing of Commonwealth Immigrants* was published in 1967. A further important paper was produced on areas of special housing need. On 8 July 1967, a

[1] Throughout this discussion, unless otherwise noted, the written sources are the N.C.C.I.'s *The First Six Months, Report for 1966,* and *Report for 1967,* all op. cit.

[2] See E. W. Hawkins, 'Three Years: The N.C.C.I. and Education', *Learning for Living* (Vol. 8, No. 3, January 1969), pp. 20–1.

[3] Ibid., p. 21.

deputation from the National Committee met the Joint Parliamentary Secretary with special departmental responsibility for the housing of Commonwealth immigrants; and later, the Minister of Housing and Local Government agreed to call a conference of local authorities. Over fifty local authorities sent representatives to the conference, which met on 21 June 1967; the purpose of this conference was 'to obtain the views and advice of those local authorities most concerned with the problems which may arise from the settlement of substantial numbers of Commonwealth immigrants', and to take account of recent reports, including those of the panels.

To a considerable extent, therefore, there is a similar pattern of activity: initial investigation, sometimes through national or regional meetings, followed by a report and probably a conference, and possibly some 'lobbying' of the relevant Government ministry. This can again be illustrated by, for example, the working of the Children's Panel, which concentrated on the problems of the pre-school coloured child. Thus, there were 'regional conferences to which both committee members and officers of local authority health and children's departments' were invited. A working party produced a pamphlet. And, subsequently, the panel supported its recommendation of a commission or inter-departmental inquiry into the care of the under-fives; a deputation met the Minister of Health on 30 June 1967. And there were also conferences: for example, the two held in 1967 were at West Bromwich on 11 February, and Leicester on 12 July. In 1967, this panel met eight times.

It is suggested that certain of the other committees worked in this way, that is, the Employment Panel, the Health and Welfare Panel, the Legal and Civil Affairs Panel, and to a lesser extent the Information Panel. This last panel saw its task as one of informing the general public, rather than acting as publicity agency for the N.C.C.I. itself. But, again, there was the preparation of reports—in this case, of a television film—and a survey of the treatment of race issues by four London newspapers. The survey was followed up, on 20 October 1967, by a conference for editors and journalists. The remaining two panels—the Training Panel and the Community Relations Panel—were possibly to a greater extent arms of the Secretariat.

As the Education Panel had been both one of the apparently

more productive and less controversial of the N.C.C.I. panels, it is not so surprising that education should continue for a time as the subject of the only C.R.C. Advisory Committee. The work of the new Committee was broad: 'With the advice of this Committee, the Commission is undertaking a nationwide campaign along the whole educational front to further the idea of "Education for a multi-racial society".'[1] The Committee set up four subsidiary groups on 'Teacher-training and curriculum development', 'Linguistic needs of the immigrant population', 'Post-school education in community relations', and 'LEA liaison and administrative group'. The most successful project was probably the summer language scheme under Professor Eric Hawkins from the University of York. Under this scheme, funded with £3,000 from the C.R.C. and via the Education Advisory Committee, 'about 100 Asian children were given English teaching for a month in a Huddersfield junior school by English students'.[2] It was also not surprising that the second Advisory Committee to be established should be on employment, for this was a field in which the then Chairman of the Commission, Frank Cousins, had long experience. Like the Education Committee, broad representation was sought, and obtained, from the Confederation of British Industry, the Trades Union Congress, the Department of Employment and Productivity, and the Central Youth Employment Executive. A number of activities were begun, including the translation into four Asian languages of a D.E.P. guide to newcomers in industry, advice to the Central Youth Executive on the production of a careers brochure aimed at the parents of coloured school-leavers, the start of a survey of in-plant language training facilities, etc. Although 'Housing probably presents one of the biggest potential sources of tension in race relations',[3] no housing committee was formed until late 1970.

(e) THE ADMINISTRATIVE STAFF

It is not easy to draw a clear and simple picture of the activities of the Secretariat, or Administrative Staff.[4] Not only was there

---

[1] C.R.C., *Report . . . 1969-70*, op. cit., p. 17.
[2] Ibid., p. 19.
[3] Ibid., p. 22.
[4] This discussion does not cover the N.C.C.I.'s organization of its internal finance, administration, etc.

continuing change over the three years of the N.C.C.I.'s existence, but its transformation into the C.R.C. marked the transferring of certain responsibilities to the Secretariat (particularly in terms of the initiation exercised earlier by the panels). If, for example, the 1966 terms of reference are set against the titles of staff of early 1968 or, for that matter, the 'functions' and 'methods' of 1969,[1] there is much apparent overlapping and interrelation between the functions and methods of the Secretariat. A simple analysis will be attempted here, considering, first, the relations with the voluntary liaison committees; second, the general information work; third, the more specialized activities or 'Special Subjects', such as education or industrial relations; fourth, advice to the Government; and fifth, research. But it must be remembered that these categories do not altogether relate to the organizational structure of the Secretariat, and also that they often tied in with the work of the panels and advisory committees.

The first category mentioned above, relations with the voluntary liaison committees, was the work of the Fieldwork, or later, Development, Officers. The growth of the local committees between 1965 and 1970 is shown in Table 11:3.

TABLE 11:3

VOLUNTARY LIAISON COMMITTEES/COMMUNITY
RELATIONS COUNCILS 1965–1970

	With full-time officer	With grant-in-aid*	Total
1965†	—	—	27
1966	—	9	32
1967	12	19	42
1968	32	35	50
1969	42	44	69
1970	47	?	81

* Grant-in-aid paid for, or approved by, the N.C.C.I.
† October 1965; for all other years, near beginning of each calendar year.
Source: The N.C.C.I.'s The First Six Months, and annual reports, all op. cit.

From the beginning, the N.C.C.I. attached special importance to the voluntary liaison committees: 'The National

[1] See Select Committee on Race Relations . . . , 23 January 1969, op. cit., pp. 57–62: the heads are Advice, Opinion Forming, Support of Local Activities, Co-ordination, Collection and Dissemination of Information, Special Subjects, Research, Training, Finance, and Staff.

Committee considers the work of the voluntary liaison committees to be of the greatest importance to community relations nationally, and its advisory service to them, with visits and assistance of all kinds, has been given high priority.'[1] The main link between the N.C.C.I. and the liaison committees, in the early days, was probably the personal activity of the General Secretary. In the first three months, the General Secretary and Deputy Secretary had accepted 'something in the region of sixty invitations to speak to groups all over the country', not all of these being liaison committees, of course. Subsequently, the task of liaison was increasingly taken over by the Fieldwork Officers, or Development Officers as they were later called; in 1968, there were three of these 'stationed at headquarters'.[3]

The creation of a voluntary liaison committee was often a long and arduous task, and in nearly all cases these committees resulted from preparation and consultation by the N.C.C.I. with the local authority. The basic concept was that the whole community should be represented, not only the immigrants; therefore, all the social organizations in an area should be invited to take part. Indeed, acceptance within the N.C.C.I. fold was sometimes withheld because representation was too narrow. It was also important that the chairman of the committee should be respected locally. In an interview (on 29 March 1968), the General Secretary pointed out one danger with respect to the committees: 'if too militant then they lose access to local authority'. Guide-lines were produced to cover key points: the creation of new committees was discussed in the 'Note for Guidance on the Formation of a Voluntary Liaison Committee' of April 1967; the functions of the officers, in 'The Duties of a Liaison Officer'; and the granting of financial assistance, in 'Procedure for Application by Voluntary Liaison Committees for Grant in Aid'. It should be remembered that the N.C.C.I.'s control over the local committees was very limited: direct financial control was initially limited to grants of about £1,500, preferably matched by local government.[4] Further, the National Committee did 'not have the responsibility for establishing functions of the committees',[5] and:

[1] N.C.C.I., *The First Six Months*, op. cit., p. 9.
[2] N.C.C.I., *The First Six Months*, op. cit., p. 5.
[3] Select Committee on Race Relations . . . , 23 January 1969, op. cit., p. 66.
[4] Interview with General Secretary, 29 March 1968.
[5] Select Committee on Race Relations . . . , 23 January 1969, op. cit., p. 72.

If we tried to take over the function [of directly organizing local community relations] under the existing terms and with the existing money, we would fail because we have neither the resources nor the capacity to do it under the existing regulations.[1]

Although the appointment of officers became increasingly and effectively a shared operation of the C.R.C. and the local councils, the direction of work still lay with the local body and the Commission's control was limited to renewing (or refusing to renew) the annual grant. The amount of this grant increased first to a maximum of £3,500, and then in 1970, to £5,000, in any one year. Local councils could also apply for grants for special work and projects.

There were also difficulties over the training of the officers: the N.C.C.I. mainly ran seminars lasting just over a week,[2] and attempted to avoid the social-worker approach, concentrating rather on community organization and social administration. However, 'there is not in this country a specific training for this kind of job ... our officers in the field at the moment have in fact a mixture of all kinds of backgrounds'.[3]

Meetings of the officers of the liaison committees, and of the chairman, were also organized. 'We have in the past had meetings of delegates, both members and paid officers of the committees, at least twice a year, one week-end and one day conference.'[4] In 1966, the committees had 'joined themselves into a Standing Conference under its [N.C.C.I.] auspices'.[5] The main links with the local committees and councils were, as suggested, primarily through the Development Officers. These were few in number (perhaps a maximum of four in the field), based in London for much of the time (although, ostensibly, in part serving far-off committees), and hard-worked, often with additional responsibilities (for example, the major task of police relations was also carried by one officer). There was, additionally, frequent staff turnover. It is perhaps appropriate, at this point, to note the emergence of more formalized points of contact, as time went on, within the

---

[1] Select Committee on Race Relations ..., 23 January 1969, op. cit., p. 68.
[2] Interview with General Secretary, 29 March 1968. For example, one at York in 1968, with another planned for 1969; see Select Committee on Race Relations ..., 23 January 1969, op. cit., p. 78.
[3] Ibid., p. 68.
[4] Ibid., p. 66.
[5] N.C.C.I., Report for 1966, op. cit., p. 10.

local community relations councils: firstly, in 1968, the local officers established ACRO (the Association of Community Relations Officers); secondly, a 1970 meeting of ACRO officers suggested the establishment of an Association of Community Relations Councils.

The written word had not been forgotten and the first issue of what became the quarterly *Liaison* appeared in June 1965.[1] This journal was aimed at the voluntary liaison committees: it gave individual committees the opportunity of describing their own success stories. Examples of this might be the Oxford Committee's 'break-through' in industrial relations, achieving the employment of Commonwealth immigrants in some Oxford firms; or the titanic struggle of the Gloucester Committee to establish a 'Multi-Racial Play Group'.[2] *Liaison* also provided some information on the N.C.C.I., and on events of major importance in the race relations world. The deputations to the Prime Minister over the difficulties of the 1965 White Paper (on 1 December 1965) and to the Home Secretary over the entry refusal of some 'Indian and Pakistani dependants' (on 15 November 1965) were recorded,[3] as were descriptions of the Race Relations Board and the Wilson Report.[4] The committees also received *NCCI Information*, a two-sided monthly news-sheet, with reports on the availability of leaflets on oil-heaters in Greek, Turkish, Hindi, Urdu, Bengali, and English; and on major N.C.C.I. activities such as the deputation on police-immigrant relations to the Home Secretary.[5] This news-sheet was replaced by a monthly, the *CRC News*. In 1969, the C.R.C. produced a successor to *Liaison* in the shape of *Community*, a glossy quarterly with a wide, free distribution.

The second area of activity of the Secretariat was given as general information work. This was the task of the Information Officer and those working in the library, and on publications and research (although research is also considered separately). This task can be interpreted broadly, with considerable importance

[1] *Liaison* was discontinued with the change to the C.R.C., the last issue appearing in October 1968.

[2] *Liaison* (No. 11, July 1968), pp. 21–2.

[3] *Liaison* (No. 3, December 1965), pp. 2–3.

[4] *Liaison* (No. 9, October 1967), pp. 13 and 16.

[5] *NCCI Information* (No. 4, September 1966). The first number was issued in July 1966. The circulation, of course, extended beyond the individual committees. See Appendix 4.

attached to 'general education' and 'opinion-forming'. 'The National Committee's primary function is undoubtedly that of education of the community at all levels and in a variety of ways.'[1] This verdict echoed a similar statement from the previous year: 'If it were necessary to sum up in one word the complicated task in hand, that word would undoubtedly be education.'[2] This great emphasis on education can be regarded as constant: 'It is fundamentally only through education that racial discrimination can be reduced.'[3]

For the moment, the rather more limited activities of the Information Officer and others will be reviewed. Within these activities, perhaps the most important lay in the range of publications produced. These covered *Liaison, Community, NCCI Information,* and *CRC News,* which have already been discussed; a series of occasional papers, of which fourteen were published in 1966–7 and which, in the N.C.C.I.'s view, 'helped very substantially in dealing with problems in particular areas';[4] and also a facts paper, short bibliographies, lists of immigrant organizations, and leaflets in various languages.[5] The occasional papers came chiefly from the work of the panels and from conferences: for example, Dr. David Stafford-Clark on *Prejudice in the Community,* or the report on *The Housing of Commonwealth Immigrants.* With the passing of the panels, the number of new publications declined: no pamphlets, for example, were published in 1969. The library work was limited and restricted to the needs of the Secretariat. The issuing of information, apart from publications and conferences, was not much undertaken; and the further extension of information work into the anti-defamation role remained largely unexplored: 'we could, if we were not careful, spend all our time answering people who make nonsensical comments'.[6]

Another activity that might be described as within the larger educational concept was the giving of talks. It will be remembered that the General Secretary and Deputy Secretary had early taken on a considerable number of talks, an activity which developed with particular importance in the sphere of police-

---

[1] N.C.C.I., *Report for 1967,* op. cit., p. 15.
[2] N.C.C.I., *Report for 1966,* op. cit., p. 8.
[3] C.R.C., *Report . . . 1969–70,* op. cit., p. 16.
[4] Select Committee on Race Relations . . . , 23 January 1969, op. cit., p. 69.
[5] For list of publications and some distribution figures, see Appendix 4.
[6] Select Committee on Race Relations . . . , 23 January 1969, op. cit., pp. 68–9.

immigrant relations. In 1967, two lectures were arranged at each police training centre in the country, and discussions over training were held with the Home Office and police.[1] In 1968, lectures were given to all police recruits in England and Wales (except Metropolitan London) 'as an integral part of the curriculum for preliminary training'. Also, assistance was provided on a number of police courses: for example, in May 1968, a pilot seminar was held for the Women's Police Branch of the Metropolitan Force, with further seminars in October 1968 and February 1969; and in November 1968, there was a one-day seminar for the Bradford City Police.

The third category, Special Subjects, is not unrelated to education. Maintaining the concept of the wider educational task, but incorporating the activities of the Special Subject Officers (and indeed the work of the panels and advisory committees), this category can be illustrated by considering the range and number of conferences held. Between 1966 and March 1969, over eighty conferences and shorter sessions were organized in various parts of the country. These covered the major conferences of the N.C.C.I., e.g. 'Racial Equality in Employment' held in May 1967; as well as 'community leadership courses' which involved local liaison committees and mainly local leaders of immigrant organizations in discussions on such topics as 'The Local Authority Social Services' and 'The Police and the Community'; and meetings of the 'Standing Conference of Voluntary Liaison Committees', for example, the annual meeting held in Bristol on 27–29 September 1968. Indeed much of the work of the Special Subject Officers lay largely in servicing the panels and organizing conferences. Subsequently, more emphasis was placed on supporting local projects. The 1969–70 annual report listed twenty-two grants, ranging in size from £3,100 to the University of York and £2,000 each to the University of Leicester and Birmingham Public Libraries, to £100 each to the Deptford Fund, Avenues Unlimited, St. Philips Church, and Moat Girls' School, with a final £64 for Wandsworth Students Housing Association. Some grants went to immigrant organizations, apparently those of a non-radical nature: for example, £1,500 was given to the Caribbean Overseas Association.

The fourth category was advice to the Government. Again,

[1] This, and following, information supplied by the C.R.C.

this activity was linked with that of the panels. Submission was made, for example, to the Wilson Committee on immigration procedures by the Legal and Civil Affairs Panel; but submission was made by the staff, for example, to the Seebohm Committee[1] on the organization and responsibilities of local authority social services in England and Wales. And there were, of course, several other deputations and discussions not here, or earlier, recorded. Under the C.R.C., the offering of advice continued, but possibly with reduced expectations: 'The Commission . . . realises that to offer advice does not mean that such advice must be accepted or acted upon.' And it was noted that changes in conditions governing 'B' voucher admissions had been made 'without prior discussion with the Commission'.[2] Nevertheless, apart from the approach to the Home Secretary over the proposed South African cricket tour, there was evidence given to the Select Committee on Race Relations and Immigration, participation in discussions, and the establishment, of the new United Kingdom Immigrants Advisory Service, and advice offered to the Northern Ireland Government which led to the establishment of a Community Relations Commission for Northern Ireland in late 1969.

The fifth area was research. A good deal of confusion is brought about by the indiscriminate use of the term 'research': from the expenditure outlined in Table 11:1, on Fair Housing Groups, multi-racial playgrounds, and summer programmes, it can be seen that the N.C.C.I. reasonably chose to concentrate on what is often called 'action research'. Inevitably, it has also been necessary for their staff to attempt some compilation of particularly relevant research and events, and this activity is sometimes called 'desk-research'. Although some of the liaison committees did move towards the policy and academic research field, attempting, for example, recruitment and attitude testing, the N.C.C.I. emphasized as priorities the more ordinary community relations activities.[3] The N.C.C.I. did, however, co-

---

[1] Jointly with the Institute of Race Relations.

[2] C.R.C., *Report . . . 1969–70*, op. cit., p. 8.

[3] 'It is arguable whether a central body of the kind here under discussion should itself attempt to undertake research (as distinct from the collection of information) into problems of community relations or whether it would not be better advised to leave this function to other bodies such as the Institute of Race Relations or the sociology departments of universities': Select Committee on Race Relations . . ., 23 January 1969, op. cit., p. 61.

sponsor with the Race Relations Board the immensely important P.E.P. report on *Racial Discrimination*, and the valuable *Report on Anti-Discrimination Legislation* by Harry Street and others.

It cannot be claimed that this section has provided an exhaustive review of the work of the N.C.C.I. and the C.R.C. Any race relations agency, in a time of tension, is subjected to many calls of an informal or extra-curricular nature which go largely unrecorded. Nor was it thought necessary or useful to describe in close detail all the work achieved, when much of it was repetitive. The intention has been to provide some indication of the range and depth of the work so that the question of effectiveness may be considered.

3. *Evaluations*

It was earlier suggested as not surprising that the N.C.C.I. should be called to court by a number of critics. The reasons then advanced were that the N.C.C.I. was of considerable size and importance within the small range and number of British race relations agencies; that it had early involved within its work many of the very few people already active in this field; and that the immensity of the social work and community relations field invited debate and dispute over role and method.[1] It was also pointed out that the N.C.C.I. was in origin basically a voluntary body; and so it relied on the part-time support of people from a variety of occupations—academics, social workers, incipient 'civil rights' workers. The following evaluations are put forward in the main by people who, for some time, were quite closely connected with the N.C.C.I., most of them serving on the panels or local committees:[2] personal knowledge and personal involvement were thus combined. This point is not altogether unimportant, as the academic criticism has so far largely originated from people who were at one time closely connected with the N.C.C.I.

One of the more valuable and forward-looking comments was that later known as the Wood proposals. These proposals

[1] In contrast, for example, with the restricted and clearly defined role of the Race Relations Board.

[2] For example, John Rex, Dipak Nandy, and Michael Dummett were on different panels. E. J. B. Rose was also on the main Committee; Anne Dummett was a local Community Relations Officer; Michael Hill was a member of a local committee; and the author has been on a local council.

were put forward as a basis for re-modelling the N.C.C.I., at the time when its forthcoming transformation into the C.R.C. became known. The proposals were as follows:

1. The advisory functions of the N.C.C.I. should be taken over by a National Commission for Racial Equality comprising 28 to 30 members. 25% should be nominated by the Government, 25% should be elected representatives of Liaison Committees, and the remaining 50% should be representatives of ethnic minority groups elected on the basis of registered membership. Included in the Liaison Committee's representation should be one full-time Liaison Officer elected by Liaison Officers from among their own number.
2. Funds should be paid direct to the Liaison Committees in conjunction with the Local Authority on an expressed statutory basis. The 'ear-marked' procedure might be suitable.
3. Reserve funds should be available in each area to finance 'grass-roots' schemes not initiated by the Liaison Committee, and an appeal against the refusal of funds at local level should lie with the National Commission for Racial Equality.[1]

None of these proposals were adopted. Thus, for example, 'the structure of the Community Relations Commission does not include representatives from functioning immigrant organizations'.[2] At the end of 1970, it did not include representatives from the local officers and councils. But the proposals themselves point to the several vital relationships outlined at the beginning of this chapter: between the N.C.C.I. and the Government; between the N.C.C.I. and the immigrant organizations; and between the N.C.C.I. and the local liaison committees. Whether it was possible with these proposals to transmogrify the N.C.C.I., is debatable: it would have meant a vast amount of trust on the part of any government so to endow with funds and authority its critics on the race relations front. At the same time, it must be admitted that the Wood proposals suggested a possible approach to closing the divide between host institutionalism and immigrant communities.[3]

---

[1] Circular from Reverend Wilfred Wood (19 March 1968) to Chairmen and Secretaries of voluntary liaison committees. The proposals were supported by six committees: see Michael Dummett, 'Immigrant Organizations' (Institute of Race Relations Conference Paper, September 1968).

[2] Rose and associates, op. cit., p. 732.

[3] It was, of course, a difficult approach: the Birmingham Advisory Council, as a more popular forum, was shed by the local council (see Institute of Race Relations *News Letter* [November/December 1968], pp. 448–51).

A further important point, made by Philip Mason,[1] is that the harnessing of the advisory and local liaison tasks in fact militated against the successful accomplishment of either. This view suggests that, at a local level, work with committees was hampered by the variety of stances the main Committee was forced to take on political aspects of race relations.

The division between immigrants and the N.C.C.I. was again, and later, denounced with some not inconsiderable vigour: 'The fundamental reason why, out of the confused variety of immigrant and interracial organisations, nothing like—I will not say a unified movement—but even a movement at all has emerged is the failure of white anti-racialists to play their proper role.'[2] The chief element in this failure is ascribed to the N.C.C.I.'s fostering of the voluntary liaison committees and their ignoring of immigrant organizations and other interracial bodies. 'By imposing on the NCCI the duty of assisting liaison committees, and ignoring the rest, a way was found to give the appearance of Government aid to voluntary effort while conveniently being able to neglect the organizations most likely to be militant.'[3] This meant the emasculation of the embryo civil rights movement, an aim 'most likely ... unconsciously pursued'. Nevertheless: 'The NCCI set about its task with consummate skill.'[4] And, indeed: 'Merely by coming into existence, the NCCI had delivered one of its most damaging blows to the embryo civil rights movement. . . .'[5] Eventually, 'unity between black people's organisations was sacrificed to the hope of influencing the Government'.[6]

The argument is clearly stated: the N.C.C.I. sacrificed the growth and effectiveness of a civil rights type movement by concentrating on the manipulation of local committees dedicated to ineffective co-operation, and the chance of influencing Government at the national level. Like the Wood proposals, this argument again covers the N.C.C.I.'s basic relationship with the immigrant communities, the voluntary liaison committees, and the national Government. In this case, it clearly attaches priority

[1] Verbal communication.
[2] M. Dummett, op. cit., p. 6.
[3] Ibid., p. 8.
[4] Ibid.
[5] Ibid., p. 10.
[6] Ibid.

of importance to the relationship with the immigrant communities.

Probably less than justice is paid to the work undertaken, particularly in the N.C.C.I.'s earlier days, with a variety of race relations organizations; but this is a minor point. The crux of the argument is that the alternative hypothesized—of a vibrant, growing movement—was possible: the balance of evidence suggests that it was not. It is, of course, quite true that the embryo civil rights leaders were, at least initially, led into divided loyalties. 'Of twenty people on the CARD Executive Committee that were elected after the national founding convention (and who served until October 1966), seven members . . . were also on either the National Committee itself or the specialist Advisory Panels'; also the Information Officer for the N.C.C.I. was co-opted onto the CARD executive.[1] It is also true that the N.C.C.I. did concentrate increasingly on the liaison committees. But there must be some measure of doubt that what mattered was the institutional location of the 'white anti-racialists', rather than their relative paucity in power and numbers. More importantly, it must be questioned whether the opportunity for a sizeable civil rights type movement against the immigrant communities had yet arisen. It will be noted that within the West Indian community 'the common view was that West Indians tend to move on a broad front, each individual jealously clinging to this individuality and refusing to place it at the disposal of any so-called leader'; and that 'Might not the whole notion of West Indian leadership in Britain simply be an indication of the grave misconceptions of those who seek it?'[2] In short, it can be argued that the West Indian community in the United Kingdom had not in 1968, for a variety of reasons, adopted to any significant extent the United Kingdom pattern of voluntary associations, of institutional structures involving leaders and the led. The position of the Indian and Pakistani communities is, of course, different, since they had established effective communal organizations. However, it is important to note that such organizations operated only within these communities, and did not act as a bridge between these and other immigrant communities. In respect of the Indian Workers' Association, the best organized and largest immigrant organization:

[1] Ben Heineman, *CARD: The Politics of the Powerless* (London, Oxford University Press, for Institute of Race Relations, forthcoming 1972).
[2] See Chapter 8.

it seems that the role of active participant in British or inter-racial associations may not be compatible with the traditional role of IWA politician. It is difficult to participate effectively in British associations if one recruits a personal following and battles for formal recognition of one's prestige within the immigrant community.[1]

The West Indians lack formal organizations and those of the Indians and Pakistanis are essentially communal: it is, therefore, less surprising that, apart from one person, the Asian leaders interviewed in the present study did not show any eagerness to join hands with West Indians in a common fight against racialism.[2] If in 1968 there was such non-cooperation, during a time of an accepted increase in the consciousness of race relations, it must be open to some doubt that the few white anti-racialists were, at an earlier period, in a position to trigger off a broad-based civil rights movement. Although it is here suggested that the main thesis,[3] as earlier outlined, cannot be wholly accepted, it is not, of course, intended to suggest that other points made in that paper are invalid, nor that the main thesis is wholly invalid. It has, instead, been argued that the main thesis has been taken rather further than the facts will sustain it.

A later re-working of this theme included a further powerful argument: essentially, the argument ran that there had been a failure in political leadership, and that the N.C.C.I. had been a part of this failure. 'In the field of race, we have had a flight from principle and common sense; inaction and confusion where there should have been positive policies; and, as the isolated remnants of original policy, the 1968 Race Relations Act.'[4] Thus, 'the Labour government bears the whole responsibility for Enoch Powell'.[5] Within this basic and national failure of political leadership and ideals, the N.C.C.I. failed to make the Government heed its advice: on the one hand, the Government 'failed even to notify it of the Immigration Bill of 1968', and on the other, the N.C.C.I. shunned publicity 'as if it was the eighth deadly sin . . . there was no way for even an MP to discover what advice it had

---

[1] DeWitt John, *Indian Workers' Associations in Britain* (London, Oxford University Press, for Institute of Race Relations, 1969), p. 158.

[2] See Chapter 8.

[3] That is, Dummett's.

[4] Michael and Ann Dummett, 'The Role of Government in Britain's Racial Crisis', in Lewis Donnelly (ed.), *Justice First* (London, Sheed and Ward, 1969), p. 37.

[5] Ibid., p. 27.

given the government'.[1] An important additional argument was introduced in relation to the links between the N.C.C.I. and the immigrants: this was the charge that the N.C.C.I. aimed at 'not the replacement of the conflict between black and white by one between exploited and exploiters but the avoidance of conflict altogether'.[2] The integrationist, consensus approach limited the effectiveness of the work, by 'providing virtually no service of encouragement or advice to black people's organizations or to interracial bodies not conforming with the liaison committee stereotype'.[3] In deploring the political vacuum which encouraged the erratic effervescence of Powellism, and in defining the failure to reach and support the immigrant organizations, the arguments seem sustained. However, the extent to which the N.C.C.I. was itself in a position to fill the vacuum and succour the Blacks is open to question.

Dummett's initial argument, on the N.C.C.I.'s emasculation of the embryo national civil rights movement, had lacked sufficient detailed evidence. Later work supplied such evidence, but on a local scale—the case of Nottingham—and also illustrated the dichotomy between the conflict and integration approaches.[4] The background to Katznelson's study of Nottingham stressed the general high repute in which the local race relations work was held, and suggested that this was due to the local political consensus that succeeded the summer disturbances of 1958, and to the fact that something in the race field had demonstrably been done. Yet what had in the main been accomplished was a system of buffering, in which the race issue was depoliticized and the Blacks placed under buffer institutions. The argument is thorough, and includes such examples as: 'When the Committee made its only political requests before 1958 for the appointment of a special welfare worker and for permission to use the city's information centre for weekly advice sessions, the Council refused.'[5] The success of the Committee was that it 'has insulated the political community from pressures for change in the racial *status quo*', but in an essentially one-sided way: ' . . . it is clear that while the

[1] Ibid., p. 61.
[2] Ibid., p. 64.
[3] Ibid.
[4] Ira Katznelson, 'The Politics of Racial Buffering in Nottingham, 1954–1968'. *Race* (Vol. XI, No. 4, April 1970).
[5] Ibid., p. 435.

city's coloured population was expected to act as if colour was irrelevant, the political community viewed coloured immigrants as a group apart'. [1]

The structure established was that:

within a year of the disturbances, the political community had established officially sanctioned access points, both within and outside the local authority, for the immigrant population. Neither access point provided for direct access to the political community; each acted instead, under the conceptual heading of liaison, as political buffers. Immigrant needs and demands were filtered through them: Irons's office dealt with individuals, the Consultative Committee with organized immigrant groups. These structural mechanisms, established when the city's coloured population numbered just over 3,000, have remained virtually unchanged to the present. [2]

Although the 'Committee on occasion did useful peripheral work', [3] it was argued that 'neither Irons's office nor the Consultative Committee has been effective in improving the average immigrant's life chances, and ensuring his access to a decent home and quality education for his children'. [4] Indeed, the overall and ultimate effect 'may not only be inadequate but actually retard meaningful black participation, the prerequisite of legitimate integration'. [5] To what extent can this study of Nottingham be applied more widely? Katznelson believes that wider application is possible: 'NCCI and its voluntary liaison committees were conceived as a political buffer that would link whites and blacks in an atmosphere of liberal good-will to promote racial harmony. Instead of blacks linked directly to the political process . . . they would be linked to the polity through officially non-political mediating institutions.' [6] He goes on to suggest a range of ameliorative measures: that the Commission and the local committees should be selected by and made responsible to 'black Englishmen'; that the C.R.C. should become more outspoken; that the advisory role should be extended beyond the present 'mock political

[1] Ibid., p. 444.
[2] Ibid., p. 436. Eric Irons was 'Organiser for Educational Work Amongst the Coloured Communities' for the Consultative Committee.
[3] Ibid., p. 434.
[4] Ibid., p. 440.
[5] Ibid., p. 444.
[6] Ira Katznelson, 'Political Relevance of Prejudice: The Claims of Black Britons', *Patterns of Prejudice* (Vol. 3, No. 4, July–August 1969), p. 4.

battlegrounds that insulate politicians from the black community'.
These arguments illustrate that the local N.C.C.I. committee did
serve to limit Black political growth, and achieved no major
structural change. They do not show that there was a significant,
repressed Black civil rights or other movement that would itself
have had major success. What pattern of development is likely to
satisfy British democracy in the long run? It can be argued that
the local committee may have provided an immediate palliative,
but that a temporarily more conflictual approach under which the
immigrant group moved at least towards pluralistic integration
would eventually achieve a more real racial harmony. One can
claim that effective Black participation, rather than buffering, is,
in the long term, necessary.

Katznelson's work covered both the relationship with the
immigrant organizations and with the local committees. One
assessment of the effectiveness of these committees was that:

The major problems—housing and unemployment—remained un-
touched by the VLCs. . . . There is no evidence to suggest that there is a
single local authority whose housing policy has been affected by the
VLCs. Nor have they played any part in affecting employment policies,
or assisting immigrant groups in industry in times of need.[1]

This comment conflicts rather starkly with what may appear
to be a contrary view: 'An enormous amount of valuable work is
being done by the voluntary liaison committees.'[2] Nandy continues his argument over ineffectiveness, stressing specific points,
including the disadvantages of the social work approach:

Those aspects which form part of traditional social welfare work are
spelt out in clear and specific detail; those which are central to race
relations are either omitted or defined in terms of vague generalities.[3]

This is illustrated in attitudes to discrimination: 'all the evidence
suggests that it [working against discrimination] has a very low
place in the list of priorities. . . . '[4] The distinction between the
act of discrimination and what might be termed the situations of
discrimination, or the relatively deprived and advantaged

---

[1] Dipak Nandy, 'An Illusion of Competence', in Anthony Lester and Nicholas
Deakin (eds.), Policies for Racial Equality (London, Fabian Research Series, 1967), p. 4.
[2] Rt. Hon. Roy Jenkins, 'Address by the Home Secretary to the Institute of Race
Relations', reprinted in Race (Vol. VII, No. 3, January 1967), p. 216.
[3] Nandy, op. cit., p. 3.
[4] Ibid., p. 5.

positions of out- and in-groups, must here be kept in mind. It is also stressed that, on occasion, in order to achieve 'harmony', a measure of confrontation and disharmony may be necessary. However, 'none of these arrangements is designed to cope with the fundamental cause from which racial tension and discrimination stem'.[1] Attention is also drawn to the selection of liaison officers, for which 'the most obvious criterion is commitment to race relations' (which is defined, *inter alia*, as 'knowledge and understanding of the broad setting of race relations problems'),[2] and to the powers that liaison officers should have, such as the right to approach city councillors and committees. The particular importance of the liaison officer is elsewhere recognized: 'The pivot of the system is the paid liaison officer.'[3]

We suggest that it would be better if there were a corps of liaison officers recruited and trained by the Community Relations Commission and seconded to serve the local community relations councils. No one would be assigned to a committee until he had been fully trained.[4]

But the local officers would be supplemented by 'regional development officers of a high calibre'.[5] Again, the shift from social work is emphasized: 'it will require a change from a preoccupation with welfare to an increasing concern with such questions as opportunities for school leavers and the policies of the local authority'.[6]

The most comprehensive study of local committees throws additional light on this second relationship, the links between the C.R.C. and the local councils. Eight local councils were investigated, and 133 out of 144 executive committee members interviewed, as well as the community relations officers.[7] Many of the points already made are also emphasized in this study. On the importance of national and Governmental leadership, the authors express this view: ' . . . above all we regard it as the case that the

---

[1] Ibid., p. 40.
[2] Ibid., p. 10.
[3] Rose and associates, op. cit., p. 728.
[4] Ibid.
[5] Ibid.
[6] Ibid., p. 730.
[7] Michael Hill and Ruth Issacharoff, *Community Action and Race Relations: A Study of Community Relations Committees in Britain* (London, Oxford University Press, for Institute of Race Relations, forthcoming 1971).

community relations movement has not been able to emerge as an effective force because of the unwillingness of the Government to back it effectively'.[1] The contradiction between the integrationist and conflict approaches is emphasized:

If one gives the Commission the benefit of the doubt, despite its disappointing behaviour in the past, and accepts that it does really want to see the rights of Commonwealth immigrants protected and community 'harmony' maintained, one still cannot escape from the fact that these two goals may be incompatible and that one may need to be subordinated to the requirements of the other.[2]

The detail of this study illustrates the significance of this view at the level of the local council. The councils were not power-based coalitions, their members were mostly middle class, and some were in any case opposed to the idea of racial integration. 'All eight committees could in no way be said to contain a cross-section of all groups, or all powerful groups, in the "host community."'[3] Further, it was argued that:

We have shown that community relations committees usually fail to involve these crucial institutions ['public and private, which determine the life chances of people in the locality'] in any meaningful way, sometimes because such institutions are not predominantly locally oriented, but mainly because these institutions resent interference which might bring about unwanted changes, and the community relations committees lack the power and influence to require their cooperation. If a committee does manage to secure some cooperation then it is usually forced to sacrifice innovation and act as a forum operating on a consensual basis composed of different interests and points of view.[4]

However, in considering the reality of the links between the N.C.C.I./C.R.C. and the local councils, the writers throw doubt upon the existence of the links themselves: 'We find that we can say very little about the relationship between N.C.C.I./C.R.C. and the local committees, because in many respects such a relationship barely exists';[5] and ' . . . despite the Press attention given to examples of C.R.C. interference with local matters, neglect has been perhaps the main feature of the relationship'.[6]

[1] Ibid., Chapter 12.   [2] Ibid., final Chapter.   [3] Ibid., Chapter 7.
[4] Ibid., final Chapter.   [5] Ibid., Chapter 10.   [6] Ibid., Chapter 10.

The Commission recognized that, by 1970, the structural relationships between themselves and the local councils needed review. Three proposals were put forward during a meeting at York in September 1970, suggesting: that all the local community relations officers should be employed by the Commission, which would also direct their work from the centre; secondly, that the officers and their work might be organized under regional committees of the Commission, in a similar way to the Probation Service; thirdly, that the officers would become local government officials. The C.R.C. made no proposals for improving the structure and representation of local views within the Commission itself.

Other evaluations have been directed at the third of the main N.C.C.I. relationships earlier outlined: the relationship between the N.C.C.I. and the national Government. It was argued that 'at the outset the National Committee *was* a political body'.[1] Of the Housing Panel, it was claimed that 'I had imagined that we were being set up as a Panel . . . giving political advice'.[2] However, 'the National Committee was gradually manoeuvred into a situation where it ceased to make policy proposals at all'.[3] It shared a common fate with the Race Relations Board: 'The truth is that both bodies did try, but that being denied even the most elementary political support, they came in time to be reduced to being at best ineffective lobbies and at worst agencies for carrying out government policy.'[4] The particular fate of the Housing Panel is adduced as evidence: eventually, 'Instead of putting further pressure to bear, someone decided that the Housing Panel shouldn't meet any more. . . . '[5] Again, this is regarded as a lost opportunity, since the important area of 'Public housing is, of course, subject to direction and control by Central Government'.[6]

[1] John Rex, 'The Race Relations Catastrophe', in *Matters of Principle: Labour's Last Chance* (Harmondsworth, Penguin Books, 1968), p. 77.

[2] John Rex in discussion, British Sociological Association Conference, 28 March 1969.

[3] Rex, 'The Race Relations Catastrophe', op. cit., p. 75.

[4] Ibid., p. 76. It does seem rather odd that the Race Relations Board, as a statutory body, should be so taken to task for carrying out 'government policy' which was in part exemplified by the race relations legislation under which the Board had been set up.

[5] Rex, B.S.A. Conference.

[6] John Rex, 'The Formation of Ghettos in Britain's Cities' (Institute of Race Relations Conference Paper, 20 September 1968).

It is probably not very important to decide whether or not the N.C.C.I. had a general 'political' role;[1] for the purpose of the particular point at issue, it is enough to consider whether the N.C.C.I. was in a position to offer advice to the Government, whether advice was offered, and whether it proved effective. One view is that, in terms of advising the Government, 'This is the field in which it has done most of its useful work'.[2] The submission to the Wilson Committee (June 1966), the deputations to the Ministry of Housing (August 1966 and June 1967) and Home Secretary on immigrant police relations (November 1966), together with the report on areas of special housing needs and the correspondence with the Prime Minister on the White Paper (of August 1965), 'are in themselves important and worthy of recognition, and some of them (e.g. the report on areas of special housing needs) of major importance. But whether more could have been done remains to be seen.'[3]

On the more general viewpoint, it can then be suggested that certain of the advice was worth-while. But there is the more basic point as to the extent to which advice-giving, in this way, was possible. The Government did not exclude the possibility of receiving advice, indeed they considered that the advice-giving role of the C.I.A.C. 'can in the future be most effectively provided as part of the work of the new National Committee'.[4] However, this task was the last recorded and least described; and the terms of reference for the National Committee were again relegated— as the last point in sequence—to 'Advise on those questions which are referred to them by Government or which they consider should be brought to the attention of Government'.[5] Given the ultimate Governmental financial control and the existing national and local government structures, it would seem very probable that advice from the N.C.C.I. would carry relatively little weight. The C.R.C., as a statutory body, had even less independence than the N.C.C.I.: 'The Commission's unhappy dilemma is that it needs to bite the hand that feeds it if it is to do what needs

---

[1] That is, political, for example, in the senses of Almond's discussion in *The Politics of the Developing Areas* (Princeton, Princeton University Press, 1960), pp. 5–9.

[2] Dipak Nandy, 'The National Committee for Commonwealth Immigrants: An Assessment' (unpublished paper, dated 20 July 1967).

[3] Ibid.

[4] *Immigration from the Commonwealth*, op. cit., p. 18.

[5] N.C.C.I., *Report for 1966*, op. cit., p. 24.

doing.'[1] The N.C.C.I. did achieve a number of polite growls, but the C.R.C. would appear to have largely given up the unequal task of advice in terms of public debate.

It is not too clear whether the attempts of the N.C.C.I. to reach and inform the host community, either relatively élitist groups or the public at large, can be termed a relationship. But, as outlined in section 2, this was an important activity of the N.C.C.I. It is argued, however, that 'it is questionable whether the expensive conferences organized by the NCCI can really be justified',[2] and that 'The Commission's faith in the efficacy of conferences seems naive'.[3] No less importantly, it is suggested that the information role of the N.C.C.I. has been ineffective; for example, the first statement 'on the dispersal policy of that circular [the D.E.S. circular on 'The Education of Immigrant Children'] came 18 *months later*'.[4] And, 'The CRC seems to place great faith in conferences, lectures, news-letters and pamphlets with little evidence that these overt media reach the right people and with no idea whether they will have any real impact. . . . '[5]

Throughout this section, the arguments have been related largely to the three relationships described: specifically the relationship of the N.C.C.I. with the national Government, the immigrant communities, and the voluntary liaison committees. It must not be pretended that this has been an exhaustive discussion of the sources quoted, or of all the sources available; rather, a number of points and themes have been introduced and broadly related to the three relationships outlined.

4. *Effectiveness*

(a) THE N.C.C.I. AND THE DISCRIMINATORY PROCESS

The crucial question remains: to what extent, and in what way, was the N.C.C.I. effective? In terms of the analysis offered in Chapter 1, it is suggested that the N.C.C.I. was concerned with the 'discriminatory process' and in particular with three of the four component parts: in-group; out-group; and their relationship to the society as a whole. It was concerned to a lesser degree with the discriminatory act. Given this emphasis on the process of

[1] Ann Dummett, 'What To Do', *Race Today* (July 1969), p. 75.
[2] Nandy, 'The National Committee . . .', op. cit., p. 5.
[3] Hill and Issacharoff, op. cit., Chapter 7.
[4] Nandy, 'The National Committee . . .', op. cit., p. 5.
[5] Hill and Issacharoff, op. cit., final Chapter.

discrimination, the measures adopted by the Committee may be termed specific, and were, therefore, aimed directly at racial discrimination.

Although the Race Relations Act 1965 apportioned to the Race Relations Board the tackling of discrimination in public places, it will be remembered that one of the instructions to liaison committees was 'To take appropriate action against discrimination wherever it occurs . . . '; and, until the passing of the 1968 Act, and so for the life-time of the N.C.C.I., the main areas of discrimination lay wholly outside the scope of the Board and, consequently, within that of the National Committeee.

It is also important to realize that the N.C.C.I., as the residual agency, might still become involved in disputes over the act of discrimination. This is, firstly, because not all the incidents occurring or complaints made of discriminatory acts will fall within the powers of the Board; and between 26 November 1968 and 31 January 1969, for example, 68 out of the 257 complaints received fell outside the Board's scope (although many of these were excluded since the Act was not retrospective). Secondly, only a, possibly, small percentage of the discriminatory acts will be reported to, and dealt with by, the Board; but the community relations situation may be affected by the total discriminatory acts. Thus, a spokesman for the N.C.C.I. believed, even of the 1968 Act: 'I am sure it will not remove racial discrimination.'[1] Inevitably, therefore, the N.C.C.I. remained involved even with the act of discrimination, although the degree of involvement might vary according to the incidence, actual or estimated, of the acts, and the effectiveness, actual and estimated, of the Board in dealing with the acts. This might be illustrated from the experience of the Community Relations Service in the United States, the organiza-tion apparently most similar to the N.C.C.I. In 1966, the Service described its main role as: 'to help communities and persons therein to cope with disputes, disagreements and difficulties relating to discriminatory practices'.[2] But the following year, it 'began turning its attention toward resolution of the factors that cause community conflict' and recognized that 'Primary responsi-bility for enforcement of civil rights laws and Executive orders

---

[1] Select Committee on Race Relations . . . , 23 January 1969, op. cit., p. 79.
[2] *Annual Report of the Community Relations Service, Fiscal Year 1965* (Washington, U.S. Department of Commerce, March 1966), p. 1.

rests with the Civil Rights Division and with other Federal agencies.'[1] Yet it would seem that the Community Relations Service was drawn inevitably into the disputes area, and in 1968, one of its three departments was Conciliation and Field Services. In short, the discriminatory act is simply a part of the discriminatory process outlined; and although it may be abstracted to a certain extent for legal and administrative convenience, it remains a part of the general social situation with which the community relations service is concerned.

In contradistinction, it must also be affirmed that the C.R.C., and its predecessor the N.C.C.I., are not simply concerned with situations of racial discrimination. Of the N.C.C.I., 'It is not enough for it to be the national committee for immigrants. The task I want you to undertake is not only to minister to immigrants, which has been your principal role to date, but to concern yourself with relations within the whole of society.'[2] There are two extensions here: to immigrants, both coloured and white; and to relations, not just racial but general. Yet how real are these instructions? The Minister then went on to say that: 'In 1953 there were 30,000 immigrants in this country.... But we have one million people.'[3] Since England and Wales in 1966 contained perhaps 837,150 'foreign' immigrants, 698,600 Irish immigrants, and some 942,310 immigrants from the Commonwealth,[4] the reference is apparently to the Commonwealth immigrants (not all of whom were coloured). The injunction to care for all immigrants, therefore, comes down, again, to caring for the coloured ones. The relationship will be correspondingly restricted, since the reference group is still the non-whites.

Although some of the points at issue will be concerned with, for example, migration factors, there thus remains a heavy emphasis on those related to race. The N.C.C.I./C.R.C. was concerned with race relations, rather than truly immigrant relations; and it was thus concerned with the process of discrimination outlined in Chapter 1.

[1] *Annual Report: The Community Relations Service for Fiscal Year 1966* (Washington, U.S. Government Printing Office, 1967).

[2] Rt. Hon. Roy Jenkins, M.P. Address given by the Home Secretary on 10 April 1968 to a meeting of the Standing Conference of Voluntary Liaison Committees, (London, N.C.C.I., 1968), p. 3.

[3] Ibid., p. 4.

[4] Figures from the 1966 10% sample census. These do not allow for under-enumeration.

(b) GENERAL EFFECTIVENESS OF THE N.C.C.I.

How effective was the N.C.C.I.? Measures of effectiveness initially advanced were the recording of incidence, variations between groups, classifications of group attainments in such fields as housing or education, and attitudes. Difficulties of measurement, it was suggested, diminished when longer periods of time were studied. But at the time when the main part of this study was undertaken, the existence of the N.C.C.I./C.R.C. had been but a short three and a half years; and it had operated during a time when the situation was in many respects deteriorating, and this will have overridden certain of the N.C.C.I.'s efforts. Indeed, the data earlier presented show that the general situation of the non-white immigrants has not improved,[1] and it is the judgement of the General Secretary that the N.C.C.I. had done little more than 'scratch the surface' and had made 'little or no impact on the problem of discrimination'.[2] In short, the N.C.C.I. was not effective in improving the general situation. But this is not to say that the N.C.C.I. was not effective at all, and that the situation would not have been still worse had the N.C.C.I. not been established.

It may be considered that the N.C.C.I. was not too likely to alter the general situation significantly, when its small size and resources are taken into account. In March 1968, the Secretariat and paid local officers together numbered about 64 persons; and the budget for 1968-9 was £200,000. The American Community Relations Service in early June 1967 had 72 permanent and 50 temporary staff with an appropriation for the 1967 fiscal year of $1,500,000;[3] but the C.R.S. was only one part of the American race relations scene. For example, the 1967 income of the National Association for the Advancement of Coloured People was $2,632,059.14;[4] and there is no comparable civil rights organization in the United Kingdom. The City of New York Commission on Human Rights had a budget of $716,165 in 1966-7;[5] and many states had such commissions. Of course, the American

---

[1] See Chapter 3.

[2] In interview, 29 March 1968.

[3] *The Community Relations Service: 1967 Annual Report* (Washington, U.S. Department of Justice, 1968), p. 15.

[4] N.A.A.C.P., *Annual Report for 1967* (New York, N.A.A.C.P., 1968), p. 123.

[5] The City of New York Commission on Human Rights, *Annual Report 1966* (New York, 1966), p. 50.

situation is a very different one; but, in some ways, the organizations there are already generally cognizant of the race relations scene, whereas the N.C.C.I. (as well as the Race Relations Board, and the Institute of Race Relations) has had to pioneer serious interest in the United Kingdom. Compared to the total race relations scene in America, the N.C.C.I. was, therefore, a relatively small organization. More importantly, when judged in relation to the situation in the United Kingdom, the N.C.C.I. was a comparatively small, quasi-Governmental body. A European example is the grant given by the Netherlands Government to the local and regional Foundations co-ordinated by the Community Relations Division. In 1969, from a much smaller national gross product than the British, this grant amounted to Fl. 25,000,000, or about £2,880,000.[1] But even this is not to say that the N.C.C.I. was in some ways under-funded; indeed, its Government allowance does not appear to have been expended in any year so far, and it has been the best financed of the race relations bodies in the United Kingdom.

(c) SPECIFIC EFFECTIVENESS OF THE N.C.C.I.

Accepting that no great contribution had been made to the general restructuring of society, how effective was the N.C.C.I./C.R.C. in its specific tasks? The specific work of the N.C.C.I. has already been reviewed and certain evaluations of it earlier considered. This assessment of effectiveness will retain the main relationships adopted when covering the evaluations—i.e. the Government, the immigrant communities, the voluntary liaison committees/community relations councils (and also the general public).

The relations with the Government were, as shown, dominated initially by the voluntary nature of the main Committee and the panels; the linking together of immigration controls and integration; and the ultimate financial control by the Government. Although the N.C.C.I. could claim that it was 'an independent body free from Government control',[2] its summary rebirth as a statutory organization showed very clearly that this was not the case. Again, although the question of immigration control

---

[1] Given in Christopher Bagley, *Race Relations in the Netherlands and Britain, A Comparative Study* (London, Oxford University Press, for Institute of Race Relations, forthcoming).

[2] N.C.C.I., *Report for 1966*, op. cit., p. 24.

must continue to impinge upon the factors of integration, the C.R.C. voice of political dissent over immigration matters was apparently silenced. Finally, the voluntary nature of the N.C.C.I. was overturned and although a smaller voluntary council remained, there was now to be a full-time chairman and the panels were drastically reformed. On the other hand, it can be argued that the Government considered the N.C.C.I. worthy of increased financial support and statutory responsibility. It remains true that the structure of the relationship with the Government has been considerably altered.

How effective was the advice that the N.C.C.I. gave? The main Committee was concerned with the immigration issue and was unable to secure any considerable change of policy in this field. But it has been claimed[1] that it was successful in getting the Prime Minister to agree to the implementation of the immigration appeals procedure in the Wilson Report;[2] although this might have been implemented anyway. It can also be argued that the Committee was able to act as a counterpoint to the more irrational and racist attitudes and behaviour at the time of the 1968 crisis of the Kenya Asian immigrants; and although it is as yet hard to evaluate this, it need not be ruled out entirely. Nevertheless, as a pseudo-civil rights movement, working to change Government policy, its success was exceedingly limited. It might be argued that the resignation of the entire main Committee would have had some effect with the Government, but this weapon could presumably only have been used once.

It is not clear that the N.C.C.I. and the C.R.C. have been able to decide exactly what 'community relations' means. Instead, 'the community life and relationships' and the plan adopted are 'to strengthen the movement for harmonious community relations by drawing on the tremendous fund of goodwill we know to exist everywhere'.[3] But a tremendous 'fund of goodwill' does not exist everywhere, and a small body of people with limited funds cannot cover all aspects of community life. Indeed, it might be argued that within a tendentious topic and an evolving situation,

---

[1] Interview with member of main Committee.

[2] Great Britain, Home Office, Committee on Immigration Appeals, Chairman: Sir Roy Wilson, *Report* (Cmnd. 3387) (London, H.M.S.O., August 1967).

[3] *Race Relations, Quarterly Bulletin of the Race Relations Board* (No. 4, March 1969), p. 8.

there is a greater need for simplicity and exactness.[1] 'Community relations', in the sense of relations between different racial and ethnic communities, must be resolved along the main areas of relationship between the groups: housing, education, employment, local government, and the police. There will no doubt be crisis situations that require the sort of fire-fighting unit devised by the American C.R.S. There will also be the long-term resolution of the factors underlying community conflict; and although much of the work will have to be attempted by the local c.r.c.s, the role of the central Commission as informant on methods and priorities, is of importance. A further confusing element of the community relations role lies in its political or apolitical nature: of the v.l.c. officer, it is suggested that 'if he has any idea as seeing this entirely as a matter for political action, he has to suppress this in the interests of being the person whom everybody can talk to'.[2] While the work at local level may not be entirely political, political factors certainly cannot be excluded: Katznelson illustrated how one local council worked as a political body to channel and neutralize Black protest; and various writers have pointed to the fundamental point that often conflict, rather than integration, is the immediate issue. It is a handicap that the N.C.C.I./C.R.C. has sometimes operated as if this was not the case.

The advice of the panels was, of course, related to specific applied fields. It can reasonably be argued that the work of the Education Panel, for example, did achieve some useful results. That part of their work relating to teacher training colleges seems likely to have affected the relative positions of the racial groups through improved knowledge and training. Or a particular incident can be noticed: when the London University special training course for teachers was being discontinued, the N.C.C.I. was successful in persuading the I.L.E.A. to take over the courses. Again, it is reasonable to anticipate some change and benefit. The same range of arguments might be advanced in favour of, for example, the Housing Panel.

One important related factor is the extent to which the panels placed an undue work load on the Secretariat, and the

[1] For example, Michael Banton, in *Roles* (London, Tavistock, 1965), p. 170: 'In a rapidly changing society people may be unable to agree just what are the rights and obligations of a particular role.' And it can be argued that there is, thus, an increased need for role definition.

[2] Select Committee on Race Relations . . . , 23 January 1969, op. cit. p. 74.

possibility that they may, in fact, have produced more ideas for action than could be administratively sustained. Thus, it can be argued that the services to the liaison committees suffered unduly. It is also open to question whether the political role was open to the panels over a long period of time, whatever the rewards that may have been reaped initially. Possibly the offering of expert technical advice to other Government bodies may in the longer term be of increasing value. However, although the over-all situation of the racial groups cannot have been significantly changed by the work of the panels, limited results were achieved.

The second relationship was with the immigrant communities. Since the immigrant organizations tend to be informal or com-munal, this relationship has not been a very close one, and the presence of individual immigrants on various committees did not provide effective links with the immigrants as a whole. The more radical immigrant organizations were increasingly unrepresented on the local committees or councils. The Wood proposals, which would have introduced local participation, were not developed; and, for example, the Birmingham Liaison Committee had shed its Advisory Council when it became too radical and it was decided that it did 'not . . . represent a reasonable consensus of immigrant opinion'.[1] Both Katznelson and the Dummetts have suggested that the effect of the N.C.C.I.'s work was to limit and buffer the contacts between, on one hand, the immigrant com-munities and civil rights movements, and, on the other, the N.C.C.I./C.R.C. and the Establishment political structure. It would also seem probable that civil rights organizations will increase in number, extent, and activity, and their relationship with the Establishment structure, of which the C.R.C. is a part, will depend upon the tackling of the series of conflict situations and factors of the future. So far, the prospect for co-operation does not look encouraging.

The N.C.C.I. would probably consider that the main link with the immigrant communities, in fact, lay through the liaison committees, which form the third relationship. The most striking feature here is the considerable increase in the number of the local committees, from 27 in 1965 to over 80 in 1970. But presence on paper can be misleading, and the question as to the achieve-

---

[1] Anon., 'Liaison Committees: Who Keeps Control of What', Institute of Race Relations *News Letter* (November/December 1968), p. 451.

ments of the committees, and the part of the N.C.C.I. in these achievements, must also be framed. The work of the committees has already been considered and is subsequently discussed, but it can here be noted that these groups varied considerably and, in terms of the harsh criterion of change within their area, did not usually achieve very much. There is little doubt that by allowing the differing councils to develop in isolation, and often in ignorance, insufficient concentration on the main tasks—housing, education, employment—was obtained. By 1970, the C.R.C. could still claim 'No two councils are alike',[1] and it is a sobering fact that no general advice on the roles and aims of the committees had ever been issued. The 'comprehensive body of doctrine' called for in 1965 had not been established: many of the projects undertaken suggested only severely limited rewards when measured in terms of improving community relations. The role of co-ordination belonged to the N.C.C.I., and it will be remembered how slender were the resources available: financial control was limited for the most time to a grant of £1,500 for a full-time officer; there was £50,000 available for relevant research; and there were some four officers[2] available for the task of co-ordination. The C.R.C. did recognize that the resources allocated to the development of the community relations councils were inadequate:

The increasing amount of activity and the growing number of community relations councils have imposed an extremely heavy load on the Development Branch. For the greater part of 1968 the Branch was seriously understaffed and it was frankly unable to provide adequately the services so much needed by new and expanding councils.[3]

There seems to have been an extraordinary diffusion of activity on the part of the local committees, with projects tending towards the social-work approach. Listing some of the contributions to one number of *Liaison* can illustrate this point: the Bolton Commonwealth Friendship Council had completed a film on the life of Commonwealth immigrants in Bolton; the Wolverhampton

[1] C.R.C., *Report . . . 1969–70*, op. cit., p. 13.
[2] In fact, the number available was less, because of staffing difficulties. In June 1969, for example, only two persons were available for fieldwork, one of whom also had responsibility for police liaison, also on a national basis.
[3] Community Relations Commission, *Report of the Community Relations Commission for 1968/69* (London, H.M.S.O., 1968), p. 14.

Council for Racial Harmony was conducting a survey 'to discover the extent of contact between the host and immigrant communities', and meeting with estate agents; the Council of Citizens of East London sponsored an essay competition for young people on the topic 'What is Prejudice?'; the Southwark Council for Community Relations were planning a film on a West Indian steel band; the Newham International Liaison Committee had taken premises for conversion into a day nursery, children's and youth clubs, etc.; the Huddersfield International Liaison Committee was 'concerned' about poor baby-care practices among Asian women and recalled that classes in English had proved 'not very successful'; and so on.[1] Relationships with the full-time officers were not always happy, and a separate association, ACRO, had been formed in 1968.

None of the officers of the liaison committees served on any of the panels or on the main Committee. Although the creation of the committees, therefore, stands as a considerable achievement, there remain some doubts over the effectiveness of the succeeding relationships. The diffusion of aims; the insistence on the comprehensive, consensus approach; the failure to involve the main interest groups, who might, in any case, be opposed to the policy of integration; increasing Government control; the erection of controls that channelled Black protest away from more effective action—these are some of the charges and the reasons for doubting the over-all effectiveness of the work of the C.R.C. in relation to local councils and the elimination of racial discrimination.

The relationship with the general public, the task of general attitude-forming, in hard fact played a less important part. However, there was continued emphasis on the importance of general education, both as a task of the N.C.C.I./C.R.C. and as a solution to racial ills. For example, in 1970 it was claimed that: 'The education of public opinion holds the key to the improvement of community and race relations';[2] and 'The Commission welcomed the statement by the Secretary of State for Education and Science . . . that "education alone" could overcome mutual ignorance and suspicion.'[3] There must be some incredulity for

[1] *Liaison* (No. 7, April 1967), pp. 5–6.
[2] C.R.C., *Report . . . 1969–70*, op. cit., p. 25.
[3] Ibid., p. 16.

those who believe that education alone can solve the racial hostility that depends in part upon deprivation in housing or employment; and the limited returns of education in changing racial attitudes were noted in Chapter 1. Although education and information undoubtedly do have a part to play in modern technological society, it would seem that the N.C.C.I./C.R.C. over-emphasized the potential effectiveness of this approach. It may also not have sufficiently considered varied methods. The Commission was asked whether it had:

given thought . . . to ways in which more direct approaches might be made . . . [than] . . . the general and traditional methods of opinion forming—production of pamphlets, organisation of conferences and so on . . . designed . . . to reach special categories of persons such as social workers, local staff and police . . . [whereas] . . . the great bulk of the people who are directly effected and whose opinions it is desired to form, are not those who read the pamphlets, go to the conferences or listen to the speakers.[1]

The 'answer at the moment' was thought to be 'no'.[2]

It has been argued that the N.C.C.I./C.R.C. was not in a position to effect the radical restructuring of society, and to be effective in a major and general way. The specific work of the N.C.C.I./C.R.C. has also been discussed and its limited success described. Some notice must be taken of comments directed at the internal operation of the N.C.C.I./C.R.C. Despite much hard and well-intentioned work, there is evidence of indecision and delay:

. . . The Commission itself has yet to make its mark. No striking initiative, not even a memorable phrase, has yet emerged, and it is other bodies which have made the running. . . . The House of Commons Select Committee on Immigration and Race Relations [sic] did a noticeably useful job in drawing attention to the crucial need to ensure equality of opportunity for coloured school-leavers in their search for employment. The Institute of Race Relations has produced its massive survey *Colour and Citizenship* which has had such a beneficial effect in dispelling hysteria (from both extremes of the spectrum of public opinion) and in marshalling the forces of knowledge and common sense. With limited resources the recently established Runnymede Trust already has to its credit a number of admirable initiatives

---

[1] Select Committee on Race Relations . . ., 23 January 1969, op. cit. p. 72.
[2] Ibid.

in promoting understanding and knowledge of what can be done in practical terms to cultivate racial and communal harmony. At the local level some of the community relations councils (which operate or are supposed to operate under the aegis of the Commission) have been experimenting with new ways of tackling communal problems at the grass roots—not always with encouragement or support from the Commission's headquarters in Russell Square.[1]

This line of argument continues:

There is a fairly uniform pattern in the criticisms which both staff still in the Commission's service and those who have left it during the past year have to make of the way in which the Commission's business is being conducted. Failure to keep staff informed on matters for which they are supposed to be professionally responsible within the Commission's organisation; little or no effort to associate them with the way in which decisions are reached; no clear direction in the allocation of tasks and priorities; far too little delegation of authority and, as a consequence, discourteous and damaging delays in dealing with matters on which instructions have been sought (with the result that the officer concerned has either to leave the matter in abeyance or to deal with it according to his or her own judgement at the risk of then receiving a reprimand for exceeding his or her responsibilities); a disagreeable atmosphere infecting not only personal relations within the office but also the conduct of business with other organisations and individuals outside with whom there should be a relationship of confidence and cordial cooperation. Such are the essentially trivial shortcomings which are vitiating this work of great national importance.[2]

This is harsh criticism, but there would seem to be at least some truth in it. Specific examples can be advanced: the Birmingham council 'had been waiting for three months for a reply to another request for an assistant'.[3] The Home Office may have assisted in the process of delay: for example, it was suggested that an application for a grant of £30 to an Oxford play group was met by a visit and then approval for the grant by the C.R.C. committee the following month; but processing by the Home Office had not been completed by five months' time—when the play group had closed. An application from Scotland took six

---

[1] John Reddaway, 'Whatever Happened to the Community Relations Commission', *Race Today* (July 1970), p. 213. Reddaway was for some time Senior Administrative Officer at the C.R.C.

[2] Ibid., p. 215.

[3] Hill and Issacharoff, op. cit., Chapter 10.

months to deal with.[1] A leader in *The Times* appeared under the heading of 'Not a Good Commission'.[2] The situation of the Commission was raised in the House of Commons, and there were publicized disagreements with local officers or councils at Oxford and Newcastle. There can be little doubt that the N.C.C.I./C.R.C. operated as an organization less efficiently than many people have thought reasonable. Had its aims been differently defined, or had the work of achieving the aims been regarded as more successful, it is, of course, possible that these operational deficiencies—which are certainly not unique to the N.C.C.I./C.R.C. —would have aroused less comment.

So it cannot be pretended that the positions of the in- and out-groups, nor the general situation, were fundamentally altered during the three-year existence of the N.C.C.I. At the same time, there were some limited and specific achievements, and a more professional structure was slowly and painfully being created. There was heavy criticism that revealed how limited these achievements were. But it is only fair to recognize also that the N.C.C.I./C.R.C. was operating with small resources and in an era of much hostility to racial integration. Had there been no N.C.C.I., no C.R.C., and no local councils (and no alternative structure), might not the situation have been worse? If the C.R.C. is organizationally developed, and its roles better defined and carried out, might not a more significant contribution be made?

---

[1] Verbal communications.
[2] *The Times* (24 June 1970).

CHAPTER 12

The Local Committees

HANNAN ROSE AND MARGOT LEVY

1. *The Work of the Voluntary Liaison Committees*
by Hannan Rose

(a) INTRODUCTION

This paper is directly based on the results of research conducted by the author from October 1966 to August 1968.[1] Some preliminary interviews were carried out in 1966–7, but the main body of the work is based on meetings with members of local committees, newspaper reporters, officials of the local authorities, and others in the areas chosen for the survey which took place between February and July 1968. To some extent, the material must, therefore, be placed in the context of the events of that period; but this is not to say that the findings presented here do not have more general reference, for it is the contention of the author that the events of 1968 only intensified already existing and inherent difficulties and contradictions in the structure of voluntary work in race relations in Britain.

The discussion of the problems in the work of the local committees does not mention the areas where the research was conducted, for those who were approached to contribute to the study were assured that confidentiality would be observed, and thus, care has been taken to eliminate material referring to specific committees, local authorities, or other bodies which would make identification possible. The study covered ten of the fifty-five committees which were in existence or in the process of formation when the major part of interviewing commenced in February 1968, and these were selected to produce a representative sample of committees in terms of geographical location (in the various regions of England) and in terms of the number of years for which they had been operating. Some further docu-

---

[1] During this period, the author was at Nuffield College on an award from the Social Science Research Council.

mentary evidence was used to establish a picture of what work was attempted in the field of race relations during the 1950s when there were a few committees which subsequently disappeared.

This material will be used as the basis for giving a brief review of the development of voluntary work in Britain in the field of race relations. This will be followed by an analysis of the working and effectiveness of the committees, and the major problems of policy and strategy which they face. There will then be a consideration of some of the immediate administrative difficulties which beset their work, and a final section will outline the basic conclusions.

(b) LOCAL WORK IN RACE RELATIONS IN BRITAIN: AN HISTORICAL PERSPECTIVE

From a very early date, the Government were asked if they had any policy with regard to the arrival of substantial numbers of coloured immigrants in Britain, a question which reflected the views of those who were hostile to such immigration and those who wished to see social policies adopted which would prevent the build-up of a 'race relations problem' in Britain. To both points of view, and on both the issue of limiting immigration from the Commonwealth and that of taking up any special policies to deal with the conditions of immigrants who had already settled in the country, the Government remained immovable through the 1950s, committed to a *laissez-faire* policy. This was exemplified by the response of a number of Government departments to the London Borough of Lambeth, which became worried by the concentration of a considerable number of West Indians in the Brixton area late in 1954.

A deputation from Lambeth went to see the Colonial Secretary in January 1955 with a number of proposals to deal with the situation. The Colonial Secretary stated that the Government were 'seriously considering the law covering the entry of people into this country ... [and] were considering whether there was some way of achieving better dispersal of coloured people when they arrive here'; but, all the proposals made by the Borough were rejected. The Borough's representatives felt compelled to issue a press statement saying that they were 'very dissatisfied by reason of the Colonial Office being unable to offer any constructive suggestions'. The Borough Council then decided

to write to the Ministry of Health, the Ministry of Housing and
Local Government, the Home Office, and the London County
Council to pursue the matter. This decision was made 'having
regard to the apparent lack of concern of the Colonial Office'.
The replies are again indicative of the situation. To a further
representation, the Colonial Office reaffirmed its previous position,
and the Ministry of Health stated: 'This is a matter for the Ministry of Housing and Local Government.' The Ministry of Housing
and Local Government stated: 'This duty to deal with housing
problems which have already resulted from immigration remains
with the housing authorities concerned' (although the Colonial
Secretary had previously 'accepted the proposition that the
problem was a national one'). The London County Council
sympathized and continued: 'It is, however, confidentially
understood that the possibility of some action on this extremely
difficult subject is contemplated by the Government Department
concerned.'

After the Nottingham and Notting Hill 'riots' of autumn
1958, committees which had been established in a number of
cities with large immigrant communities were told that the
Government were considering some action. But again, nothing
came of it, and it is now difficult to ascertain whether anything
was considered at all. Rather it would seem that the Government
were again unwilling to accept any responsibility for action; the
National Council of Social Service Working Group on the
Welfare of Coloured Workers discussed the situation with the
Home Office, and it was agreed that it would be wrong to
provide any special facilities for coloured workers, but that
voluntary committees should be established and local authorities
should be encouraged to grant-aid them.

The Government, indeed, maintained that they could not
abrogate the freedom of the Commonwealth citizen to move to
Britain and that it would be wrong to undertake any special
programmes designed to help the immigrants. These policies
were not changed until the Commonwealth Immigrants Bill
(later Act of 1962) was introduced and the 1965 White Paper on
Immigration from the Commonwealth was published. It was thus in
the face of official hostility, or at least complete indifference, that
any efforts were made by voluntary groups to help the immigrants
in the industrial areas to which they naturally were attracted

because of the pull of industry requiring largely unskilled labour.[1] Exceptionally, a few mayors or local councils went out of their way to establish contact with the immigrant communities, but generally the work was undertaken by the Council of Social Service or a churchman, or through a combined effort of the two. Those areas to which immigrants came were almost without exception already hard-pressed with a large stock of old, poor housing, strained social services—particularly in the form of inadequate and decaying schools, hospitals, etc.—and without the resources to cope with the situation.

Much of the work at this time was unofficial, and largely unrecorded, undertaken as an extra activity by some social agency or by a few individuals, and it is, therefore, almost impossible to form an accurate judgement of the position. The information available can only be taken as giving some indication of what was being done by the best organized groups, i.e. those which have left written records. Thus, in 1951, the City of Birmingham set up the Clifton Institute, which was specially designed to teach immigrants English and those skills that would help them to get better employment; this organization is still operating. Even before this, in 1949–50, the annual report of the Leeds Council of Social Service noted that there was concern that 'coloured people were experiencing difficulties about accommodation and a feeling of segregation', and this was linked with attention paid to the numbers of European Voluntary Workers also in the city. The report for the next year notes the formation of an International Centre. In the following year, 1951–2, the Council's annual report noted the formation of an International Council to ensure greater liaison between all the societies concerned with furthering international understanding: 'Its three main objects are the support and development of the International Centre, welfare of coloured people, and aid to refugees in other countries.'

At the same time, in 1951–2, the Rev. John Ragg, Social and Industrial Adviser to the Bishop of Bristol, took the initiative in setting up a 'Committee for the Welfare of Colonial Workers in Bristol', and in 1955, the Council of Social Service in Nottingham formalized its interest in this field by setting up a 'Consultative

[1] See Ceri Peach, *West Indian Migration to Britain* (London, Oxford University Press, for Institute of Race Relations, 1968).

Committee for the Welfare of Coloured People'. These organizations worked voluntarily and there probably would have been very
little co-ordination between them had it not been for the interest
shown by the Family Welfare Association in London, which had
attracted a three-year grant from the City Parochial Charities to
undertake a project in Lambeth, establishing an Advice Bureau
with special concern for the problems of West Indian immigrants.
Following this lead, Bristol and Nottingham received support
from trusts, enabling them to employ Secretaries cum welfare
officers for three-year periods; and the meetings of the Steering
Committee of the Family Welfare Association project enabled the
workers to come together periodically to discuss their experiences.[1]

Further co-ordination began in July 1959, when the National
Council of Social Service (N.C.S.S.) Working Group on the
Welfare of Coloured Workers was set up by representatives of eight
councils of social service, the Liverpool Personal Service Society,
and other groups interested in this work. The Working Group
met informally from time to time—normally once or twice a year
—to discuss their experiences and matters of general concern. At
this point, the committees were still unofficial, and without any
secure source of funds, so that when the grants from the trusts
to the committees in Bristol and Nottingham expired it appeared
that what little had been achieved would be lost. Thus, the
committee in Bristol was no longer able to employ a welfare
officer and soon afterwards lost its guiding spirit and founder and
ceased to function, while the committee in Nottingham had a
very difficult struggle convincing the local authority to support
its work and only survived through the support of the Council
of Social Service and the work of its Secretary, who continued
without pay. The Advice Bureau which the Family Welfare
Association had established in Lambeth was closed at the end of
the three-year project, although special attention to the problems
of immigrants in the Notting Hill area, was continued.

This was soon to change, for in 1959, a number of local
councils began to be involved in work in race relations; thus, for
example, meetings were held at the Town Hall in both Hackney
and Willesden in London to set up committees, and the London
Council of Social Service appointed an Assistant Secretary to
co-ordinate field-work in the London area. It appears that the

[1] S. K. Ruck (ed.), *The West Indian Comes to England* (London, Routledge, 1960).

Nottingham and Notting Hill incidents of late 1958 focused new interest on the problem, and a number of new committees came into existence in this period. As co-ordinating committees were set up, they were invited to send representatives to the N.C.S.S. Working Group, as were Councils of Social Service in towns where the proportion of coloured people had increased considerably. By January 1963, eleven Councils of Social Service and twelve committees other than those organized by Councils of Social Service, were represented on the N.C.S.S. Working Group.

At this time, the Government still refused to consider any amendment to their *laissez-faire* policies, but in 1962, after the passage of the Act controlling and limiting immigration, the Home Secretary appointed the Commonwealth Immigrants Advisory Council under the chairmanship of Lady Reading to advise him on any matters, which he might choose to refer to it from time to time, affecting the welfare of Commonwealth immigrants and their integration into the community. The Council issued three reports, in the second of which it recommended the establishment of a National Committee for Commonwealth Immigrants (N.C.C.I.) to provide advice and information on such matters and to assist in the formation of local liaison committees and regional organizations. This was implemented on 1 April 1964.

By 1964–5, a large number of local organizations, whose aim was to promote racial understanding and integration, were being established, and many adopted the name of 'International Friendship Council' or 'Association'. In the White Paper of August 1965, the Government linked more stringent control of immigration with greater efforts for integration, and the Commonwealth Immigrants Advisory Council and the National Committee were transformed into a new and larger National Committee for Commonwealth Immigrants, with greater resources and the dual tasks of advising the Government on matters affecting immigrants and promoting and co-ordinating the work of local liaison committees. The Government now officially espoused the work of the committees at local level by making money available to them for a full-time worker through the National Committee, and linking this with efforts to encourage the local authorities in the areas concerned to assist the committees with matching grants. From this point, the number of committees expanded rapidly—from the thirty or so which were in existence when the National Committee was re-structured, to fifty-five at the time when the fieldwork for this research was conducted, and with more continually in the process of formation.

It is important to note that the National Committee was set up as an independent committee, although it was receiving Government finance, and that its reports were made to the Prime Minister. In this period, further Governmental action included (i) the appointment of a junior minister with special responsibility for immigrants, who, after a short period at the Department of Economic Affairs, was attached to the Home Office; and (ii) the establishment of the Race Relations Board to implement the provisions of the Race Relations Act of 1965.

Finally, at the time when this research was being conducted, the Government were sponsoring in Parliament a second Race Relations Bill, which increased the range of legislation against racial discrimination, and thus added to the responsibilities of the Race Relations Board, while also affecting significantly the national position of voluntary work in race relations through the proposed re-forming of the N.C.C.I. into the Community Relations Commission, as discussed in the last section of this chapter.

It must be noted that the debates on these proposals became confused with the introduction, and speedy passage through Parliament, of the 1968 Commonwealth Immigrants Act and a speech by the Rt. Hon. J. Enoch Powell on immigration. This diverted attention from the Race Relations Bill which was then passing through Parliament; and passions raised by the further restriction of immigration and Mr. Powell's speech, affected reaction to the Bill. Also, discussion of the Bill was primarily focused on the extension of the forms of discrimination which were to be illegal and the powers of the Race Relations Board, rather than the structure and scope of the new Community Relations Commission.

THE POLICY AND WORKING OF THE LOCAL COMMITTEES

The background of the development of the committees to the form that pertained when this study was made, has been treated at some length because it became apparent that many of the issues which faced the committees could only be viewed as a result of the history of voluntary work in the field of race relations in

Britain, and the varying views of members of the committees on contemporary events. Thus, many questions were interrelated in the appreciation of the role of the committee that was expressed by both members and non-members of the committees. In particular, for some who found all limitations on immigration into Britain from the Commonwealth distasteful, the recasting of the structure of the national body coincided with a reappearance of the issue of immigration control, and this affected discussion of both issues, especially in view of the fact that the reaction of the National Committee for Commonwealth Immigrants to the 1968 Commonwealth Immigrants Bill, and the Government's treatment of the Committee, also gave rise to controversy. Further, in any attempt to characterize the division of opinion as to what the role of the committees should be, the history of the local committees is of great importance.

In what follows, the attitudes expressed by those who were interviewed are presented rather schematically, in the interest of clarity in a short paper, for there were many nuances of opinion, and many surprising juxtapositions of thinking on different issues which were explored as a means of ascertaining the interviewee's views about the role that the committees should fulfil. In any new organization it is not surprising to find confusion about purpose and strategy, and two points should be made about this at the present stage: firstly, the definition of a clear programme for the committees is one of the major problems for those working in the field, and this will be considered in the concluding section; secondly, on many occasions initial inconsistencies or contradictions were apparent rather than real, as committee members were able to develop their positions coherently in the course of an interview.

First, the historical material is a good guide to the differences of opinion which were highlighted by the study. Indeed, the names used by committees in varying periods clearly mark the view that was taken of the work by those involved in the establishment of the organization. Thus, as has been mentioned, the mid-1950s saw the use of such a name as 'Committee for the Welfare of Colonial Workers'—or an organization name would specifically mention 'Coloured Workers'. It is also significant that in both Leeds and Nottingham the committees put great emphasis on housing associations, especially trying to provide accommodation on a multi-racial basis (in Leeds this was the Aggrey Housing Ltd., and in Nottingham, the Coloured Peoples' Housing Association). In Bristol, the possibility of setting up a similar project was discussed on a number of occasions. The committees also showed a common concern for the idea of setting up social centres—'international clubs'—to encourage immigrants to mix into British society.

By the end of the 1950s, 'welfare' was not considered attractive to the immigrants, or a satisfactory approach, and the names of the new committees reflected a concern for 'international friendship'. When a number of new committees were established in the period between the introduction of the first Commonwealth Immigrants Bill and the formation of the second National Committee, they emphasized their political stance, and the attitude which led to their creation in opposition to the trend in Government policies by taking such titles as 'Committee for Racial Integration', and the like. Immediately after the formation of the second main National Committee, the position was unclear, reflecting the existing doubt as to the exact nature of 'the comprehensive body of doctrine which can be flexibly applied to a variety of local situations', which the White Paper said the National Committee should build up. The National Committee itself at first recommended some mention of 'International Friendship', and as the General Secretary of the N.C.C.I. had been associated with one committee which had attracted great publicity and was regarded as the leading example of what could and should be done, many of the officially sponsored groups used similar terms. Also, some committees used the straightforward title 'Voluntary Liaison Committee', as the National Committee espoused a policy of 'liaison' between the host and immigrant communities, the committee being cast in the role of a 'bridge'. Finally, in the period since the beginning of 1967, many committees adopted a title referring to 'Community Relations' and other committees changed their names to reflect this concept, even before the transformation of the National Committee was announced; and it became clear that the Government and the Committee were anxious to produce uniformity in the titles.

From this, it can be seen that there are three main trends in the work of the committees, which have built up over their history: first, there was the 'welfare' attitude, associated with the operation of international friendship; this gave way to a concept of the committees acting as a bridge between communities, as exemplified by the 'liaison' approach developed by the National Committee in its initial work; and finally, there is the 'community relations' approach, the orthodoxy at the time of writing. However, there is also a further conception of the work which accepts that the National Committee was correct in wishing to drop the phrase 'for Commonwealth Immigrants' from its name, but feels that the community relations approach is still too static. Rather, the task should be seen in terms of 'Community Development', bringing people together to take action over their common problems, giving them the information and the equipment which they need to do so, and in the process, allowing them to become fully participating members of the society.

The questions that were used to ascertain the attitude of those interviewed were as follows: Do you think that the committee should do welfare work or individual casework? What do you think that the attitude of the committee to such activities as play groups, housing associations, youth clubs, and so on, ought to be? Do you think the committee should be non-political? The second question was expanded by mentioning three possible strategies for the committees: thus, they could be pressure groups, working to ensure that the appropriate body does what they feel should be done; they could be initiating bodies, making sure that a scheme gets under way with the necessary resources and then handing it over to some other larger agency, such as the local authority, or to the local people involved, remaining at hand should they subsequently require further help and guidance; or they could build themselves empires of various kinds of organizations so as to become a power in their local area. These three themes were used as the main method of assessing views of the committees' role.

It must first be stated that many of those interviewed, including those who were members of the committees, had no clear answers to the questions and had not thought out what they felt the role of the committees should be. This apart, the greatest unanimity was found in replies expressing opposition to the idea that the committees should be welfare or social groups. For some, welfare was an inevitable and regrettable necessity, but few welcomed it. On the second question, nobody favoured the idea of the committees building empires for themselves, but a number doubted whether they should become involved in such schemes as play groups and housing associations at all. Of the others, those who had very definite conceptions of 'community development' elaborated them on many occasions without the question even having to be asked at all, but many others did not have a firm conception of how such projects might develop or be directed. The final question, concerning the political nature of the committees, produced the least clear response: many of those interviewed often felt uncomfortable about it and it seems inevitable that a small number of those who wished the committees to be completely non-political probably did so because they agreed with the sentiments that had been expressed by Mr. Enoch Powell, M.P., and feared that the committees would oppose them if they were to make public statements. The majority (about 80 per cent of respondents) clearly felt that the committees could not remain silent when issues became matters of political controversy; but, the committees should not be identified in party politics, however difficult it might be to maintain this distinction.

As will be the case in the discussion of other organizations' views of the liaison committees, much of the evidence for assessing attitudes lies in the internal structure of the interview and the way an interviewee expressed his replies, and it is, therefore, difficult to give a precise division of opinion on each question. However, a clear pattern did emerge from the interviews taken as a whole, with those who were most opposed to the idea of the committees doing welfare work being the same respondents who felt that the committees could not 'dodge the issue' by failing to make their position clear when political controversy affected their work. Also, those who can be called the more 'radical' were more likely to feel that the committees should initiate programmes of pre-school play-groups and other projects, and that these should be handed over to the people whom they concerned when they had become firmly established. However, as was mentioned before, this was not always the case; one example will show the types of variation that occurred. A small number of those who felt that the committees are morally bound to make public statements, and that they should be involved in starting schemes to benefit the residents of the areas in which they are working, also felt that the committees should not react negatively towards welfare work; in their view, the committees could only learn of the problems of the areas if people came to them to seek advice and help with their difficulties, and the very individuals they were trying to help would lose confidence in the committees if they were to be refused their first, most immediate requests.

A composite picture, drawn from all the issues raised in the interviews reveals a spectrum of opinion in which the committee members divide roughly in the following pattern: 5 per cent had virtually no idea what the committees were about; and at the other pole, 20–25 per cent were what might be termed 'radical' in their view of what the committees should be doing, i.e. they did not feel that welfare should be one of the prime tasks of the committees, rather they should lead the disadvantaged—immigrants *and* others—to becoming full citizens and they should lead the community by articulating the point of view that was likely to reduce tension. The remaining 70–75 per cent presented a spectrum of opinion ranging from those who were not willing to commit themselves to what was in effect the community development approach and expressed some reservations, to those who can be termed 'conservative', i.e. they did have a clear idea of what the committees should do, but felt that they should help the immigrants to conform to the standards of the host society, that they should not do anything that some other body such as the local authority could and should do, and that they ought not to risk offending any body or any segment of public opinion by making statements on national or even local issues that might be controversial. As should be apparent, these figures and characterizations are far from precise, for they do not do justice to the various shades of opinion and combinations of views on different points which emerged; but they are presented in the hope that the material will be put in some perspective.

Of course, not only did individuals differ in their opinions, but committees differed in their approaches. To a certain extent, these differences can be measured in terms of their activities, and in this context it would have been interesting to tabulate attitudes with such factors as main areas of interest: e.g. was the committee more concerned with establishing a Fair Housing Group or a multi-racial social centre? However, the study did not have the resources to undertake the gathering of material on a scale sufficient to make any resulting data significant, and it is doubtful

12*

whether this would be possible at all, for it would not be sufficient to ascertain merely what a committee was doing; rather, it is equally important to know also what other schemes it would wish to undertake, or which it had decided not to consider. As with the interviews of committee members and others, in any accurate assessment of approach, the attitude conveyed would, in effect, be as important as the actual activities sponsored and the position adopted. Thus, only two committees were able to establish Fair Housing Groups as a result of grants made available by the Gulbenkian Foundation through the National Committee, but there were others who had made unsuccessful applications; a committee's attitude towards the establishment of multi-racial social clubs can only be judged in relation to such factors as the needs of the community and the feelings of the coloured community organizations in the area, whatever its general conclusions might be as to the value of such schemes; the need for individual casework can vary depending upon the efficiency and the willingness of local authority departments and other voluntary agencies in dealing with cases brought in from the coloured communities, and so on. The approach of a committee could only be categorized by a combination of factors including both what it does and why. The sample studied cannot be taken as a representative cross-section of those in existence; some were only just being established and so it was too early to make a categorization, while the others could be placed on a rough spectrum corresponding to the 'conservative'-'radical' range of opinion indicated above for individuals interviewed. Those committees at the conservative end did not wish to expand their activities beyond welfare work and occasional international friendship social events, whereas the most radical committee was seeking to broaden the range of its activities, and this was clearly not just a function of its having greater resources than any other committee, but a reflection of its view (collectively amongst the members) of its work.

To some degree, the variations in the 'character' of the committees were accounted for by their particular histories, for few were so old as to have lost their founding members, and they strongly maintained the ideas that they had when their organizations were founded; but neither the period when the committees were founded nor the individuals who composed them, their own predilections, and their views, were sufficient to explain the different approaches to the committees. Rather, these were all a function of the areas in which the committees were situated, for the committees naturally tended to reflect the social environment from which their membership was drawn and in which it was working, and it is to this that the next section will turn, followed by a brief discussion of the committees' relationships with the central organization, the National Committee for Commonwealth Immigrants.

(d) THE ADMINISTRATIVE DIFFICULTIES FACING LOCAL LIAISON COMMITTEES: RELATIONS WITH OTHER ORGANIZATIONS

The basic research for this paper suggested a correlation between the orientation of a committee towards its work, in terms of responses to the major questions of its desired role (as indicated in the previous section), and the various social characteristics of the area in which it was based, in terms of the number and strength of other voluntary organizations, the individuals involved in the politics of the local authority, and other factors. An analysis of this correlation was, however, beyond the scope of the work, but it would appear that the attitudes of other local bodies to the voluntary liaison committee would be a first approximation to this and a significant measure of the committee's potential influence. As has been mentioned, interviews were sought not just with the members of the committees, but also with officials and members of the local authority, representatives of the local Press, and other officials, who were not also members of the committee. In addition, almost without exception, the committees are based on a liaison concept giving representation to many different groups, and there was thus no need to seek special interviews with these representatives or the Secretaries of local Councils of Social Service.

The most important conclusion drawn from these interviews was that committee members who represented some other interest on their committees, and were not involved solely because of a personal commitment, were more conservative in their views of the role of the committees. This does not mean that all who were ostensibly representatives were also not personally committed, for many had been involved personally in the establishment of these bodies before the organizations to which they had a prior affiliation gave their official support, and others had taken care to ensure that they would be asked to act as a representative on the committees when nominations were requested. However, the serious implication was not merely that officials of other bodies were more cautious about the value of the liaison committees, but that in many instances they had no obvious idea of what the committees' role should be.

Thus for a few voluntary bodies, the new committees seemed to pose several threats: by stealing the limelight for social work; or by gaining the energies of voluntary workers who would otherwise have helped them; or even by being too 'radical' and thus making Governmental and local authority departments suspicious of all voluntary agencies. Although there was still some doubt whether special committees were needed to deal with the problems of some voluntary organizations that felt that their work would be taken away from them by the new committees, this was a much less vital factor than the reserved attitude and, in some cases, open hostility, on the part of local authorities. This often took the form of the argument that had been used forcefully for a long period before any action in the field of race relations was admitted to be necessary: i.e. that it was morally and politically wrong to set up any organization which was specifically concerned with the needs of a minority group.

Equally, there is little doubt that some other local authorities suspected that sooner or later the committees would be troublemakers, that is, that the committees would start making demands that they would be unable or unwilling to meet. This was particularly true in those areas where (i) a committee had been formed by a group of politically committed individuals; and (ii) the local establishment had not wished to be implicated and still considered the whole underlying philosophy of the group to be dangerous, if not completely subversive. In contrast, there were other authorities which might be regarded as slightly more sophisticated, and which seemed to be calculating the minimum degree of co-operation with the committee which would prevent any outright challenge.

So bleak a picture must not be left without the assertion that a minority of those interviewed who represented an official body in one way or another, did genuinely support the work of the committee personally and desired a similar commitment from their organizations. However, this analysis would not be complete if it did not mention that within each organization there were different views of the committee in its area, particularly in the case of local authorities. The attitude of the local authority, thus, often differed from department to department; and the experience of the committee, most often through its full-time officer, often depended on the individuals within each department with whom he had had most contact. This was a much more important factor than the political control of the Council, for often there had been changes in political control during the life of the committee and these changes seemed to entail only differences in degree of attitude rather than complete changes in attitude; that is to say, in one area both major parties would be hostile (or favourable) to the committee, only more or less so.

The major conclusion must be that there has been very little done in the way of projecting the purpose and aims of the committee as a means of gaining the support of other organizations, and particularly the critical body in the area, the local authority. Some committees had begun with a hostile attitude to the authority, and over-all, there had been very little concern with any form of public relations. Indeed, it was surprising to note that only a small minority of committees had developed any regular relationship with the Press, and only half of the committees in existence in February 1968 had any systematic file of press-cuttings about their work and/or race relations in their area.

The impression gained was, thus, one of muddle and an amateur approach to the work of the committee. For example, the main committee had often set up a number of sub-committees to deal with such problems as employment, housing, legal affairs, and so on, but in many cases it did not appear that more than one or two individuals, who were the key workers in the committee, had any clear idea of what the structure should be, or what such sub-committees should be doing. Particularly for those committees which were established after the White Paper of August 1965—either because it was Government policy to encourage the committees, or the National Committee applied pressure on the local authority and other local bodies to do so—actions were often undertaken because they had been successful elsewhere and the National Committee recommended them, and not because the sponsoring committee had any clear idea of the purpose of the undertaking.

Indeed, throughout the field, the role of the National Committee for Commonwealth Immigrants, and its relationships with the local committees, were crucial. Thus, part of the difficulty that committees faced in projecting a clear impression of their work was that for a considerable period, the National Committee was obviously dissatisfied with the concept of liaison, and was searching for a new definition of the work. Indeed, the National Committee began with several disadvantages, which events only made more difficult to overcome.

Essentially, the N.C.C.I. suffered from the neglect of the issue during the 1950s. Further, many of those who were already in the field were very strongly opposed to any form of immigration control and doubted the wisdom of agreeing to support a body which had been linked with immigration control in the 1965 White Paper. Additionally, they doubted the sincerity of the Government's commitment to better race relations, fearing that the N.C.C.I. would be used, as they perceived local committees being used, for the authority to shift the responsibility for any action that might appear to be politically dangerous. These factors were only reinforced, to the National Committee's disadvantage, by the events of 1968, when the Government introduced further immigration control at the same time that they were proposing new measures designed to further racial harmony. Activists in the field found the new controls more distasteful than ever, and did not find the new Race Relations Bill to be satisfactory. Above all, the Government did not consult the National Committee before they introduced the Bill to restrict immigration, although the Committee's objections to control and to Parts 1 and 2 of the White Paper under which it was reconstituted in 1965, were so great that the Committee's first action on being appointed had been to seek an interview with the Prime Minister to state its position. This treatment of the National Committee only reinforced those who had argued that the Government were not really committed to racial justice and that the National Committee was merely their 'fig-leaf'.

To this, other factors must be added. The National Committee put great emphasis on building up the number of committees for which it was responsible—as a sign that it was active —and many of the established committees were disturbed when they had very little contact with the 'people from London'.

Thus, for many of those active in local committees, the N.C.C.I. came to be just another bureaucratic organization; this was particularly the case for liaison officers who felt that their requests got lost in the machinery, that inexperienced individuals were promoted to jobs in London, and then came to tell them what to do, and that the headquarters of the National Committee was the scene of vigorous office politicking with different groups competing for influence and favour. Indeed, by the time of the controversy over the National Committee's position in relation to the 1968 Commonwealth Immigrants Bill, and whether or not it should resign, much of the discussion about the National Committee was in terms of personalities, and a growing number of resignations and dismissals only increased the disenchantment. The political and individual dissatisfaction coalesced in the discussion of how work in the field should be organized.

It appeared that the N.C.C.I. favoured the idea of becoming a statutory board, for this gave the organization new status, especially as the Race Relations Board had been receiving much more favourable publicity in the Press and was more highly regarded even by members of local committees; but to the activists, this merely represented a formalization of the Committee's position as just another part of the Government machinery, with even less chance that the new structure would be responsive to the interests of the coloured communities or the local committees. In this, it must be recorded that the National Committee had largely failed to give any coherent public impression of its policy or direction; publicity appeared only when there was a crisis. Also, the Committee had little reality for those working on the local committees. Its personnel were, as seen from the provinces especially, individuals who descended infrequently from an office just behind the opulent Dorchester Hotel and then disappeared again just as abruptly. Regional Development Officers had been appointed, but they were based in London and not in their regions, which is where the committees wanted them to be. The N.C.C.I. had not established regional committees as had been foreshadowed in the 1965 White Paper, and had apparently gone out of its way to demolish one existing regional structure. Those members of the committees who knew about the N.C.C.I., knew all about its defects, whereas others who were unaware of any possible change in the national structure often did not even know the name of the central body and certainly had no clear idea about its purpose and policy. This extreme 5 per cent of those interviewed can best be typified by the remark of the person who suggested that the liaison committees should leave any comments on political issues to a national body. When asked whether there should be such a body, he replied: 'Well, I think there already is one; it's called that N . . . er I . . . er C . . . or something. They had a lot to do with getting the Immigration Act through Parliament, didn't they?' Of the rest of the sample, about 20–25 per cent expressed strong dissatisfaction with the National Committee, while the remaining 70–75 per cent had varying degrees of difficulty remembering the N.C.C.I.'s name, and their knowledge of the work of the central organization was limited to the information gleaned at monthly meetings from announcements—either by the Secretary or liaison officer, or in various bits of organization literature—of various conferences and other activities.

A corollary of this vacuum in central leadership was that committees did not have much more idea about each other's work than what they gained informally. Due to the dissension, meetings of representatives of the committees and their full-time paid officers were more often debates about the National Committee's policy and the way it was working—particularly making decisions first and then telling the people who were 'out in the field' about them—rather than exchanges of information. This emphasized the differences between committees, rather than allowing the weaker to use the experience of those which were richer in finances and personnel. All this put a strain on the liaison officers, or community relations officers, who have not been mentioned so far, but are undoubtedly the key figures in those committees (about half) where they had been appointed. However, it is impossible to make any other characterization of them other than that they are the most important factor in the committees where they work, for it was impossible to have any fixed criteria of qualifications for these officers, since there were no clear ideas as to what either their functions or the role of the committees, should be. Further, the National Committee had not elaborated any substantial programme for the training of the officers. Their work was thus a matter for agreement between the individual officers and their committees; thus, with a weak committee, the officer had to provide all the ideas and other resources.

All this meant that there was no coherent pattern or philosophy in response to such problems raised in the course of the study as: how the committee should treat the grievances of members of the immigrant communities, whether the committee should encourage the development of organizations specifically for members of the immigrant communities, whether the committee should invite representatives of the police to its meetings, and what the type of internal organization would enable the committee to carry out its work to greatest advantage. Each respondent's answers to these questions were more or less consistent with his individual view of the role of the committee, but over-all, the pattern was much more of case law, the committees taking positions on an *ad hoc* basis depending on both the way in which an issue presented itself and the personal views of those who had happened to attend the meeting at which it was discussed. Again, this only served to reinforce the division between those committees which were wealthy in both monetary resources and able personnel and those which were floundering with little support, if not outright hostility, from other local organizations and the local authority, and had few members with a well thought out point of view on the major issues.

Over-all, there is little doubt that those who took what might be called the more radical view appeared to have the more coherent and considered opinions, and were better able to express them. The author of this paper will not try to deny that due to his own personal predilections on the issue, he was probably inclined from the start to come to this conclusion; but, it would also appear that there are compelling reasons, concerning both organization and theoretical considerations for work in the field, whereby the more radical community development approach recommends itself. The following, and final, section of conclusions and recommendations for future action, will outline these reasons and the position.

(e) CONCLUSIONS

It cannot be over-emphasized that the work of local liaison committees, like that of all organizations in the field of race relations in Britain, has continued to suffer from the neglect of the subject through the critical period of the 1950s and up to the White Paper of 1965. With the establishment of the National Committee and the first step towards the creation of a profession of workers in the field, there has been an impatient casting around for a new rational approach to the work. This has coincided with another aspect of the sudden burgeoning of committees and other bodies which cannot be ignored: considerable attention has been paid to the subject of race relations by academic research in the social sciences. Not only was the topic neglected by the Government for a long period, but also very little was written about it. Thus, when the Government introduced immigration control, very little was known about the pattern of immigration, for little data had been collected systematically, and very few studies had been carried out as to who the immigrants were, whether they had successfully found employment, and so on. Equally, when the Government decided to support the local liaison committees, there was little background material available to enable those who had charge of the field to decide what the correct policy should be. It was immediately apparent that the old ideas of welfare were unsatisfactory, and within a short period the international friendship approach was also found to be too static. The process whereby the new policy of community relations was evolved is itself important, but in order to place this evolution in its proper context, it would first be valuable to review briefly how thinking on the subject has developed, along converging paths, amongst both academic observers and fieldworkers.

As has been mentioned frequently, the 1950s were the years of welfare. This must be related to the fact that those involved in the field were often drawn in through activities in other social organizations, or in the Council of Social Service, which acted as the 'umbrella' sheltering work for colonial workers. Equally, some of those who were drawn in from the churches, especially if the work was fostered by the Council of Churches, brought with them a tradition of missionary work. For all, the immigrants were regarded as another disadvantaged group to be helped, like handicapped children and the aged. As the numbers of immigrants grew, however, the machinery of voluntary agencies could no longer cope with individual cases, and it was recognized that all immigrants had a problem of adjustment to the new, urban society. This conception of the problem was supported by the main academic writing of that time, which emphasized that immigrants were 'strangers' to the British way of life. By concentrating on the fact that the difficulties involved *immigrants* from a poor rural background, this theory minimized the importance of race and considered the solution to be the finding of ways to overcome the strangeness which both host and immigrant groups felt towards each other.

Thus, work tended towards attempts to create activities which would foster international friendship by bringing people together to participate in schemes which were of mutual interest, e.g. play-reading groups or a jazz ballet company. (These projects were initiated by the Willesden International Friendship Council, which in the period 1961–3 was considered to be the most effective example of this kind of work, and it was not a coincidence that the person who became General Secretary of the National Committee was for some time quite active in that committee.) However, the view that all that was necessary was to bring people together to join in activities of common interest was soon felt to be inadequate; with the first Commonwealth Immigrants Act, the issue became overtly political for many in the field; and the threat of extreme right-wing candidates who were willing to make an issue of race, created a desire for much more forthright action, especially after the victory of Mr. Peter Griffiths at Smethwick in the 1964 General Election. Committees began to pay more attention to activities designed to attack prejudice and discrimination in housing and employment (and Willesden, for example, put great emphasis on the work of teams of conciliators—one white, one coloured—who visited homes where there had been friction between landlords and tenants of different racial groups, and on efforts to remove discriminatory advertisements for accommodation from local newspapers and news-agents' noticeboards).

The task was seen to be beyond the resources of a voluntary committee, and it was considered to be essential that the committees enlist the support of as many as possible of the existing social agencies, the political parties, the churches, and every other group conceivable, and especially that it have the backing of the local authority (as, again, at Willesden, where leading members of the Council had been instrumental in setting up the International Friendship Council and had secured the official backing

of the authority for its work, financing its office and the employment of a full-time officer). Thus, if the committee did not have
the resources to do the job by itself it would be assured of having
the goodwill of the other established organizations in the area,
and would be in a good position to encourage and cajole them
into doing the things that would achieve its goals. This was
essentially the concept of liaison that lay behind the White
Paper of August 1965, and the work of the National Committee
during its first months.

Still, however, this was too passive a conception of what the
role of the committees should be. It seemed to the committees
themselves that they had been called into existence merely to be
talk-shops, and this irritated the more impatient members
(especially articulate representatives of the immigrant communities who were dissatisfied with the creation of sub-committees
ostensibly concerned with the critical sectors of employment,
housing, and so on, but having little idea what they were supposed
to do) as confirming this view. The National Committee itself
wanted to demonstrate to the Government that it was not merely
establishing ever more committees but that it had a constructive
role. In addition, as has been indicated, the National Committee
itself had problems with the more militant activists in the field who
saw its creation as a token gesture by the Government and doubted
that it really had the resources or policy to be effective.

Finally, this coincided with renewed academic interest in
race relations from political and sociological perspectives. This
can best be illustrated by reference to Rex and Moore's study of
housing in the Sparkbrook area of Birmingham[1] which was
based on the belief that the problem of race relations was one of
prejudice and discrimination amongst the host community in
many fields, of which housing was only one. Prejudice and discrimination are seen as being inextricably linked to the existing
social structure in Britain, so that immigration has highlighted,
rather than caused, many of the faults in the social structure of
Britain. Thus racialism can only be cured when the social faults
have been eliminated. At the same time, many of the leaders of
the immigrant communities were coming to see immigrants as
a disadvantaged group—their disadvantage being the hostility

---

[1] John Rex and Robert Moore, *Race, Community and Conflict: A Study of Sparkbrook*
(London, Oxford University Press, for Institute of Race Relations, 1967).

of the host community and the social conditions from which that hostility resulted.

It was at this point that the direction of community relations work was injected into the field as a direct result of an importation of some of the schemes which had been undertaken in race relations in the United States, using pre-school play-groups and housing associations, for example, with the specific aim of bringing racial groups together. A grant from the Gulbenkian Foundation enabled the National Committee to invite the local committees to propose such schemes for their areas. This programme was essentially grafted on to the existing liaison conception of the work, and did not affect the structure of the committees but, rather, gave them new objectives. It was at this point that the research was conducted, and the questions inevitably arose as to whether the structure was well suited to the programme, and whether the implications of the programme had been fully considered, to produce a coherent view of what the future course of the work of the committees might be.

Here again, the effect of the long neglect of the subject in Britain has to be faced, for the result has been that there is no tradition of assessing the problem of race relations in British terms; rather, there has been a tendency to adopt American thinking both on the radical side, which has adopted the terminology of Black Power, and in the attempts to find solutions to the problems, as in the adoption of 'community relations' discussed here. The National Committee had to develop very quickly; and with many factors seemingly against it, the projection of a clear policy was apparently not possible. As a result, it would appear that the articulation of racial prejudice has increased in Britain and that the National Committee and the local committees have been powerless to prevent this. Above all, there was no clear policy for the N.C.C.I. or the local committees to promote to the public, and there are many committees which are floundering badly without the necessary resources of finance or informed and able personnel. Generally, there is confusion both in administration and conception of the problems and solutions.

Any conclusion must to some extent depend on an individual interpretation of the general situation and the likely development of official policy, but this should be more a matter of tactics and the presentation rather than the basic orientation of the programme, which depends on an appreciation of what the problems are. Theory has given two main positions, in terms of strangeness and the structural defects of the society, and the main emphasis is now put on the latter; however, it would seem to be just as possible to provide solutions which dealt with the structural defects but still leave hostile groups, just as hostility might be reduced to some extent without affecting the structural defects. Research with small groups leads to the conclusion that groups brought together to reduce tension will work best when they are provided with some tasks on which they can co-operate. This was seen in the efforts to create jazz ballet and theatre groups. However, an important additional consideration is that the groups work best when they are asked to tackle problems which are seen to be central by all, or a substantial proportion of, their members. Thus, liaison committees can only work effectively if (i) they bring people together to solve problems and (ii) these problems are of great importance to those participating in the work of the committees.

Here one further important factor appears: whom should the committees bring together? It is very obvious that at present the committees are mainly composed of individuals who would, in any case, be involved in other activities if they were not sitting on the committees, and indeed are often engaged in many other activities other than the liaison committee. On the other hand, their work is directed towards the needs of those inarticulate or disadvantaged groups which do not include typical committee members and supporters of good causes. Thus, if the committees are fully to affect the attitudes of the people for whom they wish to work, they will have to do so in ways that involve these people in groups that aim to solve their own problems. In other words, the ideal of integration and anti-racialism is the initial impetus, bringing together a group of the kind of people who join committees and enjoy talking about the possible solutions to problems; but to proceed further, the committees will have to involve members of the disadvantaged groups who might be affected by their policies—in projects directed towards immediate actions to fulfil immediate needs, rather than in committee discussions.

In political terms, this means that the committees may have to expand their commitment to programmes such as pre-school play-groups and housing associations and also to develop more along the lines of the Fair Housing Groups that are already being tested. Such activities will have obvious effects upon the organizational problems that have been discussed, and it would seem that these effects will be positive. Thus, if a body has concrete schemes which express its goals, it will more easily project an image of what it represents and what it is trying to do; a structure of sub-committees will take on relevance as these committees find themselves developing and taking responsibility for new projects within the philosophy of the organization, and so on. Above all, those groups who are concerned about their public image—i.e. whether they are seen as merely pro-immigrant pressure groups (and to the extent that they consider this to be a problem at all)—will be able to show that they are undertaking activities which are designed to benefit the whole society.

However, such programmes have political repercussions in wider spheres, both in the organization of the whole sector of work in race relations and with reference to relations between that sector and the wider political processes. Underlying this is the philosophy which is the base for these kinds of activity, for they are obviously not entailed by a concept of liaison or merely community relations, and in particular such projects as Fair Housing Groups have very different dimensions. Thus, the committees are not merely bringing people together, but they are bringing them together to participate in schemes which will directly affect the social structure in the situation of those whom they will be involving in their work. If the groups brought together to tackle common problems are to be effective, they must be given the equipment in terms of information, finance, and whatever else might be necessary to do this *for themselves*, for there is no longer a demand for, or a desire to give, better conditions in the form of welfare or things *done for* the disadvantaged. Within the field of race relations, such mobilization of energies—which enables people to participate in the schemes which affect them—is likely to entail greater impatience with a centralized structure which promulgates policy and hands it down subsequently. There is likely to be an increasing demand for the local committees to participate in the formation of policy, as has already developed to some extent, and this demand is likely to be fed by the kinds of programmes that are being encouraged. Indeed, the most con-sistent way for this to be implemented would be for the central body, now the C.R.C., to encourage local bodies, and representatives whom they might designate, to take part in this process as one step towards encouraging the outlook the programmes demand.

Unfortunately, it does not appear that such developments are likely, and dissension, from the present vantage point, or rather point of disadvantage, seems likely to grow. In this, the N.C.C.I. was not merely conforming to what might be expected of a bureaucracy which has just staked out its area and is unwilling to give up any of its new-found power; but it is anticipating what it (almost certainly, correctly) sees as being the possible reaction of outside political forces to such developments, for such schemes as Fair Housing Groups are quite likely to find themselves opposed to the policy of government at both local and national levels. This goes beyond the very difficult problem of how the committees should handle complaints from individuals or groups amongst the immigrant communities against official bodies such as the police or departments of the local authority who might be represented on the committees. One relevant warning from the experience in the United States is that the political establishments are likely to react unfavourably to such situations. This is especially critical as the groups are almost certainly going to rely upon the different levels of government for financial support. From the attitudes already developed by the most successful committees, it would seem that the British ethos might have an answer, in that open clashes will be avoided and the committees will be careful to flex their muscles only after a considerable period of development and when the issue is absolutely right. At least, this would be the policy if all the committees were well guided in terms of what they felt they could gain from the system by taking the most 'radical' approach that could be used from within the system. What is immediately clear is that this community development approach (based on mobilizing those who are disadvantaged on matters of common interest with those who are additionally disadvantaged by the prejudices of the society, to overcome all the blocks together, so that those who are at present outside much of modern society can become fully participating members of a restructured society) can provide the rational philosophy which solves many, if not all, of the organizational and conceptual problems facing those working in the field. However, it is not clear that the conditions are appropriate for such an approach. The people whom the committees would wish to mobilize might not feel that they could benefit from action 'from within the system'; the Governmental and other bodies with whom the committees would still have to work to a certain extent might not be willing to allow the use of this more radical, community development approach; and because there are already vested interests in the present structure, the creation of a new organizational basis specially suited to the tasks which would be undertaken, might not be feasible. Above all, the consequences of this theoretical view of how work in the field might be conceived must be explored further—in terms of policy, organization, and other considerations—than has been possible in this chapter.

(f) FURTHER DEVELOPMENTS

Further visits were made to a number of committees in the course of the academic year 1969–70.[1] These included all the committees which were visited in the original study in 1968. No attempt was made, however, to obtain the same number of interviews with a large proportion of the members of the committees, and extended interviews with the professional officers of the committees were relied on in the main as being sufficient to ascertain whether any of the findings reported in the original research would represent a situation which had been superseded by developments in the intervening two years.

Some changes must be noted: For example, there was considerably heightened concern about the nature of relationships between the police and the coloured communities; and a more positive attitude had generally been adopted towards the Press, particularly local newspapers, with the Community Relations Commission running a series of training seminars for community relations officers on this topic.

Yet these changes were minor developments within an over-all picture that had remained largely unchanged. The N.C.C.I. had become the C.R.C., its budget and staff had expanded, and it had moved its office to a rather less ostentatious setting; but the criticisms of its work remained the same. Its administration continued to be criticized in very much the same terms as before, while at the local level there was no clear pattern of

[1] This was made possible by a grant from the Research Board of Leicester University.

organization or policy. Above all, there was no clear national leadership as to what the goals of work by the committees should be, and what strategy and structure would be appropriate. In effect, committees are constituted on the basis that was appropriate for a liaison conception of their work, representing a variety of local interests.

The overriding difficulty is that it is not clear exactly what the committees are considered to be doing, for 'promoting good community relations' is an extremely vague definition. Unfortunately, it can only be reported that there appears to be little possibility that they will adopt the coherent and positive terms of reference that will allow these problems to be resolved.

2. *The Work of the Liaison Officers*
by Margot Levy

(a) INTRODUCTION

The appointment of full-time liaison officers by local voluntary liaison committees was sanctioned by the Government in the 1965 White Paper, *Immigration from the Commonwealth*:

The Government consider it of the first importance that each voluntary liaison committee should be served by a trained, full-time, paid official who should be the direct servant of the committee. As evidence of its wish to give tangible support to the committees, the Government is prepared, in certain circumstances, to make a grant towards the salary of such an official available to each voluntary liaison committee through the National Committee. . . . We hope that the local authority concerned will provide adequate office accommodation and secretarial support for the official appointed.[1]

As has been shown, the establishment of the National Committee for Commonwealth Immigrants in 1965 had led to the multiplication of voluntary liaison committees, and the White Paper enabled them to appoint full-time liaison officers. The National Committee defined the duties of a liaison officer in the following terms:

1. To promote and assist in programmes of public education for positive and harmonious relationships within the community.
2. To be the focal point for inquiries of any kind from the host com-

[1] Great Britain, the Prime Minister, *Immigration from the Commonwealth* (Cmnd. 2739) (London, H.M.S.O., 1965), para. 75.

munity in connexion with problems or relationships in general with immigrants.

3. To work in full co-operation with Central and Local Government Departments.

4. To participate in the activities of immigrant organizations and give help where required.

5. To assist the immigrant to use existing social services and facilities, and where necessary to form a link between the two.

6. To be available to social workers, officials of all kinds, etc., as an adviser on special aspects of immigrant problems.

7. To participate in the widest possible range of social activities designed to draw immigrants and host community together.

8. To take advantage of opportunities (e.g. at national conferences) to meet liaison officers and workers from other areas. . . .

9. To take appropriate action against discrimination wherever it occurs.

10. To act as secretary to the Committee.

11. To be responsible for the organization of the Committee's office.

It is clear from the above that the job of liaison officer is an exacting one, calling for energy and initiative and the willingness to give far more than the usual working hours. It is essential that the officer should regularly attend a wide variety of evening and week-end meetings and social activities, and become a familiar figure in the city, in whom both immigrants and host community can have confidence when difficulties arise. This is a job which cannot be done in the confines of an office or of regular office hours.[1]

As this description of the work of liaison officers shows, the post involved a very large range of responsibilities, and the widest terms of reference. In order to observe the liaison officer in action and evaluate how far he was able to carry out these duties, the Institute of Race Relations carried out a survey of a group of liaison officers, and the results are analysed in this chapter.

The material for the survey was obtained by means of interviews conducted by Martin Davis in 1968. Ten liaison officers and three non-Government officers working in race relations were interviewed. All came from a single conurbation, but the sample was selected to illustrate a variety of experiences, resources, and methods, and to provide a composite impression of the nature of liaison work at the time. The questionnaire was open-ended, and liaison officers were encouraged to speak freely on a variety of

[1] Given in Sheila Patterson, *Immigration and Race Relations in Britain, 1960–1967* (London, Oxford University Press, for Institute of Race Relations, 1969), p. 433.

subjects including their previous experience and qualifications for the job; their relationships with their committees, with the local authority, with the National Committee, and with the police; their contact with immigrant organizations; their plans and projects; and their assessment of how far they had succeeded in carrying out their aims. In order to quote their views freely, we have concealed the liaison officers' identities. Although the situation has changed since 1968 (the N.C.C.I. has been replaced by a statutory body, the Community Relations Commission; the officers are now called Community Relations Officers; and experience has led to some redefinition of their role), we believe that the evidence drawn from this survey is of more than historical interest. It illustrates continuing problems in committee structure, in relationships with national and local authorities, and in community relations work as such.

Two of the ten committees in the sample were founded in the 1950s; the remainder had been established after the formation of the N.C.C.I. in 1965. Only two officers had had predecessors in the post, and so in general, both committees and liaison officers were working out their terms of reference in a new field. Five of the liaison officers in the sample were white, four were Black West Indians, and one was Indian. Seven were university graduates, and four had professional qualifications or degrees in social administration or social work, and could, therefore, be described as qualified social workers. Four had worked in central or local government, three had industrial or business experience (either in management or on the factory floor), two had been clergymen, and the majority (seven) had experience of welfare and community work, though sometimes this was experience of a very general kind. All officers agreed it was essential to have a sound knowledge of the area in which they worked, but only two thought it essential to live in the borough so as to be available round the clock.

Officers generally thought their practical experience was their best qualification for the work—'my most helpful past experience has been local government, where I got to know various departments and people and found out who dealt with what'; 'I knew how political parties worked and was not frightened of them'; 'my business background is my strongest asset'—but some of the trained social workers deprecated the over-all lack of professional training among liaison officers. One commented that for the untrained officer, liaison work was 'a matter of trial and error'; another was 'all for professionalism. . . . The best thing in this job is to build up a body of mixed fieldworkers through training programmes and make sure . . . they won't be put to waste.' Two of the Black officers had chosen liaison work because of the pressures of racial discrimination: 'When I graduated I got the shock of my life . . . what was in the P.E.P. report was being applied to me.' The other said he had always been concerned with race relations and was 'virtually propelled into it by Powell's "rivers of blood" speech'. One or two had drifted into the work—'I did not choose the work, it just grew on me'—attracted by its flexibility: 'in the beginning I would be left to my own initiative when there was not a lot of red tape'. The most positive statement of commitment came from an officer with extensive experience as a welfare officer in the West Indies and the United Kingdom: 'This is my job: I'm a square peg in a square hole.'

Colour obviously played an important part in the selection of liaison officers, and it also had a significant effect on the individual officer's estimation of his fitness for the work. One of the Black officers knew he had been appointed because he was a West Indian 'with an awareness of Black social life and society' in the borough; three others agreed it was easier to do the job if one was Black. This view was shared by four of the white officers (one of whom had been told by his committee that they would have preferred to appoint a coloured man if a suitable candidate had been available) and was elaborated by one of them as follows:

There are some aspects of the job which could be done better by a Black man, such as gaining access to the immigrants, but then I'm not sure—coloureds as liaison officers can become white, can lose their roots. . . . I'm very conscious of the question. I would get on better with the Town Council if I were Black. Three of the new Tories, nasty right-wingers, gave me a . . . grilling. They had wanted to see exactly what we were doing here. If I had had a black face they would have been more deferential to me. It helps if one's secretary is coloured. Mine is. I've got out of her facts about the Black world, such as the West Indian housing grapevine.

Two other white officers stressed their reliance on a Black secretary or assistant, and conversely, one Black officer would have appointed a white assistant. Only two white officers did not believe that aspects of their work could be done better by a coloured man: one mentioned training and personality as more important, the other thought his working-class background a greater asset than a black skin.

(b) OFFICIAL RELATIONSHIPS

The officers had been appointed by local liaison committees, whose executive retained control over all policy decisions. Nine officers were recognized by the N.C.C.I., which paid their salaries (£1,500–£1,620 per annum) and in two cases had made an additional grant of £300–£500. All officers received a grant from the local borough council, ranging from £1,000 to £2,500 per year; in only one case, where the borough council was exceptionally progressive, did the local authority grant exceed £5,000. The local authority also provided free accommodation in six cases (other officers rented offices from charitable bodies on favourable terms), and in four cases provided telephone, stationery, and postage. Officers were, therefore, operating on extremely low budgets, the average being £3,000 per annum to cover salaries, publicity, projects, and, perhaps, overheads. Their income came from at least two sources (the N.C.C.I. and the local authority), but additionally, an officer was technically responsible to the voluntary liaison committee which had appointed him. This tripartite obligation has been widely criticized; it has been argued that financial obligation to the N.C.C.I. identifies the officer with the central Government, while the hold of the local authority (which has a voice on the committee as well as a financial whip hand) prevents the officer's opposing local government, and this, together with the executive control of the committee (a lay body of varying quality), can destroy the officer's initiative. The officers were, therefore, asked to comment on their relationships with their committees, with the local authority, and with the N.C.C.I. to illustrate how the system was operating.

Most liaison committees were set up with the co-operation of the local authority, and the committees in the survey group invariably included either borough councillors or local officials. In one extreme case, six members of the committee were representatives of the local authority, and one of these had always to be chairman. Committees had an average of twenty members. A typical committee included teachers, doctors, clergymen, and representatives of immigrant organizations. Few officers felt that their committees were representative of the community; one officer commented that although his committee was 'highly political', 'it does not represent the power structure of the local community— no leaders of trade unions, industry, or welfare'. In general, the committees lacked representatives from business, industry, and the trade unions. Only two officers felt they had a representative committee: one had expanded 'a cliquish body of the left' into a 'fully representative body', containing delegates from up to eighty organizations; the other felt his executive committee was representative—'the middle class and grass roots of the community are there'—but would have liked to include a spokesman for anti-immigrant views, and people from the business world.

The main concern of the liaison officers was inadequate representation of immigrants. A typical comment was:

most of them [i.e. the committee members] who are Black are educated and/or comfortable, and, therefore, are not really representative. We should make contact with the unclubbable immigrants who are not in touch with organizations on our committee and who could benefit greatly by them.

This officer had made increased immigrant representation a priority, and now had twenty coloured committee members; one alderman had asked him 'if this is the start of a Black Power take-over'! Other officers had been less effective in recruiting immigrant support: one blamed apathy, another the fact that too many members were 'paper representatives of paper organizations'. We shall return to the officers' relationship with the immigrant community at other points, while noting here that the majority felt there was inadequate Black representation on their committees, and several expressed resentment against the weight of local authority representation.

In addition to the executive committee, all committees had formed from three to nine sub-committees, involving a wider section of their membership. These sub-committees met at irregular intervals, depending on the nature of the projects involved. Subjects covered included employment, housing, education, publicity, social and cultural functions, research, community action, youth, conciliation, and the police. One officer had asked his members to state the committee they would prefer to join, and found that over 50 per cent chose education and housing. In one case, the committee system was encouraged, and the officer was anxious to set up more informal sub-committees; others found too much time was spent on repetitive discussion ('I'm sick to death of sitting in people's sitting-rooms'). One very useful committee dealt with 'children in trouble', and attempted to act as an early warning system for spotting juvenile delinquents; in another borough, a sub-committee dealt with complaints against the police.

The working relationship between a liaison officer and his committee had an important effect on his work. An enthusiastic committee could provide practical and moral support. One officer said: 'I have masses of self-doubt, but my committee never seem to doubt me!' Another described himself as 'a U Thant to my committee', both initiating projects and carrying them out with the committee's support:

I am able to give the executive and sub-committees all information necessary from ground level, and suggest action to be taken in the field. I know what people's reaction will be in a particular situation. I get sanction from the executive to be both executant and initiator. . . . I'm given a wide hand. . . . If I was to do anything which was to affect the policy of the council, I would first consult a member of the necessary administrative body. The treasurers, chairman, and myself carry out executive functions. . . . My committee keep a lot in touch with community relations. . . . They stick their necks in to say hello and see that I'm O.K. Some other [officers] . . . are just placators and appeasement personnel for institutions and Establishment, because of their committees. But my committee is ready, willing, and able to co-operate with me.

Five of the officers interviewed found their committees enthusiastic and co-operative, one had not been appointed long enough to make an assessment, and four were more or less critical. Three of these found their committees lacked specialist knowledge; two had experienced friction because their committees did not share their priorities ('Those most influential on the committee thought I should concentrate on educating the host community, but I thought we should spend most of the time working with immigrant communities if we weren't to become an amiable irrelevance'); three felt they were hampered by Town Hall pressure exercised through their committee members; and three complained of apathy—'they're not a working committee: they're divided into mandarins who work very hard and clergyman types who don't initiate a bloody thing'—and indifference. Difficulties of this kind were perhaps inevitable when committees were composed of well-intentioned laymen, less experienced than their officers (two officers described their relationship as 'teacher-pupil'), working in a fluid situation. As one officer explained: 'My committee have not thought out the implications of my job, because its evolution was via very few guide-lines. I put forward projects and hope they will accept them.'

All the officers found that their financial dependence on the local authority led to embarrassment or ambiguity. As one officer put it: 'It leads immigrants and the host community to misunderstand our position; the Town Hall thinks of us as one of their own departments, and when we attack them the Council are shocked.' All but one officer preferred their offices to be physically separated from the Town Hall for psychological or practical reasons: 'we don't want to be identified with local authority in the eyes of the immigrants'; 'the Town Hall image is dull and dowdy, reducing immigrants to welfare cases'. Additionally, confinement to Town Hall hours would destroy the informality people had about coming and going.

The level of local authority support for liaison work in any area reflects the borough council's commitment to community relations, and some officers were very aware that it was a low priority. Two officers related this to the fact that they were working in 'twilight areas': the declining character of the neighbourhood produced a defeatist attitude in local government, and the officers could not envisage a change of heart without a programme of urban renewal. At the other end of the scale, a progressive borough could facilitate a wide range of projects. Only one committee had been unable to spend its local authority grant for lack of projects; four officers regarded the local authority contribution as inadequate, and two of them had made unsuccessful applications for additional funds. Two other officers were anxious that rather than increase grants to the committee the local authority develop its own services in, for example, the provision of facilities for young people through the youth employment service or some programme aimed at 'keeping kids off the streets'.

13

If local authorities were providing inadequate backing, could the officers turn to the N.C.C.I. for guidance? The overwhelming consensus among the liaison officers was that the N.C.C.I. was failing to provide them with any help apart from financial support. There were criticisms of lack of direction, lack of communication, and lack of helpful publications other than the P.E.P. report and pamphlets on cultural origins. Most officers related their criticism of the N.C.C.I. to that body's close association with the Government and 'the Establishment': the National Committee was not free to criticize Government policy, and had not spoken out enough against Enoch Powell. Six of the officers had been signatories of the Wilfred Wood proposals presented during the Committee stage of the Race Relations Bill of 1968; these proposals called for democratic elections to broaden the base of the N.C.C.I. and strengthen Black representation, but they were not taken up. The officers felt that the Community Relations Commission (which succeeded the N.C.C.I. in November 1968) would suffer from the same faults and would merely be the same body with a new title. There was only one officer who did not join the prevailing criticism of the N.C.C.I., and was anxious to strengthen it; in his view, the N.C.C.I. had 'failed to link techniques with local level committees', but no voluntary liaison committee could succeed without official support: 'we want to be establishment, we want help from establishment bodies. The Wood proposals were irrelevant. Strong contacts are needed between the N.C.C.I. and Ministries like Housing. . . . ' There was one other critic of the Wood proposals: this officer was conscious of the practical difficulties in obtaining 'representatives of grass-roots organizations'. However, it is clear from the survey that there was a very low level of communication between the liaison officers and the N.C.C.I., and this weakened the contribution of both the national body and the local committees.

The liaison officers had established a better relationship with the police than with any other public body. A number of factors contributed to this: one is the public attention focused on police attitudes to immigrants; another is the positive effort to improve the situation by the police themselves, who in many cases have joined liaison committees; a third contributing factor is the fact that complaints against the police are relatively easy to define, and the police have an established hierarchy, which facilitates access. However, the liaison officers echoed the widespread criticism of the system by which the police judge complaints against their own officers; as one liaison officer put it: '[The police] should not investigate their own complaints. There should be approved lay bodies to do so. This would reduce the suspicion of the Black community. . . . People's suspicion decreases when they know they have access.'

Most officers appeared to have an excellent personal relationship with the police, describing them as 'very, very co-operative', 'most cordial'; and seven had access to the police through a Chief Superintendent, Chief Inspector, or 'general access'. Two committees had police liaison officers as observers or advisers, and one of these police officers sat on a committee panel with a solicitor and a West Indian to review complaints against the police. In one case, however, the presence of a police super-intendent on a committee had proved an embarrassment: 'we couldn't talk about the police; rather than make a formal complaint, we would give cases to him. Although he was a well-meaning man and took trouble, he . . . could not enforce discipline among his men.' The Superintendent was eventually removed from the committee and formal complaints are now made through the regular channels. Two officers felt that the police 'needed educating', but only one had experienced positive hostility: 'the police officials treat us with disgust—a nasty atmosphere'. One officer had 'lectured to police groups and talked to them and reactions have been frightening—you can see the hatred on the coppers' faces'. However, it was clear that the police were in most cases making a conscious effort to establish good relations with the liaison officers and committees. One Chief Inspector had welcomed a liaison officer at his interview by saying: 'We'd better get to know one another personally, because in future we'll be on opposite sides of the barricade'; but their relationship has proved consistently friendly.

The question remains whether the accessibility of Chief Superintendents and Chief Inspectors is a formal gesture, cloaking discrimination 'on the beat' and indifference to complaints. There were indications that in some cases this might be true, and whether complaints against the police were treated seriously seemed to depend entirely on the policy of individual superintendents. (One liaison officer drew a clear distinction between different police stations in his borough.) The number of complaints brought by liaison officers against the police was generally small, and the numbers obtaining redress were smaller still. Examples from different areas were: two cases brought, one admission by the police that they were in the wrong; one case referred by the police to the Department of Public Prosecutions; no complaints in six months; redress secured through a solicitor for three out of twelve complaints. A reason for the small number of complaints may be that because of the link between liaison officers and the police— often formalized through police affiliation to a voluntary liaison committee—victims of police discrimination may not approach the liaison officer. Several officers considered this a real possibility. One said he had had no complaints against the police: 'either police-public relations are very good, or we're completely out of touch'. In another area, the local branch of the Campaign Against Racial Discrimination claimed to have received regular complaints of police brutality, but the liaison officer felt this claim had been fabricated to gain political capital.

Because the police conduct internal inquiries into complaints, officers could not be certain whether their complaints were being glossed over; but one was convinced he was being ignored. Other officers had obtained an answer—if not a positive assurance—in every case they had referred to the police. Two officers had noticed a definite improvement in their relationships with the police since establishing a 'police panel' and a police sub-committee, respectively, and on the whole, liaison officers were optimistic about their working relationship with the police.

(c) THE LIAISON OFFICERS' INTERPRETATION OF THEIR ROLE

Official and quasi-official definitions of the work of liaison officers have been notoriously wide. In 1968, their role was open to a number of interpretations. Government policy (as expressed in the 1965 White Paper) had been that immigrants should not be provided with special services, but should be directed towards the social services available to the population at large. Were the liaison officers acting as channels to welfare departments on these terms? Secondly, were the liaison officers meant to educate the Black community for acceptance of the Blacks, or educate the Black community for integration with the whites; and which community were they meant to represent? Thirdly, how active should they be in resisting discrimination? Should they play any part in political lobbying on a national level, and did they see themselves as initiators of community developments? In order to obtain the liaison officers' point of view on these subjects, they were asked how far these roles applied to them, and where their priorities lay.

Most officers denied that they were welfare officers: their task was to refer inquiries to the appropriate department at the Town Hall or to the Citizens' Advice Bureau, and to advise immigrants to make use of existing facilities. One liaison officer was supplying welfare services not provided by the borough— i.e. an evening advisory council on legal matters and a birth control service for coloured girls. But only one officer described himself as 'generally a welfare officer—I cannot get out of it. If one refuses to supply services that are not catered for, one ignores the principle of community relations'; he co-operated on case-work with the local probation service in a 'two-way traffic'. On the other hand, seven officers considered the initiation of community development to be of prime importance. They started projects to create new social amenities and bring people into contact with each other, particularly in such activities as pre-school play-groups, youth clubs, social and cultural gatherings (these activities will be discussed later). Only one officer opposed the idea of liaison committee involvement in community development 'as a self-conscious thing to bring races together'; all the others were anxious to start such projects and obtain support from the local authority or independent bodies to do so.

The liaison officer's role as a representative and educator has been described as a choice 'between interpreting the demands for equal opportunities of the minority to the dominant white society, and, on the other hand, acting as spokesman of that society to the minority group'.[1] All the officers in the survey denigrated the concept of representing the local white population to the local Black population, though one white officer felt he attended immigrant functions in this capacity. Four white officers felt they were prevented by their colour from acting as representatives of the Black population, and one encouraged the Black members of

---

[1] Dipak Nandy, quoted in E. J. B. Rose and associates, *Colour and Citizenship: A Report on British Race Relations* (London, Oxford University Press, for Institute of Race Relations, 1969), p. 387.

his committee to speak for themselves on every possible occasion. But another white officer felt he was acting as a representative of immigrants by explaining their difficulties to white employers with 'Black problems'. One Black officer said he was playing this role '80 per cent of the time', particularly in relations with the police; but another refused to act as a representative if this meant accepting invitations from organizations which wanted to use him 'as a substitute for Black people who aren't invited . . . people will be contented enough with one Black man and won't be looking at the people they have to live with, the people they've got to understand'.

Education of the public was given priority by most respondents, but there was a sharp distinction between those who viewed their task as educating the host community and those who thought they should be educating the immigrants. This distinction was based on colour: four Black officers thought they should act as educators of the host community (though one objected to the word 'host' since it smacked of inequality by implying that other people were guests); but three white officers thought this a more or less futile undertaking, and one thought the best education was to ignore colour altogether. Those officers attempting to educate the host community did so in the belief that it was the best method of achieving co-operation. As one put it: 'Toleration presupposes compatibility; but we've not got tolerance, so we must create it by education.' The methods used included lectures to local government departments, employers, churches, and youth groups—one officer called this work 'spectre-raising'—and face-to-face discussions. Those criticizing an approach geared to the host population did so either on the grounds that it was irrelevant or ineffective—'if the hosts are prejudiced, they're prejudiced'—or on strategic grounds: 'unless we are deeply rooted in immigrant concerns we will be driven out of business by people in Black Power'.

Most officers, black and white, felt that one of their major roles was educating immigrants; but they were clearly construing education in varying terms. 'Educating the host community' appeared to mean persuading whites that Blacks could be good neighbours or employees; 'educating the Blacks' meant helping them to use social services (thus overlapping with the officers' functions in respect of welfare), encouraging self-help, or diverting immigrants from behaviour which the white community might regard as antisocial. Only one (Black) officer felt there was no need to educate the immigrant community: 'West Indians are not much different from the host community. Common sense makes them realize that they have got to behave in certain cases in certain ways, to live in the community.' This interpretation of education was very different from that of another Black officer with a large West Indian population in his borough: he felt he must educate this community 'towards self-development and self-help' by trying to persuade them to present a united front, to avoid late-night parties ('a sore point for the community'), and by teaching them 'that there is a social service to be used. Their standards of expectation may have been raised, but some of them had sub-human ones.'

Four officers stressed that they were fighters against discrimination and one considered this the most important role of all. However, as the analysis of their activities will show, they were divided in the precedence which they gave to this role, and the means they used to carry it out. There was no evenly distributed commitment to casework in discrimination and referral to the Race Relations Board; but in their role as public educators all officers were concerned with discrimination in its widest sense, and three officers were committed to political activities in a national framework to reduce discrimination.

The concept of 'liaison work' is extremely wide, and being relative newcomers to a new field, officers had not fully defined their roles. One confessed that he had never done so: 'it's one of my principal weaknesses, I try to do everything'. And another officer thanked the interviewer for giving him the opportunity to crystallize his thoughts on this subject. The interviews showed that while there is broad agreement on some aspects of liaison work, there is a lack of precision in the choice of priorities.

All the liaison officers were anxious to strengthen their links with the Black community through increasing representation on their committees and making contact with organizations and individuals. The majority said that their work was governed by the needs of the immigrant communities rather than the host community: after all, as one officer put it, 'without the immigrants there is no need for a Community Relations Officer in the role in which I'm placed'. One officer felt that the role of both

liaison officer and committee was to 'exercise positive discrimination in favour of the immigrant community', and he had had to
persuade his committee that they should not concentrate on
educating the host community: 'We have to spend most of the
time working with immigrant communities if we are not to
become an amiable irrelevance.' Three of the Black officers
claimed to pay equal attention to the needs of the white community, but felt that their links with the Black community were
the basis of their appointment.

Officers were very concerned with making contact with
accessible political or social groups in order to establish links
with the Black community at large. All but one officer considered
the immigrants in their boroughs badly or even 'hopelessly'
organized; the exception was a borough with a large Indian
population, and it was generally accepted that even when they
were the smallest minority, Indians were relatively well organized. Officers had two preoccupations: one was the low level of
political organization among West Indians (there were references
to 'fragmented loyalty', 'fratricidal groups', 'just social clubs', and
the difficulty of finding permanent representatives: 'the man who
is represented today will get axed tomorrow with the internal
change-arounds'). The other preoccupation was the difficulty
in reaching the rank and file. Several officers expressed the view
that the present Black membership on their committees was
unrepresentative because it was entirely middle class, and there
was no spokesman for 'the invisibles'.

Two of the Black liaison officers played a prominent part in
promoting political groups, one through his informal patronage
of local associations (he helped them to find premises, tried to
steer clear of personal rivalries, and thus, found himself being 'a
person who bridges gaps and brings new thoughts for action
within the groups'), and the other in his separate capacity as
leader of a West Indian organization. It was in this role that the
officer found himself 'trying to remove frustrations from persons
who aren't as in touch with the host community as I am, bringing
sentiments to a focal point', though he made this interesting
admission: 'I draw a distinction in my mode of speaking from my
liaison officer style—then [i.e. when addressing a West Indian
audience] I am speaking as a Black man; they mustn't expect me
to say anything white.' The white liaison officers could not hope

for involvement of this depth; the only officer quantifying his contacts with Black organizations estimated that he was in touch with seven out of the seventeen organizations in his borough.

Six officers mentioned militant Black organizations, and two thought that the Black population had greater confidence in the Campaign Against Racial Discrimination and Black Power than in the N.C.C.I. But interestingly enough, both thought the balance would shift in favour of the N.C.C.I./C.R.C. in the future: one, because people would be forced to recognize the value of the N.C.C.I. 'as pressures on the Black man increase'; the other, because the N.C.C.I. represented the Establishment 'in a white country which is not used to listening to protest in emotional terms'. All six officers had had some contact with extremist groups. In one case, a representative of a local group, described by the officer as 'a Maoist Black Power organization', had sat on the committee's employment sub-committee; another liaison officer had held a series of talks with 'Black Power people'. But neither of these contacts had been of long duration. Two officers thought the local militant groups were ineffective, and only one had a constructive relationship:

I've won a breathing space from the more dissident members of the immigrant community—people who would have looked at me as an Uncle Tom, organizations like Black Power and the more articulate immigrant movements. They are prepared to give us a chance. Our views might not agree, but we have a common cause and objective with them. B. [a prominent Black Power leader] has been of help through his associations—people who know him have come to be in touch with us.

The general impression of these interviews with liaison officers is that officers were making relatively slow progress in involving the Black community in their work. This was particularly true of the white officers, but it was a stumbling-block for Black officers as well.

(d) THE WORK OF LIAISON OFFICERS

The work of a liaison officer—as defined by the liaison officers themselves—has been shown to comprise casework, public education, and community development. The officers in the sample were asked to describe their activities in welfare, discrimination,

13*

publicity, and contact with employers, the local authority, and the police; the results of the survey show the liaison officer in action.

Only a small proportion of the officers (three out of ten) kept standard records of cases. Welfare cases were referred to the relevant department of the local authority. All officers tried to establish working relationships with local government officials, and, on the whole, found them helpful. The exception here were housing officers, who had generally proved intransigent. One housing officer had said: 'We don't tell you we don't discriminate, as if it were a principle!' One liaison officer found it difficult to work with local officials: 'They feel you're attacking them; . . . therefore, they get defensive.' Examples of good co-operation were an Education Officer's providing material for a liaison officer's report on local education policy; a continuous association with a Children's Department where a very high proportion of children in care were immigrants; casework in co-operation with the local Probation Service; and general assistance from the Town Clerk (singled out by four liaison officers as the most helpful local official). On the other hand, no pattern of regular consultation with heads of local government departments emerged; some officers relied on the local authority representatives on their committees to provide a link with the Town Hall, but for most, the local authority was merely a destination for welfare cases.

The liaison officers' action when cases of discrimination were brought to their notice was determined by the legislation then in force. The powers of the Race Relations Board under the 1965 and 1968 Race Relations Acts have been described in Chapter 9 of the present study. The survey of liaison officers was conducted shortly before the 1968 Act came into force, during the period when the Board's powers were limited to investigations of alleged discrimination in public places. The 1968 Act extended the Board's powers to the key fields of housing and employment, and introduced greater sanctions against discriminators. But although the Board's powers were limited at the time of the interviews, the legislation for extending its scope had already been passed by Parliament. How far liaison officers were recording cases of alleged discrimination and referring them to the Board is a matter of considerable importance, because the first Race Relations Act had not given the Race Relations Board the power to initiate inquiries, and the Board depended on liaison officers as one channel for receiving complaints.

Some of the liaison officers in the sample received a strikingly small number of complaints. One officer mentioned a figure of twenty in two years, another 'six at most', a third 'seven or eight'. These low figures were ascribed to the reluctance of complainants to come forward and the liaison officer's lack of contact with the Black community: 'It's partly because people don't know that I'm there and partly because they are not anxious to talk about their experience'; 'some people just let themselves be pushed around'. However, only three officers kept standard records of cases, and only two of these referred cases to the Race Relations Board with any regularity. One of these officers had acted as a testing agency for the Board, and issued a standard complaint form; he passed on approximately 60 complaints a year. The other officer referred between 30 and 40 cases to the Board, but the third officer keeping records 'very seldom refers cases to the local Race Relations Board—we are not in touch'. The low level of referral did not arise from lack of confidence in the Board, since officers referred to the Board and its members with approval in other contexts; the main reason seems to have been that officers did not regard themselves as being committed to casework or to keeping in touch with the Board.

What other methods did the officers use in cases of discrimination? One method was direct action by the liaison officer in individual cases, either through conciliation or the application of pressure from another source. One officer seemed over-anxious to conciliate, believing that 'there is no point in referring cases to the Race Relations Board if one can't do anything oneself', and confessed that he had 'smoothed over' at least one dispute at the Pakistani complainant's cost. Some officers had had successful negotiations with employers and secured jobs for victims of discrimination: in one case, the officer had received support from the Ministry of Labour against an employer who openly discriminated; one had an 'excellent' contact at the local Labour Exchange, and claimed to have found a job for everyone who had come to him for help; and another had used 'situation testing' (i.e. sending a white applicant for a job when an Indian had been told there was 'no vacancy') to persuade an employer to change his policy. Officers had had little success in dealing with cases of discrimination in housing, partly because of the attitude of the local housing authorities, and two found that housing problems most commonly involved Black landlords and tenants.

Only two officers were aware of discrimination in pubs in their boroughs. One of these had approached the local M.P. 'as a last resort', but the other had obtained a considerable improvement through prompt action: 'When I heard that no Blacks were allowed in a certain saloon bar, I planted the Labour leader of the Council and myself as witnesses. The brewer put pressure on the landlord concerned and he was forced to stop.'

A second method was holding discussions with employers on the general issue of employing coloured labour, and four officers had been to see local employers for this purpose. One of them had convened a conference of employers and trade unions on the subject, but found the employers split into two groups: 'those who were already converted and those who stood firm against new ideas, just confirming our feelings of their attitudes'. No other officer had made any approaches to trade unions, and none had approached building society managers or housing trusts. It was more common for officers to undertake public speaking and lectures with local bodies, i.e. schools, churches, rotary clubs, the local Chamber of Commerce, and the like. Some officers were sceptical of the value of such talks, but one described them as 'spectre-raising', serving a useful if limited purpose, and two were anxious to establish training seminars and group consultation on local problems.

Small attendances were reported at meetings addressed by visiting lecturers: 'there is nothing more ghastly than listening to experts talking', said one officer; and informal private or group discussions were preferred at all levels.

The value of good publicity was appreciated by all the officers: it could be used for attracting a wider membership and publicizing their work. One officer had taken on a part-time public relations officer and regarded his 'propagandist' functions as very important. He had good personal contacts with Press and television reporters, and issued regular press releases, as did two other officers. But four other officers were suspicious of the Press—because stories would be sensationalized, because they felt the local Press was hostile, and because frequent press releases might inhibit free discussion: 'people just look at you as a publicity stunt man . . . When you start coming up in the Press, people hesitate to discuss things with you.' One officer had resisted his committee's suggestion to publicize a case of discrimination in employment, on the grounds that this would increase his difficulties in approaching employers. Relations with the Press depended on the officer's personal contacts: if funds became available, two officers said they would employ a press officer. All the committees issued news-letters, generally once a month. The mailing list usually consisted of institutions or middle-class groups —i.e. schools, churches, welfare departments, doctors—and the total circulation ranged from three to six hundred. Four newsletters were changing their style to suit a wider readership: one officer described the existing news-letter as 'fairly intellectual, the working class wouldn't understand it'; it had been sent to 'six hundred carefully selected whites plus heads of welfare in the area'; the new version would 'have a style of its own', and would be orientated towards the Black population. Other methods of communication included scattered leaflets, hand-to-hand invitations and posters for social events, which generally have obtained a very good response: one officer had obtained an audience of 800 people for an international concert, and was almost overwhelmed by the immigrant response to social invitations. The most ambitious publicity exercise undertaken by any officer in the survey was a sophisticated campaign against racial discrimination including exhibitions, concerts, leaflets, and car-stickers. Other officers would have liked to undertake further publicity campaigns, given the expertise and the necessary funds, since publicity would help in attracting the local Black population; however, two officers were reluctant to receive a flood of inquiries whilst they lacked the staff to deal with them, and two felt that the best publicity would be an attractive office on a main road—their existing dingy accommodation could never attract people to their door.

The range of projects undertaken by the officers either through their committees or in co-operation with other organizations, varied greatly because of the disparity in their available resources. The most comprehensive range of projects undertaken by any committee in the sample included:

Community Housing Association building a block of flats incorporating purpose-designed pre-school play-group; leasing of four large houses and converting them into family units, decorated and furnished by volunteers; home tutor service; language classes; summer camps; youth workshop; music, art and drama course; school leavers' survey including analysis of working of youth employment service; 'discovering London' project; child-minding service.

Other officers, with fewer resources, had a more circumscribed range of activities. Three ran pre-school play-groups, three concentrated on youth activities (including youth clubs, summer camps, facilities for games and socials); one had established a subcommittee on 'children in trouble' which was conceived of as an early warning system for juvenile delinquents; and two were involved in conferences or research projects dealing with coloured school-leavers. Other activities included language classes, mothers' clubs, a 'housing surgery', and a Credit Union for developing group saving.

It is difficult to generalize about the activities of the committees because of the divergence in the projects undertaken and the resources available, but increased local and centralized efforts are necessary if those officers at present engaged in only one or two activities are to achieve the range of activities carried out by the most successful committees. The position at the time the interviews were carried out does show the officers' preoccupation with children and young people, and their concentration on the second generation was further evidenced by their plans for future activities if they had additional funds.

Officers were asked how they would spend an additional £5,000 (for most, this would double their present resources). Their choices were: (i) engaging and training a full-time youth employment officer; (ii) employing a woman assistant with special responsibility for Asian women, and extending playgroups; (iii) pre-school play-groups and an interracial coffee bar; (iv) engaging a public relations officer, a female social worker, and another secretary; (v) employing two other staff to deal with office administration and founding a housing association; (vi) extending existing play-groups, starting an international centre for immigrants, and forming a housing association; (vii) equipping a recreational centre and taking on an assistant for youth work; (viii) creating an international youth centre, engaging part-time youth workers, and founding a housing surgery; (ix) starting a pre-school play-group and developing activities for youth; (x) taking on extra staff.

These responses show that the officers were most conscious of the need for additional trained staff, for more social facilities—especially for young people—and for pre-school play-groups. The need for staff arose partly from the lack of trained personnel in social work, partly from the fact that most officers were over-worked and needed secretarial assistance to free them for out-of-doors work.

In the final section of the questionnaire, liaison officers were asked how well they believed they had succeeded in achieving their objectives within their chosen spheres of activity. Their answers are given individually below, in order to illustrate the officer's own views. The officer's colour and number of years as a liaison officer have been included for the sake of comparison.

A. (Black, one year): I have not failed at all in making progress, in making people learn more about the immigrant population, in increasing the awareness of employers who, unlike the teachers here, had not dedicated themselves to the tasks of a multi-racial society. . . . Things can be solved if there is a willingness among persons.
B. (White, two years): I've not succeeded well at all, partly because I've never had my aims clear-cut. I'm never able to sit back and plan the next move—I deal with too many things by rule of thumb. . . . There is an inherent contradiction in this kind of work—one is trying to work oneself out of a job.
C. (Black, two years): I haven't yet made the impact on the immigrant community that I hoped to have made by now—I would like to open the doors to them. . . . My effectiveness relates to the feeling of the Black community at the time. I'm unable to make contact with the young second generation. This is where the trouble lies—no communication beyond going up to people in the streets. . . .
D. (White, one year): I have succeeded in getting into the Establishment, but we have a lack of experts. . . . I want to get people to think and advise on techniques. . . . I dream of becoming a professional stimulator.
E. (White, one year): I've tried to do too many things at once. The only possibility of ultimate success is the establishment of a strong relationship with the coloured people of the borough. . . . My initial ideas of the impossibility of the liaison officer's role have been confirmed—I can only hope to cushion the blow for a few individuals.
F. (Black, one year): I have failed in employment and in getting a unified team out of my committee. . . . I have had success in public education, in subtly changing the senior police and Town Hall officers. I have built up an effective bridge-head so that people are coming to

me. . . . People know me by name and it is more important to build
up a reputation as an effective spokesman for the immigrants against
the Establishment.

G. (Black, one year): There have been failures—this is communica-
tion. . . . One has to get through people's preconceived ideas. . . . When
I approach whites I must offer myself as a hostage, with Black groups
I must offer myself the same way. . . .

H. (White, three years): I have fitted into this job better than any
other I've ever done. It has been a great success; we have 730 members
and do more than any other committee. . . . In spite of that, we are
still ineffective and will continue to be so until the Government treats
us seriously. . . . This is a most disillusioning job, and yet I enjoy
doing it.

I. (Black, under one year): I can't say yet. . . . I'm still in the process
of building up local relationships.

J. (White, twelve years): I have failed in all aspects of my job . . .
though individual people have had individual problems solved . . . the
situation is intractable—nothing we do locally will be of any use with
Powell blaring forth.

These comments make depressing reading. Only two of the
officers were optimistic about their achievements, and the prevailing mood was one of qualified pessimism. Their conditions of
work were extremely difficult: pay was low, hours were long (it
was not unusual for officers to work thirteen hours a day), and
secretarial help was inadequate. The interviewer described all but
two of the offices he visited as 'buried in the labyrinth of the Town
Hall or tucked away in a side street', presenting an unpromising
exterior which could not attract the public. It may be that the
eleven-point description of the liaison officer's duties set out at the
beginning of this section, postulates a range of activities beyond the
capacity of any individual officer—unless he is unusually well-
trained, strongly supported with ancillary staff and a team of
expert advisers, and able to build up sufficient confidence among
immigrants to confront the Establishment and compel its co-
operation. Under the conditions existing in 1968, liaison officers
were being asked to do the impossible.

(e) NON-GOVERNMENTAL OFFICERS: A BRIEF COMPARISON
To establish whether the difficulties experienced by liaison officers
were common to all fieldworkers in race relations, interviews
were carried out with the race relations officers of three religious

bodies. The first was a West Indian social worker appointed to run a neighbourhood centre for community relations financed by a religious body. He regarded himself as a social caseworker, dealing primarily with youth and education; one of his four assistants was a qualified social worker concentrating on projects for children, which included a play-group and an adventure playground. This officer had a detailed knowledge of the Black population of his borough, and had investigated housing conditions and schools. He ran a legal advice centre, and mediated in landlord-tenant disputes. He was confident that he was in closer touch with immigrants than the secretary of the local liaison committee, who was operating from the Town Hall in the capacity of Immigrant Welfare Officer, under the aegis of a basically conservative borough council.

The second officer in this group was a minister of religion and adviser on race relations to a large religious body. He was principally concerned with submitting ideas to his committee—'we are in solid agreement on everything'—and identifying areas for community development where his Church could make a contribution; he was anxious to 'get away from the image of my faith as a ghetto Church, just looking at our own people. I want to make them responsible to the wider community, especially the immigrants.' He was, however, conscious of the advantages that belonging to a religious hierarchy gave him in communicating with M.P.s and local officials, but said he also had 'a deep understanding of Black Power—I get on very well with them. They have pointed the way to the future. I am all for militant organizations.'

The third officer was secretary of a religious organization's committee on race relations. Their contribution was concentrated on 'education and practical involvement'. The officer was an active public speaker and conference organizer; and his committee produced a wide range of publications, carried out research, and ran an information service. The committee co-operated with other organizations, including militant Black groups, and the officer felt it was vital that they were distinct from central and local government: 'We are independent and in a position to do things because of this.'

The optimism of these officers shows that field-workers can feel confident that they are making a positive contribution to community relations. The officers were able to concentrate on a chosen range of activities—community development, public education, or research—and act as a ginger group to voluntary and statutory bodies. The organizational framework in which these three officers worked presented none of the conflicts and contradictions which have featured in the survey of liaison officers. There was agreement on ways and means between officer and committee, financial security, money for projects, and scope for development. All three officers stressed the importance of their independence from central and local government, whereas the tripartite system of appointing and subsidizing liaison officers has been shown by the survey to create tensions and ambiguities which can seldom be resolved.

The survey of liaison officers showed that officers lacked a sense of direction and that their energies were being wasted through an effort to do too many jobs at once, through lack of guidance on a national level, and through conflicts with committees and local authorities. Only a firm national commitment can alter this situation by providing adequate training, imaginative guidance, and flexible resources.

CHAPTER 13

Other Measures Against Racial Discrimination

NICHOLAS DEAKIN AND BRIAN COHEN

1. *The Government*
by Nicholas Deakin

Although the main theme of this volume is measures taken by Governments to abate discrimination against minorities, this theme entered comparatively late into official policy in the United Kingdom. Initially, the policies of the United Kingdom Government were directed almost exclusively towards the restriction of immigration. Subsequently, such policies were broadened to include measures designed to integrate those who had already entered the country; but even here anti-discrimination legislation as such was a comparatively late addition to the official armoury.

When Oliver Lyttleton (now Lord Chandos) became—much to his own surprise—Colonial Secretary in the in-coming Churchill Administration of 1951, the first communication he received was from Field Marshal Lord Montgomery. It was about the Malayan emergency and urged the Colonial Secretary to find a man. Once he had a man, Lord Montgomery added, it would then be possible to devise a Plan.

On one particular issue, among the many that he inherited from his predecessor, Mr. Lyttleton had neither Man nor Plan: this was the question of what was then known as colonial migration. The absence of a clear-cut policy was not particularly sinister; rather, it was chiefly due to the fact that the Labour Government had attached no particular importance to the issue. It is true that they had been responsible for the passage of the British Nationality Act; but, contrary to a persistent myth, that Act made no change in the position of colonist subjects who wished to come to the United Kingdom. Generally, the Colonial Office under the Attlee Administration had been content to deal with problems as they arose on a rule-of-thumb basis. The voyage of the *Empire Windrush*, more significant (according to one recent essay) than that of the *Mayflower*, aroused the passing indignation of the Minister of Labour; but steps were promptly taken to house and find jobs for the new migrants. In conducting this operation, the Colonial Office and Ministry of Labour had the experience of the war-time scheme for colonial workers on Merseyside to fall back on; there were also standing welfare arrangements, including hostels for seamen as well as for students. An Advisory Committee sat (as was the fashion in the Colonial Office of the period) and some statistics were collected. The possibility of some form of control was discussed, both publicly and privately, without acrimony but also without enthusiasm. All this activity, though hardly adding up to a systematic policy, was sufficient to earn the praise of visiting American social scientists, who saw the British Government's willingness to intervene directly on behalf of colonial citizens as an agreeable contrast to the supine behaviour of their own Federal Government.

During Churchill's prime ministership most of these admittedly fragile initiatives withered. There seem to have been two main reasons for this. The external pressures of decolonization which began to get under way towards the end of his administration, caused increasing stress to be laid on the significance of the status of Africans and West Indians in Britain, as citizens of countries shortly to become free and equal partners in a multiracial Commonwealth. The dignity attached to this new situation, and to the common possession of the rights attached to the status of British subject, was held to preclude the introduction of any special measures that would invidiously single out the newcomers from their fellow-subjects. Measures devised by the Colonial Governments or by High Commissions in Britain were naturally a different matter—hence the British Government's willingness to collaborate in the setting up of the British Caribbean Welfare Service, or with the highly successful Barbados Immigrants Liaison Service, both established in the middle fifties. But these initiatives were also held to relieve the Colonial Office of their Departmental responsibility for the subject. Their residual functions passed, by an analogous process of internal decolonization, to the Home Office, the traditional keepers of the gate. And the complaints that began increasingly to be heard from local authorities and that led to a number of deputations visiting various Whitehall departments, were firmly ignored. Local government was exhorted, as Duncan Sandys exhorted Lambeth in 1955, to paddle its own canoe.

The assumption of the major share of the responsibility for the question of colonial and Commonwealth immigration by the Home Office had a decisive effect on the development of policy over the ten years from 1955 (when Sir Anthony Eden decided not to proceed with the possible introduction of legislation to control immigration) to 1965, the year of the Prime Minister's White Paper on immigration. To look through official documents of the period in search of a definition of the goals of official policy, or of the meaning of the integration which was generally agreed to be a desirable objective, is a frustrating business. No sign of a Plan—still less a Man—can be detected. This may be less surprising than it seems at first sight. There seems to have been a widespread assumption that equal citizenship not merely conferred equal rights, but threw a kind of cloak of invisibility over the newcomers, which would protect them against any danger of being singled out for unwelcome attention, until that not far distant day when the purpose of the exercise was achieved and they became 'assimilated' —or 'integrated' (the words are interchangeable in the protocol of the period)—that is to say, like the majority in all significant respects. In this situation, definitions were irrelevant. But such an assumption (if I have correctly interpreted it) means that the investigation is reduced to an attempt to extrapolate policy from the activities of Government and since these were often ineffective and even contradictory in their consequences, the task is not altogether straightforward.

One temptation is to see official policy during the period merely in the context of the Home Office's gate-keeping role. It is true that this function assumed increasing importance throughout this period: but those responsible for policy did, it is clear, have other considerations in mind apart from the need to devise an efficient and smoothly functioning system of immigration control —despite the impression left by the recent study of this subject by the Chief Immigration Officer at London Airport, T. W. E. Roche.[1] From the earliest stage in their consideration of the

---

[1] T. W. E. Roche, *The Key in the Lock: A History of Immigration Control in England from 1066 to the Present Day* (London, Murray, 1966).

subject, Home Office officials were concerned with a broader issue: the problems, which also arise in the context of aliens policy, of the acceptability of newcomers in terms of language and customs, and the extent to which they would make a positive contribution to the economy, or place strains upon the social services. On this issue, some guidance had already been provided by the *Report of the Royal Commission on Population*.[1] Obsessed —as all commentators of the period had been—by a falling birth-rate and the probability of substantial emigration, the Commission had considered the possibility of a policy of sponsored immigration to make good the population loss, coming to the conclusion that 'such could only be welcomed without reserve if the migrants were of good human stock and were not prevented by their religion or race from intermarrying with the host population and becoming merged in it'. In practice, some steps had already been taken towards implementing such a policy, though not quite in the way suggested by the Royal Commission. As Isaac[2] points out, in the first five years after the War the population of Britain was increased, as a result of immigration, by over one million. Some of these were British subjects returning from the Empire, including Anglo-Indians in both definitions of the term (though the numbers of 'Eurasians' never equalled those of the Dutch East Indian 'repatriates': it is interesting to speculate about what might have happened if they had). But two other groups are of particular interest in this context: the Poles, in part former soldiers from General Anders' Army; and the European Volunteer Workers recruited from the D.P. camps after 1947. They are of interest because in the first case, very considerable effort involving substantial expenditure was made, through the establishment of the Polish Resettlement Corps and the provision of separate educational facilities in the Polish University College, to promote speedy adjustment without destroying the cultural identity of the groups concerned; and in the second, because a planned opera-tion was undertaken, consisting of recruitment to meet specific economic needs in specific industries and areas, during which very stringent restrictions were imposed on the individuals involved. Either set of devices—or a combination of both—might have been adapted to meet the case of the Commonwealth

---

[1] *Report of the Royal Commission on Population* (Cmnd. 7695) (London, H.M.S.O., 1947).
[2] Julius Isaac in *The Positive Contribution by Immigrants* (Paris, UNESCO, 1955).

immigrants: in practice, a common citizenship did duty for positive measures. The ritual incantations of 'Civis Britannicus Sum' filled the policy vacuum.

The disturbances—by the standards of Bogside they can hardly be called riots—of 1958 did create a considerable degree of anxiety in Whitehall: there was even some question of resurrecting the notion of control but, as the Colonial Secretary of the day, Alan Lennox-Boyd, told the Conservative Party conference, if it would be tragic to end the right of free entry it would be unthinkable to do so on grounds of colour. No action followed; incipient patterns of discrimination against coloured newcomers became increasingly entrenched.

While the Government were content to rely upon the sonorous phrase-making of Mr. Justice Salmon, sentencing the Notting Hill nine and celebrating the right of all citizens to walk through the streets in peace and with their heads held high (no matter what kind of accommodation they had to return to at night), the Labour opposition was developing a different theory of action. Integration was not taking place with sufficient rapidity: what was needed to accelerate the process was the removal of some of the existing blemishes on our society: the use of language calculated to incite racial hatred, or colour-bars in public places or employment. The succession of Bills introduced into the Commons by Fenner Brockway—latterly with official Opposition endorsement—during the later fifties and early sixties at first embodied both these aims but later concentrated more on the first, which was both technically easier to achieve and likely to command wider support.

But even this much corrective intervention in the natural processes was too much for the Government to accept: not even the further anxieties provoked by the Kelso Cochrane murder in North Kensington in 1959 or the Parliamentary lobbying activities of the all-party British Caribbean Association could change this. And the dismal failure of Sir Oswald Mosley's attempt to mobilize popular support on the immigration issue in North Kensington at the 1959 General Election seemed at first sight to justify a holding policy, rendered easier by the fall in immigration produced by the recession of 1958.

The apparent stability of the situation rapidly proved illusory. In part, the abandonment by the Macmillan Government of their *laissez-faire* position on immigration can be seen as part of a general process of withdrawal from the red-blooded Toryism of the earlier fifties. The housing policies of successive Conservative Governments which interlocked in several crucial respects with the evolving issue of race relations, can serve as a paradigm; without going into the broader issues, it can safely be said that the Rent Act of 1957 failed in its proclaimed objective of making available a greater quantity of rented accommodation in the conurbations. Instead, it provided the springboard in several areas for the exploitation of the decontrol provisions by unscrupulous landlords, the best known of whom now has a secure foothold in history through his largely fortuitous association with the Profumo affair. The failure of Conservative policies of concentrating on private building and slum clearance and leaving the private rented sector to work out its own salvation became steadily more apparent by the end of the fifties; and Members for constituencies affected—mostly in the inner belts of London and Birmingham—made a clear association between the increasing difficulties of the areas of multi-occupation and the development of racial tension. Local authorities pressed increasingly strongly for some form of additional power to enable them to bring the situation under control. The result was the Housing Act of 1961, a clear reversal, with its emphasis on local authority interventions, of previous Conservative housing policy. The Act enabled authorities to intervene—either indirectly through improvement grants or in a last resource, directly through taking over the property—in housing in the city centre. Introducing it, Henry Brooke, the Minister of Housing, spoke of 'conditions so foul that most people would not believe they still survived in this country of ours', and of one particular experience he had had while visiting such property: 'I do not know exactly on whom rested the responsibility for the state of that house, but I felt, there and then, that unless I did something about it, part responsibility would be on me.' The Opposition was quick enough to assure him that he and his predecessors were strong candidates for that responsibility: their reproaches were, perhaps less predictably, echoed by a number of Conservative back-benchers sitting for such areas. Members, like Colonal Cordeaux (Nottingham Central), with their talk of 'social life poisoned and racial relations envenomed'—all within the last six years—were in effect indicting the failure of *laissez-*

faire to meet the needs of the inner city, of whose population Black newcomers were now an increasingly conspicuous part.

Similarly with the Commonwealth Immigrants Act of the next year. This is a tale too often told to need repeating. But two of the most striking features of the episode were the final collapse of the old Colonial Office-C.R.O.[1] open-door lobby, which had been sustained throughout by the Treasury (who saw immigration as an unmitigated economic benefit) in the face of the arguments for social stress deployed by the Home Office, and the total absence of constructive policy initiatives. This vacuum was laid painfully bare in the course of the long scrutiny to which the Opposition subjected the Bill. For if the Labour Party was too willing to swallow the whole case for rejecting control, the Conservative Government were only too glad to see control as the be-all and end-all of the new initiatives required. 'The greater the numbers coming into this country', said R. A. Butler, introducing the Bill, 'the larger will these communities become and the more difficult will it be to integrate them into our national life.' *Ergo*, reduce numbers and integration will follow. Only the establishment of the Commonwealth Immigrants Advisory Council (a curiously neglected body) prevented the Government from lapsing into complete inactivity after the passage of the Act in March 1962.

The advice provided by the Council under the energetic Chairmanship of Lady Reading covered most of the important areas of social policy, i.e. housing, education, and employment; in some cases, the Government were prepared to make some form of (largely token) response. The philosophy behind the Council's recommendations was simple: a number of social problems had arisen as a result of immigration, but special measures directed specifically to the needs of immigrants should be avoided wherever possible. Instead, immigrants should be encouraged to adapt as speedily as possible to their new surroundings: integration would then occur naturally. The blemish, in other words, lay in the immigrants' strangeness: but this could be removed without too much difficulty. Of education, the Council wrote: 'a national system cannot be expected to perpetuate the different values of immigrant groups'. If too many children accumulated at individual schools, and difficulties arose as a result of language problems

---

[1] Commonwealth Relations Office.

or the inassimilability of children with different cultural needs or values, the solution was to disperse them to other schools. The level at which a school ceased to be able to 'integrate' the minority was fixed at the point when they constituted 30 per cent of the school population (this became known facetiously as Boyle's Law, after the Conservative Minister of Education who first formulated it).

The Labour Party, in the first afterglow of its opposition to the Commonwealth Immigrants Bill, had examined the implications of the failure of the Government to produce any coherent integration policy, and issued a pamphlet designed for local authorities and entitled *Integrating the Immigrant.* Harold Wilson, succeeding to the leadership in 1963, delivered in Trafalgar Square a speech in which he not only pledged that a Labour Government would introduce legislation against incitement to racial hatred but spoke of special aid to areas affected by immigration. This undertaking was incorporated in the 1964 Election Manifesto: but its importance for integration policy—for it represents a sharp break with Conservative policy—was initially obscured by Labour's painful conversion to the principle of immigration control, begun during the Expiring Laws Continuance debate of 1963 and consummated immediately upon the Party's arrival in office, in the aftermath of Patrick Gordon Walker's defeat at Smethwick.

The strategy devised by the new Labour Government to meet the situation with which they were confronted was described by Harold Wilson in March 1965 as 'an attack on three broad fronts'. The first sector was concerned with what the Prime Minister, for tactical reasons, chose to term 'evasion'. In practice, this meant that after the failure of the foredoomed Mountbatten Mission to Commonwealth capitals in search of a bilaterally negotiated immigration policy, far stricter immigration controls were introduced. The second front consisted of the appointment of a junior minister specifically designated as responsible for integration; the third, of the introduction of legislation against 'the evil of incitement against racial hatred'. The whole was designed, as Wilson put it, to promote 'integration, in the widest sense of the word, in terms of housing, health, education and everything that needs to be done to minimise the possible social disturbance arising from this problem'. As an objective, this statement was both more limited in its immediate implications and less sweeping in its rhetoric than the conclusions of the Prime Minister's White Paper of August 1965, in which these initial aims were put into more concrete form. To the draftsmen of the White Paper, the objectives of the policy were to produce 'positive measures designed to secure for immigrants and their children their rightful place in our society'—a duty laid upon us in 'the good name of Britain, or relations with other members of the Commonwealth and, above all, justice and common humanity'.

The White Paper is particularly important because it represents the first attempt at a co-ordinated policy—and one that had been in several respects the basis for official action until the end of the Labour Government in 1970. The provisions for additional controls in Part II of the White Paper, with their very substantial reductions in numbers, the virtual elimination of the unskilled migration, and in the case of the entry of dependants, the *de facto* shifting of the burden of proof from the immigration officer to the migrant, constitute the final triumph for the Home Office in their long struggle to impose their view of the proper workings of a control system on their tender-minded colleagues, although some of these provisions had to wait until 1968 and the Kenya Asian panic to be fully implemented. But not merely was control presented in the 1965 White Paper in the context of integration, as the Government's predecessors had presented it: the embryonic machinery for co-ordination of Government action in the field of integration was transferred from the Department of Economic Affairs to the Home Office, as the most suitable locale. The first constructive act taken to translate good intentions into action was the bringing together of the voluntary organizations— which had in the past received fulsome praise but no practical assistance—under the umbrella of an officially funded body (the National Committee for Commonwealth Immigrants) which also assumed the advisory functions of the Commonwealth Immigrants Advisory Council. The second was the introduction of the Race Relations Act of 1965, changed in mid-stream by the Home Secretary from a Bill providing for criminal penalties for acts of discrimination in public places—as well as for racial incitement— to one establishing a statutory agency for conciliation. The significance of this new body, the Race Relations Board, lay less in its immediate powers—which were limited, and extended only to areas in which discrimination has a largely symbolic significance—than in its potential. Finally, there were the powers eventually obtained in Section 11 of the Local Government Act of 1966, providing for grants to local authorities to defray the cost of staff employed in consequence of the presence of immigrants with 'language or customs differing from the rest of the community'. These special grants, which were compared by the Minister of Housing to those granted simultaneously to defray the burdens imposed on local authorities by the presence of derelict land, were defended in terms of 'certain problems peculiar to immigrants from the Commonwealth' and welcomed by one perceptive back-bencher 'because this is the first occasion on which money has specifically been set aside for authorities which suffer from this problem'.

But these grants represented the limits to which the Government were prepared to go. Members who raised the question of special provision for housing in twilight areas were slapped down on the grounds that immigrants were in no greater need than anyone else. 'The sole test for action in the housing field', observed the White Paper sternly, 'is the quality and nature of housing need'—this, despite the fact that both local authorities (in the 1966 Act) and immigrants (in the 1965 Act) were now recognized as facing special problems. Moreover, the implementation—in the Department of Education and Science Circular 7/65—of the provisions of Boyle's law underlined the Department's acceptance of the theory of special problems associated with immigrant concentrations. As for employment, the White Paper commented flatly and unconvincingly that 'this complex issue is being tackled in a number of effective, if unobtrusive, ways'. The deficiencies in the programme of 1965—a confluence of Labour Party thinking in opposition and Home Office doctrine—are already clear enough: basically, they are that it failed to go to the root causes of inequality, particularly in housing and employment. Instead, it perpetuated the notion that patching up the more unsightly blemishes that had appeared in ten years of neglect would prove sufficient to allow the natural process of integration to take place. But within its limits, the programme was a coherent one: all that the Plan lacked was a Man. He duly materialized at the end of 1965 in the shape of Roy Jenkins.

Jenkins's record as Home Secretary has already been the

subject of endless discussion. As far as race relations is concerned, his achievement (in my view) consisted of two things. First, that he breathed life, and hence credibility, into the programme already drawn up by his predecessors. In particular, the protracted series of negotiations finally brought to a triumphant conclusion in the Race Relations Act of 1968, which extended the anti-discrimination legislation into the critical fields of housing and employment, realized the full potential of the Board as an instrument of policy. Second, he provided the blueprint for a further advance, which can conveniently be crystallized in his well-known definition of integration as 'equal opportunity, accompanied by cultural diversity in an atmosphere of mutual tolerance'. In taking the trouble to devise an operational definition of integration instead of merely making the usual obeisance to the desirability of the process (like Enoch Powell two years before),[1] Jenkins was opening the way to a new view of the situation in which immigrants are not assessed merely in terms of their significance for the efficient functioning of the existing social system and their rights no longer depend either on an obsolescent system of citizenship or a willingness to conform by shedding their separate cultural identity. But in practice the new departure was not followed through. The new provisions in the Race Relations Act of 1968 are of very considerable importance, especially those relating to the purchase of housing. However, to claim, as Jenkins did in his Abingdon speech of July 1969, that 'as a result of these two [Race Relations] Acts I believe that [we] have done a great deal to avoid disfiguring social strife in the decades to come. I do not believe that those who wish to exploit this issue for their own petty purposes will now succeed', is to pitch the claim too high.

The precariousness of the favourable climate produced by the initiatives of Jenkins's Home Secretaryship was shown by the rapid deterioration in the atmosphere produced by the episode of the United Kingdom citizens of Asian origin in East Africa and the effective extinction of their rights of citizenship by the Commonwealth Immigrants Act of 1968. Its significance in the context of integration is that the inability of successive Governments to devise a viable immigration policy that can be assimilated to a positive programme of action in domestic race relations policy

---

[1] In Paul Foot, *The Rise of Enoch Powell, An Examination of Enoch Powell's Attitude to Immigration and Race* (Harmondsworth, Penguin Books, 1969).

has left an exposed flank which can always be turned by those either sufficiently obsessed with or unscrupulous about the question of immigration to raise a scare. The Kenya Asian episode provided such an opportunity, which was duly exploited. The result was not merely that the passage of the Race Relations Bill became a far more complex and hotly disputed exercise, but that the first major initiative in the new ('pluralistic') direction that Jenkins had mapped out was nearly upset at the outset.

The Urban Programme derived from a number of different strands of thinking about social policy: principally, the notion of positive discrimination in favour of areas of cumulative underprivilege, first systematically enunciated in the Plowden report on primary education; in part, notions about poverty and the most effective means of relieving it which has been developed by a number of academics and whose relevance to race relations was first systematically explored in a paper by Peter Townsend in late 1966;[1] and, in fact, ideas devised from the War on Poverty Program in the United States. The initial announcement of the programme was made by the Prime Minister in Birmingham on May Day 1968: in making this pronouncement, he implied, first, that the funds made available would be raised by a levy upon areas not affected to subsidize those areas that he described as 'unfortunate' and, second, that the programme constituted a practical answer to the propaganda of Enoch Powell. The effect was to promote a widespread delusion that the programme was designed as a measure to aid areas of immigrant settlement—a belief encouraged by a number of Midlands authorities, who eagerly put together cases for funds based on an assessment, *per capita*, of the burden they were compelled to carry through the mere presence of immigrants. In fact, those responsible for devising the programme had always intended that it should be directed towards those in need, not towards immigrants as such.

Nor did the first phase of the programmes, which the Home Secretary announced in July 1968, altogether dispel their misunderstanding. A total of £3·5 millions was allocated by the Home Secretary in grants to 34 local authorities, whose eligibility was determined by either the presence of housing need (defined in terms of overcrowding) or the presence of immigrants (defined

---

[1] In Anthony Lester and Nicholas Deakin (eds.), *Policies for Racial Equality* (London, Fabian Society Pamphlet 262, 1967).

in terms of the presence of 'immigrant' children on the school roll). It was not until after the passage of the Local Government Grants (Social Needs) Act at the beginning of 1969—which authorized the payment of grants by the Secretary of State 'to local authorities who in his opinion are required in the exercise of any of their functions to incur expenditure by reason of the existence in any urban areas of special social need'—that all the implications of an immigrant aid programme were finally shaken off. In the second stage of the programme, which is intended to run alongside the Educational Priority Area programme and the newly announced community development programme (also under the control of the Home Office), a further £4 millions was allocated to 89 local authorities—and through them to voluntary organizations—to fund projects covering a far wider field than the nursery classes and children's homes of the first stage.

The introduction of a programme of selective aid from central Government resources to deprived areas represents a decisive break with past policy. Such programmes are of immense importance for the future of race relations: they deal for the first time with one of the major causes of interracial tensions, i.e. the competition for scarce resources in the inner city. But in order for such programmes to become an acceptable device for policy in this field, it is necessary to discard, first, earlier views that integration is a natural process, promoted by time and, if necessary, public education, in which the intervention of Government is unnecessary (this was the view that prevailed for a decade in the middle fifties); and, second, the view, which developed in opposition and prevailed from 1965, that there were certain limited special needs that were generated by immigration. These, together with the increasing hostilities of a small number of the majority, constituted the obstacles within the existing system that would have to be removed by special measures. But should the needs of immigrants overlap with those of other groups or be generated by deficiencies that could not be removed by simple ameliorative measures, then action must be resisted, as it was by the Ministry of Housing and Local Government in 1965 and both sides of industry in 1967. The important change partly discernible since 1968—the synthesis, if you like—is that the possession by Blacks of needs in common with other people in the same geographical or social situation has become a ground for satisfying those needs, not for passing them over. This strategy, which I have called elsewhere 'strong universalism',[1] is an acceptable device in terms of race relations as well as in general terms because it fits the new definition of integration as a process in which rights are secured without uniformity being imposed.

Alongside this changing definition of the legitimate focus for action, there has been a shift in the definition of responsibility. Initially, central Government were disqualified from intervention, for fear that the newcomers' status might be compromised. The problem, as Lord Gardiner subsequently put it, was 'just thrown on the desks of local authorities'. In the second stage, limited intervention by central Government to correct malfunctions was acceptable, but the main onus still remained on local authorities. Thus, housing authorities were expected to meet all the foreseeable needs of immigrants in the course of their normal housing programmes: problems of entry into local authority accommodation or of voluntary dispersal would resolve themselves naturally as a result of existing practice. The P.E.P. report on the extent of discrimination effectively dynamited this notion, as it did the idea that the 'unobtrusive' processes taking place in industry were coping with problems of discrimination in employment. In a third stage, the specific measures designed to eliminate discrimination and deal with those difficulties inseparable from the early stages of migration have been reinforced by the beginnings of a comprehensive attack on the causes of underprivilege in the inner city, in which central Government have made the first tentative steps towards assuming responsibility for matters that have indirectly been the problems of local authorities.

Alongside the progressively greater assumption of authority by central Government and a changing definition of tasks, there have been the beginnings of a shift in the internal division of responsibility. A subject once rigidly excluded for consideration by social policy departments has moved from the periphery, in the Colonial Office, to the Home Office. Here, for the moment, it remains: but there are those who feel that the increasing share of responsibility assumed by other departments, which would be further increased if some housing functions come—as they should

---

[1] In Chapter 29 of E. J. B. Rose and associates, *Colour and Citizenship: A Report on British Race Relations* (London, Oxford University Press, for Institute of Race Relations, 1969).

do—within the scope of the Urban Programme, should be reflected in a further move.

This review of policies affecting anti-discriminatory measures and integration has necessarily involved over-simplification, and the kind of distortions of perspective inevitable when one issue is pulled out from a range of issues with which it intersects, and examined in isolation. The delusion that this is an area in which solutions can be left to time, education, and goodwill has disappeared, and the manner of its departure has been painful: but the lesson that lasting solutions will involve change in our own society is not yet thoroughly learnt. The sentimental (though attractive) delusion persists that it will be different in the next generation; they will know our language and our tribal customs; there will be no need for disputes about loyalties or whether to honour the citizenship of those who may not be 'belongers'. We have even gone so far as to make this distinction into law: for the purposes of the 'racial balance' clause of the Race Relations Act 1968, the children of immigrants educated here count with the white majority.

Yet all the evidence so far available suggests that the search for policies, so far from ceasing to be pressing when a generation of Black Britons emerges, will have to be intensified if intense frustrations are to be avoided, and that any solution must encompass another second generation, the white children now growing up in the twilight areas with every prospect of a life circumscribed by limited access to job opportunities or tolerable housing and every incentive to blame the available—because visible—scapegoat who faces the same handicaps. New developments provide some hope that such solutions can be achieved: but for the present, the best one can say, as another student of policy in this field puts it, is that so far: 'Race relations policy . . . has not really resulted in any exclusively novel solution for social policy. Perhaps what it has done is to bring into focus for policy-makers emerging concepts of community development, the need for participation, the need for redress for societal mishandling, and the desirability of "selective" compensatory services: But these concepts are the ones dominating the debate on how to aid all underprivileged or stigmatized groups, and even so, they are not yet translated into service reality to any appreciable degree.'

2. *Employers, the Private Sector*
by Brian Cohen

In a discussion of the effectiveness of measures against racial discrimination there is a danger that attention is only directed towards those measures that emanate from Government, and that the possible potentialities of other measures will be overlooked. This is especially so in the field of employment where the majority of opportunities are under the control of private individuals and organizations who often wield great economic power and influence. An example of the possible scope for private and voluntary measures are those that have been undertaken in the United States under the title of Plans for Progress, and other schemes. While these schemes have not been as successful as one could have hoped, they are potentially a valuable adjunct to the legislative and administrative measures of the Federal and State governments of the United States. As yet, the activity of private companies in Great Britain has been minimal and any measures that have been carried out have nearly always been individual and personal. The growing involvement of American companies, not only in the field of employment opportunities but also in the wider society, has not been matched by British companies.

(a) EMPLOYERS AND DISCRIMINATION

Most major companies in Great Britain have, when challenged, stated that they do not discriminate and that they judge all applicants on their merits. These statements are usually made in response to allegations of discrimination and must be seen in terms of an affirmation of the general credo of equality and not as a statement of policy. No major company has made a public statement, in a non-reactive situation, of a fair employment policy in the manner in which some American companies have acted. As far as it is known, by 1969 only one major company in Great Britain had developed any machinery to ensure that the company practises a fair employment policy. The more general policy of large companies has been to state that they deal fairly with all applicants for most types of job. This eliminates any need to specify and actually apply this approach throughout those levels of their companies at which decisions on recruitment, training, promotion, etc., are taken.

A large exception to these statements of fairness has been the declarations by some employers that due to major constraints they have been unable effectively to operate an open employment policy. These constraints are cited by employers as being the opposition of their white employees and of trade unions to the employment of coloured workers and the reactions of their customers. This point of view was put forward by one leading employer in the following terms:

The employer is not, however, an entirely free agent when engaging employees. He has to take into account the attitudes of his other personnel and in the case of industries serving the public, he will have to take into account the attitudes of his customers.[1]

In its discussion of the survey of people in a position to discriminate, the P.E.P. report summarized this point in slightly different terms:

But whether informants' convictions that other white people were hostile and resistant to coloured people were based on an extension of their own beliefs or on an objective assessment of the situation, the practical consequences were the same: a very great deal of the discrimination practised against coloured people was justified by employers in terms of the resistance or hostility of white employees, customers or clients.[2]

Because it is generally believed that these constraints exist, employment opportunities for coloured workers have been severely limited in certain types of job, especially those involving customer contact. Furthermore, in certain concerns, because of this assumed hostility of white workers, managements have been reluctant to recruit coloured workers for certain grades or for any position. However, in spite of this there are companies that have employed coloured workers in these jobs and grades and have reported no significant adverse effects either from customers or from co-workers.

Another factor which has seriously affected the achievement of equal opportunity has been the question of coloured workers' skills. The contradiction between declared policy and practice

---

[1] N.C.C.I., *Racial Equality in Employment* (London, N.C.C.I., February 1967), p. 2.
[2] W. W. Daniel, *Racial Discrimination in England* (Harmondsworth, Penguin Books, 1968), p. 93.

is often explained by the assertion that no coloured workers sufficiently well qualified have ever applied for the particular jobs in question. This assertion in some cases deteriorates into the grossest form of stereotyping which assumes that all coloured workers on the labour market are unskilled, indolent, slow to learn, and inherently incapable of fitting into a modern, industrialized environment. While the grosser extensions of these beliefs are patently incorrect, certain credence has been given to this belief by aspects of the current situation.

Most coloured workers were born and educated in a non-industrial environment and some either speak no English or have a limited command of the language. For some of those who speak English, difficulties of dialect or non-comprehension of idiomatic usage can make communications difficult. The average educational standards of coloured workers are generally lower than those of white workers, and qualifications gained overseas are not necessarily of the same level as those gained in the United Kingdom. Cultural standards, attitudes to work, and the general pace of life differ between the countries of origin of many coloured workers and the United Kingdom. All the above are statements which possess a certain general validity for the existing situation in this country, but they are no more than generalizations. Because the presence of coloured workers in the labour force is intimately related to immigration, most major employers have at some time or another been approached by ill-qualified coloured job applicants claiming what seem to employers to be spurious qualifications. Thus, many employers have taken the objective fact that a higher proportion of coloured workers are ill-qualified and have extended it to a blanket suspicion of the skills of all coloured workers. The basis, therefore, of stating that no coloured worker is qualified for a specific post is an unjustifiable extension of the particular to the general.

An example of the effect of these beliefs is to be seen in the practice of a large international company in the selection of its graduate management trainees. The company has received each year some three to four hundred applications for ten posts. As the company found it difficult to evaluate overseas qualifications, all persons with degrees obtained outside the United Kingdom were excluded. Also excluded were all those persons born in India, Pakistan, and other countries who had obtained English university qualifications—usually post-graduate. The reasons for excluding these applicants can be summarized as follows:

(i) These foreign applicants were likely to return to their countries of origin, and if the company were to recruit them, it would be done by the branches based in the applicants' countries of origin and not by the English end of the company.

(ii) Past experience had shown that overseas applicants with paper qualifications equivalent to those of English applicants were not judged suitable at the interview stage due to poorer command of the language and imperfect understanding of the cultural background.

(iii) For reasons of cost-effectiveness, it was necessary to reduce the number of applications to manageable proportions and as it was felt that the majority of overseas applicants would be ineligible due to reasons (i) and (ii), all were excluded as a matter of course.

The above is an example of a recruitment policy that is certainly discriminatory in effect, although the reasons for this policy were seen to accord with good business practice and were not overtly racialist. It should also be stated that the company concerned had on another occasion shown considerable courage in fighting a strike called by white workers against the employment of coloured workers.

The practice described above was operated with some degree of disquiet by the company concerned but many other companies have made far more sweeping conclusions about the quality of coloured workers. Some companies having had bad experiences or having heard second- or third-hand accounts (often wildly exaggerated) of the lack of skills of some coloured workers, have come to the conclusion that these workers are unfit for any type of work or are only capable of performing the most unskilled types of work. It is significant to note that the normal ability of employers to distinguish between different grades of skill for white workers is often suspended for coloured workers.

A pointer to the general attitudes of management to coloured workers is the reasons given by employers for initially employing them or, conversely, for not employing them. Studies have shown that the original reason for employing coloured workers has usually been the existence of grave labour shortages for particular grades with little or no prospect of recruiting suitable white labour. A few companies have stated that coloured workers were

initially employed as a matter of course when they started appearing on the labour market, but this reaction has tended to be
concentrated in the larger, more modern, and expanding companies. In these companies, recruitment policies are more often
determined by well-trained, powerful personnel departments
rather than the employing departments. In a very few instances,
it can be said that coloured workers are first employed for reasons
of humanitarian sentiment or social responsibility. An example of
this is the case of the personnel manager of a large company who
felt that his company ought to employ some coloured workers
and convinced his directors of the necessity of this. These cases
are, however, very limited and often take place against a background of previous exclusion; and the fear of future political
repercussions are often as important as 'humanitarian' reasons.

In contradistinction, many companies not employing
coloured workers have explained that the reason for this is that
there is a sufficient supply of local or English labour for their
needs. Many of these companies do not consider that their
practice is discriminatory and feel that their policy of keeping to a
known labour supply is justified. Many also are unwilling to
experiment and, as discussed by Bob Hepple in Chapter 6, are
unwilling to disturb the delicate balance of industrial relations;
thus, they opt for a conservative policy.

(b) A CASE STUDY OF AFFIRMATIVE ACTION
It is worth examining in detail at this point the actions of one
company which was in the process of carrying out the nearest
approach, in the United Kingdom, to a policy of affirmative
action. In this respect the company was probably unique and its
experience gives a good insight into the problems of translating
policy into practice. The company is a large group with a major
retail chain of stores in most of the larger cities in the United
Kingdom. It employs over 5,000 full-time sales staff and over
5,000 part-time and Saturday sales staff. The company has
employed coloured workers for some years, but until recently
there have been very few on the sales staff. As a result of an
initiative by the Deputy Chairman and Managing Director, the
company has evolved a specific policy towards the employment of
coloured sales staff.

Over a period of about two years, the Group Personnel

Manager had sent a series of requests to store managers, asking them to employ more non-European sales staff. This proved to have little effect and in November 1967, a circular was sent to all store managers stating that as a matter of company policy at least 5 per cent of all sales staff had to be of non-European descent, except in those areas where it could be established by the Department of Employment and Productivity that there were no suitable applicants. This circular was signed by the Sales Manager, the direct superior of the store managers, who were responsible for recruitment, rather than by the Personnel Manager who only had advisory powers in relation to store managers.

A further circular was sent out in February 1968 when it was seen that nearly half the stores had failed to reply to the original circular. In April 1968, the Personnel Department—in its four-weekly returns of staff turnover—began to collect the number of non-European staff in each store. Further letters and circulars were sent to store managers, area managers, and regional Personnel Officers, as a means of chasing stores which either had not completed forms or were considered to be dragging their feet. In July 1968, it was believed that progress had been made and that some stores had already reached their minimum levels but that it would take time and constant pushing to educate the laggards. It was stated that if any store managers continued to disregard the policy over a long period then there was a strong possibility that they would be dismissed as their action would be in opposition to the company's declared policy.

As can be seen, considerable resistance or possibly inertia was displayed against this company's policy by some of those directly responsible for employing sales staff. It was thought that most of the progress made was due to the fact that the Deputy Chairman of the company was the prime mover and this meant that there had been little resistance in the top management. At lower levels, however, resistance did occur and in one branch situated in an area with a high proportion of coloured people, staff opposition was fairly open. In this branch the female staff threatened to walk out *en masse* if any coloured staff were employed, but subsequently when coloured staff were engaged, the threats evaporated.

The lessons to be learned from this company's experience are that a statement of policy which is not administratively implemented will have little effect. There is a clear need for an unequivocal directive on policy to be sent to those responsible for recruitment; and once such a policy is set out, progress must be continually evaluated. If this does not occur, then the opposition or non-enthusiasm of any individual in the management hierarchy can defeat the objectives of the policy. Furthermore, at the lowest levels, pressures will often exist which impede the carrying out of a policy of equal opportunity and these can only be overcome by a firm and clear commitment from top management which is seen to be determined to implement its policy. In the whole of this process, the role of evaluation and the keeping of careful statistics is of the utmost importance, otherwise policy-makers become too detached from practice.

Recently, a greater interest in the position of coloured employees has been shown by a number of major employers with a view to re-examining their practice. The catalyst for these moves would seem to have been the introduction of the Race Relations Bill 1968 to Parliament. In a similar fashion to the moves made by the Confederation of British Industry and the Trades Union Congress, and the Engineering Employers Federation and the Confederation of Shipbuilding and Engineering Unions to enact voluntary machinery when legislation was mooted, as described by Louis Kushnick in Chapter 9, so certain employers have consulted outside bodies specializing in race relations or have conducted internal enquiries. These attempts by some employers to put their house in order is one positive side-effect of the Race Relations Act 1968. It is doubtful, however, if much of this activity would have occurred without the spur of legislation. This new interest was also shown by bodies associated with industry, and there have been a number of conferences and seminars aimed at directors, managers, personnel officers, and others. The greater interest shown and the discussion of what industry can do to tackle the existing problems were almost unknown previously and they are another undoubted effect of the 1968 Act. It is, however, too early to determine whether the employers concerned will modify their earlier practices to any great extent, but it is at least a promising sign that some have begun to talk in this fashion. It is, however, unlikely that the engrained habits of prejudice and discrimination built up over a long period by many companies will disappear in the short term.

Part IV
Conclusions

CHAPTER 14

Conclusions

SIMON ABBOTT

1. *Immigrant Groups and the Receiving Society*

In Chapter 1, racial discrimination was defined through the concept of a discriminatory process, involving an in-group, an out-group, the act or process of discrimination, and their relationships to society as a whole. The purpose of this concept was, firstly, to illustrate that discrimination went much further than the occasionally detected act of racial discrimination; and, secondly, to provide a simple scheme of analysis for discussion of this more general idea of discrimination in relation to the so-called 'coloured' immigrants to Britain and the receiving society. The first part of this volume considered in particular the general situations of the in-group (generally, the receiving, British society) and of the out-group (generally, the coloured immigrants). The situations of these groups and their relationships with society as a whole became apparent through the examination of the migrations to Britain, and through analysis of the relative positioning of the immigrants and natives in the stratification system. The second part of this volume went on to consider 'the process of discrimination', which—in the terms of the concept above—shifts the emphasis on to the third factor of 'the act or process of discrimination'. And the third part of this volume reversed the emphasis to consider attempts to check or eliminate this same process of racial discrimination, particularly by evaluating the development and work of the Government race relations agencies. This final chapter will conclude with a discussion of the fourth factor of the concept outlined above: the relationship of the discriminatory process to society as a whole. But it will be discussed, no doubt in a preliminary and unsatisfactory way, by projection against the fundamental, underlying issues of racial discrimination: How is discrimination eliminated? How is social change achieved? What kind of society permits or encourages basic structural change or simply the elimination of discrimination based on race?

(a) THE MIGRATIONS TO BRITAIN

The history of earlier immigrant groups did not serve adequately to prepare the way for the more recent coloured immigration. Sheila Patterson outlines the changing climates of opinion with respect to the Commonwealth immigrants: a combination of *laissez-faire* on such issues as housing, education, employment, among others, and 'uncontrolled, unselected, undirected immigration' gave way to a policy of immigration restrictions and integrationist attempts, and also to increased displays of populist hostility towards the immigrants.

A fundamental problem in the discussion of race and migration situations, is the use of terms. Sheila Patterson discusses concepts in immigration theory, starting from Eisenstadt's definition of absorption. Assimilation is described as 'complete adaptation by immigrants or a minority and complete acceptance by the absorbing society in all areas of social relationship, private as well as public'; and integration is used in the sense of 'pluralistic integration' or 'cultural pluralism' to cover the adaptation of a group to acceptance 'as a permanent member in a society in certain universal spheres of association' such as employment or politics, while retaining its group identity based on such elements as religion or language. The tendency of certain groups to self-segregation is noted. Accommodation is regarded as 'a minimum *modus vivendi* between newcomers and the receiving society', but consistent with peaceful co-existence and the socialization of the newcomers, adaptation and acceptance being greater in institutionalized spheres such as housing or social services. Variables affecting absorption are defined under four heads: demographic, socio-economic and cultural, structural (e.g. policies over immigration control), and specific (e.g. such a factor as, in the British case, the Commonwealth connection).

The early history of migration into Britain was dominated, as described, by official *laissez-faire* in economic and social matters; but the smaller, early groups—i.e. political refugees and those seeking work—were effectively assimilated. In the case of the two main earlier groups, the Irish and the Jews, the process of absorption has varied considerably: for the Jews, for example, from individual assimilation to anti-assimilationist self-segregation and pluralistic integration. The coloured groups have been in Britain for only a short period, mainly arriving after the mid-

1950s, and have not had the advantage of earlier, sponsoring groups, as did the Jews and Irish. The benefit of the Government's integrationist policy was offset by two main difficulties: the immigrants were recent arrivals, who were experiencing the problems of adjustment/adaptation to the new society, and they were highly visible by their darker complexions. Within the framework of migration theory outlined, none of the coloured groups could be said to be assimilated, and as groups they at present fall short of pluralistic integration or cultural pluralism. Instead, the coloured groups lie largely in the state of accommodation. There are considerable differences in the situations of the different groups, as instanced in their tendency to be self-segregating, for example. Of the Yemenis in the Midlands, the ascribed status and traditional pattern of life persist in their home-life; and at work, in ethnic groups with leadership based on achieved status, 'the migrants ... achieve accommodation by isolating themselves'.[1] This may be contrasted with the West Indians: in one area investigated during the present study, it was found that they were using, for example, the same pubs as the white British. Generally, the coloured groups are still influenced by both the immigration and the race relations factors although, with time, the weight shifts increasingly to the race relations side.

Under the pressure of the effects of war, a plan to resettle some 150,000 Polish ex-servicemen and their families had been evolved. It covered housing through the use of camps and hostels, education in English, and also instruction for employment. Beyond this, the Poles were left free to retain their own culture and language. A smaller, but successful, scheme was adopted for the Hungarian refugees in 1956–7. But such planning, for alien whites seeking political refuge, did not serve as a base and example for the coloured immigrants seeking economic security.

Apart, then, from the case of the Poles and Hungarians, earlier Government action had been concerned primarily with immigration control—for example, the 1905 Aliens Act following the 1903 Royal Commission on Alien Immigration. Such immigration control combined with *laissez-faire* in, among others, the field of housing permitted the continued growth of poor, urban

[1] Badr Ud-Din Dahya, 'South Asian Urban Immigration with Special Reference to Asian Immigration in the English Midlands' (M.A. thesis for University of London, 1967).

reception areas. But the introduction of coloured immigration control in 1962 and the increased restrictions that followed in 1965, both eased the host's fears of a coloured avalanche,[1] and determined that immigration should continue as a major issue in British race relations. For the immigrants, migration control represented a continuous hazard and lottery to the reunification of families and to travel between countries. For the receiving society, control developed into a potent political debate, with further restrictions viewed as concessions, victories, or as necessary compromises. However, the integrationist policy for those already arrived, hinted at by the Conservatives in 1962, was later much extended in terms of institutions under the Labour Government. This policy received its most quoted definition from the then Home Secretary, Roy Jenkins, who said of integration that 'we must aim, not at a flattening process of assimilation, but at equal opportunity, accompanied by cultural diversity, in an atmosphere of mutual tolerance'.[2] Through the White Paper and the Race Relations Act of 1965, the N.C.C.I. and Race Relations Board were set up; and these bodies were later strengthened in 1968. Thus the Government's new policy was a compound of migration control and integration. It is pointed out, however, that the policy of integration has had negative, as well as positive, aspects: the anti-discrimination measures are 'preventive rather than positive', and the emphasis has perhaps been on neutralizing the race factor in the hope that the general social structure will then work satisfactorily.

(b) THE DEMOGRAPHIC AND STATISTICAL DATA

The testing for effectiveness of particular measures in particular situations will probably not indicate the general relative situations of the coloured and white groups in British society. Further, the existing data for specific measures—such as the race relations legislation—cover both a short time period and a relatively small field of activity. Despite the drawbacks of the census and other basic data (such as the migration statistics), it is, therefore, important to use them in estimating the position and mobility of the

---

[1] However, if fears were temporarily eased, they were certainly not assuaged: the panic and rush of the 1968 Act aimed at excluding Asians from East Africa, illustrate this.

[2] Address by the Home Secretary to the Institute of Race Relations, reprinted in *Race* (Vol. VIII, No. 3, January 1967), p. 216.

different groups within the stratification system. What effect have the various measures and the general situation had upon the coloured immigrant groups? The data here analysed give some answers.

Brian Cohen first sets out the figures for the migration to Britain of the coloured groups. Using data from the 1951, 1961, and 1966 censuses, and also from the Migrant Services Division and the Home Office, he shows the now well-established pattern of the migration: the arrival, mainly after 1955, of the West Indians as the first and largest group, with the numbers of women (never small) and children coming to exceed male arrivals by 1959–61; followed by the Indians, with a lower proportion of women and children; and, finally, the Pakistanis, with pre-1962 arrivals being perhaps 90 per cent male. Before 1962, return migration could be quite high: for Indians and Pakistanis up to 1960 the number of returnees was equal to more than half the number of arrivals. After 1962 and the introduction of control, the flow reflected the migration of the preceding period, with Asians now in the majority and their dependants exceeding voucher-holders by 1964.

At the time of the 1966 Census, the coloured population in England and Wales numbered about 924,200, of whom 213,300 were children born in Britain; and by mid-1968, there were about 273,800 Jamaicans, 180,300 other Caribbeans, 223,600 Indians, and 119,700 Pakistanis. In 1961, 47 per cent of coloured Commonwealth immigrants lived in London, 14 per cent in the West Midlands, and 71 per cent in the six conurbations combined; while in 1966, the percentages (of people from India, Pakistan, and the West Indies) were 44·3 per cent in London, 14·7 per cent in the West Midlands, and 70·5 per cent in the six conurbations. In 1966, in none of the 700 London wards did new Commonwealth immigrants form a majority, the highest concentration being just over 30 per cent. Distribution was unequal both in density and as between ethnic groups and area; for example, West Indians formed the largest group in Huddersfield, and Pakistanis the largest group in near-by Bradford.

The evaluation of the census data is complicated by a number of factors; but for racial analysis the chief difficulty is that the census asks no questions directly related to race or ethnic origin. Data on birth-place are collected and for 1971 these had to be extended to birth-place of parents. The availability of varying census data is listed, and problems such as the number of white Indians and under-enumeration are discussed. Unfortunately, 'a wide range of social data' for comparisons between the 1961 and 1966 censuses can be presented only for four broad areas of investigation.

A comparison of the different immigrant groups—from India, Pakistan, Jamaica, the rest of the Caribbean, British West Africa, Cyprus—with the total population reveals certain conclusions on economic position: in the two conurbations of London and the West Midlands, males in the groups are proportionately more active economically than the total population; and despite a slightly higher number out of employment, the proportions in employment are still higher than for the total population. If one excludes students, the economic participation rate is still further increased. For females, the Caribbean migrants generally have considerably higher participation rates, but the Indians and Pakistanis have lower rates. A comparison of data between the censuses for London reveals very little change in the rate of participation.

Taking a different dimension, industrial status, Brian Cohen shows the differing rates for climbing 'out of the ruck'—in this case, the 'other employees' category: one in four of the total population have managed this, one in ten of the Indians, and three in one hundred of the Jamaicans and Pakistanis. The data here illustrate also, for example, the different position of the Jamaicans as compared to the slightly superior status of the other Caribbeans. A third dimension is that of occupation: looking now at 'white-collar jobs' and at the West Midlands (where the problem of white Indians and Pakistanis enumerated under 'coloured' groups, is considered to be less), 'all the immigrant groups are badly under-represented in white-collar jobs and the representation of Pakistanis and Caribbeans is minimal'. The evidence from Chapter 7, on coloured applicants for white-collar jobs, suggests that this situation may still be poor, in that a majority of these applicants with suitable qualifications may be likely not even to receive interviews; and, of course, the percentage of immigrants with such suitable qualifications will be relatively small compared to the national population.

General conclusions are that: distribution differs from the

general population and between immigrant groups; occupational distribution is generally less favourable for the immigrant groups, and it is also less favourable in the West Midlands conurbation than in the London conurbation; and 'there has been no indication that during the five-year period from 1961 to 1966 there has been an improvement in the occupational position of the immigrant groups'. It is suggested that London may be attracting the more skilled and able immigrants, and that 'in areas where immigrants are less favourably received, a proportion of the most able amongst them will move to areas where they are given a better reception'. The case of the Caribbean women is selected to illustrate possible under-utilization of human resources: Caribbean women are heavily over-represented in nursing, and their 'white-blouse' nursing ratio in London is about 1:1, as compared to 13:1 for the total population. Brian Cohen then suggests both that there are probably more Caribbean women capable of taking on 'white-blouse' jobs and—since the abilities of Caribbean females are unlikely to be grossly superior to males— more Caribbean men capable of white-collar occupations.

The present available statistics allow only broad comparisons, and the main issue must be the indicated lack of upward mobility between 1961 and 1966. Whatever the skills and job opportunities of the immigrant workers (the Caribbean workers came in largely before 1962), there must be some hopeful expectation that longer residence in Britain will produce signs of upward mobility. So far, this has not happened. However, it must also be pointed out that there is a need for comparative material that relates selected coloured birth-place groups to white groups that are more similar in terms of economic, migration, and other factors. A major task of investigation must be to gauge the effect of the race factor, which can be more easily done when white and coloured immigrant groups are matched in terms of occupation, industrial status, etc. How well are the Jamaicans doing, compared to Cypriots, Maltese, Poles, or Italians? Studies attempting to answer this question may well prove valuable.

2. *The Process of Racial Discrimination*

The initial discussion of the discriminatory process in Chapter 1 was extended to consider the factor of *racial* discrimination. It was suggested that there are situations, particularly visible, perhaps, during testing such as was undertaken for Chapter 7, where the fact of social race is shown to be primary in the discriminatory process (and this was called first-order racial discrimination). There are also situations where race, previously of historical primary importance, as in the creation of the North American ghettos or in the colonial relations between Britain and the West Indies, is now of secondary and supportive importance (and this was called second-order discrimination). The essential point of defining acts or processes of discrimination in this way—of first- and second-order discrimination—is that it forces recognition of the present effect of previous acts of discrimination. The North American ghettos were 'created', 'maintained', and 'condoned' by whites;[1] what is often now termed white institutional racism effectively placed Negroes into the ghettos because the Negroes were Black; and the present exclusion of Blacks from employment because of poor education, etc.—apparently on non-racial and rational grounds—is consequently shown as the result of earlier racial discrimination. Of course, first-order racial discrimination also exists in respect of Blacks from the ghetto.

While it is evident that racial discrimination does affect the non-white minorities—it was noted that the P.E.P. testing found it to range from 'the massive to the substantial' and the report in Chapter 7 found 'substantial differences between the success rates of white and coloured immigrants'—it is yet difficult to show the exact extent of its influence in the lives of the immigrant groups. This is because other factors are also potent: there are the factors of migration, such as language, dress, food, or hygiene; there is the social structure of the English receiving society itself. Taken together, these may produce a situation such as Elizabeth Burney describes in respect of one aspect of council housing where 'Direct racial discrimination has played very little part'; but which may, at the same time, be laying a foundation for increasing polarization and conflict between racial groups.

If we have a certain amount of first-order racial discrimination, albeit wrapped around by the other differences of the immigrants and by the in-built discrimination of British society, it might yet be concluded that there is little second-order racial

---

[1] See the *Report of the National Advisory Commission on Civil Disorders* (the Kerner report) (New York, Bantam Books, 1968), p. 2.

discrimination, similar say to that found in the case of the American Negro and ethnic ghettos. This is true inasmuch as the immigrant groups are recent arrivals and much of their lives has been lived in their original home-lands. But can the historical relationships, for example between Britain and the West Indies, be considered free of racial factors? In terms of historical, overseas relationships, one can therefore suggest that the position of second-order racial discrimination does indeed exist. This relationship will not be a very real one for many people: it is difficult to feel oneself bound by the actions of one's precursors in faraway lands. However, this individual sense of freedom from involvement does not mean that British society, as a whole, is not affected by its national history. The West Indies, from which many of the coloured Commonwealth immigrants have come, was in many senses created by the British: in terms of population, when 'Negroes . . . were stolen in Africa to work the lands stolen from the Indians in America';[1] in economics, where 'it is not possible to deny that these societies owe their very existence to economic exploitation';[2] in political control, under such as the crown colony system. It is a direct result of these historical links that the West Indians arrived in metropolitan Britain, as relatively poor, dependent, Black relations.

The discussion of the discriminatory situation fell easily into three main areas—housing, education, and employment, being those areas most critical to the lives of the minority groups. Additionally, the attitudes of some minority group leaders were surveyed.

(a) HOUSING

The situation of housing was divided into the categories of private rentals, owner occupation, and local authorities. But the general position of coloured immigrants was first described as 'strikingly different' from that of the population as a whole; and figures for persons per room, and those sharing households, illustrated this point. However, the primary reason for these differences was the poor housing stock available in the reception areas, and not racial discrimination. On the other hand, racial discrimination was

[1] Eric Williams, *Capitalism and Slavery* (London, André Deutsch, 1964), p. 9.
[2] Malcolm Cross in *The Varied Heritage* (London, Oxford University Press, for Institute of Race Relations, forthcoming).

likely to be primary in restricting movement out into the suburban housing.

Private rentals had fallen between 1961 and 1966 from 32 per cent to 24 per cent of all households. Coloured immigrants were heavily dependent on this diminishing supply, and particularly so in the case of furnished rentals and in London. Restrictive measures against coloured landlords, such as in Birmingham, smacked more of persecution than solution. The Race Relations Act 1968 could outlaw some discriminatory notices, but the solution of the problems depended on enabling the immigrants to compete equally in terms of economic status and for improved housing.

The rapid tendency towards owner occupation means that over half of all the households in England and Wales were in this category. The immigrants are well represented, and in the West Midlands 60 per cent of all coloured immigrant householders were in 1966 shown as owner occupiers, compared with 42 per cent of English householders. But this must be offset against the relatively low quality, multi-occupation housing into which many immigrants have moved. The limited knowledge possessed by the newcomer, and the tendency to stay close to other immigrants, limit the housing sought or acquired. But racial discrimination operates through the denial of loans, the practice, common among estate agents, of directing immigrant house-seekers to inferior property, and the restricted access offered to estates by developers. The strengthened laws will certainly make it harder to discriminate in this specific area: the first case to go to court under the 1968 legislation concerned refusal to sell an estate house to an Indian.

In the United Kingdom, a considerable part of the population lives in publicly owned housing. In London, for example, 22·2 per cent of the English were so housed in 1966; but only 4·2 per cent of the coloured immigrants had achieved the same status. The statistics do not show how far coloured families are moving into ordinary council estates. Access to this housing is of need heavily discriminatory: waiting lists usually give high importance to long residence; and long residents are again favoured under redevelopment schemes. But the coloured people are newcomers and so tend disproportionately not to be involved in re-housing under redevelopment, or in access to council estates. Further, when contact with housing departments is achieved, the traditional paternalism and Victorian values of public health officials tend to relegate the newcomers to inferior housing.

The housing situation, then, is a discriminatory one that is weighted against newcomers, against people of lower class with such alleged encumbrances as large families, and against those living in London and other urban areas. The coloured immigrants are thus in a relatively poor position—which, as recent migrants, must no doubt be expected. In terms of outward mobility, the race factor appears important and operative in situations of first-order discrimination. Testing of estate agents, study of council housing procedures, and access to loans, all suggest this.

(b) EDUCATION

Racial discrimination has not generally been perceived or acknowledged as a central problem in education. Yet there has been recognition that the immigrants, or coloured children,[1] may be deprived because they came generally from disadvantaged economic and social backgrounds.

Certain racially discriminatory situations are, however, apparently developing. Although there were in 1969 few if any 'all-immigrant' schools, the next few years may see an increase in the number of all non-white infant (5–7 years old) and, possibly, junior (8–11 years old) schools. Such segregated schools may appear as the large number of children now under four years old in immigrant households enter school for the first time —the assumption being that there is not much residential dispersal among immigrants, especially West Indians, but that the dispersal of young, white English families continues. There are, however, considerable regional variations: in the London borough of Haringey with the highest proportion of immigrant pupils, the West Indian population is widely dispersed; in the outer London borough of Brent, concentration is greater. In Inner London, concentration is low, whereas in Birmingham—the next largest educational authority but with a much lower over-all proportion of immigrant pupils—concentration is again probably greater. There has so far been little outcry at heavy concentrations which are seen as the natural consequence of residential patterns. There has been one

---

[1] According to the Department of Education definition, an immigrant child is one who was either born abroad or born in Britain to parents who arrived in the last ten years.

case of criticism of an education authority for creating a mainly coloured (mostly West Indian) new school; but this school (Grove School, Wolverhampton) was also praised by the Press as successful. It would seem possible, however, that there is a tendency in some mixed areas—for example, in Birmingham—to move towards segregated schools not because of residential patterns so much as placement policy or practice. A local organization has drawn up a list of pairs of schools within one and a half miles, of which one group is all white and the other is 30 per cent to 76 per cent immigrant. Thus, there are moves to segregation, some reflecting increased residential concentrations and some reflecting apparent under-the-counter racially discriminatory practices of placement. There is a distinction to be drawn between these moves: on the one hand, there are increasingly mono-racial schools that reflect local residential patterns and parental choice; and on the other hand, there is racial segregation fostered by the action of other parents, administrative officials, or teachers. In terms of earlier discussion, and regarding the native British as the in-group, only the second of these would be racially discriminatory.

It must seem somewhat contradictory to advance, as a further example of discrimination, the practice of dispersal by a few L.E.A.s. It is, however, the case that the immigrants (the out-group) increasingly regard dispersal and bussing as discriminatory. The schemes have been operated mainly for Indian and Pakistani children, and have been opposed because the rights of choice of school for immigrant (but not indigenous) parents have been removed. The schemes have met with opposition on other grounds: travel arrangements have sometimes gone awry with children being left at the wrong stop or lost; reception arrangements have been discriminatory; the children have been removed from assemblies and general activities, and have been banded together into all-ability, all-immigrant classes; and the children are removed from their own locality and culture. There is one additional racially discriminatory element within the present practice: this lies in the fact that only immigrant children are moved.

A further controversy is over the question of banding. The Haringey scheme which proposed to disperse lower ability pupils amongst secondary schools was heavily criticized by West

Indians on the grounds that this measure was *racially* discriminatory. Against this view is the argument that the scheme is allegedly based on merit: however, the National Foundation for Education Research, who supplied the tests, claimed that these could not be used to predict accurately the ability and attainment of some years ahead. Since West Indians tend at present to fall disproportionately into lower streams, apparently reflecting different cultural backgrounds and relatively low socio-economic statuses, a system of selection that places them *en masse* into lower bands, and from which there is little escape, may well appear also as a discriminatory practice affecting a racial group. (Here is another possible example of second-order racial discrimination.)

The general stereotyping of immigrants as a problem group in education is regarded by immigrant organizations and their spokesmen as perhaps the most important form of racial discrimination. This applies not only to the banding schemes such as at Haringey, and to statements labelling the West Indians as a group of particularly low ability and lower intelligence, who are not well motivated towards learning; but it applies also to the observation—expressed by both academics and Government officials—that immigrant school-leavers have unrealistically high aspirations. In some cases, statements indicating inferiority may be linked with tests applied only to immigrants; many immigrants have been wrongly classified as educationally sub-normal and sent to special schools or classes. The expression of hostile views, the misuse of tests, and the placement of children, have to be seen in relation to the general allocation of resources to immigrant pupils: the Asians and Southern Europeans have had a good deal of attention, whereas the West Indians were for some time comparatively neglected.

The arrangement of the children between and within schools is important: the curriculum content is no less so, particularly as this is an area in which ideas and facts about non-whites are conveyed to white children throughout the country. Little research has been done on this problem, but the little that has appeared tends to suggest that, to some extent, traditional stereotypes of superiority-inferiority still often appear in schoolbooks and in classroom teaching.[1]

[1] E.g., Janet Hill (ed.), *Books for Children: The Homelands of Immigrants to Britain* (London, Institute of Race Relations, 1971).

The educational system is necessarily a selective one: but certain of the selective procedures may be seen as partially discriminatory in racial terms, such as the bussing of immigrants only. There are also the wider issues of the content of the curriculum, and the attitudes towards coloured immigrant groups.

(c) EMPLOYMENT

Bob Hepple's main discussion of immigrants and employment was in relation to the system of industrial relations as a whole. The considerable majority of the working, economically active immigrants are in employment in industry, as shown in Chapter 3; few are self-employed; and there have been no longitudinal studies yet completed, due to the recency of the migration. But the situation is quite varied in detail, and immigrant groups in each of Sheila Patterson's stages of industrial absorption can be found in British industry. Hepple argues, however, that the matter of racial discrimination 'cuts across the generations [and] is of primary importance only in the second'. Some observers may feel that, for the first-generation immigrants, it may also prove particularly important for the small, skilled élite, and in such terms as promotion, it is also important for the ordinary workers. However, for the second generation, British education and higher aspirations may make the discriminatory barrier more obvious and more vital in the history of minority group relations in Britain.

By relating racial discrimination to the system of industrial relations as a whole, it is possible to give an integrated view of the total complex of factors—such as managerial decisions and trade union rules—which influence the position of ethnic minorities at work. Referring to rules, or the means by which jobs are controlled, three areas were examined: 'the technological characteristics of the work place and the work community'; 'the market or budgetary constraints which impinge upon the actors'; 'the locus and distribution of power in the larger society'. For the first, the rules may lie in public attitudes towards particular roles, immigrants being acceptable as waiters, or in higher status, but depersonalized, occupations, e.g. as doctors. Generally, low-status, public roles—for example, railwaymen or busmen—were acceptable. Such rules were affected by locality; also they could be changed; and Brian Cohen's study within the wool industry found that new investment in high-cost machinery led to the employment of Pakistani men, contrary to the general assumption that immigrant labour could only be associated with old, under-capitalized businesses.

The effect of 'market or budgetary constraints' can be appropriately illustrated by the tradition of racial differentiation in British shipping. Legislative discrimination, largely against Asian sailors on British ships, was removed only in 1970, but many forms of racial discrimination on these ships are specifically excepted from the provisions of the Race Relations Act 1968, so permitting traditional segregation to continue. Particular economic conditions explain why the wool industry employed immigrants, whereas in another industry, such as engineering, the economic factors may have worked to exclude newcomers. The size of particular firms may also prove crucial: in the case of light engineering, in Croydon, some larger firms had developed techniques for the selection and training of coloured workers, whereas smaller firms tended to favour particular groups, excluding others. More generally, the national economic situation will affect the operation of such as redundancy rules.

Hepple then writes that 'the power context is crucial in defining the status of managers, local labour core, ethnic minorities, and Government and private agencies'. Unlike earlier ethnic groups, such as the Poles, the tendency has been for coloured immigrant groups to participate in and support the existing trade unions, rather than to found new ethnic or racial organizations. However, communication between the union and its immigrant members may be very poor, as Peter Marsh showed in his study on the strike of Punjabi workers in Southall; and immigrants do not yet participate in the trade union leadership. Managements have also defined rules; and the Government agencies do this, with the Department of Employment and Productivity claiming some success for its policy of withdrawing employment exchange facilities from racially discriminating employers (but exercised only once up to November 1967, for example).

It is possible to define such rules as internal, i.e. affecting jobs within enterprises; and external, i.e. depending on persons outside the enterprise. The internal rules—such as shop-floor 'understandings' or establishment of ethnic work units—are discriminatory and strongly resistant to change. The external rules—such as the legislation and official trade union policy on race—tend sometimes towards the anti-discriminatory. However, the effective external rules were achieved largely from voluntary processes, and not through legislation. In the case of the Race Relations Act 1968, the first legislation to cover discrimination in employment, the industrial relations system dominated the requirements of the anti-discrimination laws, as shown in Chapter 9; and this is not surprising since the use of the law was 'strenuously opposed' by both the Trades Union Congress and the Confederation of British Industry. 'Peace' has been considered more important than justice for individual victims of discrimination. All employment complaints go first to the Department of Employment and Productivity, and then to a suitable voluntary industrial body if it exists; and 'racial quotas' are legalized. This is not to say that the Act will not have some good effect; for example, it may open certain middle-class jobs to immigrants, or protect employers against the real or fancied prejudices of customers, employees, and competitors. The setting up of such special machinery, to deal with complaints, is important as it brings together management and labour in joint decisions.

There has been little activity outside of industry, since the local voluntary liaison committees (discussed particularly in Chapter 12) were unsuited to the task of handling individual complaints; and since the coloured immigrant groups have not produced bodies comparable in influence to, say, the Trades Advisory Council of the Board of Deputies of British Jews.

In the field of Government employment, there has been little active pursuit of 'equal opportunity'. Government contracts did not, until 1969, contain an anti-discrimination clause (which is, in any event, mainly of declaratory effect); a quota was believed to have been operated by the Army; cases of discrimination in nationalized industries did not bring Government intervention; local police authorities have been reluctant until fairly recently to recruit coloured people; and some councils have, for example, banned the wearing of turbans by busmen.[1]

The picture painted of Britain's industry is one of a traditionalist, discriminatory, largely unchanging industrial relations

---

[1] For two illuminating case studies, see David Beetham, *Transport and Turbans: A Comparative Study in Local Politics* (London, Oxford University Press, for Institute of Race Relations, 1970).

system. The progress of the newly arrived immigrant groups depends much upon general economic conditions, the particular industry, area, and size of business. The 1968 anti-discriminatory legislation has been moulded to fit only the traditional system, retaining some discriminatory practices in law, but may still have some beneficial effect in changing the rules.

(d) WHITE-COLLAR WORKERS

Because there was little information on the position and progress of coloured white-collar workers, a study was commissioned for this volume. In contrast to the broad survey of Bob Hepple, the content of Chapter 7 by Roger Jowell and Patricia Prescott-Clarke covers simply the treatment of applications for white-collar jobs: in all, 128 genuine job vacancies were applied for by 256 'applicants' (i.e. two matched applicants per job, one British-born white and one immigrant). The letters of application were constructed to test discrimination on grounds of race (country of origin), level of education, and country of schooling; and although the letters were not then sent by genuine applicants, the employers approached did not know this and treated the applications as genuine. Four job types were applied for (sales and marketing vacancies, accountancy and office management, electrical engineering, and secretarial) in four areas (Greater London, Birmingham/Wolverhampton, Nottingham/Derby/Leicester, and Reading/Windsor/Slough). The applications were matched for such factors as age, marital status, present and previous employers, date of despatch, style of letter.

The results were, firstly, that, in the authors' words, 'Using colour as an independent variable, we found substantial differences between the success rates of white and coloured immigrants.' For white immigrants (Australians and Cypriots), the success rate was 74 per cent, and for coloured immigrants (West Indians and Asians), the rate was 52 per cent. This over-all colour difference disguises the more extreme variation between a success rate of 78 per cent for Australians and 35 per cent for Asians. Only country of origin (race) emerged as a significant variable: the differences between job types, areas, qualifications, and schooling, were not considered significant.

What do these results mean? Certain factors need stressing: that in the granting of interviews, discrimination is presumably less severe than in the granting of jobs; that the pool of potential white-collar applicants created had education and qualifications probably far in excess of their real counterparts; and that the discrimination here exposed would in all likelihood be hidden from those discriminated against, and from the Race Relations Board. Although the findings of this limited study do not necessarily apply more widely, within the scope of the study there was severe discrimination against coloured people with *equal* qualifications to the whites.[1] If this pattern is more widely applicable, it means that there may be a burying of the coloureds at the foot of the social structure, rather than the correction of a disadvantaged position. Additionally, the use of the testing techniques here developed should provide more information on aspects of discrimination.

(e) THE ATTITUDES OF SOME MINORITY GROUP LEADERS

The immigrants are not in a position of much power within British society. They are consequently less concerned with controlling the introduction and implementation of anti-discriminatory measures, than with the experience of the effectiveness of such measures. Leaders from the West Indian and Asian communities were therefore interviewed, and it will be remembered that it was originally suggested that it is important to test the perceptions of immigrants within the process of discrimination. So we move from the act of discrimination and from the in-group to the attitudes of the out-group.

The West Indian community had few formal organizations and few formal leaders. Indeed, to suggest a common 'umbrella' leadership is to impose a unity and conformity among the Caribbean islanders themselves, and also the mainland Guyanese, that does not as yet exist. It is also to cover over the considerable ethnic differences that exist in parts of the Caribbean, such as Trinidad and Guyana. Some of those interviewed queried the concept of leadership as alien and European, and the attitudes expressed were generally the articulate and thoughtful views of individuals. But the lack of community organizations and formal leadership should not lead one to suppose that the views are simply those of individuals: they may also be to an increasing

---

[1] In defence of optimism, one might applaud the fact that the success rate for West Indians and Cypriots was similar at 69 per cent. Whether this rate would, in fact, be sustained with more West Indian applicants for white-collar jobs, is open to question: the present limited numbers of such applicants may make them appear unduly exotic.

extent representative of the West Indians in Britain, although they have not so far found much institutional expression.

Manderson-Jones suggests a tentative division into a 'conservative-moderate' and a 'radical-militant' leadership, on the basis of the interviews conducted; but it must be remembered that this apparent division is also mainly based on divergencies over the strategy to be employed in dealing with discrimination, and the ultimate end sought. It can, in practice, be modified to the extent that certain leaders will, on different occasions and before different audiences, display different attitudes. This may reflect a continuing ambivalence to integration into British society, that can bring the chairman of CARD (believed by many to be a quite militant organization) into the Community Relations Commission (regarded as Governmental and conservative) as a Deputy Chairman.

All the West Indian leaders interviewed were born or brought up in the West Indies. The militant-radical identifies with Blackness and Afro-internationalism; the conservative-moderate has a 'Euro' identification with aspirations directed towards the upper (and so whiter) stages of the class structure—in short, he hopes to become 'an upper-middle class West Indian domiciled in Britain [but] able to return "home" for sunny vacations at Christmas'. Both would like an England free of racial prejudice: the first sees the system so prejudice-filled that it must be abandoned, and the second still hopes to see it purged. The emphasis on violence was still, in 1968, muted, with both categories expressing 'a preference for peaceful means'.

These general attitudes partly determined more specific attitudes over anti-discriminatory measures. The community relations effort by the N.C.C.I. was apparently unknown or considered unimportant; but those interviewed were well aware of the legislation. The arguments in favour of the law were clearly put by one leader: 'The law creates and is itself the norm. Consequently the racists of society are placed outside the law, which therefore tends to weaken their support and legitimacy.' And another referred to the law as 'the leadership given by Government to public opinion for change'. The radical viewpoint, however, in the words of one leader, is that 'the destruction of the system . . . is the prerequisite to any form of meaningful change'. And supportive points can be cited such as: the inclusion of the racial incitement clauses in the 1965 Act 'as a "whip" to be used against the back of the Black man'; the limited scope of the 1965 Act condoning by implication racist behaviour in other areas; the 'impotence' of the Race Relations Board; the absence of machinery for immigrant organizations to elect to the Board; the so-called Asian legislation (the 1968 immigration Act restricting the ingress of Kenya Asians and others); the 'racial quota' system in the Race Relations Act 1968; etc. Other measures, such as employers' efforts to increase the ratio of coloured employees, received varying responses.

The movement of feeling is towards the radical and violent approach: one conservative commented that 'Up to 1967 . . . people thought that integration was a practical reality. . . . The West Indians here feel that they gave their hand but that the clasp was refused and so they have to withdraw it'; and another that 'counter-violence . . . certainly . . . seems to be the developing trend'. There is a general acceptance that British society is racially discriminatory, that the Governmental counter-measures have not proved effective, and that a new emphasis must be placed upon self-help.

The Asian leaders depended much more upon institutional organizations, over half coming from religious or socio-cultural societies. All had been born outside Britain, but the home-land values were diminishing in importance: on the one hand, traditional factors, such as caste and economic help, had been undermined by a more equal access to wealth through employment; on the other, new demands, such as knowledge of English, created a new élite.

There was general agreement over the existence of racial discrimination: it was suggested that 'It was a dream for a coloured man to get a council flat.' In the fields of employment, education, and housing, and in relation to treatment by policemen and by white doctors, discrimination was alleged. The respondents generally thought that prejudice was stronger amongst the lower classes, offering the widespread support for Mr. Powell as an example; but they also felt that it was more difficult for the well-educated immigrant to get a job. However, three leaders offered different views, ranging from the view that there was no racial discrimination, to the views that there was much less than was usually alleged and that it was the fault of the immigrants. Most leaders, however, regarded the receiving society as the culprit. What of the prevention of racial discrimination? 'The N.C.C.I. was almost unknown to most of those interviewed and those who knew of it did not see much hope in it'; and it was felt that the gap between immigrants and community was not being bridged. The Race Relations Act 1968 received various comments, mostly critical and some mistaken; however, its value was considered much offset by the Commonwealth Immigrants Act 1968 which 'stinks of racialism' by restricting the entry of Kenya Asians because they were 'a bit more tanned'. The Board was held to have only a symbolic status, largely, it seems, because of weak enforcement powers. In general, opinion of the Government's policy was poor.

There was complete agreement that the Indian and Pakistani communities should contribute to the solution of the problem. But only one of the leaders argued for a united effort by all coloured groups, and the leaders generally saw little value in co-operating with West Indians. None of the leaders favoured violence.

Those West Indian and Asian leaders interviewed were well aware of the discriminatory society in which they lived; and they also knew, often in detail, of the anti-discrimination legislation; but they knew much less of the community relations activities. They generally had a poor view of the Government's intentions, and of the effectiveness of the Government's and others' anti-discriminatory measures. The West Indians were concentrating increasingly on racial solidarity and self-help, and the Asians saw value in contributions from their community towards integration. The interviews with the leaders suggested that there was little effective co-operation between these two communities; but there have been successful organizations involving different communities, notably CARD during a period of perhaps two years, the Joint Council for the Welfare of Immigrants, and—for shorter periods—various Black Power coalitions.

3. *The Prevention of Racial Discrimination*

In this study, particular emphasis was placed on specific anti-discriminatory measures and organizations. The first of these to be analysed was the Race Relations Board and the legislation that framed and empowered its work. The methods of measuring effectiveness outlined in the first chapter, included the recording of incidence of acts of discrimination and the use of comparisons in time and between groups. Especial emphasis was laid upon the need for comparisons in time and for the use of historical perspective, when the divide between attitudes and behaviour may be considered decreased and when the movement of groups within a stratification system is more clearly visible.

(a) THE HISTORY OF THE LEGISLATION

Since the period of race legislation is a short one, beginning as late as 1965 with the Race Relations Act of that year (that is, if, as seems reasonable, one excludes the immigration legislation), it is all the more important to examine closely the evolution and the intent of its makers. Louis Kushnick argues that the fact of the recency of the migration, the relatively small size of the coloured population, and the respect for the rule of law commonly believed to be inherent in the British nation, all inclined politicians and others to consider the colour problem a small one. The newness of the problem meant that there was little rigid and entrenched opposition to legislation; but this newness also meant that the legislation was ineffective. Because the problem was viewed as a minor one, the Home Secretary had argued that it was 'as much a question of education as of legislation', and that the legislation was likely to have 'less emphasis on the enforcement side than on the declaratory nature of the Act itself'.[1] Additionally, the politicians feared that the general public would not accept stronger measures. Kushnick stresses the importance of allying legislation to 'positive Governmental programmes', and the need for vigorous political leadership, as for example evinced by timing and implicit assumptions of the Government's replies to Enoch Powell's speeches: the Prime Minister did not reply to the speech of 20 April 1968 until a fortnight later, and the Home Secretary talked in terms of 'our people' and 'them'.

The Labour Party, through the involvement of a few individuals like Fenner (now Lord) Brockway, had become committed to the implementation of anti-discrimination legislation on reaching office. But the Bill introduced in April 1965 was restricted in scope to places of public resort, based on criminal penalties that could only be invoked by the Director of Public

[1] *The Sunday Times* (28 January 1968).

Prosecution, and contained sanctions against incitement to race hatred in speech or writing. This last element had been introduced largely because of Jewish pressure, and it was to prove ineffective and possibly an embarrassment to the Race Relations Board and to the local conciliation committees that were formed under the Act. The principle of conciliation was adopted during the progress of the Bill, but it was felt unnecessary or impossible to provide for much in the way of enforcement machinery. Louis Kushnick has suggested that the meaning of much of the North American experience was ignored. On the committee, some seven Labour and two Conservative M.P.s failed to get even shops included within the Act; and it is a notable and consistent feature of racial issues within British politics that the division has not been along strictly party lines. However, throughout the passage of both Acts, the Conservatives were generally more opposed to legislation than were the Labour Government.

The 1965 Act was thus the fulfilment of an earlier commitment, but was regarded by its makers as having a largely declaratory nature, and was not provided with much enforcement machinery.

That the 1965 Act was, in fact, held to be inadequate, in a number of ways, was illustrated by the willingness of the next Home Secretary, Roy Jenkins, and the Chairman of the Board, to consider extensions to the legislation. Here it is important to note that the research findings in the P.E.P. report had the very direct effect of winning wider support for such extension. For example, *The Times* changed its position following publication of the report; and a House of Commons motion for extending legislation appeared within a week, and was supported by over one hundred Labour M.P.s.

The 1968 Bill was introduced by a new Home Secretary, James Callaghan. There was again the reliance on conciliation, and again also the restricted powers for the Board. For example, conciliation committees still had no authority to enforce the attendance of witnesses. A second major difficulty lay in the field of employment where, as described, the traditional industrial relations system prepared to take over the role of investigator. Nevertheless, by extending the scope of the Bill (to cover housing, employment, credit and insurance facilities, education, all places of public resort including shops and offices, and the Crown), a 'courageous step forward' had been taken. Kushnick counter-balances this credit with the observation that 'its enforcement measures included a number of thoroughly obnoxious and dangerous loop-holes'. On the enforcement side, again the North American experience—now presented for British consumption through the Street report—was largely spurned. Apart from the fact that (i) the Board was given no powers of subpoena, and (ii) part of the machinery for conciliation in employment cases was placed with the Department of Employment and Productivity and industry's own voluntary grievance machinery, the Board was given no powers to make positive orders for the provision of the job, accommodation, etc., in dispute, or of the next available ones. The obnoxious clauses included the preservation of segregation in the merchant navy; the introduction of an (undefined) 'racial balance' as cause for refusing employment (although this clause could not be used to exclude non-whites wholly or mainly educated in Britain). But, at 1971, the Board believed its powers to take to court had in practice ensured attendance of witnesses, and the offering of jobs, etc.

It is relatively easy to discuss the 1965 Act in relation to the subsequent Act; at the time of writing it was, of course, not easy to discuss the 1968 Act in relation to its actual working. The arguments in favour of particular American experience are therefore hypothetical inasmuch as they rely upon cross-cultural estimates of the future development of the race situation. Against the arguments in favour of the American experience, which point out the need for stronger powers, for example, can be set the belief of the Board that by mid-1969, no single case had been delayed or adversely affected by its present limited powers. The validity of the alternative viewpoints will probably become clearer over the years.

The discussion of legislation is also based on the assumption that such legislation is indeed beneficial. It can here be noted that such as the American and Canadian experiences do suggest the specific effectiveness of certain legislation[1]—a thesis that is also supported by some of the British experience now reviewed.

[1] For example, see John H. Denton, 'The Effectiveness of State Anti-Discrimination Laws in the United States', *Race* (Vol. X., No. 1, July 1968), pp. 85–92; and Daniel G. Hill and C. Marshall Pollock, 'Human Rights Legislation in Ontario', *Race* (Vol. X, No. 2, October 1967), pp. 193–204.

(b) THE RACE RELATIONS BOARD

The Board was constituted in 1966 and its functions were, of course, limited to the letter of the 1965 Act. Its major tasks were the appointment of the local conciliation committees (eleven were set up in 1966–8), the employment of officers to service the committees, and the decision to remit cases to the Attorney-General for possible prosecution. The composition of the local committees, who had the powers of investigating complaints and attempting conciliation, had to satisfy a number of criteria, including knowledge of race relations, industry, and housing. Brian Cohen believes that the Board was able to effect better selection for its committees than was the N.C.C.I.; and this was followed up with better liaison. Because of the small number of committees, a headquarters representative generally attended the local committee meetings; the local conciliation officers had a monthly one-day meeting in London; and the headquarters kept a copy of all complaints and conciliation decisions.

In size, the Board grew, for example, from an over-all total (headquarters and local permanent staff) of 14 in March 1967, to 68 in April 1970. In income, the amount rose from £46,833 in 1967–8, to £161,076 in 1969–70. These totals are, of course, less than those for the N.C.C.I./C.R.C.

Officially limited to the brief scope for action allowed by the 1965 Act, some of the Board's activity fell into the area of extending legislation, under the guise of research and through co-sponsorship of the P.E.P. and Street reports, and the subsequent publication of these reports. In 1966–7, some 70 per cent of complaints had fallen outside the scope of the 1965 Act; in 1967–8, this was so for some 83 per cent of complaints.

The experience in cases that fell within the Act related largely to public houses (pubs). Here it seems that a real, albeit limited, achievement was reached, largely by the behind-the-scenes negotiations held with breweries, the Licensed Victuallers' Association, and others. It seems that clear-cut displays of race discrimination did diminish. Yet certain more sophisticated forms of discrimination may have replaced those initially practised; virtual segregation may have developed by the practice of serving coloured people only in one bar, or overcharging them or keeping them waiting for service. The number of complaints about public houses did not diminish during the last six months of the old Act.

The period before the 1968 Act, then, did see some success in the area of public houses, although more detailed case studies would be needed to estimate the degree and kind of effectiveness achieved. More importantly, the old Act was of such limited scope that the Board was inevitably drawn into the really crucial fields of housing, employment, and education.

The review, by Marna Glyn, of the complaints received by the Board, serves not to illustrate the incidence of discriminatory acts in Britain, but simply to provide some details about the referral of some of these acts. While, for example, the total of 3,040 complaints received up to 19 November 1969 cannot reflect the extent of racial discrimination, neither can the influence of the Board—so it is argued—be judged in terms of single cases settled: 'one finding of unlawful discrimination may affect many people throughout a large enterprise or whole industry'. Regional variations in the numbers of complaints are related to the vigour of local groups, and the majority of complaints fall into the areas of employment and housing. During the first year of the 1968 Act, just under half of all the complaints concerned housing.

Since the 1968 Act, it is suggested that the only major source of complaints falling outside the scope of the Board is complaints against the police. But a constant factor has been the high proportion of findings of 'no unlawful discrimination', for example, in 545 out of 1,562 cases investigated in 1968–9. While the reasons for this are not clear, it is thought that inadequate understanding (among the population at large) of the powers of the Board, and poor communications (as between employer and employees) may contribute.

Despite the poor appreciation of the Board's showing by the immigrant leaders, the Race Relations Board had achieved something of a success at least amongst workers in the race relations field. Charged to fulfil limited legal undertakings, and operating reasonably effectively, it would seem to have made some impact against racial discrimination both in terms of leadership factors and small changes in certain fields, e.g. pubs, housing, and employment.[1] But some question marks remain over the

---

[1] Further evidence on success can be gleaned from the Board's 'Case Histories': in housing, a South of England property company refused to let to a coloured woman and 'In using her rights under the law the complainant not only won the apology to which she was entitled but made sure that when other people approach this company

future: firstly, there is the view of Louis Kushnick that the penalties will be found insufficient for sustained effect; secondly, it is not yet clear how wide the Board's effect is, nor how much value is ascribed to its work by the immigrant communities more generally; thirdly, it is not clear how much support will be given over a longer period to the Board by the Government and the native British.[1]

(c) THE NATIONAL COMMITTEE FOR COMMONWEALTH IMMIGRANTS, THE COMMUNITY RELATIONS COMMISSION

The second Government agency was the N.C.C.I., re-formed after the Race Relations Act 1968 as the C.R.C. It was older in origin than the Board, being set up in 1965 and having links with earlier national bodies (the C.I.A.C. and the first N.C.C.I.) and earlier local committees. It was larger than the Board; its permanent headquarters and local staff numbered about 70 in early 1969 (as opposed to 59); and its expenditure was over £284,408 in 1969–70, as opposed to £161,076 for the Board.

Its aims were set out in the 1965 White Paper as 'providing advice and information' and 'assisting in the formation of local liaison committees and regional organizations'. In 1969, with the establishment of the C.R.C., these dual aims remained; but there had, in fact, been real changes in policy and practice. The provision of advice and information had been performed at a high level by the main, governing council of the National Committee, and chiefly on the issue of immigration. From 1969, the direct link with the Prime Minister was discontinued, and the main

---

they will not be treated in this way'; in employment, a coloured worker was discharged, but 'Both the firm and the manager gave assurances against further discrimination and the firm also paid the complainant £44 . 8s.—the actual financial loss he had suffered because of the sacking.' (From Race Relations Board, press release issued 25 November 1970).

[1] The complaints procedure has led to a series of harrassments levied at the Board by white British, some of whom have the apparent intention of ridiculing its work. Perhaps the most publicized case was that of the Scottish porridge. The Board had the statutory duty of having to investigate all complaints submitted to it, and had no discretionary powers in this respect. In this particular case, a complaint was made because advertisement for a 'Scottish daily' was, in effect, advertising by national origin. It is worth noting that a modicum of literary ingenuity and legal knowledge would have enabled the advertiser to seek a skilled maker of 'plain cooking' and Scottish porridge without involving the wrath of the law.

immigration topic was largely abandoned.[1] Advice had also flown from the specialist advisory panels set up by the N.C.C.I. to national Government, local government, and agencies in the field; and these panels (excepting the group on education) were initially discontinued. However, to a certain extent, it is possible to see these changes as the necessary preliminaries to substituting specialist, professional advice for the earlier, predominantly voluntarist advisers. Such advice may be less spectacular and public, but need not be less effective. However, it would also seem that Government departments, such as the D.E.P., have been building up their own specialist expertise, and it is not clear how much they will rely upon the C.R.C. for advice. The second main aim of assisting with local committees continued with little change, although it is possible to see a weakening of the already tenuous links with the civil rights bodies and immigrant communities.

These, and supplementary, aims covered a broad area of community work that was sometimes weakly defined: it was noted that the Chairman of the C.R.C. had claimed that the Commission had 'broad terms of reference incorporating all aspects of community life and relationship', and that the plan adopted was 'to strengthen the movement for harmonious community relations by drawing on the tremendous fund of goodwill we know to exist everywhere'. The linking together of the immigration-integration debate confused these ill-defined integration aims still further; and the use of voluntary advisers was to a considerable extent abandoned after three years, in favour of a statutory status that confirmed the Government as the real master. By mid-1969, the local committees had received instructions on how to apply for grants, and a code of rules for their local liaison officer (if any), but no general instructions on national or local priorities or programmes had yet been issued.

The working of the N.C.C.I./C.R.C. was reviewed under a number of heads. These included the main Committee, which was not successful in changing Government policy on immigration. Also there were the advisory panels, of which some—for

---

[1] 'Asked whether he believed in the restrictions on commonwealth immigration in the 1967 and 1968 Acts, Mr. Cousins [the Chairman of the C.R.C.] said that he did not believe that the Commission needed to have a public attitude on this': in *The Times* (26 June 1969). See also Chapter 11.

example, those dealing with housing and education—would seem to have had some effect. Through a pattern, often of investigation, publishing a report, organizing conferences, and lobbying the relevant department, some impact was made; thus the Education Panel did achieve results in respect of teacher training colleges. The third head was that of the Administrative Staff, who may have been overburdened by the vigour of the main, voluntary Committee and the voluntary panels to the detriment of their work in assisting with local committees. But in mid-1969, some time after the end of the panels, there were only two officers in the field who were primarily engaged in the co-ordination of the local committees, or councils. Other tasks of the Administrative Staff included publications; a certain amount of limited information and library work; and organization of a considerable number of conferences, often in conjunction with the activities of the panels. More emphasis was placed upon giving grants for local projects. Some of the N.C.C.I. activity was thus changed in 1968, but of that remaining, perhaps most important was its role as co-ordinator of the local committees, with the provision of professional advice for central Government also important.

It is more difficult to estimate the effectiveness of a community relations organization, such as the N.C.C.I./C.R.C., than one charged with a specific task, such as the Race Relations Board. But it has already been suggested that the N.C.C.I./C.R.C. was not very effective in its three main relationships: those between the N.C.C.I./C.R.C. and the Government, the immigrant committees, and the local committees. In the case of the immigrant communities—and without accepting the hypothesis that the existence of an N.C.C.I. has effectively destroyed the civil rights movement—it is yet possible to argue that the local officer and committee could act as a buffer between host and immigrant, in such a way that immigrant community development was stunted at a local level. Specifically, their political consciousness and action were channelled into the local committee and away from the customary political structures. In the case of the local councils, it was argued that the wide organizational representation did not include the interest groups that in fact controlled the life chances of the immigrants, but did include undue middle-class representation, and was, in any case, sometimes opposed to the aims of racial integration. In the case of the Commission itself, the total lack of representation from the local community relations councils and officers, let alone the radical grass-roots control envisaged by Wilfred Wood, coupled with the inadequate links emerging from the N.C.C.I./C.R.C. itself, did mean that the links with the councils were often insufficient. The survey reported on by Margot Levy in Chapter 12 confirms this: in 1968, only one of the committee officers interviewed was satisfied with the support received from the N.C.C.I. In the case of the relationship with the Government, the decrease of publicly offered advice has been noted, as well as the failure to change Government policy, while the provision of professional advice was, at the end of 1970, still at an early stage.

The N.C.C.I./C.R.C. was, therefore, not very effective, nor indeed—given its resources and the existing situation—was it likely to be successful in achieving any major change in British society. There were, however, some limited achievements in the educational field and in the creation of a more professional body of community relations officers. Despite the challenging argument that the N.C.C.I./C.R.C. participated in an era of poor political leadership, it is possible to argue the contrary to the extent that first the N.C.C.I., and then the C.R.C., stood as evidence of the Government's commitment to action against racial discrimination. The importance of this commitment is often ignored because it has been imperfectly sustained; but it should not be left out of the account.

(d) THE LOCAL COMMITTEES

One of the two main tasks of the N.C.C.I. was to assist with the formation and work of the local voluntary liaison committees. Hannan Rose writes of ten of these committees, first recounting their historical origins which lay in such local organizations as the Committee for the Welfare of Colonial Workers in Bristol, set up in 1952, and the Consultative Committee for the Welfare of Coloured People, set up in Nottingham in 1955. They were the product of local initiative, often sponsored by bodies like the National Council of Social Service, and sometimes receiving special financial grants from charitable trusts. At this time, the national Government were rejecting requests for support. It is suggested that the Nottingham and Notting Hill incidents of 1958 helped to accelerate the creation of new committees, loosely linked with the National Council. In 1965, the National Committee took over responsibility for the committees.

The development of a broad policy can be seen in the names of the committees: the early emphasis on 'Friendship and Welfare' gave way to 'Liaison', and the idea of providing a 'bridge' between communities; and in early 1967, this in turn gave way to the concept of 'Community Relations'. However, 5 per cent of members of the local voluntary committees, when interviewed, had 'virtually no idea' over the question of role: 20 to 25 per cent of the interviewees opposed the welfare approach, while supporting the need for political expression through, for example, public statements; and the remaining 70 to 75 per cent covered a wide range of views, extending to the conservative concept that the immigrants should be helped 'to conform to the standards of the host society'. The activities and attitudes of the committees as a whole also varied, mainly reflecting the influence of the remaining founding members and the particular localities. Generally, members representing institutions tended to be more conservative; and local authorities facing committees founded by politically committed individuals, were also conservative. Political control of the local council by the main political parties did not seem so important as the personal contacts made with the different local government departments. Little attention had apparently been paid to the problem of promoting effective relations between the committee and local government, and the working of the local committees and their sub-committees often seemed 'one of muddle and an amateur approach'.

Hannan Rose argues that the N.C.C.I. took on a difficult job that had been neglected during the fifties and early sixties; and that, partly because of the increasing number of local committees, those in operation had 'very little contact' with the national headquarters. Further, regional structures were not established as forecast in 1965 and the Regional Development Officers were based in London, all of which helped to create a 'vacuum in central leadership'. A heavy strain was thus placed upon the local liaison officer.

Because of the newness of the problem, the tendency has been to import American thinking to articulate 'community relations'. In fact, a scheme of 'community development' may have to be adopted, with increasing emphasis placed on involving the

15*

minority groups in projects 'directed towards immediate action to fulfil immediate needs'. This involvement in pre-school play-groups and housing associations will, however, demand reorganization of policy and administration, and will face political difficulties.

The second study in Chapter 12, by Margot Levy, was an evaluation of the work of thirteen local officers in a conurbation. The survey illustrated continuing problems in committee structure, in relationships with national and local authorities, and, more generally, in community relations work. The officers felt practical experience was their best qualification, and—not surprisingly—that colour played an important part in their work, with multi-racial teams evidently being developed (i.e. if the officer was white, then the assistant or secretary would be Black, etc.). On the committee structure, the officers mostly felt that there was inadequate immigrant representation and, sometimes, overmuch local authority representation. About half were happy with their committees. On the relationship with the local authority, there were ambiguities: since grants were given to the local com-mittees, the authorities resented attacks against them and all but one of the officers preferred to have their offices away from the Town Hall. At the time of the survey, in 1968, only one of the N.C.C.I. officers was not dissatisfied with the links with the National Committee, the 'overwhelming consensus' then being that 'the N.C.C.I. was failing to provide them with any help apart from financial support'. There appeared to be good relations with the police, although it should be noted that there has been an apparent deterioration in police-immigrant relations since 1968.[1]

In discussing their role and work, the officers generally opposed a welfare orientation, but were often drawn into welfare work. Four Black officers were the most optimistic about educat-ing the white receiving society towards less hostile attitudes; and the officers were generally in favour of educating the immigrants, but in the wider sense of using social services and other facilities. The Blacks apparently had the better links with immigrant communities, and two were active politically. There was emphasis

---

[1] For example, in a talk at the Institute of Race Relations (2 March 1970), Jeff Crawford, then Secretary of the West Indian Standing Conference, who had earlier been optimistic about relationships, stated that the police were 'the biggest scourge of the Black community'. See also article on the trouble over the Mangrove restaurant, in *Race Today* (October 1970), p. 376.

on publicity—all issuing news-letters, etc.—and there was a variety of projects under way. Perhaps because of the pioneering factor and pressure of their work, only three out of the ten kept records of cases. From an earlier argument, it will be remembered that the councils could reasonably be regarded as involved in anti-discriminatory work, particularly in terms of correcting more general situations of discrimination: four officers stressed that they were 'fighters against discrimination', but there was no consistency in their relationships with the Board. One officer passed on about 60 cases a year, but most referred very few; some officers favoured personal conciliation rather than referral, and another adopted the technique of direct action. They assessed their general success with 'qualified pessimism'.

A contrasting footnote was provided by the interviews with the officers working for religious organizations, who benefited from clear and effective support from their employers, more exact role definition, and even claimed what would seem to be more effective links with the Black Power organizations.

(e) SPECIFIC AND GENERAL MEASURES

It was suggested in Chapter 1 that it is possible to distinguish between specific and general measures: specific being those directed at some part of a process of racial discrimination and general being those directed at situations not primarily of racial discrimination but which in operation may affect racial and minority groups. Much of the earlier discussion has centred on organizations and measures designed for effectiveness in relation to the race factor, such as the Race Relations Board, and the Community Relations Commission and its local committees. But the possible effectiveness of general measures should not be forgotten.

It is clear that such measures may have certain advantages. Firstly, they may not be seen by the host community as favouring an (unpopular) minority. Overt discrimination in favour of racial minority groups has been repeatedly attacked: 'racial discrimination is just as bad when it is in favour of races different from the rulers of the community as when it is discrimination against minority and other races. . . .'[1] Secondly, general measures may

---

[1] Quoted by Louis Kushnick in Chapter 9.

not be viewed by the minority racial groups as paternalistic, or even as racially oppressive. The Race Relations Act 1965 was heavily criticized by many of the West Indian leaders interviewed, not for what it did, but for what it left undone; and it was 'the general view that the legislation in existence is racial and acts against the Black man'.[1] Thirdly, general measures may be larger in scope than those designed expressly for minority needs. Put simply, is it the case that a general programme of urban renewal—that improves the housing, education, or employment prospects in an area containing a non-white population—is more effective than specific, racial measures?

Nicholas Deakin, in Chapter 13, first reviewed Government action in respect of the immigrants, in an account which necessarily emphasized the negative aspects—i.e. *laissez-faire* and minimal paternalist involvement set against a concern over the problems that the immigrants might present during integration. In moving on to record the increasing commitment to integrationist measures, notably under Roy Jenkins, he also stressed the debilitating effect of the repeated restrictionist immigration laws. Next, for the first time in this volume, there was a review of Government measures, which might be termed general in respect of minority groups, particularly the Urban Programme. The sum allocated was comparatively small, first £3·5 millions, and subsequently £4 millions. But Deakin argues that 'Such programmes are of immense importance for the future of race relations: they deal for the first time with one of the major causes of interracial tensions, i.e. the competition for scarce resources in the inner city.'

This stage, it is suggested, marked a shift from central Government's dropping immigrant problems on to the desks of local government, through limited intervention by central Government to correct specific malfunctions, to the assumption that the central Government must accept some responsibility for urban and community redevelopment. The former responsibility of the Colonial Office has also moved to the Home Office, a Department with capacity for considering social problems—although, unfortunately, immigrant questions are sometimes apparently subordinated to the supposed demands of immigration

[1] See Chapter 8.

control, and there are strong arguments for preferably moving the integration aspects a stage, or department, further.[1]

In Britain increasing emphasis has been placed upon special area programmes, such as the Plowden Committee's advocation of educational priority areas, or the Seebohm Committee's priority areas for community development. But general measures, such as these and the Urban Programme, can come to be regarded as inadequate. In respect of measures against poverty, for example, it is suggested that 'programmes aimed at reducing the incidence of poverty . . . may do little for, or even divert resources from, the majority of the poor, and may not significantly reduce the number in poverty in the whole country'.[2] Although general measures may thus appear impressive in size and scope, they may yet impinge less upon particular groups as a whole and on members of groups in particular areas, than at first thought.

The relative advantage of specific and general measures can be viewed in a further dimension, in respect of specific anti-discriminatory measures implemented not by specially established race relations agencies but by long-established and important parts of the general society. Brian Cohen discusses the limited measures taken by the police and by non-Government employers. In a draft paper, he argues that the race issue must be set alongside difficulties in police-public relations stemming from such problems as motoring, drug-taking, and political dissent. The police have an important community relations role and considerable powers of discretion, and have claimed that there is no particular racial discrimination in the police force, nor, consequently, is there any need for special measures. However, the police have introduced some limited teaching on race into their training programmes, and have appointed a number of liaison officers. Some immigrants have made strong allegations that the police do discriminate on grounds of race, including among examples of discriminatory behaviour, the planting of drugs; and there has been only a small handful of coloured recruits to the police force. Unfortunately, the police continue largely to control the investigation of complaints against the police force, and it is not possible to provide much

[1] See, for example, Nicholas Deakin, *Whitehall and Integration: An Unauthorized Programme* (London, Institute of Race Relations Briefing Paper, 1968). He argues that the Home Office is inevitably affected by its watch-dog, policing role. This Department controls both the immigration officials and the police.

[2] Adrian Sinfield, 'Poverty Rediscovered', *Race* (Vol. X, No. 2, October 1968), p. 205.

definite proof for or against allegations of discrimination. But police outlooks continue as traditional and authoritarian, and the present measures of education and co-operation seem inadequate.

In British society, there is clearly much opportunity for anti-discriminatory action in the non-Governmental area; but Brian Cohen's discussion indicates that, in the field of employment, very little has been done. Even when one substantial firm adopted a positive programme of recruitment, it required repeated direction and checking from senior management to ensure that the declared policy was being partially implemented. The advent of the 1968 legislation, however, did cause a flurry of debate on the part of a number of employers; but it is as yet too early to see how much practices have, in fact, changed.[1]

Finally, the discussion of measures, specific and general, must not be regarded as exhaustive. There are a number of agencies, working in the race field in Britain, that have made a variety of contributions. These include the Race Relations Committee of the Society of Friends, which has undertaken conferences, pamphlets, and welfare work; the Runnymede Trust, with a significant programme in the trade union field; and the Martin Luther King Foundation, which runs an employment agency. It also includes the Institute of Race Relations, which has been active in the information and research field in Britain; and, in the research area, a number of other institutions and individuals in universities and elsewhere. The importance of the P.E.P. report has several times been noted, and other research has had some effect.[2]

It can, therefore, simply be said that both specific and general measures can affect and ameliorate race situations.

4. Discrimination and the General Society

In this, the final section, the attempt is to focus more clearly on the relationship of racial discrimination to the general society. This was the fourth part of the concept of discrimination originally outlined, and so stands additional to the related situations of the in-group, out-group, and the act of discrimination.

---

[1] Indeed, the evidence of Chapter 7 suggests that some employers will find ways round the legislation, when they choose to do this.

[2] For an account that includes discussion of the effectiveness of research, see Simon Abbott, 'Race Studies in Britain', *Social Science Information* (Vol. 10, No. 1, February 1971), pp. 91–101.

(a) STRUCTURAL RELATIONSHIPS

Viewing the general society as a whole, what is racial discrimination and how is it eliminated? Many of the chapters—such as those on education, housing, and employment—have illustrated that much of the discrimination against racial minority groups is not simply racial discrimination, but is part of a more general discrimination within society. Although the given scope of this study was to scan specifically racial discrimination, and this more general and final discussion is therefore brief, it must be a main contention that the complete elimination of racial discrimination in certain situations depends upon the major restructuring of society. This is argued because the race factor is repeatedly shown as closely related to the main structural factors of society, i.e. to the allocation of social, economic, and political resources. If these resources are unequally divided, and if different race is firmly tied to unequally endowed groups, then race and class or social group are increasingly and firmly correlated.

This line of argument can be exemplified, for example, by the suggestion that, even if the race factor were to be removed from black-white relations in the United States, it would take sixty to eighty years before the American Negro obtained occupational parity, because of these broad social factors.[1] Rather than thinking in completely racial terms, in certain countries 'one can think of race relations in terms of inter-group power contrasts'.[2]

This relationship of racial discrimination—in the broad sense—to class discrimination, has important implications for the effectiveness of measures against race discrimination. One criticism aimed at the C.R.C. was that:

The existence of the Community Relations Commission, and of local committees supported by it, is often pointed to as evidence that something is being done about race relations in this country, but we will show that . . . as far as the social structure as a whole is concerned this is mere tokenism.[3]

[1] S. Lieberson and G. Fuguitt, 'Negro-White Differences in the Absence of Discrimination', *American Journal of Sociology* (No. 73, 1967).
[2] H. M. Blalock, *Toward a Theory of Minority-Group Relations* (New York, John Wiley & Sons, 1967), p. 109.
[3] M. Hill and R. Issacharoff, *Community Action and Race Relations: A Study of Community Relations Committees in Britain* (London, Oxford University Press, for Institute of Race Relations, forthcoming 1971).

Indeed, how could an organization with such tiny resources on the national level significantly change the major structuring of British society?

Talk of the general society should not be taken to imply that, even in Britain, such a society is everywhere similar and uniform. Rather, there are significant regional differentiations that may be seen in racial terms as differing situations between, say, the more explosive Wolverhampton and the more quiet Brent, in the period 1967–9; and this contrast is the more pointed by the greater concentration of immigrants in Brent. Talk of the national society, even for an insular Britain, must not be taken to mean that, in many important ways, the issues are not international. This can be seen in terms of issues at Government level, such as Rhodesia and South African cricket tours and armaments, as also at minority group level, such as in the creation of new alliances (CARD was founded following a visit from Martin Luther King, and the setting up of Michael X's RAAS succeeded a visit from Malcolm X). It can be seen also in the economic interdependence, or in many ways dependence, existing between Britain and certain of the countries from which the coloured immigrants have come.

Having stressed the extent to which the race factor is part of and governed by the general society, including the international society, let the importance of the race factor not be underestimated. The attempt to dismiss race as insignificant and wholly subsumed, for example, within the class concept is—in my view— overturned by experience and analysis. Black Power leaders rightly claim that ' . . . we must realize that race is an overwhelming fact of life in this historic period'.[1] Academics can argue that, 'In fact, race and ethnic factors in America are significant realities that require direct theoretical and empirical focus.'[2] And such as the careful testing of coloured white-collar job applicants in the present study confirms the sometimes salience of race. The structural conditions that surround men are the same: the factors of education, housing and neighbourhood, employment, relation to the ownership of production, etc., confront all

[1] Stokely Carmichael and Charles V. Hamilton, *Black Power: The Politics of Liberation* (New York, Vintage Books, 1967), p. 54.

[2] From the Institute of Race and Community Relations, 'Proposal to the Regents of the University of California', July 1968, p. 4.

men. But in certain societies, the social ascribing of race as a symbol of inferiority does add a qualitative difference. This qualitative difference, however, can vary as between different societies. And it can be argued that the difference is not explicable solely in terms of the distribution of resources and structural factors, but that other, cultural factors, also operate.[1] If this is so, then it follows that it may in some cases be possible to change or diminish race factors within certain societies without always changing in an equal way the related major structural factors.

(b) POSSIBILITIES OF SOCIAL CHANGE

Accepting both that the major factors in society lie in the basic distribution and use of resources, and that race is an additional factor of significance, in what way, then, is more general social change achieved and social discrimination eliminated? One answer[2] lies in the concept of the integrationist state. Gunnar Myrdal's *An American Dilemma* is usually taken as advancing this thesis: ' . . . the conquering of color caste in America is America's own innermost desire', and 'the great reason for hope is that this country has a national experience of uniting racial and cultural diversities and a national theory, if not a consistent practice, of freedom and equality for all'.[3] Admittedly, Myrdal suggests that this is only one of the choices open, but there is the opportunity outlined of assimilating the minority into the society of the majority: and, 'it has been observed by writers concerned with oppressed minorities that the problems are essentially not minority problems at all, but majority problems'.[4] So *Colour and Citizenship*

[1] For example, see Christopher Bagley on 'The Prediction of Prejudice in a National Sample', *Race* (Vol. XII, No. 2, October 1970), pp. 234–6. In particular, 'In our view a large part of the variation in prejudice in Britain can be accounted for by *cultural* factors.' He argues this partly in relation to a comparative study between Britain and the Netherlands. Of course, a relationship between prejudice and race is established.

[2] In the following discussion, it is accepted that the views expressed are simplified, and that quotations do not always necessarily represent the full or current viewpoints of those quoted; and, indeed, that the quotations may have been used rather out of context in the attempt to delineate three possibilities of change.

[3] Gunnar Myrdal, *An American Dilemma* (New York, McGraw Hill, 1964), p. 1021.

[4] Robert Bierstedt, 'The Sociology of Majorities' in Raymond Mack, *Race, Class and Power* (New York, American Book Co., 1963), p. 20.

ended with some eighty pages of recommendations directed largely at national and local government.[1] The Jenkins philosophy of 'equal opportunity accompanied by cultural diversity, in an atmosphere of mutual tolerance', would seem to be a political expression of this 'integrationist' viewpoint. It seems unarguable that the weight of power in Britain does lie with the majority; but how just is the society for the relatively deprived groups?

A second answer lies in the concept that society needs radical restructuring to achieve a satisfactory social justice. It may be that ethnic, racial, and class groups will coalesce as increasingly recognizable entities in British society. The situation may be developing 'When conflict groups encounter each other in several associations and in several clashes, and the energies expended in all of them will be combined and one overriding conflict of interests will emerge.'[2] Rather than assimilation or pluralistic integration, is not crude conflict a more real description of the relationship that may come to apply to the coloured groups in Britain and the receiving society? In this second case, of course, the coloured groups would be subsumed within a class grouping that would provide the base support for the radical, 'revolutionary', and socialist reorganization of British society. Not, in this case, the integration of 'a *process* whereby units or elements of a society are brought into an active and coordinated compliance with the ongoing activities and objectives of the dominant group in that society',[3] but radical change engineered by a minority in terms of apparent power.[4] It seems unarguable that much of British society is insufficiently just;[5] but this major restructuring does not appear imminent or immediately possible. Nor do radical plans always sustain either their founders or intended forms in situations of rapid social change.

[1] E. J. B. Rose and associates, *Colour and Citizenship: A Report on British Race Relations* (London, Oxford University Press, for Institute of Race Relations, 1969), pp. 675–756.

[2] Ralf Dahrendorf, *Class and Class Conflict in an Industrial Society* (London, Routledge & Kegan Paul, 1959), p. 215.

[3] R. A. Schermerhorn, *Comparative Ethnic Relations: A Framework for Theory and Research* (New York, Random House, 1970), p. 14.

[4] In this discussion, majority and minority are used in the sense of power, and not numbers of people.

[5] This is not intended as a unique condemnation of British society alone. What country, in fact, fully achieves its proposed ideals? Indeed, in terms of ethnic and race relations, the sometimes declared absence of problems might prove hollow if subjected to independent and skilled testing.

A third answer to the changing of society and the elimination of racial discrimination can be drawn from the action of a *racial minority group*. In Britain, the most politically conscious and articulate racial minority has been the West Indian. The strong influence of the United States on members of this group has already been noticed in the establishment of activist organizations in Britain following visits by Martin Luther King and Malcolm X, and other visitors, such as Stokely Carmichael, have also made an impact.[1] As there has been little effective action by racial minority groups in Britain, it is easier to select a model from the United States. And because of the existing links between Afro-Americans and West Indians, it is more relevant to choose the concept, or concepts, of Black Power, rather than ideas drawn from another racial minority such as the *Chicanos*. Of course, Black Power is not the only black American philosophy, and there are variant movements of Black Power in different countries. But Black Power in the United States has been articulated in clear, varied, and compelling terms, and it is discussed here as a movement based at some stage specifically on racial cohesion and that may affect social change. The action by one racial group, or possibly in the future by members of various racial minority groups, to eliminate or at least diminish racial discrimination is in contrast to the two earlier possibilities outlined. In the case of Black Power, it is argued that 'there is no "American dilemma" because black people in this country form a colony, and it is not in the interest of the colonial power to liberate them'.[2] The argument for colonial status is sustained when one sees 'some major developments in Black Protest—the urban riots, cultural nationalism, and the movement for ghetto control—as collective responses to colonized status';[3] and when the 'four basic components of the colonization complex' are present, specifically 'forced, involuntary entry' into the dominant society, great impact on the culture and social organization of the colonized, the colonized being 'managed and

---

[1] 'Stokely Carmichael had visited an Islington meeting in July and left his imprint. Members were impressed with his theories of antagonism and polarization by coloured people as a prelude to power.' Benjamin W. Heineman, Jr., *The Politics of the Powerless: A Study of the Campaign Against Racial Discrimination* (London, Oxford University Press, for Institute of Race Relations, forthcoming), Chapter 5.

[2] Carmichael and Hamilton, op. cit., p. 5.

[3] Robert Blauner, 'Internal Colonialism and Ghetto Revolt', *Social Problems* (Vol. 16, No. 4, Spring 1969), p. 393.

manipulated by outsiders in terms of ethnic status', and 'racism'. [1] So, 'It is the objective relationship which counts, not rhetoric . . . or geography', [2] and 'the vital first step' is 'a new consciousness'. [3] In essence, 'The concept of Black Power rests on a fundamental premise: *Before a group can enter the open society, it must first close ranks.*' [4] And the first plank of the Black Panther programme is: 'I. We want freedom. We want power to determine the destiny of our Black Community.' [5]

There are different ways forward: in one view, 'Black Power in the ghetto is the only viable solution'; [6] and yet 'The Negro wants a full stake in society. He wants to own some of this country. He has to share its wealth.' [7] But the drive forward by the minority into the existing capitalist majority of America is not everybody's way: 'For more than 300 years, we tried the impossible—integration. Now let's be rational.' [8] This means that 'the only viable alternative is for blacks to separate themselves from this insanity called the United States of America' and get 'land for a separate nation'. [9]

But much of Black Power is more outward-looking: 'It is also clear that "being black," to many, is more than skin color. It is an attitude, a state of mind, a way of looking at life.' [10] And being minority based, much of it is radical: 'Our view is that, given the illegitimacy of the system, we cannot then proceed to transform that system with existing structures.' [11] For some, 'We are attempting to transform an oppressive capitalist society into a socialistic society. . . .' [12] It does seem unarguable that white America has not offered the Blacks a just deal, and also that much of American society does not reach up to the image of the Great American Dream; but critics have questioned how much Black Power will

---

[1] Blauner, op. cit.

[2] Carmichael and Hamilton, op. cit., p. 6.

[3] Ibid., p. 39.

[4] Ibid., p. 44.

[5] 'October 1966 Black Panther Party Programme', to be found on back of any issue of *The Black Panther*.

[6] Sterling Tucker, *Beyond the Burning: Life and Death of the Ghetto* (New York, Association Press, 1968), p. 105.

[7] Ibid., p. 132.

[8] Julius Lester, 'The Necessity for Separation', *Ebony* (August 1970), p. 169.

[9] Ibid., p. 168.

[10] Charles V. Hamilton, 'How Black is Black?', *Ebony* (August 1969), p. 45.

[11] Carmichael and Hamilton, op. cit., p. 42.

[12] Huey P. Newton, 'The Black Panthers', *Ebony* (August 1969), p. 108.

achieve even in the States (although, surely, the growth points of radical social change have repeatedly gone without due contemporary acknowledgement?).[1] In Britain, the chances of a powerful colour coalition are probably much less: but the example of change deriving from the pressures of a racially distinct minority group remains.

Other possibilities for social change in Britain might be discussed, including the display of some public sentiment for measures of racial segregation, with repatriation to the original homelands of the settlers. But such policies have received little comprehensive and logical formulation, and may in effect rather be viewed as a white racist variant within the integrationist position whereby non-whites will be 'integrated' at the foot of the social pyramid. This is not to say that under different circumstances these views would not deserve critical analysis and discussion.

(c) LEADERSHIP

These three possibilities for change have been set out in an abstract and theoretical way. But people, and in this instance individual people or leaders, can be of great importance. Although 'the leadership status itself is within a group, and not outside of it' and the 'Leader himself is not immune from sanctions, . . . in critical situations, leaders tend to take over the reins.'[2] Of course, too much must not be made of the room for manœuvre of the leader: 'it is precisely in the most crucial issues that he must be exemplary of the group's values and stay within their narrow bounds.'[3]

But the importance of the leader in respect to race issues remains: it has, for example, been suggested that some prejudice declines when 'the elite leaders or spokesmen do not define such big events ("events touching on relations") vehemently or adversely or where they define them in the direction of racial

---

[1] See, for example, Bayard Rustin, 'Where is the Negro Movement Now?', *Dissent* (November–December 1968), pp. 491–504; and his '"Black Power" and Coalition Politics', *Commentary* (No. 42, September 1966), pp. 35–40, reprinted in Joanne Grant (ed.), *Black Protest* (Greenwich, Connecticut, Fawcett, 1968).

[2] Muzafer Sherif (ed.), *Intergroup Relations and Leadership* (New York, Wiley, 1962), pp. 17–18.

[3] Muzafer Sherif, *Group Conflict and Co-operation* (London, Routledge & Kegan Paul, 1966), p. 136.

harmony. . . . '[1] Conversely, the disruptive effect of the demagogue speaking on race relations is well known. The point here is not whether harmony or conflict are intrinsically preferable, but that leaders do influence people, even on race issues. Some social scientists seem to quantify their subjects into unthinking vegetables, but such abstraction is less real than the societies in which we live. Although individuals are surrounded and in many senses dominated by their environment, some do have opportunities for affecting change that may significantly affect the lifestyles of others In my view, this does operate both at the grassroots, community level, and at the national and international level.

(d) THE FUTURE

It is not intended that this brief discussion of change, here arranged around 'integration' and 'radical' and 'racial minority group engendered', does more than indicate the basic necessity for setting the discussion in this book against further discussion of the nature of society and social change. The pattern of possible relationships between the newcomers and the receiving society was investigated, and it was suggested that most of the immigrants were in a state of accommodation. The present and past positions of the immigrants were examined, particularly in terms of census data, and it was seen that there had not been significant change. But will there be a continuing movement by the majority to absorb (or reject) the minority? Discrimination in the fields of housing, education, and employment was discussed, with the aid of studies of white-collar job applications and immigrant attitudes to discrimination and anti-discriminatory measures; and it was found that the general society was in part discriminatory, that there was racial discrimination, and also that there was sensitive and perceptive awareness—on the part of the leaders interviewed —of racial issues. Will there be an increasingly effective radical movement, perhaps partly defined in racial terms, aimed at a general restructuring of society along socialistic lines? The operation of the anti-discriminatory measures was reviewed: specific bodies such as the Race Relations Board, and the N.C.C.I./ C.R.C. together with its local councils, and such general measures

---

[1] Herbert Blumer, 'Race Prejudice as a Sense of Group Position', in Jitsuichi Masuoka and Preston Valien (eds.), *Race Relations: Problems and Theory* (Chapel Hill, University of North Carolina Press, 1961), p. 226.

as the Urban Programme, were judged of limited effectiveness. Are such measures nugatory, or should they not, rather, be strengthened and extended?

This study started by commenting upon the necessarily limited state of our knowledge, caused in part by the recency of the moves against racial discrimination in Britain. It is also the case that, in many ways, racial factors are in their infancy of examination and in dispute as to the extent of their raciality, while their reframing as part of broad social questions is imperfectly under way. The quantifying and computerizing of human attitudes and behaviour can, on occasion, induce an unreal sense of knowledge and achievement, and provide an imperfect platform for predicting the future. However, the present study may yet serve to indicate ways in which race and discrimination may be better judged, and it may also provide to some degree a necessary base-line for future assessments and more definitive analyses. Finally, there is the hope that the attempt in Britain to resolve racial and social issues will be of wider value to an international audience, and that this volume will indicate a society that contains both racial discrimination and a critical freedom designed to reduce that discrimination.

Appendices

Appendices

Documentation of Main Research Instruments of White-collar Worker Survey

1. Standard Letters of Application[1]

Dear Sir,

With reference to your advertisement in *The Daily Telegraph* of nth July, for the post of *Electrical Engineer*, I wish to apply for the vacancy.

I am 29 years old and received my secondary schooling in *Karachi*, where I obtained six 'O' levels *and three 'A' levels*.

I arrived in England from *Pakistan* in *1958*. After leaving school I attended *Bristol University* and obtained a *B.Sc.(Hons.) degree in electrical engineering*. I am now permanently resident in Britain *and am married with three children*.

On leaving *University* I joined '*Y*' *Industries* and was employed there for *five* years. My responsibilities concerned *the application of solid state control schemes to the company's range of synchros and fractional horse power machinery*. I left in *1966* to take up my present job in a leading *paper machinery* company where I am now *engaged on design problems related to manufacturing machinery for various grades of paper and corrugated board*.

From the description of the advertised vacancy, I feel that I would be interested in the kind of work involved. I would certainly be pleased to attend an interview, if you think my qualifications and experience are suitable.

Yours faithfully,
(signed) Ahmed Khan

Dear Sir,

I was interested to read of the vacancy in your organisation for the post of *Electrical Engineer*.

I think my experience is suited to this position and I would be glad of the opportunity to visit you and discuss it in more detail.

I am *28* years of age and have been working as *Design and Contract Engineer* with a major company in *the paper industry* for the last *three years*. The work includes *consideration of all aspects of design techniques in*

---

[1] The italicized sections in all letters are exclusive to the particular applicant.

the electrical components of heavy machinery. I am married and have two children.

My educational qualifications are as follows:

Six 'O' levels ⎱ obtained at a *grammar*
Three 'A' levels ⎰ school in *Basingstoke*

B.Sc.(Hons.) degree in Electrical Engineering from London University.

My first job on leaving *University* was with *'X' Industries as a machine designer working on small motors.* I stayed there for *five* years before moving to my present post.

I hope that the description above will enable me to obtain an interview.

Yours faithfully,
(signed) John Robinson

2. Standard Letters of Refusal

Dear Sir,

Thank you for your letter *of nth July* inviting me to attend an interview *at 9.30 a.m.* on *nth August.*

Since writing to you in answer to your advertisement, I have been offered and accepted a post elsewhere. I would like, however, to thank you for asking me to attend this interview.

Yours faithfully,
(signed) Ahmed Khan

Dear Sir,

Since my recent application to you for the post of *Electrical Engineer*, I have had a discussion with my employers and, as a result, have decided to remain with my present organisation.

I thank you for considering my application and apologise for any inconvenience.

Yours faithfully,
(signed) John Robinson

3. Standard Names Used by Job Applicants

Nationality	Male	Female
British	John Robinson	Mary Robinson
Asian: Indian (Sikh)	Santokh Singh	Ranwi Kaur
Pakistani	Ahmed Khan	Sushma Khan
Australian	Paul Harris	Avril Harris
Cypriot	George Demetriades	Helen Demetriades
West Indian	Errol Gardiner	Eva Gardiner

4. 'Addresses' of Applicants

In selecting the two addresses for each area, an attempt was made to locate them in a fairly 'mixed' neighbourhood. All our possible contacts for addresses in and around the Reading area happened to be in 'white', middle-class areas, and to avoid the possibility (however slight) of an applicant claiming to live in the same street as a prospective employer, or even one near by, it was decided that all candidates for jobs in Reading/Windsor/Slough should be currently resident in London. The following list indicates the general locality of each address.

Base Area	Address	
	Letter A	*Letter B*
Greater London	London, S.E.1	London, N.1
West Midlands conurbation	Great Wyrley, Nr. Walsall	Great Barr, Birmingham 22A
Reading/Windsor/Slough	London, S.W.15	London, N.W.3
East Midlands	Nottingham NG7 1BB	Nottingham NG7 1DW

5. *Newspapers Used as Advertised Job Sources*

NATIONALS

The *Daily Telegraph*
The *Sunday Times*

LOCALS

Derby Evening Telegraph
Leicester Mercury
Evening Post and News (Nottingham)
Evening Post (Reading)
Birmingham Evening Mail
Slough Observer
Windsor, Slough and Eton Express

Suitable trade journals were initially also scanned as sources of suitable job advertisements, but proved unproductive and were discontinued. A large majority of these advertised vacancies were duplicated in the daily Press.

6. Detailed Table of Results

	Total	0						−1					+1
		Both interview	Both application forms	Both refused	Both no reply	1 refused 1 no reply	Acknowledgement only	1 interview 1 refused	1 application form 1 refused	1 interview 1 no reply	1 application form 1 no reply	1 interview 1 application form	
ALL	128	51	26	16	5	1	3	12	3	5	2	1	3
Area													
Nottingham	32	13	5	6	3		1	3					1
Reading	32	13	6	3		1	1	3	1	2	1	1	1
Birmingham	32	11	8	5	2			3	1	1			1
London	32	14	7	2	1		1	3	1	2	1		1
Nationality													
Australian	32	17	8	4	1		1			1			1
Cypriot	32	13	8	5	1			3	1				1
West Indian	32	15	6	4	1		1		1	2	1		1
Indian	16	4	1	2		1	1	4		2		1	1
Pakistani	16	2	3	1	2		1	5	1		1		2
Job type													
Sales marketing	32	4	14	3	1			1	3	3	1		2
Electrical engineering	32	12	5	4	2		3	4				1	
Accountancy	32	17	4	4	1	1		4		1			1
Secretarial	32	18	3	5	1			3		1			2
Immigrant's qualifications													
Equal	64	23	11	10	3		1	7	2	5			1
Higher	64	28	15	6	2	1	2	5	1		2	1	2
Immigrant's schooling													
U.K.	64	31	12	9	1	1	1	3	3	2	1		1
Abroad	64	22	14	7	4	1	2	9		3	1	1	2
Immigrant's colour													
Coloured	64	21	10	7	3	1	2	9	2	4	2	1	1
White	64	30	16	9	2		1	3	1	1			2
Native language													
English	64	32	14	8	2		2		1	3	1		1
Not English	64	19	12	8	3	1	1	12	2	2	1	1	2

Interview Schedule for West Indian Leaders

Personal History

1. Age group.
2. Country of origin.
3. Length of time in U.K.
4. Employment: (a) before immigrating; (b) subsequent to.
5. Religion, if any.
6. Political activity: (a) before immigrating; (b) subsequent to.
7. Membership of group concerned with anti-discrimination (size of group).
8. Areas of residence.

Discrimination/Integration

1. Do you distinguish between racial discrimination and racial prejudice? How do you identify both?
2. Do you see discrimination mainly in terms of an individual's experience or that of a group?
3. Is racial discrimination of any kind justifiable?
4. Have you heard of Black Power? What do you understand by the term? How feasible is it?
6. Is a multi-racial society possible? What do you understand by the term?
7. Do you think a foreigner resident permanently in this country should conform as much as possible to the established customs of the host community? How do you define 'as much as possible' —matters of religion? dress? food? turbans?

Host Community

1. Did you anticipate prejudice and discrimination in Britain? What manifestations did you expect? Has discrimination been greater or lesser than expected?
2. How do you see the white section of the host community? (Simply as 'white' implying homogeneous, or as multi-national, etc.)

3. Do you distinguish between discrimination as against Jews, Pakistanis, Poles, West Indians, Greeks, Africans, Indians, gipsies? If so,
4. Do you think that the white section of the host community distinguishes between West Indians, Africans, Indians, and Pakistanis? If so, does this have any implications for the degree of discrimination towards the various minorities? If not, what reasons can be attributed for this?
5. The most unpopular form of discrimination suffered by your group.
6. Has your experience of discrimination in Britain been general (on a national basis) or limited locally?
7. In what strata of white society do you find the greatest degree of discrimination?
8. Extent of discrimination in Britain; in your area?

Measures Against Discrimination

1. How effective do you think the Government's legislation has been (nationally and locally)? Reasons.
2. How seriously do you think the Government views discrimination? Reasons.
3. Are you very familiar with the legislation against discrimination?
4. What are your main criticisms of the existing legislation?
5. What areas would you rank as first priority for further legislation?
6. To what extent is legislation an answer?
7. What do you expect from forthcoming legislation?
8. In your opinion, what are the effects of the work of various anti-discriminatory groups (CARD, for instance)?
9. To what extent has legislation in other areas—i.e. not directly anti-discriminatory measures—and not specifically motivated by the racial problem, been helpful? (E.g. general legislation on housing, etc.)
10. What importance do you attach to non-legal measures against discrimination (taken by businessmen and others, private firms, societies, individuals)? How do you see this aspect of the situation developing?
11. Do you think a greater influx of West Indian immigrants would complicate or aid the progress towards integration, and how do you view the matter of Commonwealth immigration?

Roles

1. What role do you think you have as a leader; in promoting integration?

2. Do you identify on an international level with your race? If so, in what ways and with what effect on your attitudes towards the specific situation in Britain?

3. What do you think of (a) the other leaders in the various anti-discriminatory organizations? (b) the organizations themselves?

4. Marcus Garvey or Malcolm X, Martin Luther King, or any other. Which one(s) do you think most relevant to your present cause?

5. In connection with your role, what type of action do you envisage —individual/collective; within or outside the existing framework?

6. Extent to which attitude of the West Indian immigrant in Britain is thought to correspond to your own, both in relation to discrimination and to action.

7. Do you think the situation lends itself to a range of alternative forms of action, or just the one specified?

8. How would you consider yourself on the leadership spectrum?

9. Which groups would you consider most radical and which least? For what reasons?

10. Do you envisage collective action within economic structures— such as West Indian insurance companies, West Indian housing companies, etc.—as a necessary forward step to integration? Economic boycotts? Unionism?

11. Have you had useful assistance from interested host parties (individuals and groups) in: (a) the work of your group; (b) furthering the cause of anti-discrimination?

12. Any comments on the role of the news media in race relations.

Interview Schedule for Asian Leaders

Personal History

Name
Age
Country of origin
Resident of U.K.
Occupation: at home; in U.K.

Political/Community Activity

Political philosophy
Active or passive: at home; in U.K.
Member of any organization concerned with anti-discrimination
  policy
Formal structure of organization: numbers; leadership; relation of
  respondent to other leaders and followers

Racial Discrimination

1. Do you think it exists in this country?
2. In what fields does it prevail the most?
3. Were you ever discriminated against?
4. What do you think about the Commonwealth Immigrants Act?
   Is it racial in character?
5. Do white people discriminate equally against all coloured
   communities?
6. What do you think is the reason for such prejudice?
7. Do you think the Indian or Pakistani community is partly responsible for making their prejudices stronger? How would you compare
   this situation with that in the U.S.A.?
8. If racial discrimination is bad then:
   (a) How would you justify the caste system that exists in India
       or Pakistan? What would you say about the hostility between
       two groups of different religion and belonging to different
       states?

(b) To what extent do such differences (based on different caste, religion, or state) prevail amongst the Indians and Pakistanis living here?

Government Policy

1. What is your opinion about the Government policy in this matter?
2. Do you think that the measures taken by the Government would be effective?
   (a) Race Relations Bill
   (b) Race Relations Board
   (c) N.C.C.I. appointment of voluntary committees.
3. If the Government is not taking the proper steps, what do you think would be the best policy for the Government to follow?
4. Education: dispersal?

As a Community

What do you think Indians or Pakistanis can contribute, as a community, towards the improvement of such prejudices?

Role of Leaders

1. To what extent do you think the community leaders can contribute?
2. Whom will you call a leader?
3. What should be the method to approach this problem? Violence?
4. Do you think all minority groups should combine in their efforts to achieve their rights?
5. What do you think of 'Black Power'?

Future

What do you think is the future for coloured communities in this country? Do you think it is possible to create a harmonious multi-racial society in Britain?

APPENDIX 4

Complaints Received under Race Relations Act 1965

ANALYSIS OF COMPLAINTS RECEIVED UP TO AND INCLUDING 31 MARCH 1967

TOTAL RECEIVED—327

A. COMPLAINTS INVESTIGATED OR UNDER INVESTIGATION—89

Establishments

Public Houses	54
Hotels	12
Cafés	7
Clubs	11
Miscellaneous	5

How dealt with

Settled by conciliation...	20
Not substantiated ...	28
Referred to Race Relations Board	1
Referred to Attorney-General	2
Under investigation ...	38

Conciliation Areas

Northern	—
Yorkshire	3
Manchester and District	7
Liverpool and District	1
West Midland ...	17
East Midland	4
Eastern	3
Berks., Bucks., and Oxon.	—
Hants.,Surrey,andSussex	1
Kent	7
South Western ...	2
Greater London ...	41
Wales and Monmouth	—
Scotland	3

B. COMPLAINTS NOT INVESTIGATED AS BEING OUTSIDE SCOPE OF THE ACT—238

Subjects

Employment	101
Publications	24
Housing	37
Shops	7
Financial facilities ...	12
Police	14
Miscellaneous ...	43

Conciliation Areas

Northern	1
Yorkshire	19
Manchester and District	41
Liverpool and District	1
West Midland	19
East Midland	8
Eastern	2
Berks., Bucks., and Oxon.	8
Hants.,Surrey,andSussex	10
Kent	10
South Western ...	3
Greater London ...	111
Wales and Monmouth	4
Scotland	1

ANALYSIS OF COMPLAINTS RECEIVED FROM
1 APRIL 1967 TO 31 MARCH 1968

TOTAL RECEIVED: 690

A. COMPLAINTS WITHIN THE SCOPE OF SECTION 1 OF THE ACT—108

Establishments

Public houses	78
Hotels	0
Cafés	10
Clubs	5
*Hospitals	1
*Public transport ...	7
*Municipal entertainments centre ...	0
*Public utilities ...	2
*Police stations	1
*Town halls	3
*Places of public entertainment or recreation	1
	108

Conciliation Areas

Northern	2
Yorkshire	15
North West	11
West Midlands ...	23
East Midlands ...	6
Eastern ...	7
Berks., Bucks., and Oxon.	4
Hants., Surrey, and Sussex	0
Kent	4
South Western ...	1
Greater London ...	33
Wales and Monmouth	0
Scotland	2
	108

How dealt with

Settled by conciliation	35
Not sustained	46
Referred to Attorney-General ...	2
Under investigation ...	25
	108

B. COMPLAINTS OUTSIDE THE SCOPE OF SECTION 1 OF THE ACT—574

Establishments

Public houses ...	37
Hotels and guest houses	3
Clubs	10

Subjects

Employment	254

Conciliation Areas

Northern	3
Yorkshire	77
North West	63
West Midlands ...	59
East Midlands ...	34
Eastern	13
Berks., Bucks., and Oxon.	17

Subjects—cont.

Publications	...	...	19
Housing	...	...	61
Shops	...	...	9
Financial facilities	...		21
*Car hire	...	...	4
Police	...	...	74
*Religion	...	...	1
*Display notices		...	2
Miscellaneous		...	79

574

Conciliation Areas—cont.

Hants., Surrey, and Sussex	...	...	19
Kent	...	...	35
South Western		...	8
Greater London		...	226
Wales and Monmouth			13
Scotland	...	...	7

574

* Complaints under these headings were classified as 'Miscellaneous' in the Board's annual report for 1966–7.

ANALYSIS OF COMPLAINTS RECEIVED UNDER SECTION 1 OF THE RACE RELATIONS ACT OF 1965

1 April to 25 November 1968

(The Race Relations Act of 1968 came into force on 26 November 1968)

CATEGORIES OF COMPLAINTS	Inside the scope of the 1965 Act	Outside the scope of the 1965 Act
Establishments		
Public houses	39	—
Hotels and guest houses	2	4
Cafés	8	—
Clubs	15	10
Hospitals	1	—
Public transport	4	—
Places of public entertainment	3	—
Subjects		
Employment	—	184
Publications	—	11
Housing	—	45
Shops	—	8
Financial facilities	—	15
Car hire	—	8
Police	—	40
Religion	—	2
Display notices	—	2
Miscellaneous	—	60
	72	389

HOW DEALT WITH	
Settled by conciliation	20
Not sustained	34
Referred to Attorney-General	1
Under investigation (at 25.11.1968)	17
	72

CONCILIATION AREAS	Inside the scope of the 1965 Act	Outside the scope of the 1965 Act
Northern	1	6
Yorkshire	9	38
North West	4	35
West Midlands	9	38
East Midlands	3	22
Berks., Bucks., and Oxon.	3	17
South Western	1	5
*Greater London	38	211
Wales and Monmouth	4	9
Scotland	—	8
	72	389

*Includes East Anglia, Essex, Hants., Kent, Surrey, and Sussex

APPENDIX 5

Complaints Received under Race Relations Act 1968

EMPLOYMENT COMPLAINTS, BY TYPE OF COMPLAINT, 26 NOVEMBER 1968 TO 31 MARCH 1969

Type	Total number received	Outside the scope of the Act*	Opinion: discrimination†	Opinion: no discrimination‡	Under investigation	Complaint withdrawn§
(1) *Section 2*	3	—	—	—	3	—
(2) *Section 3*						
Recruitment	88	13	—	17	58	—
Terms	24	6	1	1	16	—
Conditions	20	4	1	1	14	—
Training	4	1	—	2	1	—
Promotion	12	1	—	1	9	1
Dismissal	54	6	—	13	33	2
(3) *Section 4*						
Trade unions	7	1	—	—	6	—
Employers' organizations	—	—	—	—	—	—
(4) *Section 6*	23	7	—	4	12	—
(5) *Section 12*	1	—	—	—	1	—
Total	236	39	2	39	153	3

(1) Section 2 covers the provision of goods, facilities, and services.

(2) Section 3 covers employment.

(3) Sections 4 covers trade unions and employers' and trade organizations.

(4) Section 6 covers advertisements and notices (in this table, relating to employment).

(5) Section 12 makes it unlawful deliberately to aid, induce, or incite another person to discriminate unlawfully.

* Many of these complaints concerned incidents which occurred before the Act came into force.

† The opinion was formed that unlawful discrimination had occurred. Satisfactory settlements were obtained and assurance, where appropriate.

‡ The opinion was formed that there had been no unlawful discrimination.

§ The complainant wished to withdraw his complaint and in the cases enumerated here the Board decided not to continue its investigations.

Complaints other than Employment Complaints, by Type of Complaint, 26 November 1968 to 31 March 1969

Type	Total number received	Outside the scope of the Act*	Opinion: discrimination†	Opinion: no discrimination‡	Under investigation	Complaint withdrawn§
(1) *Section 2*						
Public resort	33	1	1	7	23	1
Hotels	—	—	—	—	—	—
Insurance	4	—	—	—	4	—
Education...	7	—	—	—	7	—
Police	22	13	—	—	8	1
Other	108	32	—	16	58	2
(2) *Section 5*						
Private housing (rent) ...	36	4	—	12	20	—
Private housing (sale) ...	8	1	1	—	6	—
Public housing	15	3	—	—	12	—
(3) *Section 6*	32	—	3	5	24	—
(4) *Section 12*	6	2	—	—	4	—
Total	271	56	5	40	166	4

(1) Section 2 covers the provision of goods, facilities, and services.

(2) Section 5 covers housing accommodation, and business and other premises.

(3) Section 6 covers advertisements and notices.

(4) Section 12 makes it unlawful to aid, induce, or incite another person to discriminate unlawfully.

* Many of these complaints concerned incidents which occurred before the Act came into force.

† The opinion was formed that unlawful discrimination had occurred. Satisfactory settlements were obtained and assurances, where appropriate.

‡ The opinion was formed that there had been no unlawful discrimination.

§ The complainant wished to withdraw his complaint and in the cases enumerated here the Board decided not to continue its investigations.

EMPLOYMENT COMPLAINTS (OTHER THAN THOSE HANDLED WHOLLY BY
INDUSTRY MACHINERY) BY TYPE AND OPINION FORMED,
1 APRIL 1969 TO 31 MARCH 1970

Type	Total number on which opinion formed	Opinion: discrimination	Opinion: no discrimination
Section 3			
Recruitment	202	21	181
Terms	43	1	42
Conditions	47	2	45
Training	4	—	4
Promotion	28	3	25
Dismissal	176	7	169
Section 4			
Trades unions	11	1	10
Employers' organizations	—	—	—
Section 6			
Advertisements and notices	37	32	5
Section 12			
Aiding, inducing, or inciting	2	1	1
Total	550	68	482

APPEALS AGAINST FINDINGS OF INDUSTRY MACHINERY

1. Number of cases completed by industry machinery   137
2. Number of appeals to Board against findings of industry
   machinery   36
3. How disposed of by Employment Committee of Board
     (i) not further entertained 28
    (ii) investigated by Board
           Opinion: discrimination 1
           Opinion: no discrimination 5
   (iii) Withdrawn 2
                                 36

COMPLAINTS OTHER THAN EMPLOYMENT, BY TYPE AND OPINION FORMED
1 APRIL 1969 TO 31 MARCH 1970

Type	Total number on which opinion has been formed	Opinion: discrimination	Opinion: no discrimination
Section 2			
(i) Public places			
Public houses and hotels	64	31	33
Clubs	8	4	4
Public transport	4	2	2
Other	20	9	11
(ii) Goods, facilities, and services			
Insurance: motor*	8	5	3
Insurance: other	3	—	3
Financial and credit facilities	12	—	12
Education: facilities	12	1	11
Education: grants	11	—	11
Services connected with employment	18	2	16
Social services	9	—	9
Medical services	14	—	14
(iii) Other	46	2	44
Section 5			
Private housing (rent)	36	4	32
Private housing (sale)	5	3	2
Estate agents	32	3	29
Public housing	12	2	10
Section 6			
Advertisements and notices	116	111	5
Section 12			
Aiding, inducing, or inciting	2	—	2
Total	432	180	252

* Including car hire.

APPENDIX 6

N.C.C.I. Publications

Periodicals

Liaison: A quarterly magazine for voluntary liaison committees containing a review of N.C.C.I. activities and local news about the voluntary liaison committees. First appeared in stencilled form in June 1965. First printed edition appeared in December 1965; last printed edition, in October 1968. (Average print run: 1,200.)

Information: A monthly news-sheet. First appeared in 1966. Available after mid-1967 in Bengali, Urdu, Gujerati, and Punjabi as well as English. (Distribution: English 6,000; Urdu 3,000; Punjabi 3,000; Bengali 1,500; Gujerati 1,500.)

Occasional Papers

PUBLISHED IN 1966
Health and Welfare of the Immigrant Child: an address given by Dr. Simon Yudkin at the N.C.C.I. conference on Immigrants and their Babies, March 1965.

Prejudice in the Community: an address given by Dr. David Stafford-Clarke at the N.C.C.I. conference on Immigrant or Citizen, September 1965.

The Pakistani Family in Britain by Dr. Farrukh Hashmi.

Psychology of Racial Prejudice by Dr. Farrukh Hashmi.

PUBLISHED IN 1967
Towards a Multi-Racial Society: symposium from the N.C.C.I. seminar, Towards a Multi-Racial Society, July 1966.

The Young Englanders: an address given by Stuart Hall at N.C.C.I. conference, The Second Generation, March 1966.

The Housing of Commonwealth Immigrants: report prepared by the N.C.C.I. Housing Panel.

Areas of Special Housing Need: a corollary report by the Housing Panel.

Practical Suggestions for Teachers of Immigrant Children: prepared by a group of educationists.

Research and the Teaching of Immigrant Children by Dr. Ronald Goldman.

The Indian Family in Britain by Dilip Hiro.
Racial Discrimination: a summary of the P.E.P. report.
Anti-Discrimination Legislation: a summary of the Street report.
Race in the Curriculum: report of the N.C.C.I. seminar, April 1967, published in an edition of the *World Studies* bulletin.

Other N.C.C.I. Publications

Your Vote: leaflet outlining electoral registration procedures published in English, Urdu, Punjabi, Bengali, and Gujerati. (Distribution: English 10,000; Urdu 30,000; Punjabi 25,000; Gujerati 15,000; Bengali 10,000.)

Facts and Figures about Commonwealth Immigrants in Britain

Calling All Women: in association with Women's National Cancer Control Campaign. (Distribution: approximately 500.)

C.R.C. Publications

A Bibliography for Teachers of Immigrants: compiled by the N.C.C.I. Education Panel. (Print order: 5,000.)

Index

Absorbing society, and integration of minority groups, 29; stability due to territorial links, 30; and structure of pluralistic society, 30; effect of its ethos and structure on minority groups, 31, 35–6; varying indices of accommodation, 33 and n.; in sponsoring or black-balling roles, 36; need to meet expectations of immigrant children, 38; promotion of informed public opinion, 40–1; need to accept foreign cultural elements, 41; and élitist groups, 42; benefits from assimilation of refugees, 43; subsidence of hostility after absorption, 52; dislike of newcomers, 155

Absorption, changing orientation towards integration, 24; definition of author's use of term, 27; defined by Eisenstadt, 27, 155 and n. 2; into complex societies, 30, 31; time span, 32, 48; factors influencing its processes, 34–6, 39–41,; via stratified class system, 40–1; of early British immigrants, 42; aided by residential dispersal, 48; and employment, 155, 173–4

Accommodation, changing orientation towards integration, 24; earlier phase of migrant-host relationship, 32, 33; defined, author's use of term, 32 and n. 2, 33, 410; retention of social differences, 33; beginning of re-socialization process, 33; its progression, 33–4; conflicts during, 34; variables affecting, 35, 410; in employment situation, 156

Aden, 49, 100

Adorno, T. W., and analysis of prejudiced people, 10 and n. 2

Aliens Act, 1905, 46 and n. 1, 411

Allport, G. W., aspects of discrimination, 4 and nn. 1, 2

America see United States

American immigrants, ease of absorption, 39 n.

Anders, General, Polish Army, 388

Anglo-Indians, 388; rapid assimilation, 49 n. 1; numbers of, 69; in employment data, 74

Anglo-Jewry, 26; Orthodox communities, 31 n. 4, 34; self-segregation, 32; and Eastern European refugees, 45; assistance to newcomers towards integration, 46 and n. 3; and Race Relations Bills (1965), 241, (1968), 431; fear of fascist revival, 241–2; press for anti-racial legislation, 242

Anti-discriminatory legislation, 5–6, 18; adverse and beneficial effects, 8; its effectiveness, 8–9, 21; based on considerations of host group, 9, 169; its newness, 14–15, 17, 97, 234–5, 430; need for expertise, 22; attitudes towards, 22, 206, 208, 226, 427–8; growth of public concern, 22–3; and housing, 97; and building societies, 104; and private vendors, 105, 106; use of housing authority records, 109; and industrial relations system, 169, 424; common opposition to, 169; compromises in 1968 Act, 170, 432; prompts joint policy decisions, 171; need for participation of discriminated, 207; distinction between physical and psychological freedom, 207; limited scope, 208; 'incitement to racial hatred' clause, 208, 428; need for redress against humiliation and harm to victim, 209–10, 243; and complaints against Government, 210; its enforcement, 234, 240, 242, 247, 265; political implications, 235; and Government programme, 235–6, 385–90; and elimination of prejudice, 236; history of, 238 ff., 390 ff., 430–2; Jewish

17*

1961, 97–8; duties of local authorities, 102

—owner-occupation, 417; immigrant-English comparison, 99, 100, 102–3; national increase in, 103, 417; coloured immigrants as purchasers, 103–5, 222; attitude of vendor, 105, 106; Colorado clause in 1968 Act, 261

—private rental, 417; immigrant-English comparison, 99, 100; decline in, 100, 436; racial discrimination, 100–1; coloured landlords with coloured tenants, 101; effect of 1957 Rent Act, 390

—shared accommodation (multi-occupation), 4; increase in since 1961, 97–8; between owner-occupier and tenant, 101–2; aggravated by ethnic differences, 102; local authorities and, 102; associated with racial tension, 390

Housing Act 1961, reversal of Conservative policy, 390; and local authorities, 390

Housing of Commonwealth Immigrants, 297, 304

Howe, Geoffrey, 255 n. 3

Huddersfield L.E.A., dispersal policy, 133–4; Spring Grove School, 133–4

Hughes, Everett, 27

Huguenots, full assimilation in Britain, 28 n. 2; and host society, 42, 46

Hungarian immigrants, 16; refugees after Budapest Rising, 48; resettlement scheme, 1956, 53, 411

Hunt, John, M.P., 246

Immigrant communities and groups, impossibility of complete transplantation, 31 n. 3; adaptation to universal roles of host society, 31 and n. 3; 'third-generation' reaction, 34 and n. 1; adaptation-acceptance balance, 33–4; varying expectations and aspirations, 91; resistance to singling out, 113; advantages of geographical dispersal, 227; N.C.C.I./C.R.C. relationship, 326, 437; work of voluntary associations, 334–5; association with deprived areas, 335; failure to produce negotiating organizations, 424 *see also* Minority groups

Immigrant-host relationship, range of variable factors, 34–6; importance of

cultural kinship, 35 n.; lessons learnt from past immigration, 52; position of v.l.c.s, 343; voluntary associations and, 353; hostility based on social conditions, 354–5

Immigrant labour, reactions of local labour force, 91, 155, 163, 401–2, 403; association with old, run-down industries, 160; willingness to work unpopular hours, 160, 162–3; customers' objections to, 161, 401; roles and spheres, 161, 401, 422; influence of economic factors, 163; redundancy rules and, 163; and separate unions, 164; and trade unions, 164–5, 167; shop-floor rules concerning, 166; in non-unionized industries, 171; attraction to industrial areas, 334–5; criticism of their skills, 402; stereotyping, 402; lower educational standards, 402; effect of labour shortage, 404; affirmative action by major company, 404 ff.; levels of resistance, 405; lack of upward mobility, 415

Immigrant pupils, arrival in British schools after 1962, 111, 112–13; D.E.S. definition, 113, 419 n.; failure to qualify, 113; results of ten-year rule, 113, 118 and n.; numbers and concentrations in schools by birth-place (1967), 116; % in maintained schools, 117; % distribution, 118; distribution by age-groups, 118; English language teaching *see under*; their handicaps, 121; dispersal policy, 121 *see under*; alleged association with lowered standards, 126–7, 146, 152; association with deprived areas, 129; inferior stereotyping, and dangers of, 140, 151, 152–3, 421; compared with English contemporaries, 142; effect of 'banding' scheme, 145, 420–1; ancillary aids and resources for, 148; assessment of current situation, 150; differing situation of English-born, 150; treatment by other children, 222; growth in all-immigrant schools, 419

Immigrant-receiving society, 21, 408; development of social climate, 21–5; hostility aroused by threats to community core, 25–6; movement towards assimilation, 28; rejection of large groups of newcomers, 38; interaction

situation, 213, 216, 221; alleged responsibility of immigrants, 224-5; implications of Powellism, 237; limited returns from education, 329

Ragg, Rev. John, Committee for the Welfare of Coloured Workers, 335

Ramsay, Dr., Archbishop of Canterbury, 295 and n.

Rastafarians, 31 n. 4

Reddaway, John, 'Whatever Happened to the C.R.C.?', 329-30, 330 nn. 1, 2, 359 n.

Ree, Harry, and language teaching, 137

Religion, area of community sub-culture, 29; acceptance of alien cultures, 41 n. 2; powerful communal tie, 47

Religious organizations, and immigrant community work, 335, 382-4, 441

Rent Act 1965, 'harassment' provision, 102; effect on social problems, 390

Rex, John, 307 n. 2; 'The Formation of Ghettos in Britain's Cities', 317 and n. 6; 'The Race Relations Catastrophe', 317 and nn.; with R. Moore, *Race, Community and Conflict*, 354 and n.

Richard, Ivor, M.P., 246

Richmond, A. H., definition of discrimination, 3 and n. 2; *Colour Prejudice in Britain*, 158 and n. 2

Robb, James H., *Working-class Anti-Semite*, 157-8, 158 n. 1

Robertson, Sir James, 295 n.

Rogers, Margaret, and ATEPO, 140; and multi-racial classes, 140, 142

Roman Catholicism, as alien religion, 41 n. 2; among Irish immigrants, 44, 47-8; Irish-born priests, 45; of Southern European exiles, 49

Romanian exiles, 48

Rose, E. J. B., 307 n. 2; *Colour and Citizenship*, 447-8

Rose, Paul, M.P., 246

Royal Commission on Alien Immigration, 1903, 46

Royal Commission on Population, and sponsored immigration, 388

Royal Commission on Trade Unions and Employers' Associations, 173

Russia, *émigrés* in Britain, 43

St. John Stevas, Norman, M.P., 246, 247

Sandys, Duncan, 387

Scandinavians, amalgamation in Canada, 28 n. 2

Schools, British, lack of preparation for multi-racialism, xvii, 112, 150; effects of arrival of immigrant children, 111, 126, 127; immigrant pupil statistics, 116, 117, 123; responsibilities of D.E.S. and L.E.A.s., 119-20; dispersal policy, 121, 123 ff. *see under*; changing social composition, 127; neighbourhood, 129; comprehensive system, 143

School-teachers, and discrimination against immigrant children, 111, 112; D.E.S. and L.E.A.s and, 119; personal responsibilities, 119; raising of quota for immigrant concentrations, 121-2; and arrival of immigrant pupils, 125-6; and falling attainment in schools with immigrants, 127; anti-dispersal groups, 128-9; contact with parents, 132; individual attention to immigrant pupils, 133, 149-50; and English as second language, 133, 134, 136, 137, 138, 141, 149, 150; voluntary groups, 137, 138, 141-2, 149-50; assessment of numbers in need, 139; and comprehensive system, 143; and 'banding' system, 143-4; and assumptions of immigrant inferiority, 152-3; acceptance of coloured staff, 161

Schools Council, and curriculum development, 119; and teacher-parent contact, 132; assessment of Leeds Project, 139, 140-1, 142; and Birmingham Project, 148-9

Schwerner, George, on U.S. enforcement agencies, 265

Scotland, Irish immigrant population, 43

Scott, Nicholas, M.P., 260, 261, 262

Scottish Highlanders, 31

Seamen, merchant, 57; 1968 Act and, 163, 256, 258, 261, 262, 423

Segregation, based on class and colour bar, 31 n. 4; in sub-communities, 34; condemned by educationists, 111; form of discrimination, 279; move towards, in schools, 420

Self-segregation, in Britain, 31 n. 4, 410; among Orthodox Jewish communities, 31 n. 4, 45, 410; author's use of term, 31-2; evolution from rejection and alienation, 31 n. 4, 40; part of accommodation process, 32; voluntary ethnic